Race Mixing

Race Mixing

Southern Fiction since the Sixties

Suzanne W. Jones

The Johns Hopkins University Press
Baltimore and London

The Johns Hopkins University Press
2715 North Charles Street
Baltimore, Maryland 21218-4363
www.press.jhu.edu

Library of Congress Cataloging-in-Publication Data

Jones, Suzanne Whitmore.
  Race mixing : Southern fiction since the Sixties / Suzanne W.
Jones.
      p. cm
  Includes bibliographical references and index.
  ISBN 0-8018-7393-2 (alk. paper)
    1. American fiction—Southern States—History and criticism.
2. American fiction—20th century—History and criticism.
3. Racially mixed people in literature. 4. Interracial marriage in
literature. 5. Southern States—in literature. 6. Race relations in
literature. 7. Miscegenation in literature. 8. Sex role in literature. 9. Race in literature. I. Title.
  PS261.J66 2002
  810.9′355—dc21
                                                    2003006812

A catalog record for this book is available from the British
Library.

For Frank

For better or worse, our customs and laws, our culture and society are sustained by the myths we embrace, the stories we recirculate to explain what we behold. I believe that racism's hardy persistence and immense adaptability are sustained by a habit of human imagination, deflective rhetoric, and hidden license. I believe no less that an optimistic course might be charted, if only we could imagine it.

—PATRICIA J. WILLIAMS,
Seeing a Color-Blind Future: The Paradox of Race

Contents

Acknowledgments

My research has been funded by the National Endowment for the Humanities, the Virginia Foundation for the Humanities and Public Policy, and the University of Richmond. I am grateful for all this support.

I appreciate the kindness of friends and colleagues who read and commented on portions of this work: Thomas Allen, Edward Ayers, Vanessa Dickerson, Susan Donaldson, Michael Kimmel, Carol Manning, Sharon Monteith, Velma Pollard, Diane Roberts, Maureen Ryan, Peter Wallenstein, and Patricia Yaeger. Discussions with students in seminars at the University of Richmond and at the University of Virginia stimulated my thinking about this project, as did comments from those who attended talks I gave at East Carolina University, J. Sargeant Reynolds Community College, the University of Mississippi, the University of Richmond, and Rhodes College and conversations at meetings of the European Southern Studies Forum, the Modern Language Association, and the Society for the Study of Southern Literature. I am especially indebted to my husband, Frank Papovich; my editor, Robert Brugger; my copy editor, Lois Crum; and an anonymous reader for the Johns Hopkins University Press for reading the entire manuscript and offering sound advice on style and content.

I would also like to thank Rosellen Brown, Thulani Davis, Ellen Douglas, Ernest Gaines, Anthony Grooms, Josephine Humphreys, and Dori Sanders for talking with me about their work. Finally, I am fortunate to have received such thoughtful replies to so many questions e-mailed out of the blue; many thanks to Eric Gary Anderson, Martyn Bone, Paul Gaston, Richard Godden, Richard Gray, Barbara Ladd, John Lowe, Sharon Monteith, Noel Polk, Peggy Prenshaw, Scott Romine, Maureen Ryan, and Bob Skinner for their expertise and time.

Reference librarians Keith Weimer and Marcia Whitehead at Boatwright Library at the University of Richmond and reference librarians Bryson Clevenger and Sajjad Yusuf at Alderman Library at the University of Virginia were generous with their time and patient with my questions. At the Press, Mahinder

Kingra and Carol Zimmerman always responded promptly to my queries, large and small.

I owe a special thanks to Melody Herr and Lee Campbell Sioles for their help in the early stages of production and to Annie Pruett for her assistance with the index.

Some portions of this book were published previously, and I would like to thank the publishers for permission to use these materials here: an earlier version of part of chapter 2 appeared as "Dismantling Stereotypes: Interracial Friendships in *Meridian* and *A Mother and Two Daughters*" in *The Female Tradition in Southern Literature,* ed. Carol Manning (University of Illinois Press, 1993); an earlier version of part of chapter 3 appeared as "Reconstructing Manhood: Race, Masculinity, and Narrative Closure in Ernest Gaines's *A Gathering of Old Men* and *A Lesson before Dying*" in *masculinities* 3. 2 (1995); a portion of chapter 3 appeared as "Refighting Old Wars: Race Relations and Masculine Conventions in Fiction by Larry Brown and Madison Smartt Bell" in *The Southern State of Mind,* ed. Jan Nordby Gretlund (University of South Carolina Press, 1999); and some material in chapter 4 appeared in *South to a New Place: Region, Literature, Culture,* ed. Suzanne W. Jones and Sharon Monteith (Louisiana State University Press, 2002).

Race Mixing

Writing Race Relations since the Civil Rights Movement

> [O]ur fictions are a measuring rod by which one may gauge the histori-
> cally conditioned changeability of deeply entrenched human desires. . . .
> literature becomes a panorama of what is possible, because it is not
> hedged in by the limitations or the considerations that determine the
> institutionalized organizations within which human life takes its course.
> —WOLFGANG ISER, "DO I WRITE FOR AN AUDIENCE?"

In the spring of 1994, African American journalist David Nicholson, who knew
the American South only through books, television, and movies, decided to
take a trip through the region that was his grandparents' home. He admitted
that "in some secret place" in his heart, he had "wanted to be refused service
or told to go to the back door just to see what it felt like" and to discover how
he would react. He left his desk at the *Washington Post* as a deluge of southern
news items poured in: the seemingly endless debates about the Confederate
battle flag still flying over various state capitol buildings and the fallout from
an Alabama high school principal threatening to cancel the prom rather than
suffer interracial couples dancing together. But during Nicholson's three-week
journey, he did not find the South he expected: "Everywhere I went, people
were far more open and congenial than in the North, even in the most casual
interactions. And everywhere in cities and small towns, I saw blacks and whites
working together, walking down the street together, talking together. Only
once did I witness any ugliness." He found that the "pictures indelibly im-
printed" in his imagination of "rabid rednecks, fragile belles and servile blacks
co-existing in a place taut with hostility and sudden inexplicable violence"
needed updating. But underneath the southern hospitality and interracial bon-
homie, Nicholson became aware of a legacy of distrust that lingers alongside
efforts to lift the burdens of southern racial history.[1]

About the same time, white journalist Tony Horwitz, who had recently returned from covering civil unrest in Ireland, Bosnia, and the Middle East, awoke one morning to an eerily familiar sound in his own Virginia backyard—the crackle of musket fire. With the sound lingering in his head, Horwitz decided to make sense of the phenomenon that had produced it: the craze to reenact Civil War battles. Roughing it with reenactors over the next few months, he found the modern men in gray to be an odd mix of liberal white southerners disaffected with the pace of contemporary life and unreconstructed neo-Confederates disgruntled with affirmative action. In *Confederates in the Attic: Dispatches from the Unfinished Civil War*, Horwitz details not only periodic battlefield reenactments but also the rebel mania present on a small but troubling scale throughout the rural South. Sons and Daughters of the Confederacy still gather in living rooms laden with Confederate kitsch, Children of the Confederacy meet in rural high schools, weekend bazaars feature Confederate paraphernalia at derelict service stations, and tony international tourist destinations like Charleston are still home to Confederate museums on side streets. But Horwitz also found a parallel strain of black nationalist ideology and activity. In an alternative school for teenagers in Selma, Alabama, students learn that all whites are suspect and that African American activists in favor of integration, like Julian Bond, are sellouts. How does one square Nicholson's dispatches with Horwitz's?[2]

Seeing the South clearly has never been easy, and at the turn of the twenty-first century it may be more difficult than ever to get a handle on race relations in a region that has exported both racism and the civil rights movement, a fondness for guns and the Southern Poverty Law Center, high rates of black imprisonment and Habitat for Humanity. For the most part, black-white relationships in the South today differ little from those in the rest of the country. Although some contend that race relations are different in the South (some think better, others worse), Patricia Williams's belief that "racism is coded differently in the North of the United States than in the South" may help explain that perception of difference, whatever the reality.[3] One point of real difference is the deep need among black and white southern writers to think and write about black-white relationships. Peach farmer Dori Sanders tells of the sight one Saturday afternoon that propelled her to write her first novel, *Clover*. After observing two segregated funeral processions pass by, she became preoccupied with how to bring the sad little black girl at the head of the first line of cars together with the lonely young white woman at the head of the second.[4] Longtime novelist Josephine Humphreys believes that writing about black-white relationships is one of the few remaining distinctive characteristics of "southern literature."[5]

Many writers who grew up in the segregated South or who have family there, as well as a younger generation of writers who graduated from its newly integrated schools, have created fictional worlds in which they examine race relations, analyze interracial relationships, dismantle racial stereotypes, and imagine integrated communities. Their narratives demonstrate how damaging post-1960s de facto segregation is to the human spirit and to any community's health, but they also reveal promising new cross-racial relationships and repressed histories of interracial intimacy. These writers use gender and class and sexual orientation to complicate thinking about race relations. They question the usefulness of monolithic definitions of racial identity, and they reconfigure the racial contours of family life. But the way southern literature is often studied as a regional literature, separate from mainstream American literature, means that many of these southern writers' interesting interventions into current debates about race relations may not be read by as wide an audience as they deserve. Over two decades ago, Michael O'Brien noted that Americans "feel little need to assimilate what may be said [in southern fiction], except when they decide to understand the South, a thing clean different than understanding the United States." More recently Patricia Yaeger persuasively argued that one of the reasons modern southern women's writing needs to be reexamined is its potential to provoke "new ways of thinking about racial epistemologies in American women's literature." With *Dirt and Desire* (2000), Yaeger sought to widen the audience for southern writing because of the South's significance in encoding "American ways of racial knowing: of both overconceptualizing and refusing to conceptualize an obscene racial blindness."[6]

If we look beyond the parameters of Yeager's study, there is another compelling reason to read and study literature about the South. Because the federal government mandated the dismantling of southern apartheid, the South's liberal-minded intellectuals and artists, politicians and educators were forced, unlike those living elsewhere in the United States, to rethink black-white relationships. As a result contemporary fiction set in the South can now help imagine new ways of racial knowing, but this fiction needs a wider audience and a more central place in American literature and in the field of American studies. Ironically, many American studies scholars in Europe have seized on contemporary southern literature's centrality in thinking about race, perhaps because Faulkner and Welty were already staples in their syllabi, perhaps because southern literature fit neatly into their units on the American civil rights movement, but surely because racial and ethnic relations in European countries have grown more complex and tense in the last two decades.

In this book I examine the cultural work that contemporary literature set in the South—by men and women, blacks and whites—has performed in the ongoing dialogue about black-white relationships. How do these texts read race relations? What contemporary social situations are they attempting to mediate? Do they offer alternative models for interracial relationships? How do they try to change readers' perceptions about racial identity and race relations? And how do some of the works unwittingly reinforce stereotypes? Sociologists Michael Omi and Howard Winant have argued that it is crucial "to understand race as *an unstable and 'decentered' complex of social meanings constantly being transformed by political struggle.*"[7] For contemporary writers, native and nonnative to the South, the region continues to be the fictional setting of choice for representing America's evolving thinking about black-white relationships and racial identity. The South's history of slavery and legal segregation and its present demographic changes, which reverse the African American out-migration that began at the turn of the previous century, make the region crucial for examining black-white relationships. In the 1860s Albion Tourgée, a novelist and counsel for the plaintiff in *Plessy v. Ferguson,* predicted that "Southern life would furnish to the future American novelist his richest and most striking material."[8] His prediction has proved true, particularly as regards the representation of race relations—from Tourgée's contemporaries Mark Twain, Charles Chesnutt, and George Washington Cable on through such southern renaissance writers as William Faulkner, Robert Penn Warren, and Richard Wright and into the present with the novelists I discuss.

Because of the explosion of such fiction in the past two decades, I am restricting my analysis to black-white relationships, but since 1990 the South's growing population of immigrants from the Caribbean, Mexico, and Southeast Asia, especially Vietnam, has complicated the region's predominantly biracial history. In *Natives and Newcomers* (1995), southern historian George Brown Tindall pointed out how these new immigrants have made race relations in the region quite literally less black and white. These new demographics augur a new direction in literature. In Josephine Humphreys's *Rich in Love* (1987), Lucille Odom spies a Vietnamese family fishing, as she meditates on the havoc new condominiums are wreaking on South Carolina's pristine coast. The Vietnamese immigrants recede into the background, however, as Lucille and Josephine Humphreys home in on the changes caused by developers and women's liberation. Five years later, however, Vietnamese immigrants appear at the center of the stories in Robert Olen Butler's *A Good Scent from A Strange Mountain* (1992).[9] Now stories about the newest Americans are being written by first- and second-generation immigrants themselves. Roberto G. Fernández's *Holy Radishes!* (1995), Lan Cao's *Monkey Bridge* (1997), and Susan Choi's *The Foreign Student* (1998) see the South through different eyes and tell new stories of race relations that realign racial confrontations and change the mix of cultural cross-pollination. In *Holy Radishes!* Cuban-American writer Fernández tells a story of two displaced women in a small town in the Florida Everglades—one from Tallahassee and the other from Xawa, his fictional Cuba. They connect through the fantasies they share, spun from pasts constructed in large part out of familiar southern and Cuban stereotypes, some overlapping. In Vietnamese immigrant Cao's *Monkey Bridge,* Mai Nguyen finds herself caught between two worlds, much like the Asian-American protagonists in fiction set in California, but Mai lives in the more unfamiliar immigrant literary territory of Virginia. In Choi's *The Foreign Student,* a Korean exchange student at Sewanee "locates himself" in tense moments through the Tennessee hills that remind him of home.[10] But it is his relationship with a wealthy young woman from New Orleans that will not allow him to forget the complexities of border crossings, and it is his presence in America that forces him to rethink the American presence in his homeland. Such new southern novels encourage readers to reconsider the South and southern identity, and they remind readers that in the twenty-first century race relations in southern literature will no longer be simply black and white and that the South through immigrant eyes looks a lot like America.

Despite these recent changes in southern demographics and literary history, race relations in the South for the past three decades have primarily been written in black and white. These narratives look much as Donald Noble suspected they would in the mid-1980s: "The stories of gross cruelty, lynching, and brutality will be fewer and give way to more subtle examinations of race relations in an integrated society."[11] However, I would add that in contemporary fiction set in the urban South, as well as that set in the past, injustice and violence still figure prominently. In *Inventing Southern Literature* (1998) Michael Kreyling persuasively argues that white southern renaissance writers' preoccupation with "race, tragedy, moral turbulence, blood violence, and guilt and expiation" can be interpreted "as an evasion strategy"—"voiding the need for cultural change or social action."[12] I do not find such evasion in the work of contemporary writers, where models for social action and social change coexist with the injustice and violence that necessitates them. For the generation of black and white writers who grew up during the 1950s and early 1960s, jumpstarting King's dream of integration is one of their main concerns. While contemporary white novelists are writing beyond the "racial conversion narratives" that preoccupied guilty southern white writers before the civil rights movement,[13] a few African American writers are fruitfully exploring this formerly all-white literary terrain by examining black characters' stereotypes about white people. Although variations on older plots still show up, new plots have emerged that turn on previously forbidden romantic desires, on social uncertainties in personal friendships, on questions about how racial identity should be defined, on subtle and institutional racism, and on community conflicts provoked by racial isolation, economic disparity, and residential segregation.

Michael Kreyling, in *Inventing Southern Literature*, rightly sees contemporary parodies of southern modernism as evidence of the end of "southern literature" as it has been defined by many, but parody is not the southern literary line's only issue. Many contemporary white writers are attempting both to reconstruct the South and to interrogate whiteness. Such writers as Elizabeth Spencer and Christine Wiltz have moved beyond white guilt and the sins of the fathers to envision social changes that an earlier generation of southern modernists could only begin to imagine. Others, such as Ellen Douglas and Madison Smartt Bell, are exploring not simply the South's racism but also outsiders' perceptions that all white southerners are racist.[14] These writers create out of a sense not of "inherited exhaustion" but of "unrealized possibility."[15] At the same time they have a healthy ironic sense that life rarely turns out as one hopes. After listening to a smooth-talking Klansman on a radio talk show and hearing of the arrest of a friend who had demonstrated against the Klan, Madison Smartt Bell told a reporter that he was so angry he decided to break his own rule and set his next novel in the South. He wrote *Soldier's Joy* not just to denounce the Klan, but to reclaim the South as a place for liberal-minded whites: "I especially wanted to deny their pretense of representing me or the great majority of other white Southerners—rural or urban, rich or poor—for whom they do not speak and never have." Bell believes that America's lingering persistence in thinking of racism as more prevalent in the South, despite the evidence otherwise, results not only in stereotyping the region but also in ignoring the national scope of racism, a truth confirmed for him by living much of his adult life in urban slums outside the South.[16]

For southern white writers who were young adults during the civil rights movement or for those who were only children, improving black-white relationships means rethinking whiteness. Whiteness has been rightly equated with racial blindness and prejudice, with power and privilege. But even before the sixties, there were discordant, albeit marginalized, southern white liberal voices, like Lillian Smith's and James McBride Dabbs's. Others were silenced, and some did not have the courage to speak. When Diane McWhorter was researching *Carry Me Home* (2001), a Birmingham resident said, "[T]he difference between now and then is that the good people back then were silenced. Now they've found their voice."[17] There may be some wishful thinking about the "good people back then" in this comment. But when David Shipler was interviewing Americans for *A Country of Strangers* (1997), he made this assessment about the present: "There are few white people in America more passionately perceptive about our vexing national problem than liberal-minded whites from the South, especially those who lived through the turbulent years of the civil rights movement. Lacking the detachment that allowed most Northerners to make judgments without making commitments, Southern whites who valued justice were forced to confront themselves, their families, their place of privilege."[18] Surely the concern about race relations of recent southern presidents Johnson, Carter, and Clinton provides public testimony to this statement.

Because of such white southern racial self-consciousness, feminist philosopher Linda Martín Alcoff has looked to the South, both to think through recent attempts to define whiteness and "to observe attempts at antiracist transformation." Worried about white backlash disrupting efforts to combat racism and construct integrated communities, Alcoff argues that thinking about white identity should probably be revised. She finds problematic both older strategies of antiracism training that raise awareness but offer few ideas for change and newer strategies based on anarchist acts disavowing whiteness, such as those promoted by the journal *Race Traitor.* Inspired by a new mandatory course to combat racism and sexism at the University of Mississippi, Alcoff suggests that whiteness can best be understood by employing a version of double consciousness: "an everpresent acknowledgment of the historical legacy of white identity constructions in the persistent structures of inequality and exploitation, as well as a newly awakened memory of the many white traitors to white privilege who have struggled to contribute to the building of an inclusive human community."[19] This is the very strategy that southern white writers who write about race relations have employed, especially in the last two decades.

Not surprisingly, for many African American writers, the South summons deeply troubled memories of "slavery's old backyard," as Eddy Harris terms it in *South of Haunted Dreams*.[20] Many contemporary African American writers, no matter their region of origin, have found that at some time, no matter how briefly, they must go South in their fiction to understand their history, to confront old enemies, and to heal, or at least anneal, old wounds. This turn south for nonnatives is often made in historical fictions recounting slavery or segregation, such as Sherley Anne Williams's *Dessa Rose*, Bebe Moore Campbell's *Your Blues Ain't like Mine*, and Albert French's *Holly*. In David Bradley's *The Chaneysville Incident*, Toni Morrison's *Song of Solomon*, Gloria Naylor's *Mama Day*, and Octavia Butler's *Kindred*, contemporary northern and western urban characters delve into their ancestors' rural southern pasts in order to understand their family history.

In the 1990s African American writers became increasingly interested in southern self-fashioning. Historian Nell Irvin Painter has pointed out that during the era of segregation, "*[t]he South* meant white people, and *the Negro* meant black people. . . . *The South* did not embrace whites who supported the Union in the Civil War or those who later disliked or opposed segregation."[21] For some today, these limited and limiting connotations of the word *South* still hold. A recently formed white reactionary political party calls itself the Southern Party, and an ultraconservative magazine is entitled *Southern Partisan*. But other southerners, black as well as white, are attempting to loosen the neo-Confederate stranglehold on the word *South*. In her analysis of the recent and more racially inclusive definition of "southern" culture, Thadious Davis argues that the return migration of African Americans to the rural South is not just "flight from the hardships of urban life," which figures in the ending of Bebe Moore Campbell's *Your Blues Ain't like Mine*, but also "a laying claim to a culture and a region that though fraught with pain and difficulty, provides a major grounding for identity."[22]

It is equally important to understand the love-hate relationship with the South that blacks who never left the region have experienced. In Anthony Grooms's *Bombingham* (2001), set in Bull Connor's Birmingham, Uncle Reed explains to eleven-year-old Walter why he stayed put despite the danger for black men:

[T]here were good jobs in Detroit and Chicago—but we were comfortable in the South. A colored somebody being comfortable in Old Dixie? People up North laugh at that. It ain't that we like Mr. Jim Crow—but this here is our home. This is where we belong—we the ones that tilled the field and built up the buildings, just as much as the white man. So folks who say we crazy for staying here, they just don't have any pride in what we done here. And I tell you one thing—most of them will come crawling on back down here, I can see it in their eyes when they come for a visit how much they miss down here. They always talking about country cooking. . . . Can't they cook collards in Detroit? It's not the collards they're craving—it's the whole thing. It's home. It's in their blood.[23]

And yet Grooms makes very plain the complexity of Uncle Reed's relationship to his "home," because this praise of place prefaces the telling of a long-suppressed story about the injustice that befell Walter's grandfather, who died in jail for a crime he did not commit. The prediction Uncle Reed makes in 1963 about reverse migration is a safe one, since Grooms completed his novel at the end of a decade in which record numbers of African Americans returned "home."

The 2000 U.S. census revealed that in the 1990s more African Americans moved to the South than to any other region in the country, making it the only region where more black Americans arrived than left. Encouraged by better economic opportunities, improved race relations, and old family ties, the gradual return of African Americans to the South, which began in the 1970s, increased dramatically in the 1990s, giving the South 55 percent of the country's black population.[24] And yet the statistics do not tell the whole story. Martin Luther King Jr. dreamed that Americans would live together with mutual respect in a "beloved community," but desegregation, affirmative action, and reverse migration have not yet totally fulfilled that dream in either the South or the rest of the country. In fact, as communication scholars Leonard Steinhorn and Barbara Diggs-Brown point out, "it is entirely possible to desegregate without integrating," since integration, after all, is about "the realm of life governed by behavior and choice, not by statutes and institutions."[25]

In interviewing both blacks and whites, David Shipler was struck by "how easily an experiential gulf translates into a racial caricature, imputing personal traits to all those of a certain color."[26] In the United States, race continues to be the too-easy way to explain differences between people who do not know each other. Differences caused by class, age, politics, hometown, and an individual's attitude and temperament continue to be overlooked. But at the same time selectively looking for similarities such as class or gender or politics can also create problems. As whites see more blacks on television and at the office and in the job market competing with them for the same jobs, many perceive economic disparity between the races as a thing of the past. A 2001 national survey found that large numbers of white Americans believe that blacks are as well off as whites in terms of jobs, schooling, incomes, and health care. However, government statistics show that "blacks have narrowed the gap but continue to lag significantly behind whites in employment, income, education and access to health care."[27] Such white misperceptions create problems in personal interactions as well as in debates about public policy.

Cultural critic Benjamin DeMott argues that contemporary advertising and the popular media have promulgated a misleading and simplistic assumption: that racism has to do "solely with the conditions of personal feeling" between blacks and whites—a shallow understanding of the problem that omits racism's "institutional, historical and political ramifications" and ignores the survival strategies many black people have adopted to cope with racism, in both its current and its past forms. Setting fiction or film in the South means that the troubled history of race relations in America can more easily be invoked. But a southern setting does not guarantee that institutional racism will emerge as a concern or that a southern narrative will delve much beyond what DeMott terms "friendship orthodoxy." Although *Driving Miss Daisy* (1989) won accolades from the white establishment (a Pulitzer Prize for the play and several Oscars for the film, including best screenplay and best picture), many African Americans judged it a feel-good film for whites. In telling examples ranging from television's *The Cosby Show* to Hollywood's *White Men Can't Jump* (1992) to a smorgasbord of Madison Avenue's commercials, DeMott argues that popular culture never moves beyond fantasy about black-white friendships.[28] Even the provocative and well-acted *Monster's Ball* (2001), which was nominated for an Academy Award for best original screenplay and won Halle Berry a best-actress Oscar, is ultimately disappointing in its treatment of interracial love, because the film facilely uses sex to work through racial tensions and solidifies the interracial union only by creating a social vacuum.

And yet fantasy can transform thinking even as it offers up illusions. Afrikaner policeman Eric Taylor confessed to the unsolved killing and burning of four black activists in Craddock, South Africa, after he saw *Mississippi Burning* (1988), a film in which a southern white sheriff aids in the murder of three

American civil rights activists. Moved by the film, Taylor was prompted to read Nelson Mandela's autobiography, which eventually led to his appearance before the Truth and Reconciliation Commission, where he publicly confessed and expressed remorse.[29] That the families of Taylor's victims refused to meet with him as he had hoped and assumed seems to confirm DeMott's thesis that "historically oriented cultural productions" like *Mississippi Burning* in actuality twist history to support "friendship orthodoxy." DeMott argues that such films diminish black grievances and restage black life in accordance with white mythology—refiguring the main conflict as one not between blacks and whites but between good and evil whites, most of whom at this stage in the history of race relations want to think of themselves as good.[30] Obviously such films can also work to increase familiarity, to improve understanding, and to dismantle some stereotypes, as *Mississippi Burning* did for Eric Taylor, even though, to take the same example, they may make the solutions to problems involving race appear too easy.

In the decades since the civil rights movement, the United States has passed laws to foster racial equality, but real economic and social inequities still exist. During the 1990s it became obvious that blacks' and whites' perceptions of the problems as well as the solutions to racism were troublesomely divergent. Many whites have come to believe that America's race problems were solved with the civil rights legislation of the 1960s and the affirmative action programs instituted shortly thereafter. Most African Americans, however, continue to experience subtle racism and at times outright discrimination. Where whites see blacks as overly sensitive, blacks see whites as oblivious to the daily stresses of blacks' lives caused by the color of their skin. Recently scholars have been debating just how much progress the United States, and particularly the South, has made since the civil rights legislation of the 1960s ended legal segregation and outlawed discrimination. Some scholars, like Andrew Hacker in *Two Nations: Black and White, Separate, Hostile, Unequal* (1992), focus on how far we have to go, while others, like Stephan and Abigail Thernstrom in *America in Black and White: One Nation, Indivisible* (1997), emphasize how far we have come, protesting what they believe to be Hacker's distortion. In the 1990s a few scholars, such as Shelby Steele, began to argue that African Americans' continued preoccupation with white racism obscures personal responsibility for their failure to get ahead and that their continued reliance on racial preferences fosters dependency. But still others, like Douglas Massey and Nancy Denton, see racism deeply embedded in such American institutions as banks and real estate agencies, which not only continue to discriminate racially but actually work to discourage integration.[31]

How American scholars could have such different perspectives on the same problem can be explained in large part by ideological differences, which Leonard Steinhorn and Barbara Diggs-Brown believe are influenced by how readily Americans buy into the "integration illusion": images of racial integration served up ubiquitously by whites in power, from the rhetoric of politicians to the color-blind casting of Broadway shows to the black and white buddies that are de rigueur in television commercials and big-budget films. Steinhorn and Diggs-Brown worry that white Americans especially have allowed the rhetoric and images of integration to blind them to the reality that despite working together, many black and white Americans do not choose to live together, socialize together, worship together, or go to school together (if whites can afford not to). They argue that since the sixties black and white Americans have learned "to accommodate one another in the public spheres that required interaction" but "remain distant in the private spheres that involved choice and any form of intimacy." Because it is no longer socially acceptable to exhibit prejudice, Americans, particularly whites, do not fully realize the extent of distrust and disrespect between blacks and whites. It takes highly publicized events like the O. J. Simpson trials or the beating of Rodney King to reveal the depth of misunderstanding that underlies the mannered way we have come to "coexist in separate realms, interacting when necessary and occasionally crossing over, but ultimately retreating to our different worlds."[32] The contemporary fiction that I am interested in takes readers beyond the "friendship orthodoxy" DeMott has identified and penetrates the "integration illusion" Steinhorn and Diggs-Brown have observed. It accomplishes this goal by giving readers varied perspectives on the same situations. To better understand self and other, Mikhail Bakhtin argues that we must know the other's language, because understanding occurs "on the *boundary* between one's own and someone else's consciousness."[33] Narrative techniques such as dialogue and multiple perspectives allow readers to enter vicariously a dialogic process that at the very least can provide what reader-response theorist Wolfgang Iser calls "anxiety free access" to the unspoken and the unknown and at the most can reformulate thinking about race relations and racial identity.[34]

Critics have debated how best to represent southern race relations for a century, beginning with Mark Twain's early critique of the South's propensity for the romance, which ironically gave *Huckleberry Finn* its odd schizophrenic form: realism in the first half of the novel when Huck decides he will go to hell rather than help to reenslave Jim, and romance in the concluding chapters when Huck goes along with his white friend Tom Sawyer to stage Jim's prolonged fantasy escape. Like Twain, Sterling Brown and Alain Locke also praised realism as the form mostly likely to dismantle stereotypes about black people. But Albion Tourgée argued that the intensity of southern life was more suited to the heightened effects of romance than to the "trivialities" favored by realists. Seventy years later Leslie Fiedler agreed, pronouncing "symbolic gothicism" the only form adequate to the complexities of life in the American South.[35] Most recently Henry Louis Gates Jr. has praised Toni Morrison's use of myth in *Beloved,* arguing that black writers have too rigidly produced works of social realism and in doing so "have conceived their task to be the creation of an art that reports and directly reflects brute, irreducible, and ineffable 'black reality,' a reality that in fact was often merely the formulaic fictions spawned by social scientists whose work intended to reveal a black America dehumanized by slavery, segregation, and racial discrimination, in a one-to-one relationship of art to life."[36]

Rather than using myth or gothic romance or social realism, some of the writers I discuss experiment with other forms. Ellen Douglas turns to metafiction, Connie Mae Fowler to magical realism, Raymond Andrews and Lewis Nordan to parody, and Dori Sanders to the novel of manners. The unfamiliarity of reading race relations written in these forms may have produced some of the debate about their novels. On one hand, certainly it is false to assume that literary forms themselves are direct reflections of ideology; such forms are always used within historical contexts and to address aesthetic problems. On the other hand, given the increasing racial tensions of the last decade, I can see how the techniques of metafiction could be misunderstood, how magical realism could be seen as promoting easy solutions, how parody may seem to diminish the subject's seriousness, and how the novel of manners could be viewed as revealing only a small portion of the story. But each of these new fictions tells an overlooked part of the complex story of contemporary race relations.

Wolfgang Iser argues: "The production of the meaning of literary texts . . . does not merely entail the discovery of the unformulated, which can then be taken over by the active imagination of the reader; it also entails the possibility that we may formulate ourselves and so discover what had previously seemed to elude our consciousness."[37] And much regarding race relations needs reformulating in the minds of Americans. Readers will find some of these reformulations in this fiction set in the South. But while some readers will read themselves, their communities, and race relations anew through this fiction, others reading from old paradigms may misread these new narratives, as the rare criticism of Sanders's *Clover* makes obvious. Although reviewers were almost unanimous in their praise of *Clover,* the story of a black girl and her white stepmother, an African American writer questioned Sanders as to why she had chosen social customs rather than social justice for her focus, while another doubted the reality of a black family owning a peach orchard in the South, unaware that Sanders had modeled the orchard after her own family farm.[38] Whereas Iser believes that by revealing "unrecognizable realities" and by repatterning "culturally conditioned shapes," writers perform their most imaginative work, Peter Rabinowitz reminds us that misreadings can occur when readers apply the wrong paradigms or read their formal or ideological presuppositions into texts.[39]

In an interview with a *Washington Post* reporter, Sanders defended the optimistic ending she chose for *Clover:* "If I write from the view that things can work out between the races it's because I'm drawing on my youth." She explained, using an example from her background as a peach farmer, that "all farmers are affected by the weather, so if you need help to harvest before a storm, you call in the other farmers, you don't think black or white."[40] The suspicion of the happy ending may have something to do with the present dichotomous thinking that attaches the happy ending to popular fiction and rarely to serious literature, but it surely has something to do with writers' fears that readers will lapse into the "integration illusion" if a story about race relations ends happily. Does this fear mean that readers should find suspect those narratives in which relationships between blacks and whites work out and thus should only want narratives in which interracial relationships fail? The criteria for judging novels that end happily should center on how intricately conflict is presented and how believably conflict is resolved, rather than simply whether the conflict ends happily. In the case of *Clover,* the happy ending between the black girl Clover and her white stepmother, Sara Kate, seems justified and earned, given their misinterpretations and reinterpretations, confrontations and growing communication. But the grand finale in which Sara Kate becomes a full-fledged member of the rural black community by saving her black brother-in-law's life after a bee sting and learning to drive his tractor so that she can keep the farm going during his recovery seems not only far too facile but even far-fetched. In Alison Light's discussion of feminist utopian fiction, she argues that part of the "fear of the happy ending" has been a definition of radical politics that "conceives its job as one solely of critique" and rarely of desire fulfilled.[41] Could the same be said of fictions about race relations? In writing about race relations, many writers that I discuss in the following chapters have found a way to model better interracial relationships or to promote racial reconciliation without succumbing to "friendship orthodoxy" or "the integration illusion." They often manage this difficult feat through double endings, which produce a happy ending for an interracial pair even as they withhold racial reconciliation for the larger community. Such endings suggest that solutions are not simple and yet simultaneously engage readers' desires to produce them. The result is fiction that haunts readers long after the last word.

Embedded within many of these recent narratives are concerns with how best to tell stories about race relations and how to read race more sensitively. These preoccupations suggest not only that race relations and constructions of racial identity must be rethought, but that new narratives of race relations, perhaps these very stories, are necessary for reading race anew. Unfortunately, public policies and economic changes have produced behaviors that can confirm stereotypes on both sides of the color line. Predominantly white calls to end affirmative action seem insensitive to African Americans who see the black middle class as only finally beginning to grow *because* of affirmative action. White misperceptions of life for the majority of blacks in the United States make African Americans lose hope that whites will ever really see beyond the images on *The Cosby Show*. Ironically, the problem of status that began for African Americans when white slave ships brought them to America was exacerbated after the civil rights movement when the urban industrial economy throughout the country began a downturn from which it has never recovered. As a result, many see contemporary race relations as caught in the vicious circle that Steinhorn and Diggs-Brown aptly describe: "The resulting rise of the urban underclass defied easy solutions, fed racial stereotypes, reinforced antisocial behaviors among [lower-class] blacks, further divided black and white opinions on how to achieve racial progress, and offered white Americans yet another reason to retreat into their protected suburban enclaves."[42]

The fictions that I analyze disrupt the popular discourse about race and race relations, but their representations of race relations vary depending on the nature of the relationship portrayed. Chapter 1 takes a backward glance at the

civil rights era through recent coming-of-age novels that feature young protagonists who seek racial equality but who sustain painful personal loses in the
process. It concludes with a forecast of how novels about children and race relations might take shape in years to come. Chapter 2 examines strategies for
dismantling stereotypes and imagining interracial friendships between women,
both fostered and complicated by the politics of the contemporary women's
movement. Chapter 3 suggests that something more than the comradeship
black and white men have experienced in war and sports is needed to produce
real interracial friendship. Several novelists suggest that rethinking masculinity may be the best way to move beyond superficial male connections. Chapter 4 shows contemporary southern fiction eager to uncover repressed stories
about past interracial love but reticent to investigate contemporary romance
other than in pulp fictions. Chapter 5 explores the reemergence of the racially
mixed character in interesting new guises as a provocative figure for new understanding of racial identity. Even such novels that foreground personal relationships before a segregated communal backdrop could run the risk, as Benjamin DeMott has argued, of making us unable to "think straight about race"
because they carry the potential of suggesting that "the race situation in
America is governed by the state of personal relations between blacks and
whites."[43] But new narratives about the urban South as well as new stories
about familiar rural communities, which I discuss in chapter 6, prevent readers from growing sanguine about the integrated small worlds of friends and
lovers and take them into the larger political, economic, and social realities
that perpetuate segregation.

Pierre Nora argues that history has become the substitute for imagination
in contemporary France, that memoirs, oral history, and historical novels are
"stand-ins for faltering fiction."[44] The fiction I discuss in this book is evidence
that despite the same vogue for historical forms in the United States, there is
no call yet to mourn the loss of imaginative literature, especially not literature
about black-white relationships. Novelists who write about the South are too
busy seeking "beyond history" for what Audre Lorde called "a new and more
possible meeting."[45] And those who embrace historical forms are not recycling
old stories. For as Ralph Ellison has argued, "one of the important roles which
fiction has played, especially the fiction of southern writers," is "to tell that
part of the human truth which we could not accept or face up to in much historical writing because of social, racial, and political considerations."[46] If Wolfgang Iser is right that "literature becomes a panorama of what is possible, be-

cause it is not hedged in by the limitations or the considerations that determine the institutionalized organizations within which human life takes its course,"[47] we need these fictions to help us imagine our way out of the social structures and mind-sets that mythologize the past, fragment individuals, prejudge people, and divide communities.

CHAPTER 1

Lost Childhoods

Black and White and Misread All Over

[T]he supreme court required children to do what adults had not—
desegregate the nation.

—JULIUS LESTER, *AND ALL OUR WOUNDS FORGIVEN*

In the late 1980s *Eyes on the Prize* brought back to the national consciousness the violent images of southern white resistance to court-ordered desegregation and the courageous efforts of civil rights activists working tirelessly to end discrimination. For many writers, both white and black, who grew up during those turbulent times, the haunting images of that television documentary must have stirred vague memories only partially understood. Perhaps these writers had simply reached an age of reminiscence, but within a decade following the airing of the documentary, John Gregory Brown, Bebe Moore Campbell, Mark Childress, Elizabeth Cox, Thulani Davis, Connie Mae Fowler, Anthony Grooms, Nanci Kincaid, and Lewis Nordan all completed fiction about young people set during the civil rights era. While civil rights activists favored memoirs about the movement, these mostly younger writers sought the expansiveness of historical fiction to express their emotions and voice their views. Perhaps initially overwhelmed by events that had "not yet settled into understanding," this group of writers finally had the necessary "frames of reference" to tell stories about the civil rights struggle.[1] Their novels attempt to provide readers with intimate perspectives on recent public history, but at the same time they reveal contemporary concerns about the movement's aftermath. Historian Hugh Davis Graham has pointed out that the "surprising civil rights successes of the post-1965 decade in the South, as demonstrated by the rapid collapse of the Jim Crow system, the relative absence of urban rioting, the detoxification of southern politics, and the rapid pace of school desegregation, lost momentum in the 1970s."[2] By the 1980s pessimism about the future of race relations had replaced sixties idealism. Recent novelists of the civil rights movement often seek to capture both emotions by using the frame narrative: adults reflecting on their childhoods during the sixties.

The novels that I discuss in this chapter, except for Sanders's *Clover*, take place during the 1950s and 1960s, a tumultuous time of lost innocence and momentous change, which parallels the stormy nineteenth-century period that captured Mark Twain's imagination. Like Mark Twain, contemporary writers have found the child, particularly when employed as naive narrator or fallible filter character, invaluable in examining the impediments to better relationships between blacks and whites.[3] The child protagonist has reemerged as a staple both in reconceptualizing the civil rights era and in clarifying thorny contemporary social issues involving children, such as interracial families and mixed-race identity. The child's perspective allows a writer to question a society's shortcomings from the vantage point of someone incompletely trained in a society's assumptions and customs.[4] In his writing notebook, Twain characterized Huck's momentous decision to stand by Jim this way: "In a crucial moral emergency a sound heart & a deformed conscience come into collision & conscience suffers defeat."[5]

The vulnerability of the young characters in novels written since the 1960s magnifies the turmoil during the time when these authors grew up or came of age: both the injustice and violence of southern racism and the hope and disillusionment of the civil rights movement. Racism causes black children to lose their innocence much earlier than most white children. But in this contemporary fiction, the age of innocence—when children, naive about the ways of the world, believe in unlimited possibilities and feel safe and secure—is foreshortened on both sides of the color line because of racism. Novelists writing about race and childhood have embraced Lillian Smith's 1940s view that "the warped, distorted frame we have put around every Negro child from birth is around every white child also. Each is on a different side of the frame but each is pinioned there."[6] Novels focusing on childhood and the civil rights struggle are punctuated with real-life references to lost innocence: the brutal slaying of fourteen-year old Emmett Till, the deaths of black children in Birmingham bombings, the murders of idealistic young black and white civil rights workers in Mississippi, the sit-ins at lunch counters in Greensboro, the uneasy desegregation of schools in Little Rock, and massive resistance in Virginia.

Novels set during the 1950s like *Your Blues Ain't like Mine* and *Wolf Whistle*, which fictionalize Emmett Till's murder, explore not just racism's young victims but the cycle of victimized children who grow up to be victimizers. Novels set during the sixties, like *1959, Bombingham, Crazy in Alabama,* and *Crossing Blood,* pinpoint the catalysts of youthful activism but then go on to explore the psychic wounds activism engendered. Novels set in the 1980s, like *Clover* and *Half a Heart,* which focus on more recent concerns, such as racially blended families and biracial identity, situate young people at the center of private family turmoil. These children, torn emotionally by adults who pressure them to choose racial sides, often become mediators for adults who behave like children. Indeed, in all of this more recent fiction about race and childhood, adults figure frequently as impediments to progress in race relations.

Novelists interpreting the civil rights struggle take as their task one that Shoshana Felman describes in her analysis of Camus's *The Plague:* "to demolish the deceptive image of history as an *abstraction* (as an ideological and/or statistical, administrative picture in which death becomes invisible) by *bearing witness to the body.*" She argues that "the specific task of the literary testimony is, in other words, to open up in that belated witness, which the reader now historically becomes, the imaginative capability of perceiving history— what is happening to others—*in one's own body,* with the power of sight (of insight) usually afforded only by one's own immediate physical involvement."[7] Humiliation comes unbidden and often unexpectedly to the characters in these novels, repeatedly to all black children and occasionally to the few white children who side with them and who thereby become "nigger lovers." These novelists use unexpected violence to disrupt their plots, recreating the shock of the senseless tragedies that occurred during the civil rights movement but also echoing the American gun culture, which still thrives. In *Bombingham* Anthony Grooms's narrator Walter ponders the difficulty of making readers "belated witnesses" when he compares the stories that he heard about lynchings with his experience as a boy in the violent streets of Birmingham and as a soldier in the killing fields of Da Nang: "stories, as terrifying and brutal as I imagined them, could never describe real violence. Violence has odors, both loud and subtle as the heightened senses pick them out. The stories my uncles told about lynchings always happened at a great distance."[8] Grooms, like many of these novelists, juxtaposes sharply contradictory sensory experiences in an attempt to shock readers into "immediate physical involvement." Finally, by exploring the history of the civil rights movement in fiction, these novelists raise questions about the fictionality of history. They ask what we have remembered and what have we forgotten, and why.

A number of American writers have attempted to give readers "sight" and "insight" into the brutal murder of Emmett Till, the best-known young victim of southern racial violence. James Baldwin and Toni Morrison wrote plays, Gwendolyn Brooks and Audre Lorde wrote poems, and many other writers have alluded to his death in their work. But more recently, given some distance from the event and some changes in the racial climate, novelists Bebe Moore Campbell and Lewis Nordan, in a departure from these earlier chroniclers, have begun with the murder and have written hope into its aftermath. Both writers have modified the customary list of victims, examining how children of both races grow up psychically warped by white racism but also speculating about other causes that lead some to reenact the hurt they experienced as children and others to seek to ameliorate pain. When Campbell's Emmett Till character, Armstrong Todd, looks into the face of his white murderer, he wonders, "Where did all that hatred come from?"[9] This is the question that leads both Campbell and Nordan to imagine the childhoods of everyone directly and indirectly involved in the racially motivated murder of a teenage boy.

The 1954 *Brown v. Board of Education* ruling encouraged southern blacks to mount voter registration campaigns, but it sparked angry indignation among most southern whites, who, much like their antebellum ancestors, viewed the federal government as meddling in states' affairs. White hysteria found expression in an upsurge of violence—killings, beatings, burnings—by lower-class white men, who took up the old work of the Ku Klux Klan, and in economic reprisals by middle-class whites, who formed Citizens' Councils. Named the "white-collar Klan" by civil rights activists, the Citizens' Council's purpose according to one council leader was "to make it difficult, if not impossible, for any Negro who advocates desegregation to find and hold a job, get credit, or renew a mortgage."[10] Because black people outnumbered whites in many voting precincts in the South, whites were determined both to keep their political power by discouraging black voters and to maintain social segregation, which led to the formation of private all-white academies throughout the South, many of which exist today. In Mississippi white hysteria over black voter registration led to two racially motivated murders in 1955. Neither made the national news. But Emmett Till's murder in Money, Mississippi, was different. His youth and the photographs of his mutilated, partially decomposed body fueled international media interest, finally bringing southern racist violence to the nation's attention. Myrlie Evers, wife of the slain civil rights activist, perhaps best summed up the significance of Till's murder: "The Emmett Till case shook the foundations of Mississippi, both black and white—with the white community because it had become nationally publicized, with us blacks, because it said even a child was not safe from racism and bigotry and death."[11]

Visiting from Chicago, fourteen-year-old Emmett "Bobo" Till had been hanging out with friends in front of Bryant's Grocery and Meat Market, when he showed them a picture of a white girl, whom he claimed was his girlfriend. To test his boasting, the boys dared him to speak to one of the young white women clerking in the store. While the exact nature of their exchange is disputed, Emmett's friends remember him saying "Bye, Baby" to Carolyn Bryant, but she later claimed he called her other offensive names and wolf-whistled at her. At the time of the encounter, Mrs. Bryant and her sister-in-law Mrs. Milam agreed not to tell their husbands, but ironically, Emmett's cousin told Roy Bryant. Soon after, Bryant and his half brother J. W. Milam abducted Emmett from his great-uncle's house, beat him, shot him in the head, and dumped his body, weighted down with a cotton-gin fan, into the Tallahatchie River. At first some white Mississippians were shocked by Till's murder, but defensiveness grew in direct proportion to the number of national reporters who came to town. Bryant and Milam were charged with the murder; however, they claimed they had only warned Emmett Till, a defense that won them acquittal by an all-white jury. Later the two men confessed to Till's murder in a paid interview in *Look* magazine but maintained that killing a black man who showed disrespect to a white woman was not a crime. As in other periods of crisis in the South, white men sanctioned racial violence in the name of a white women's honor. For them, white womanhood was the repository of racial purity and the foundation of southern civilization; thus, to show disrespect for a white woman was to show disrespect for both a way of life and the authority of white men.

In *Your Blues Ain't like Mine* (1992) Campbell adds psychological complexity to several characters that James Baldwin introduced in his 1964 play, *Blues for Mister Charlie,* and she develops the connection between racial violence and gender oppression that Gwendolyn Brooks established in her 1963 poems "A Bronzeville Mother Loiters in Mississippi. Meanwhile, a Mississippi Mother Burns Bacon" and "The Last Quatrain of the Ballad of Emmett Till." Although Campbell was only five years old when Emmett Till was murdered, she seeks to answer the question that black teenagers in Mississippi asked after viewing photographs of his mangled body: "How could they do that to him? He's only a boy."[12] To answer this question, Campbell probes the psyches of Armstrong Todd; Floyd Cox, the white man who murders Armstrong; Floyd's wife, Lily;

and Jake, the dark-skinned black man who works in Floyd's pool hall, where Armstrong and Lily encounter each other. Given the race, gender, class, and color hierarchies involved, these four characters make up a volatile quartet, and Campbell suggests that insecurity, envy, and a desire for power motivate all four people. She represents their actions as stemming from childhood wounds that affect adult reactions. Using flashbacks, Campbell proposes that seemingly inexplicable human behavior can be understood and that apparently transparent actions are more complex than they seem.

The behavior of Jake, the black man who tattles on Armstrong, seems especially paradoxical, but Campbell uses a flashback to Jake's childhood as insight. When Jake was growing up, black children taunted him about his physical appearance: "Black Jake. Ugly as a snake!" (12). As a result, Jake takes an instant dislike to Armstrong Todd because he is light-skinned and handsome and he lives in the very city where Jake has dreamed of playing his harmonica in jazz clubs. To punish Armstrong for being the person he can never be, Jake makes disparaging remarks about Chicago; and when Armstrong responds by calling him "ugly," the word reverberates with the pain of Jake's childhood. Jake retaliates by telling Floyd that Armstrong has flirted with his wife Lily. Thus Jake uses the racist white power structure, which he hates, against Armstrong, just as black children have used a white standard of beauty against him. Jake does not recognize his envy of Armstrong and so makes their tense encounter Armstrong's fault, rather than in any way his own. Uncomfortable with the black youth's self-confidence and sophistication and angered by the familiar retort, Jake denigrates the very qualities that he envies by saying Armstrong is "trying to be white" (78). When Jake hears of Armstrong's death, he represses his role by mentally chastising Armstrong for breaking the very racist code that he himself detests: "Yella bastard shoulda kept his mouth shut" (81). By implicating Jake as an accessory of sorts to Armstrong's murder, Campbell suggests that racism's victims can become its perpetrators.

In a similarly complex way, Campbell examines Armstrong's motivations for speaking to the white women, representing the action not simply as an impetuous boyish response to a dare, but as a conscious refusal to let the southern racial code define him. Campbell's Till figure is keenly aware of how subservient his country cousins are to white people, and he does not want to be seen in the same light, either by the black "country fools" with whom he plays pool or by the "poor-white-trash" for whom they work: "He deliberately made his voice loud and condescending, so that everyone understood that he was a

Chicago boy, born and bred, city slick and so cool that nobody better not mess with him" (11, 13). Jake's disrespectful comment about Armstrong's father, whom Armstrong rarely sees, only increases Armstrong's determination to set himself apart from other black people so as not to be a stereotypical fatherless black boy. To the uncomprehending black men in the pool hall, he shows off the French phrases he learned from his father, a World War II veteran, "*Voulez-vous danser avec moi ce soir? Vous êtes belle mademoiselle.*" Nonsensical in this context, they simply suggest bravado. But when he unwittingly repeats the phrases in front of a white woman, they produce a different effect, although it is significant that Lily Cox does not comprehend them either and so does not sense any provocation in his remarks. With their connotation of intimacy, however, they suggest to readers just how daring Armstrong's subsequent eye contact and exchange of laughter with Lily is, transforming their chance encounter into a deliberate flirtation, which is exactly what Floyd Cox will accuse him of. That Campbell portrays the encounter as accidental only amplifies the reader's shock at its outcome.

To establish the link between southern race and gender oppression, Campbell represents Lily Cox as pleased by Armstrong's attention. Lily unexpectedly experiences a powerful moment of sexual attractiveness and social daring, because her encounter with Armstrong functions as a double defiance of southern racial conventions and her husband's order to stay in the truck. Making Lily's free minutes coincide with this encounter focuses attention on how inextricably southern white womanhood is linked to racial attitudes in the South. While the stolen time exhilarates Lily, it threatens her husband's control over her body. Immediately before her encounter with Armstrong, Campbell depicts Lily as eager for sex with her husband, Floyd, who has been away on a job, but sexually repressed by his belief that only whores initiate intercourse. Campbell portrays Lily as a woman trapped—horrified by Armstrong's murder but economically dependent on her husband. This feeling of powerlessness inhibits Lily from acting on her better instincts and telling the truth, thereby ruining a budding relationship with Ida, a black woman Lily has come to know, who shares Lily's restlessness with life in Money. The only way that Lily can live with Floyd's emotional and physical brutality is to construct a narrative of his heroism in protecting her from the black male beast, even if he is really an innocent boy. She consoles herself by thinking, "I've got a man who'll kill for me" (64, 150). As with Jake, Campbell uses Lily's childhood to explain her convoluted thinking about sex and sin and race. Lily is haunted by memories of an uncle who sexually abused her. Campbell flashes back to these awful memories whenever Lily doubts herself in the present, such as wondering whether her sexual desires for her husband are normal and whether the chance incident with Armstrong was her fault.

Finally Campbell probes the psyche of Armstrong's murderer and once more follows a trail of psychic wounding back to childhood. She links both Floyd's need to control his wife and his decision to kill Armstrong not simply to his society's sexist and racist ideology, but to deep uncertainty about his own manhood, caused by a feeling of inferiority to his older brother, and to a fear that his father loves his brother more. Floyd's insecurities manifest themselves in violent behaviors—both toward those he avowedly loves, like Lily and his son when they disappoint him, and toward those his society has taught him to hate, like Armstrong. Floyd's father first questioned his manhood during Floyd's first hunting trip. Only nine and afraid of blood and guns, Floyd throws up. His father's callous response—"I didn't know I was taking a girl hunting" (121)—influences Floyd's choices for the rest of his life because he is forever trying to win his father's love by proving his manhood. As Campbell makes clear through Floyd's thoughts—always worried about his father's reaction, ever conscious of how his brother would act—attempting to prove his manhood governs his reaction to Lily's encounter with Armstrong. The southern racial code his father has instilled in him requires Floyd to confront Armstrong to prove his manhood. Only when Floyd has pulled the trigger that he could not pull at age nine does he win his father's qualified approval: "Well, you might can't fix everything that needs fixing, but damned if you can't make some things right." The warmth that Floyd gains from finally "knowing that his father, at last, was satisfied with him" (43) is short-lived as his father blames him when all three Cox men are arrested for the murder. Then the cycle of violence begins all over again as Floyd discharges his emotional pain onto Lily, who absorbs his blows because of her own insecurities. For Campbell, then, the psychological wounds that Floyd experienced growing up, combined with his society's racism, provide the answer to Armstrong's question, "Where did all that hatred come from?"

Campbell's decision to intersperse scenes set in Chicago with those in Mississippi draw a clear line for the reader from southern slave quarters to northern housing projects,[13] from sharecropping in the rural South to the end of good factory jobs in the urban North, from hopes of a promised land up north to the despair of urban ghettos. The two settings remind readers that blacks who migrated north still had deep roots in the South (family ties, cooking, the blues, jazz), and at the same time they also illustrate that even outside the South, African Americans were not out of the reach of what Campbell sees as the twin legacies of slavery and segregation: white racism and an "overidentification with being a victim."[14] For although in the first half of the novel, Campbell shows all of her characters, white and black, to be victims in one way or another, in the second half she focuses on those characters who rise above their unfortunate childhoods.

After Floyd's trial, chapters alternate between the Todds in Chicago, struggling to make a life after Armstrong's death, and the Coxes in Mississippi, struggling to make a living in a town shell-shocked by the bad national publicity they brought down on their community. This juxtaposition of the black and white families points up the irony of Campbell's title, *Your Blues Ain't like Mine.* Muddy Waters and Robert Johnson are not Hank Williams and Patsy Cline, but Campbell links the pain that the lyrics of blues and country music give voice to and the solace they provide—blues to poor blacks and country music to poor whites. Both families are dysfunctional, with the sources in childhood abuse and society's race, class, and gender biases that take an early toll. Both black and white mothers struggle with poverty and single parenthood as their husbands are increasingly absent. Both black and white fathers and sons are crippled by narrow notions of masculinity and by drugs. By linking poor black and white families who because of racism have been unable to see similarities, Campbell prepares the way for a fictional racial reconciliation between the working-class people that has always eluded them because of racism.

The psychological realism that Campbell employs to probe the motivations of the characters linked by Armstrong's murder gives way to a more sweeping exploration of social change in Mississippi over the succeeding three decades. Campbell needs those thirty years in order to arrive at her surprisingly happy ending, which leaves the reader with hope that Mississippi may rise above its notoriously racist past and that poor Mississippians may understand that they share an economic struggle despite their racial differences. The unexpected happens. Armstrong Todd's father and his younger brother W.T. flee Chicago's violent, drug-infested streets for a bucolic sojourn in Mississippi. Clayton Pinochet, a prominent liberal white man who has cowered behind his racist father's bank account, splits his inheritance with his biracial half sister Ida, a character I discuss in more detail in chapter 5. Floyd and Lily Cox's daughter Doreen reaches across the color line during a labor dispute at the new catfish farm where she works with Ida, who has emerged as a spokesperson for labor. While incidents like all of these can and do occur in the South, to conclude with all three surely gives a very rosy picture of racial reconciliation in rural Mississippi.[15]

But simply to chalk up Bebe Moore Campbell's happy ending to the generic demands of popular fiction, as some reviewers did,[16] is to miss how the successes of her triumphant characters, also victims of a variety of social prejudices, drive home Campbell's belief in the possibility of rising above one's social circumstances. Doreen Cox, unlike her father, has encounters with African Americans at school and at work that broaden her perceptions, encounters that allow her to see the humanity of black people. Watching an acclaimed documentary on America's civil rights years, surely a reference to the PBS television series *Eyes on the Prize*, Doreen gains a different perspective on her father and mother's past. For each of Campbell's characters, white and black, to improve their lives, they must first face their racial misperceptions. For example, Delotha Todd's attempt to bring Armstrong back to life by having another baby backfires when she begins to ignore her husband, to spoil her younger son W.T., and to blame his problems on the white teachers and white policemen, who tip her off to his drug-related activities. At first Delotha thinks she is protecting W.T. from white people, but eventually she faces up to the truth of her role in the family's breakdown and the truth of a black friend's assessment of her family life in Chicago: "The streets is killing more black boys than the white folks ever could. We always had more than one enemy" (407). Only at that point do Delotha, W.T., and Wydell begin to function as a family. By covering two generations of characters, Campbell does not ignore history, but she finds it problematic to read past racial incidents solely through the lens of race and to see contemporary interracial interactions only through the prism of past race relations.

Lewis Nordan was the first white writer to fictionalize Emmett Till's death. In crucial ways his characterization of the white people involved in Bobo's murder and the aftermath are similar to Campbell's. Nordan builds his story with characters broken during their childhood. Some characters, like Solon Gregg, who murders Bobo, are filled with bitterness but, failing to identify the source of their pain, displace it onto those whom their society denigrates. Other characters, like Smoky Viner, a thick-necked white boy who is made the brunt of jokes because of his appearance, identify with Bobo and chastise the other white boys who make jokes about his death. Still other white characters, like Alice Conroy, who teaches tolerance, know the complex sources of personal pain but understand it to be partly of their own making. She has had a love affair with a married man that ended unhappily. Nordan depicts empathy as an act of the imagination that allows people to know the pain of others, but he suggests that empathy is often accompanied by painful guilt. Alice, who imagines a world without prejudice, feels guilt and then failure when she cannot make it a reality. She foresees Bobo's death in a raindrop and is saddled ever afterward with wondering "whether there was not more she could have done."[17]

Unlike Campbell, Nordan had a real-life connection to Emmett Till's murder. Till was killed near Nordan's hometown of Itta Bena, Mississippi, when Nordan was sixteen. Nordan has said that the day he found out about Till's death changed his life but that he hesitated to write about it because he did not feel it was his story to tell:

> I felt an outsider to the story because I knew the murderers. My father was a friend of one of the guys who killed Emmett Till. We knew their family and yet when it happened, we withdrew into a cocoon of silence, even at the dinner table. We never spoke of the murder. I never said, did Mr. Milam really do this? I never said anything, and nobody else said anything about it either. We were horrified by it. We were so shocked we couldn't deal with it at all, couldn't even talk about it, let alone take responsibility for it.

Eventually Nordan realized that a part of the story was his: "The white trash version of the Emmett Till murder. I had the story of the people who were on the periphery of this terrible thing, who didn't know what was going on, didn't quite understand their own culpability in the situation. That was the story I had to write, the murderers' story, the family of the murderers, the friends and drinking buddies of the murderers."[18] In limiting himself for the most part to the white perspective, Nordan followed Eudora Welty's lead in "Where Is the Voice Coming From?" (1963). Written on the August night when she learned that Medgar Evers had been shot, Welty's story is narrated from the chilling first-person perspective of his killer. But Nordan created his own unique literary vehicle in *Wolf Whistle* (1993)—a combination of burlesque and magical realism, filtered through many white perspectives, men and women, old and young, rich and poor. Reviewers alternated between praise for Nordan's creativity and misgivings about his unorthodox approach, given the sensitivity of the subject matter.

Randall Kenan's mixed review in the *Nation* directly addresses a concern about point of view that Nordan thought he had finessed. Aware of Nordan's reluctance to usurp Emmett Till's story, Kenan extols his artistic virtuosity and his compassionate sensibility and so grants him the "right" to explore the hearts and minds of characters on both sides of the color line. This is the "right" that some writers and scholars in 1968 thought William Styron had not earned when he wrote *The Confessions of Nat Turner* (1967).[19] Because Kenan believes that Nordan writes with much thought and care, he judges the absence of the Till character's perspective a failure of imagination:

> In the spaces that are crowded out by young white boys dealing with their igno-
> rance and bigotry, and with white husbands reconciling themselves with their
> own sense of worth and white women finding solidarity and strength among
> their own number, this reader longs for a space in which the undeniable pain and
> physical scars of oppression and miscarriages(s) of justice are explored. Or in the
> words of Douglas Turner Ward's play *Day of Absence,* 'Where de nigras at, Luta?'
> One cannot help but sigh in regret, imagining what profundity might have been
> attained had the author attempted to imagine what is apparently still the unimag-
> inable to too many Americans.[20]

In *Your Blues Ain't like Mine,* Campbell gives readers access to Armstrong's consciousness the night that Floyd Cox kills him and thus allows us to become "belated witnesses" to his murder. We experience the mundanity of the hot summer night when the white men drive up to his grandmother's house, Armstrong's futile attempt to reason with the Cox men, the shock of his pain as they kick him, his struggle to remember self-effacing tactics for dealing with white people, and his vain attempt to placate his attackers with what little money he has in his pockets. Campbell represents the kaleidoscopic last minutes of Armstrong's life by alternating descriptions of his body's realization that he is going to die (urine runs down his leg, his bowels release) with his imagination's desperate struggle to stay alive.

Clearly Kenan expected no less from Nordan. One might counter that Nordan decided against exploring black pain for aesthetic reasons. *Wolf Whistle* pokes fun at all sorts of white southern pieties: from the South's famous sense of the past (one-hundred-year-old talking buzzards bear the names of racist governors), to its highly touted hospitality (Solon Gregg offers to take Bobo fishing before he murders him), to its beloved feeling of community. Arrow Catcher, Mississippi, which has always thought of itself as "a good place to raise a boy," is forced to look at itself through the eyes of *Look* magazine as a town where a child was murdered (215). The delicious caricatures Nordan employs to topple familiar southern character types work well enough to introduce a streetwise and cocky Bobo, who brags about white girlfriends in Chicago while flashing a wallet-sized picture of Hedy Lamar. But perhaps Nordan thought it inappropriately irreverent to use parody to probe Bobo's pain. As a result, one could perhaps understand why Nordan chose not to enter Bobo's consciousness at the time of his murder, as Campbell does, but to create instead a fantastical few hours after his death to catalog racial oppression. From the perspective of a drowned Bobo's dangling eyeball, Nordan gives readers the "worlds invisible" to Bobo before his death (175): the hatred and self-hatred of impoverished white men, like Solon Gregg; the compassion of an idealistic young white teacher, Alice Conroy; and the beauty of the Mississippi landscape. Bobo's eyeball penetrates the "black water" of Roebuck Lake, which is home to both beauty and danger, good and evil: bright bluegills and submerged logs, "schools of minnows and a trace of slave death," and "baptizings and drownings" (181).

Such a mixed vision reflects Nordan's own conflicted feelings about Mississippi: love of the Delta's landscape and horror at its social geography, a need to acknowledge white racism but a desire to show that not all whites are racist. Nordan employs this signature image across his fiction to suggest that people must get beyond seeing their own reflection in the world in order to probe its depths.[21] Identifying Roebuck Lake as the "geography of my heart," Nordan remembers the day of Emmett Till's death as the day when he penetrated the surface of his hometown—the day when he knew he would have "to leave Mississippi and try to find a larger world, a world in which everybody might say, 'It's not right to talk like that about a boy, it's just not right.'"[22] These words, which Nordan remembers hearing that day, are the words his white character Roy Dale hears after school the day of Bobo's murder. Like Nordan, on that day Roy Dale realizes that racism is wrong. On that day he sees himself and then his hometown in a different light.

For Roy Dale, the realization of his own racism emerges simultaneously with a diminished view of himself, an uncomfortable feeling of shame that Nordan depicts as seeking an outlet—the other side of the coin of the teacher Alice Conroy's white guilt. That Smoky Viner, a white boy Roy Dale despises, has understood the horror of Bobo's murder wounds Roy Dale's pride; he can no longer think of himself as better than Smoky. So when the arrow-catcher coach asks him to pair with Smoky during the afternoon practice, Roy Dale shoots him with a blunt arrow, thereby taking all of his pent-up anger out on Smoky: his rage at his mother for leaving his father, the emptiness in his relationship with his father, and the loss of his sense of himself as superior to Smoky. This scene parallels the scene in which Solon Gregg targets Bobo for the hurt Solon experiences at being snubbed by a rich white woman who responds more favorably to Bobo's flirtations than to his own. Through flashbacks, Nordan makes sure that readers see Solon's violent act in much the same way as Roy Dale's—as a product of Solon's past pain at watching his father molest his sister and of his current confusion about his own sexuality. By linking two very different characters, the reprobate Solon and the adolescent boy Roy Dale, Nordan, like Campbell, shows that the potential to scapegoat is present in everyone and that those people whom society marginalizes provide the readiest target. Roy Dale's horror at hurting Smoky is so great and his relief so powerful at not having harmed him worse by using his one prized steel-tipped arrow, that he breaks the arrow. Nordan makes this a symbolic break with an old way of dealing with hurt. Roy Dale has been driving the steel-tipped arrow into his bedroom wall every night to release his rage at his parents. After this momentous day, he turns his back on ineffectual outrage; he acts to change the home life he hates, by breaking his silence and talking with his mother and telling his father he loves him.

Thus, certain realistic scenes push their way up through *Wolf Whistle's* burlesque, as if Nordan were personally too close to the emotional pain they portray to stylize them: Roy Dale's realization that he is a racist, his alcoholic father Runt's pleading telephone conversation with his estranged wife, and the beauty of the Mississippi Delta. Nordan's biography suggests that the moments of pain in this novel—broken marriages, distant fathers, white epiphanies about racism—are rooted in his own experience. Because realism has a place in this narrative as a vehicle for expressing emotional pain, one finally cannot let Nordan off the hook for failing to express Bobo's emotional and physical pain. Perhaps the specter of William Styron's attempt to enter Nat Turner's consciousness cast a troublesome shadow on Nordan's imagination.

His decision to stylize Bobo's pain is not race specific, for Nordan resorts to magical realism to transform Smoky Viner's physical pain when Roy Dale shoots him during arrow-catcher practice:

The atmosphere rarified.

Birds fell from the air.

Cattle toppled over in a field.

Car motors stalled on the highway.

To emphasize the significance of Roy Dale's dawning empathy and to contrast it with Solon's lack of empathy, Nordan also imagines a reversal of Bobo's fate: "The body of the Bobo-child, dressed in a heavy garment of fish and turtles and violent death, reversed all its decay . . . and bad manners and disrespect and a possessive disdain for a woman became mere child's play, a normal and decent testing of adolescent limits in a hopeful world" (208–9). This wishful, magical transformation of past tragic events that should have been viewed as adolescent playfulness parallels the real transformation of white boys like Roy Dale by Smoky's empathy with a black boy. The narrator terms the startling occurrence of interracial empathy in a racist town "a miracle" (210). Nordan punctuates other miraculous moments in the novel with magic. When a black man does the unthinkable and testifies against Bobo's killer, Runt's parrot flies over and lands on Solon's head: "It shit down Solon's back, great farting blobs of liquid white bird dooky. *White!* it seemed to say, *White, white, white!*" (255). When Alice and her fourth graders sit in the balcony with the black people, Nordan fills the courtroom with "magical identification" (232), and a white woman who is married to a racist man is transformed by a sense of solidarity with Alice.

By using magical realism and parody, Nordan complicates his readers' view of Mississippi and expresses both his love and his hate for his native state. But by using magical realism to transform Emmett Till's mangled body into Bobo's magic eyeball, he distances painful memories. And yet, even as Nordan attempts to reclaim the Delta with his loving descriptions and with a reorientation to the future, he tempers his hopeful fantasies with reservations: *"Begin again,* the mallards say, *Begin,* the rice fields whisper. . . . What do the cotton fields say when the green leaves are gone, and the square and the blossom and the boll? . . . Do they say, *Shouldn't our ancient suffering be more fruitful by now?"* (150). In *Wolf Whistle,* only the white people begin again: Roy Dale's father, Runt, drops the nickname he has always hated and becomes Cyrus, Roy Dale's mother comes home, and Cyrus and Roy Dale vow to express their love. Despite the novel's stylistic innovations, then, its intervention in race relations is not unlike that in earlier southern novels, such as William Faulkner's *Intruder in the Dust* (1948), or more contemporary novels, like Padgett Powell's *Edisto* (1983) or Kaye Gibbons's *Ellen Foster* (1987), in which an encounter with a black person makes a white youth think differently about race but goes no further. Certainly white racial conversion before the civil rights movement was momentous, as Nordan shows, because so few white people even thought about whether segregation was right or wrong. And because of this, Nordan's use of magic as a metaphor to represent such unlikely imaginative breakthroughs makes the novel innovative despite its reliance on the old white racial conversion theme.

John Dittmer has pointed out that the young people who were leaders of the Student Nonviolent Coordinating Committee (SNCC) in the 1960s were "in a real sense members of 'the Emmett Till generation,'"[23] a contention echoed by former civil rights activist Julian Bond, who wrote that "the movement succeeded because the victims became their own best champions."[24] Novelists who write about the sixties have cast their child protagonists as civil rights activists, thereby reminding readers how much the civil rights movement depended upon the actions of young people. They integrated the schools, sat in at the lunch counters, picketed the stores, participated in the marches, rode buses to desegregate interstate travel, and formed their own organizations, most notably SNCC. Much of the recent novelists' focus on young activists may be wishful thinking: that they had been old enough to be activists themselves during the movement, or that their novels will act as catalysts for a social movement they participated in and remember vividly but that now seems stalled. Some white writers, like Mark Childress, who was born in 1957, too late to participate in the movement, remember childhood epiphanies about the absurdity of southern racial apartheid: "I remember one time when I was 7 going to a Dairy Queen with my cousins and unwittingly walking up to the window marked 'Colored.' My cousins made fun of me for that, but I had a very clear sense that it was the same ice cream, so why different windows? I felt humiliated for not 'knowing my place' in the 'white' line, and I guess my very small sense of injustice awakened then." Others, particularly African American writers like Thulani Davis, who was born in 1949, participated in voter registration drives through their churches and joined boycotts and marches in their communities. Younger black writers, like Anthony Grooms, whose wife grew up in Birmingham, have heard many tales about the movement from family members. White writers of the same age have heard almost nothing, probably because their parents have something to hide—either overt or covert racism or a failure to act on liberal beliefs.[25] In *Carry Me Home: Birmingham, Alabama: The Climactic Battle of the Civil Rights Revolution* (2001), white journalist Diane McWhorter relates how the bomb that killed four black girls her age meant merely a canceled play rehearsal for her. Only decades later did McWhorter delve further into her earlier suspicions about her father's clandestine activities that fateful week.

In Diane Roberts's review of Grooms's *Bombingham,* she pointed to the lack of complexity with which most people view the sixties: "most Americans see the civil rights movement in cartoon simplicity: eloquent preachers, thuggish cops, virtuous marchers, snarling Klansmen," but the reality, as *Bombingham* makes clear, was "not quite so black and white."[26] Those novelists who have revisited the sixties through the eyes of a child have attempted to recapture the mixed emotions and the ideological variations among both blacks and whites that the popular imagination has evened out. In explaining his reasons for writing *Crazy in Alabama,* Mark Childress said, "I wanted to write something that showed the complexity of racism in the South—whites beating up on black people; whites with good instincts who were afraid to do anything; blacks who didn't know what to do, either; blacks pushing too hard; whites like Peejoe's grandmother who had a good heart but was devoted to George Wallace— in other words, a full range of people."[27] While his range of characters is broad, Childress develops his white characters more fully than his black characters. One must read Thulani Davis and Anthony Grooms for more three-dimensional black characters, although conversely Davis's white characters are not three-dimensional. Because the authors have created fiction out of the segregated communities of their childhood, these movement-era novels need to be read together to get a more complete picture. Only in Nanci Kincaid's *Crossing Blood* do both black and white characters play major roles and emerge as three-dimensional figures, but then Kincaid bases her novel on her own childhood experiences of living next door to a black family.

All of these novels portray the terror and the violence that accompanied civil rights activism in the face of white backlash. Although young protagonists of both races challenge the conventions of southern race relations, they experience the struggle differently, with blacks fearing more for their lives and whites more for their reputations. Mark Childress's Peejoe remembers the shock he felt when a black boy he did not know died trying to integrate the neighborhood pool; Anthony Grooms's Walter, in contrast, remembers the pressure of his friend Lamar's dead body against his shoulder the day Lamar was shot while riding on the handlebars of Walter's bicycle. Surprisingly perhaps, black and white protagonists have similar emotional antagonists, because they must defy family and friends who disapprove of their activism. Walter's parents forbid his participation in the demonstrations, and they only allow him to go to movement workshops to learn black history. He rebels, but secretively. In contrast, Peejoe becomes something of a pariah in his neighborhood and within his family for supporting the freedom movement. Youthful idealism about the civil rights movement and loss of childhood's illusions of safety and justice are recurring themes in these novels. Thulani Davis sees integration as inextricably linked with the loss of a familiar way of life.

This sense of loss may seem paradoxical, especially to white readers, but in the face of Jim Crow, African Americans created their own communities by establishing businesses, professional institutions, and churches and by nurturing their own music and art and culture in order to provide solace and sustenance. Anthony Walton, whose parents left Mississippi for Illinois during the 1960s, talked with family members who stayed and found that this "sense of community was the other half of the black experience in Mississippi, the palliative to the difficulties of Jim Crow, and the unifying glue—the larger, self-contained and self-sustaining bond—that some felt had been lost with the advances of the civil rights age." Thulani Davis, who grew up in Hampton, Virginia, recreates this sense of community in her fictional Turner, but not quite with the same nostalgia that Walton's interlocutors reminisce about the "good old days."[28] Examining class divisions within the black community, *1959* (1992) also explores how black adults came of age politically along with, and often because of, their children.

1959 covers Willie Tarrant's tumultuous thirteenth year. The new social terrain of dating and the new knowledge that her father had contemplated giving her up for adoption when her mother died make Willie's emotional life difficult enough to negotiate without having the social geography of her town complicated by boycotts and sit-ins. In addition, because Willie is smart, a committee of black citizens selects her as one of six black children who will desegregate a white junior high school. Davis parallels Willie's loss of innocence about self and family with loss of innocence about race and community. Such a layering of plot lines suggests that growing up black in the sixties meant that the political became personal for black children whether they chose to be involved in the movement or not.

Reviewer Melissa Fay Green finished Davis's *1959* disappointed that "the much-vaunted desegregation does not occur within the novel's time limit," thus making it feel like "a strong plot line inexplicably abandoned."[29] But Davis's project is not to explore the pains of desegregation; instead, she wants to recreate the relative calm and then mounting anxiety before the storm, to show how a fractured community came together, and to explain how a girl interested in clothes and music and boys becomes a budding social activist. Noting the "dailiness of all the past" in the segregated 1950s, which had no need for monuments, Davis suggests that the time has come for a memorial because memories are fading.[30] With *1959* she provides a verbal monument to a neighborhood that white city leaders erased in the sixties when they turned the wrecking ball on black-owned buildings in the name of "urban renewal" (296). Davis links the white power structure's decision to raze Turner's black-owned homes and businesses to the black sit-ins and boycotts of white-owned businesses. Suggesting that the black neighborhood fell victim to white fear of black solidarity, Davis points to the white remaking of a black place with a new architectural design that militated against community: "parking lots and garden apartments could not revive a place that had died when all the front porches were turned over" (4–5).

By conjuring up the sights and sounds and smells and preoccupations of Turner, Virginia, in 1959, Davis counteracts the erasure of black social history and lays physical and emotional claim to a place white people assumed was theirs because they ran both the city and state governments. Willie tells the story of her thirteenth year retrospectively. The "sound of the birds, the smell of the tide" (5) function for her as a "lieu de mémoire," or site of memory, to use Pierre Nora's phrase, because the "milieu de mémoire," or setting, in which memory is part of daily experience, no longer exists. The lengthy and loving reminiscence evoked by the place functions as the adult Willie's explanation of how Turner nurtured her commitment to activism and her need to tell forgotten or suppressed stories. Pierre Nora argues that when society loses its memory or becomes alienated from its past, it becomes "obsessed with understanding itself historically," a reason why memoirs, oral histories, and historical novels have such an important role today.[31] The United States is now two generations beyond the civil rights era, and these generations of young people, black and white, do not fully understand our country's painful racial history.

Willie Tarrant grows up nurtured by adults who consciously supplement her white-authored and white-sanctioned history books with lessons that reveal white injustice and black resilience. Willie's father, Dixon, a professor at fictional Turner College (modeled on Hampton University), makes sure that she knows her local history: that the first settler of Hampton Roads was an ailing African woman left to die by a slave trader and that Turner was founded by freed slaves. Willie's teacher at the black school, Mrs. Taliaferro, explains the power relations that shaped U.S. history: how during the Civil War rich whites paid poor whites to fight in their place and how brave black men escaped slavery in order to join the Union army and fight for the freedom of all black people. Mrs. Taliaferro alerts her students to the continued suppression of the truth about race relations. White-owned newspapers do not include news about the white man who killed an innocent black teenager and was never brought to trial, or about the black boycott of white-owned stores in Turner, or even about the ongoing debate concerning school desegregation. Mrs. Taliaferro uses current events, such as the local sit-ins by black college students, to explain old American practices like civil disobedience, thereby giving her students the knowledge and the courage to practice principles that would otherwise have been mere abstractions.

As *1959* revisits black history that white readers and some black readers may not know, it also reveals class tensions within the black community that some black readers may try to repress. Through the personal history that Willie learns from her grandmother Louisa, Davis suggests that black people themselves have suppressed personal stories of slavery because of the pain such history holds. Dreaming of better lives for their children, the Tarrant family does not care to be reminded that their family matriarch is the daughter of a slave. The suppressed history Louisa shares with Willie becomes a story not only about how whites treated blacks, but also about how elitist her husband's family, the Tarrants, are.

The hidden U.S. history and the dirty family laundry that the adults in Willie's life make sure she knows parallel the potentially lost local history that Davis shares in *1959* with her readers. By choosing a middle-class black child as her protagonist, Davis spotlights an emotional side of school desegregation that some white readers, aware of white fear of desegregation, may never have considered—black fear of white hysteria and the reluctance of black middle-class parents to have their children attend school with lower-class whites. Having seen terrifying television images of school desegregation in Little Rock, Willie worries about what might happen to her: "The white people came after those kids like animals every day. The mobs of crazed housewives and men yelling, 'Lynch them, lynch them,' outside that school were the first crackers I'd seen out being like folks said crackers were. Worse. Little old ladies spitting on school girls. Nobody would ever want to go near people like that. . . . Any fool knew there had to be lots of people like that across town waiting to leave their ironing and soap operas and jobs and babies to come out and kill" (51). Davis also lays bare the mixed feelings of middle-class black parents, like Willie's father, reluctant to volunteer his daughter for a cause that threatens both her physical well-being and her self-esteem: "She's only twelve. My God, does she have to have grown people throw rocks and eggs at her, spit on her, to learn about the real world, as you call it, to find out about the man in the cage at the bank who thinks I'm a boy, to find out that she's supposed to be dirt? I'm not going to do it. You may think it's the wrong attitude, or that I'm not for change, or rocking the boat, but I'm not tough enough to send my kid to take the kind of shit we took from these crackers in Turner" (98–99).

Because the Supreme Court did not include instructions on how desegregation was to be accomplished, most southern state governments and local school boards openly defied the court order or stalled for time by agreeing to admit a few black students to selected schools. All across the South, whites banded together to form private segregationist academies in order to circumvent the ruling altogether. In *1959* bigoted white school board members oppose school desegregation with bureaucratic foot-dragging, and their business cronies attempt to control the level of black activism through threats of job layoffs. Willie begins her reminiscence about her childhood with the time when black parents sue the town council in order to bring the public schools into compliance, but the parents are divided about how to proceed.

Thulani Davis recaptures the emotional impact of what J. Harvie Wilkinson called the "unwitting slight" that integrationist ideals dealt blacks: "*Brown* implied first, that black schools, whatever their physical endowments, could not equal white ones; second, that integration was a matter of a white benefactor and a black beneficiary."[32] As children grow up, their perspectives change and their physical horizons widen when they begin to see self, family, and community through the eyes of others who are different. For white children living in a racist community, like Nordan's Roy Dale, this means seeing one's town through northern eyes when *Life* magazine reporters stare at the locals "like people visiting the zoo."[33] For black children in the segregated South, like Willie, this means seeing self and community through white eyes: "I could still remember when I didn't know what the word 'segregation' meant, when I hadn't noticed the white side of town and its seats at the front of the bus. It seemed as though I had just gotten big enough to go out on my own and see the town when it began to look blighted" (134). When white school board members invade Willie's classroom in order to help choose the black students who will desegregate the white school, Willie's pride in her teacher and her own accomplishments withers under their condescending gaze: "Before that week no one had ever expected us to be dumb, or fail, or waited for us to act like savages. No one had waited for us to mess up—they had waited for us to do it right, whatever it was" (120).

The white characters that Davis introduces after the school board members become increasingly more violent. As black activism increases in Turner, so do the threats of the white store owners and policemen. First the white customers in Woolworth's physically abuse the nonviolent demonstrators. Then the policemen use German shepherds to attack the black women and children who are boycotting the department stores. None of Davis's white characters ever rise above their prejudice or vary from the racist roles in which she first casts them.

A telling vignette about Charlesetta, who hopes to become a writer, suggests that Davis has made a conscious choice to flatten her white characters and to end her novel before school desegregation so that she can hold the focus on the black community, even though race relations are central to her plot. In Charlesetta's story, a black woman wants to bury her beloved dog Minxie in a pet cemetery. But because the cemetery is segregated, she cannot; so she prevails on the kindness of a white acquaintance, who pretends the dog is hers. The black woman poses as the white woman's maid in order to attend the funeral, only to realize too late that she will never again be able to visit the dog's grave. Out of the blue, the story ends happily when segregation is miraculously outlawed. Charlesetta's mentor, Coleman, a creative writing professor, suggests that the unexpected ending needs explanation, but Coleman's wife Lillian simply judges the story "bad" on several counts: "the worst thing about the story is there's no story without the kindness of the white woman who doesn't really want to help. Such *brief* kindness. There's gotta be a better way to tell the story. Is everybody happy after integration? . . . Once you put her in there it's no longer about the Negro, it's about the race question, the ways of white folks and all that" (79). In constructing the plot of *1959*, Davis seems to consciously avoid two pitfalls that Lillian mentions: using a white character to save black people and presuming that integration will be a panacea. Davis positions her white characters as the "enemy" (120) on all fronts: at Willie's school, where they look for a way to forestall integration; in Willie's father's college tales about how he had to work twice as hard to make his white college professors recognize his ability, and in Aunt Fannie's life story, in which the white employer who promises to help Fannie enter nurse's training betrays her trust and uses her as a servant.

1959 exhibits the tension typical of the coming-of-age novel, the tension between the dreams of youth and the restrictions of maturity. Because it is white people who threaten to restrict Willie's dreams, Davis employs the black adults in Willie's life to delineate a range of reactions to white society. For Willie's father and his friends Coleman and Ralph, who all went north to white colleges, integration meant first being treated like a cultural oddity, then being expected to assimilate into the white collegiate world, only to be denied entrance to the larger white world after graduation. Davis orchestrates two lengthy discussions—about school desegregation and about the sit-ins at Woolworth's—to represent three different ways of dealing with unfulfilled dreams and white society's barriers: Coleman is bitter and elitist, Dixon resigned and passive, and Ralph angry and politically active. Coleman maintains his sense of self-worth by patterning his life after upper-class white people and positioning himself above his black neighbors. He continues to teach creative writing at Turner University, even though the job has left him unfulfilled. Publicly Coleman shows no interest in black culture, but privately he listens to jazz on Sunday, as if resting from the effort of aping white culture during the week. Willie's father, Dixon, has returned to Virginia exhausted after his northern white college experience and without the fire for a fight against discrimination at home. Comfortable enough as a professor at a black college, he is "inclined to take life as he found it" (204). Ralph, who trained to be an engineer, found his career path blocked by racism, so he became a barber. Unlike Coleman, Ralph channels his frustrations by turning his back on white people, their culture, and their businesses and by making his shop a center of black culture and a shrine to his favorite jazz musician, Dexter Gordon. Gordon's music helps Ralph "keep his edge" in the "soft easy belly of his hometown," where friends like Dixon have grown complacent (171). As a movement organizer, Ralph turns complaining diatribes about white people into focused discussions about what black people can do. Ralph's mantra—"It's our dance. . . . It's not about white people" (96)—parallels Davis's approach to storytelling and predicts Willie's epiphany about how to deal with white people: "After six months of watching them watch me, I was tired of white folks I didn't even know and had lost my curiosity about who they were. I had incorporated the white school across town into my imaginary life side by side with my comic books, TV shows, a new boy who had visited church, the need to have a pair of red flats, and the snow that too rarely fell on Turner" (199).

Willie has other life guides as well. She does not arrive at such a philosophy of life without her father's guidance in helping her understand the dynamic of self-doubt that the white men's presence in her classroom has created for her, a feeling he experienced in college. But it is hearing Martin Luther King Jr. explain how white power and privilege exist at the expense of black people that cleanses Willie of the shame she was beginning to feel about her race. Davis describes Willie's new understanding in the language of a religious conversion. King "took away the shame" like sin, and his "story of Montgomery" leaves her feeling "full of power . . . soaked in a feast of spirit" (134, 136). Davis suggests that King's power as a speaker came from the way he fashioned civil rights protests into narratives, "full of heroes and heroines" (134). Through his stories rather than through the abstract arguments about social justice, Willie senses that she too can be a heroine, which is why she feels so powerful after listening to King. Davis parallels Willie's political education in nonviolent protest with her father's growing willingness to become politically active after he sees his college students sit in at Woolworth's. Davis champions metaphor as an aid in grasping the unimaginable. For Willie, consumer of comic books and creator of her own *Nancy La Haute Couture* mystery stories, the imaginative leap occurs because King uses a heroic plot she is familiar with. For her father the instigating "metaphor" is the visual image his students create simply by sitting at the lunch counter: "They let you see how stupid the law is. A law that doesn't make any sense. As long as nobody really looks at the law, we go along. Those fool kids didn't bother about going to court and arguing the law and all that, they just went over there and sat down and everybody could see it" (209).

Davis represents the civil rights movement as the catalyst that heals the economic, generational, and ideological rifts in the black community. By joining in the movement's protests, Willie recaptures a closeness with her father that she has not experienced since she discovered that he had thought of giving her up for adoption. In meeting new people through her voter registration drives, she even grows closer to her dead mother, because neighbors tell her stories about her mother's successful activism. At local movement meetings, Willie's father finally assuages his loneliness, meeting people outside his social circle, most especially a spunky and attractive working-class woman who has been marginalized by the black elite. In order to become a truly effective community organizer, Willie's cousin Maddie sheds her reluctance to associate with lower-class black people. For Davis, recalling the civil rights era summons a story about the black community's solidarity rather than a story about integration. Closing the frame around her coming-of-age narrative, the adult Willie refuses to allow integration to be the grand finale of her story (or Davis's): "I've never been in the public library in Turner, Virginia. I did swim in the water reserved for whites on Turner's beach where they left an African woman to die after being declared a slave. The barbed wire put up to keep us out was left standing in the water. I've never eaten lunch at a Woolworth's counter. It just turned out that way" (297).

Anthony Grooms covers similar but more violent southern territory in *Bombingham* (2001), and perhaps as a result he tells a less consoling story about the civil rights movement. Like Davis, Grooms focuses on the black community, employing a few whites only as minor characters. However, less concerned than Davis that white characters will reduce his narrative to "the ways of white folks," he uses a cast of more ideologically varied white characters in ways that challenge readers' expectations. For example, Grooms includes the death of William Moore, a real-life activist, thereby reflecting the white presence in the movement, even as he uses the enormous publicity and public outrage following Moore's murder to focus on racial imbalance in media coverage and in response to murder. Thus Grooms avoids the pitfall of representation that Davis self-reflexively highlights as well as the pitfall some readers might say she falls into by casting all of her white characters from the same mold.

Although Grooms's first-person narrative of growing up in the 1960s is an activist conversion story, similar to Davis's, his 1970s frame demonstrates the personal costs of activism, rather than its benefits to black solidarity. Grooms's 1960s coming-of-age story focuses on how Walter, a rather sheltered middle-class black boy, becomes a "race man." His path to participation in the movement is paved with roadblocks: his mother thinks Martin Luther King Jr. is a "troublemaker" (49), and his father grounds him for accompanying his friend Lamar to a civil rights demonstration. Like Thulani Davis, Grooms explores in some detail black reluctance to get involved in the movement: from Walter's mother's fear that he will be injured to his father's practical concerns about his own job security and about his son's ability to get into a good college if he is arrested during a demonstration. Because Walter's mother's father has been incarcerated for a crime he did not commit, she embraces racial separation as a means of self-protection: she works for the richest black man in Birmingham, trades in black-owned stores, and travels in the best black social circles. Walter's father deals with racism much as Willie's father does—by not calling attention to himself, by staying passively in his place, and by hoping someone else will change his world.

But the night that Walter hears the real-life Reverend Shuttlesworth speak defiantly to the white fireman who attempts to break up their meeting changes Walter's life, much as hearing King changed Willie's. For the first time, Walter experiences black power in black solidarity. Much like Davis, Grooms details his protagonist's growth as an activist in the language of a religious conversion, which is not surprising given that movement organizing occurred in black churches. Thus, when Martin Luther King Jr. asks for volunteers willing to go to jail, Walter is inspired to offer himself up, thinking, "It felt like a calling" (203). Like Davis, Grooms shows that it was easier for teenagers and children to become movement activists than for adults, because young people had more time and no job to lose by being affiliated. In attending a march, Walter and his sister Josie not only defy their parents; they consciously differentiate themselves from their parents. But Walter and Josie do not become passionately committed to the movement until white violence directly touches their lives, which is where Grooms's story parts company with Davis's and where Alabama's civil rights history contrasts with Virginia's. Josie's defining moment comes when a white policeman's German shepherd kills their dog Bingo. Josie counters Walter's easy platitude that "eventually everything will be okay" with a call to action, "Not if we don't *do something*" (225). Josie's anger replaces her fear of Bull Connor's dogs, and eventually Walter's does too, although their courage alternates with terror in the presence of snarling dogs and high-pressure fire hoses. The defining moment in Walter's political education comes when he watches his father humiliate himself before a white police officer by pleading on bended knee for Josie's release from the state fair grounds, where she has been penned in a cattle stall with other young demonstrators. Walter vows that he will never stoop before a white man as his father has done, no matter the reason. He sees continued activism as the answer, despite his parents' remonstrations.

Bombingham actually opens in Vietnam, a decade after the Birmingham bombings. Grooms uses Walter's story about coming of age during the civil rights era to explain the adult Walter's callous thoughts and cruel actions, both on and off the battlefield. The novel provides an answer to white Americans' questions about why it is so difficult for many black Americans to put this past behind them. Grooms repeats words and situations in his '60s and '70s narratives so as to telescope time. He sets up puzzling situations in the 1970s frame, when the adult Walter's reactions seem disproportionate to the incidents that provoke them, but repetitions in the adult frame and the childhood narrative provide clues. Random sensory experiences in the present trigger painful past memories. For example, in Vietnam Walter thinks "All-American" when looking at a southern white comrade's friendly gap-tooth grin and well-proportioned build, only to be overcome with seemingly inexplicable anger. Walter's anger does not make sense because the man, whom Walter has nicknamed Bright Eyes, defers to him, openly acknowledging his superior intelligence and his ability to write. Thus, some readers, especially white readers, may be surprised to learn that Walter sees Bright Eyes only as "the white boy, the little rabbit": "I didn't mind him, but there was always going to be that problem between us: He was white. In the field, that meant nothing. He was a GI. He died as easily as I died. But in camp he was a rabbit. A peckerwood. A likeable peckerwood, but a peckerwood just the same" (283). By the end of the novel, readers discover that the lean, freckled white teenager who shot and killed Walter's childhood friend Lamar similarly made Walter think "All-American" (106, 297). Grooms's repeated use of this particular adjective further reminds readers that for too long this phrase only connoted white Americans. Grooms makes painfully clear that in order to understand why Bright Eyes will never be more than a "peckerwood" to Walter, why Walter is the most cold-blooded killer in his platoon, and why he will not tell his army buddy Haywood about the civil rights movement in Alabama, readers must fully understand Walter's childhood. The device Grooms uses to excavate that story is the death of Haywood, an event that thrusts Walter back into his memories of the 1960s when Lamar was killed right before his eyes.

Until 1963, Walter's eleventh year, he was a sweet boy, who loved his family, looked after his little sister, delivered daily newspapers with his best friend, Lamar, went to church regularly, and aspired to become an astronaut or a doctor—really an all-American boy who followed the "rules" of his family and his church. But in his eleventh year, the unchecked white terrorism that gained Birmingham the name Bombingham among black residents made it difficult for Walter to follow the rules he learned in Sunday school: "When you are chased by dogs and beaten down with clubs, how many times do you turn the other cheek? When your friends are shot and blown up to chunks, how do you love? . . . How do you love without hating a little?" (206). Walter's friend Lamar was blown "to chunks" while riding on the handlebars of Walter's bike en route to the Sixteenth Street Baptist Church to examine the damage from the bomb that killed four black girls their age. The white teenager's callous shooting of Lamar kills Walter's budding idealism about being an activist. In an attempt to imprint the horrific event on readers' minds and hearts, Grooms describes the scene in great detail. Positioning the murder at the end of the novel, Grooms employs it to explain Walter's lack of compassion for an old Vietnamese man, whom he shoots unprovoked. But it is the loss of hope that makes this incident in Walter's childhood so heartbreaking and *Bombingham* a book with so little consolation. In order to make sense of a senseless universe, young Walter turns from his scientist father's rationalism to his Lutheran mother's fatalism, assuming he has no control, that whatever happens is "just God's will" (300). How else to explain that his best childhood friend and his best adult friend are shot while he watches? How else to explain that he is fighting the white man's war, just as his father did in Korea?

In the years between the 1960s narrative and its 1970s frame, Walter loses a great deal: his mother to cancer, his childhood dream of becoming an astronaut, and his adolescent hope that he can change his society. In a decade that saw the assassinations of Martin Luther King Jr., Malcolm X, John F. Kennedy, and Robert Kennedy, as well as the Watts riots and the escalation of the Vietnam War, Walter has not been able to keep hope alive. In Vietnam, he and his black comrades wonder if they are there because they "don't matter" (2). Are they the expendable Americans who fight their country's wars of whatever kind? In many respects the novel's lingering question is "How do you keep hope alive?" *Bombingham* offers no easy solutions. Walter concludes that "to hope will only set you up for disappointment" (299). But Grooms makes sure readers understand that without hope, Walter has no dreams; without dreams, he has no direction; without direction, he finds no attachments; without attachments, he has no compassion. Walter keeps saying he feels "loose," a word that summarizes his emotional state surprisingly well. What Walter does know from remembering his childhood is that "suffering connects one body to the next," a result that happiness does not always have: "What we learn from suffering, from grief, is what every other person is learning. It's human compassion" (302). Walter sees this sense of connection in the black community after repeated racist attacks. But he also sees it the day of his mother's funeral when the white policeman who stops traffic to let the funeral procession pass removes his hat to honor the dead, even the black dead. He sees it most unexpectedly when the policeman who gave a German shepherd enough lead to attack and kill Bingo says he is sorry and offers Walter and his sister a ride home. But how to sustain this fleeting sense of mutual humanity is not Grooms's subject, any more than integration is Davis's. Grooms is more interested in moving Walter beyond cynicism, and yet he shows how this goal is dependent on understanding both the other and the self.

Memoirist Patricia Hampl argues that a healthy relationship with the past means not only telling our stories but also listening to what our stories tell us; otherwise "we carry our wounds and perhaps even worse, our capacity to wound, forward with us."[34] Near the end of *Bombingham,* the adult Walter begins to reflect on the past, and in doing so he becomes something of a memoirist, writing his reminiscences about Birmingham. At this point the hope he has lost actually flickers in an unexpected form in the last chapter when he finally completes the letter to Haywood's parents that he started in the first chapter. Walter has difficulty writing a consoling letter about loss because he does not believe one can be consoled. Thus he wonders what approach will simply best fulfill his promise to Haywood.

The succession of drafts could be seen as a catalog of different ways to cope with the disillusionment that has followed the civil rights era and a variety of approaches to the very type of novel Grooms is writing. Before Haywood's body is even cold, Walter mentally begins a draft suffused with soothing, clichéd lies about family and home: "I was with your beloved Haywood at the end, and I can assure you that it came quickly and without any pain. In his last breath he whispered about you, about home, about home sweet home" (7). Abandoning that tack, Walter next relates a soothing story of a global community of people of color that might displace the pain of Haywood's death. In this second draft, he tells a story Haywood related of a North Vietnamese soldier who did not kill him when he could have, saying, "Sssh, black Brother . . . it's not you we want" (83). In yet another draft, Walter attempts to console by making a more universal human connection between the Jacksons' loss of Haywood and Walter's loss of his mother: "losing a mother, or losing a son, is the deepest loss you will ever feel" (178). But watching a lizard catch a beetle, he decides to dispense with illusions of human connection altogether, to give voice to the cynicism he feels, and to focus solely on race, "Dear Mr. and Mrs.

Whatever Your Name, As you well know, since you are Negroes, life is an illusion of comfort, prosperity, and happiness. . . . Whoever told you to hope for anything? Some preacher? The Reverend Ike? The Reverend A. A. A. Or maybe the Reverend King. King. King?" (184). Knowing he will never mail this cynical letter, Walter marks a large X through it and starts again, but the very act of verbalizing his bitterness seems to exorcise it somewhat.

Walter's final attempt to write the letter arises out of his own feelings of vulnerability, which he has hidden from his comrades, who call him Mr. Tibbs, after the cool, confident detective played by Sidney Poitier in the 1967 film *In the Heat of the Night*. Walter begins this version of the letter with complete candor, "Maybe I will tell you the truth if you want to hear it. And that is that I am not very happy and I am scared. So were Haywood and everybody else. I would like to say that we were heroes somehow, but honestly, we are just average guys" (184). The last chapter of the novel, which includes the scene of Lamar's death, is printed entirely in the same italic type as Walter's drafts of the letters he never sent and thus suggests that in order to complete the more truthful letter he has begun, it must contain his reminiscences about Lamar and the civil rights movement, the very subjects he refused to share with Haywood before he was killed. In seeking to tell the Jacksons the truth about Haywood's death, Walter has to relive Lamar's death and thus reconnect with his childhood feelings—both bad and good.

The last chapter contains Walter's most thoughtful musings; his introspection enables him to see the past more clearly than his cynicism has allowed. He finally articulates the effect Lamar's death has had on his ability to hope. Surprisingly, but, as Grooms presents it, necessarily, Walter also speculates on the complexity of the motives of Lamar's killer. He wonders if the "strange" expression on the face of the white teenager who killed Lamar registered not hatred or even confusion but rather hope, much as his and Lamar's did on the way to the civil rights demonstration: "Could he have been trying to fulfill a dream impressed upon him by his minister, or his Scout master, or Governor Wallace—some dream of a world in which he might be happy and secure. I know the dream" (297). Significantly, right after his attempt to understand the thinking of the white racist who killed his best friend, Walter realizes that he has shot the old Vietnamese man in similar racist circumstances. He dehumanized him by looking at him as "more a monkey than a man" (300). Finally, by observing how much the landscape of Vietnam resembles Alabama, Walter links all people through their human suffering: "We are always ready, are we not, to point out the obvious differences? But just below the surface—or maybe just on top of it, visible to those who would see it, invisible to those who would not—is the incontrovertible proof that the world is a tumultuous place and every soul in it suffers" (302).

As the result of these imaginative leaps—seeing self in other and other in self—Walter begins to wish he had told Haywood about the civil rights movement in Birmingham, because it was a time of dreams and hope and compassion, not just a time of violence and death and loss. By ending his novel this way, Grooms encourages his readers not simply to keep hope alive, as Jesse Jackson implores, but to use the mind's ability to make connections as a faculty for transcendence. Writing the letter to Haywood's parents is a small act, but it is an important step of self-reflection and connection to others. By having Walter complete the letter, Grooms holds out the slim possibility that hope can be rediscovered. The shape of *Bombingham*'s framed narrative enacts the tension in coming-of-age stories between a dream that enables and the reality that falls short of the dream, and it explains how Walter's childhood experiences during the civil rights era helped shape the alienated adult he became. But perhaps even more importantly, the narrative structure of *Bombingham* points to the value in listening to our own stories, in reflecting on what types of stories we are telling.

Just as Thulani Davis and Anthony Grooms are intent on dismantling monolithic notions about black reactions to the civil rights movement, Mark Childress wants to remind readers that not all white southerners were racist. In a complementary move, Childress is interested in identifying those moments that actually provoke a liberal-minded white person to activism in a racist society. A former journalist, Childress examines the power of the media in shaping public perception during the civil rights era. Although Selma, Alabama, readily calls to mind white policemen beating black civil rights demonstrators as they crossed the Edmund Pettus Bridge in March 1965, only movement historians may remember that a much smaller group of about seventy white Alabamians marched to the courthouse in Selma the day before to demonstrate against police violence and for voting rights for blacks. Childress's *Crazy in Alabama* (1993) focuses his readers' attention on one such liberal family. The novel contrasts the reactions of twelve-year old Peejoe with his Uncle Dove. Although both are sympathetic to black victims of injustice, Dove, like the adults in the African American novels, is more reluctant to act on his convictions because he has a lot more to lose. Childress intertwines Peejoe's first-person narrative about the civil rights movement with his Aunt Lucille's women's liberation story, featuring a wacky cross-country road trip. While some reviewers viewed this dual story line as schizophrenic, most saw the thematic similarities and noted the final irony that while murders of black people go unsolved by the dozens, Lucille gets away with murdering her husband by offering sexual favors to the judge trying her case. Reviewers judged the two intertwined stories as very different genres—"comic adventure" and "dramatic narrative," "comic exaggeration and sudden, fist-in-your-face realism."[35]

But the ostensibly different forms share at least one important similarity. The fantasy of Louise's cross-country sexual adventures and shopping sprees, her winnings in Las Vegas, and her triumph in Hollywood, appears in Peejoe's story as well—from testifying before a grand jury against a racist sheriff, to meeting Martin Luther King Jr., to appearing on the cover of *Life* magazine giving solace to a frightened black girl. What liberal white southerner who was a child in the sixties does not wish he or she had been so involved? At seven Mark Childress himself did not remain in the "colored line" for ice cream or lecture his cousins about their racism, but surely decades later he wishes he had.[36] In *Life* magazine in 1965, there were no photos of little white boys protecting little black girls, even unwittingly. The photos that spring were of white-on-black violence in Selma and Montgomery. The headlines read, "Selma Beating Starts the Savage Season," "Montgomery March Ends in Murder," and "The KKK Rides Again." The only picture of white children in any of the spring 1965 issues of *Life* shows them dressed in Klan robes, acting as mascots for their parents' parade of hate.

In *Crazy in Alabama,* the community pool becomes contested ground: the site of sit-ins, police brutality, murder, speeches by local leaders, and visits by both George Wallace and Martin Luther King Jr. Because Peejoe and the black boys who try to enter the pool are about the same age, Childress portrays Peejoe as tasting "their humiliation" when they are thrown out of the pool.[37] When they return with Taylor as their leader, Peejoe admires Taylor, who is "confident, arrogant, so superior" that it takes his breath away (106). Childress prepares readers for Peejoe's surprising empathy by staging a previous scene in which Peejoe's brother, Wiley, humiliates him in order to impress his girlfriend, and Peejoe does not respond with Taylor's aplomb. Childress gives Peejoe his own youthful white innocence. As a boy Peejoe cannot quite penetrate what he considers the oddity of his grandmother's unexplained racial customs:

calling black people "colored people" to their faces but "nigger" behind their backs, and reserving a chipped cup for them to drink from. Because *nigger* is a forbidden word, one of opprobrium, Peejoe senses that black people are somehow different and for some reason unworthy, but he cannot discern how, and the adults in his life do not tell him, a not uncommon practice in middle-class white homes during that time. As a result, Peejoe is stunned by the injustice and illogic of the absurd world he finds himself in—where the sheriff and his deputies hurt people, where a boy is killed because he wants to go swimming, where you cannot take a dead black body to a white-owned funeral home. The first time that Peejoe decides to ally himself with the black boys, his older brother, afraid that Peejoe will be arrested, discourages him, but Peejoe assumes that his age will protect him from police violence. Of course, it is Peejoe's white skin that protects him, although he is oblivious of the fact, and Taylor's dark skin that makes him a target for white violence.

The innocence and the luxury of acting without thinking about the consequences distinguishes the child Peejoe from his Uncle Dove, recalling the difference between the children and the adults in *1959* and *Bombingham*. As the town coroner, Dove has witnessed the results of white terrorism against black people, but he has not seen fit to do anything about it, despite encouragement from the black undertaker in town, whom Dove likes and respects. Childress does not try to excuse the inaction of southern white liberals during the civil rights era so much as he attempts to understand it; it is similar to the way Davis and Grooms interrogate the motivations of reluctant black adults. When the sheriff jails the only black undertaker, Nehemiah, for unlawful assembly, Dove agrees to embalm an old black woman, much to his wife's disapproval. The murder of this innocent woman in an act of white terrorism and the incarceration of Nehemiah for speaking freely about desegregation push Dove to act on his principles—at least after dark. But Dove cannot camouflage his racial politics for long and soon loses his white clients, his white employees, and eventually his social-climbing wife, who is mortified when her friends begin to shun her. When Dove backpedals on testifying to the grand jury against the racist sheriff, in hopes that he will go easy on his sister Lucille, Peejoe, exhilarated from participating in a demonstration at the pool, calls Dove "scared." Dove, trying to explain his contradictory actions and his torn allegiances, lectures Peejoe about the difference between them: "it's easy to know what to do when you're a kid. You see everything in black and white" (352). Eventually, however, the cold-blooded murder of Nehemiah provokes Dove to a level of political activity that even his black employee Milton cautions him against. Feeling like he has nothing left to lose and determined to prove to Peejoe that he is not "scared," Dove not only embalms Nehemiah's body but opens his funeral home for the viewing. Racist whites retaliate by burning down the funeral home and lynching Milton.

When Peejoe sees these horrible sights, he finally understands his uncle's former reluctance to act. Childress depicts this moment as the white boy's coming to manhood; he marks it by changing the chapter title from "Peejoe" to "Peter Joseph" and by placing a glimmer of light in Peter Joseph's blind eye. His eye, wounded in a mowing accident, becomes a symbol of both the personal price Peejoe has had to pay for "seeing too much" too young and his growth from personal loss: "Had I finally seen everything I was supposed to see?" (378). Until the night of the arson and lynching, Peejoe has closed the door on things he did not want to look at: Wiley making out with cousin Mabel in the hall closet and Uncle Dove getting drunk in the embalming room. But in this horrific final scene in 1965, Peejoe, like Davis's Willie and Grooms's Walter, is forced to see more than any child should ever see of human hatred. The difference, of course, is that the hatred is not directed at Peejoe. Although Lamar's death profoundly affects Walter, because the boys were close friends, Taylor's death, much like Bobo's for Roy Dale in *Wolf Whistle,* functions more abstractly to initiate Peejoe's political education.

Like Grooms and Davis, Childress shows the enormity of the movement's price for those who participated: Dove leaves Alabama, supposedly to join Lucille in California, and Peejoe never sees him again. This loss of his beloved Uncle Dove may explain why Peejoe shuns human connection, much as Grooms's Walter does, but without Walter's bitterness. While we do not know what happens to Dove, Peter Joseph retreats to a life of art. The 1993 frame that brackets the 1965 civil rights story emphasizes Childress's concern with the media's representation of southerners. Peejoe grows up to be Peter Joseph, a screenwriter living in San Francisco, who has just sold a screenplay, resembling *Crazy in Alabama,* to Paramount Pictures. That Mark Childress, like Peter Joseph, lived in an apartment in the same neighborhood at the time links the writer's and the character's desires to tell fresh stories about the South. Aunt Lucille's encounter with the cast and crew of "The Beverly Hillbillies" makes clear Childress's criticism of Hollywood's early stereotypes of white southerners as hillbillies and buffoons.[38]

The space Childress devotes to the media—the way photographs are framed and stories reported—demonstrates that he is interested in dissecting the media's influence on the way we understand our world and the way we act in it as much as in complicating popular knowledge about the civil rights era. The novel is suffused with references to television shows, network news, and popular magazines. Grooms seems to focus on how to convey violence through words, but Childress seems concerned with the way children process violence on television. When Taylor is killed at the swimming pool, Peejoe's first reaction is to watch the brutality "like something on TV" (129). Never having seen such violence except on television, Peejoe's first reaction is conditioned passivity, although his second is empathy, because he has not been sufficiently socialized to racism. To script his actions in his subsequent quest for justice, Peejoe uses television shows like *Perry Mason,* in which the toughest cases are always cracked and justice is always served. Peejoe makes sense of the large number of people who attend Taylor's funeral by comparing the mass meeting that evolves out of it to the news reports about Selma, but as he comes closer to the violence of the racial conflict himself, Peejoe thinks, "This was nothing like Selma. Selma was a TV show in broad daylight, it was over in two minutes. This was real it was live it was happening now, it went on and on in the dark" (178). Later bullets "ricochet *piyaaiiing!* like on 'Gunsmoke'" (184), with one crucial difference: an innocent old black lady whom he knows gets shot in the back. Childress's portrait of Peejoe's naive understanding of what he sees on television and its relationship to the racial reality that he lives in Industry, Alabama, parallels J. A. Appleyard's analysis of the different roles readers assume as they grow up. Peejoe has an "intermittent grasp" on the "boundary between fantasy and reality"; he sees himself as "the central figure in a romance" that will end happily like *Gunsmoke* or *Perry Mason.*[39] Thus he is confused when the white "bullies"—Sheriff Doggett, his deputies, and the state troopers—win at the swimming pool, and not the black people who are the "good" guys (347). Eventually Peejoe substitutes Martin Luther King Jr.'s lessons about the "golden sword of nonviolence" for those he has learned about guns on *Gunsmoke* (347), but as Peejoe's language indicates, he still romanticizes the possible outcome.

Crazy in Alabama is the story not only of Peejoe's political education but also of his media education. Childress shows how stories become embellished to suit the teller's purposes. For example, Peejoe watches George Wallace in a triumphant face-off with a few black people at the pool, and the six o'clock local news program shows a strong segregationist governor, backed by force. But from a black adult Peejoe learns that Wallace has come a day early in order to avoid facing off with King and the crowds who will flock to hear him. For young children, the authority of interpretation is not an issue, but Peejoe learns that he must make interpretation an issue.

An incident in which Peejoe appears at the center of a radio news report drives the point home with uncomplicated force. While mowing an old white woman's lawn, Peejoe is struck and blinded in one eye by a rock. When the old woman sees his bloody head, she dies of a heart attack. Upon hearing that an old white woman has died and a white boy has had an eye put out, the town's radio announcers allege that black people are responsible, and the sheriff arrests two black men. Blacks, on hearing the same story, allege white racist revenge, since Peejoe, the injured boy, "helped" Taylor. In each case, the town's preoccupation with race relations overdetermines the shape of the story. Although Peejoe sympathized with Taylor and instinctively stepped out to defend him at the pool, Peejoe just as instinctively stepped back when police directed their billy clubs toward him. But when black people hear that Peejoe, Taylor's "defender," has been "shot," they assume he has performed other heroic acts in the name of civil rights. Some say white deputies have ambushed Peejoe as a warning to other liberal white boys; others say a white deputy shot out Peejoe's eye at the pool while he was defending Taylor. Childress does not leave the explanations for how the story takes on a life of its own at the level of social relations, but he shows how individuals' psychological needs shape the public narrative as well. When the white sheriff has to release the black men he has falsely charged, he blames Peejoe for the false accusation to protect himself. Even Peejoe is not blameless in the making of this small-town legend. When a black woman at Taylor's funeral thanks Peejoe for defending Taylor and putting his own life on the line, he tells her his injury was an accident, but he does not press the point when she dismisses his protestation, and he does not correct her version of what happened at the pool: "I might have tried harder to convince her of the truth, but I rather like her version. It wouldn't be too hard for me to start believing it myself. I *had* stood up for Taylor. For a minute, anyway" (172).

If *Wolf Whistle* reminds readers that becoming conscious of racism is not the same as helping to end it, *Crazy in Alabama, 1959,* and *Bombingham* remind readers that demonstrating against segregation is not the same as ending it. At the conclusion of *Crazy in Alabama,* all the white liberals have left the South for California, and all the significant black characters have been murdered. Similarly, neither *1959* nor *Bombingham* suggest that Willie or Walter will ever live in the South again. While these novels about the segregated South teach tolerance, their segregated physical and social geography means that race mixing is necessarily limited. As a result, readers learn much about the ugliness of racism but little about how we can all get along. How to sustain the feeling of mutual humanity that Childress represents in brief scenes in *Crazy in Alabama* is the subject of novels about southern childhood by Nanci Kincaid and Dori Sanders. The main difference between these novels and those by Childress, Davis, and Grooms is that the social geography in which the children grow up is integrated, by chance in *Crossing Blood* and by design in *Clover*. Ruth Frankenberg has pointed out that the racial "landscapes of childhood are important because, from the standpoint of children they are received rather than chosen."[40] When the other is viewed at a distance, the other remains more object than subject, more racial signifier than individual. Because Lucy Conyers, the first-person narrator in Nanci Kincaid's *Crossing Blood* (1992), inhabits a different racial social geography than Willie, Walter, and Peejoe, her story reveals a different dynamic in race relations, even though she too comes of age in the segregated sixties.

Drawing from the social geography of her own childhood, Nanci Kincaid puts twelve-year-old Lucy on the racial "dividing line" in Tallahassee, Florida: "about as close to French Town as you can get and still be a white person."[41] The physical proximity of working-class white and black families in the segregated sixties makes for what Ruth Frankenberg terms "a complex system of interactions and demarcations of boundary, rather than complete separation."[42] The novel opens with a series of approach-avoidance behaviors, as the white and black children try to attract each other's attention as soon as Lucy's family moves to California Street. The white children, whose race has previously ensured that they do not have to earn black respect or attention, unconsciously expect to receive it. The black children, not subject to a power relationship with white children in their own neighborhood, flaunt what little power they have by seeming to ignore the white newcomers and thus, in a racial turnabout, make the white kids feel invisible and "unwelcome" (56). As a result, Lucy is unceasing in her attempts to get Skippy and his sister, Annie, to notice her so that she can be certain they like her, whereas Skippy is more ambiguous in his efforts, drawing attention to himself and then dismissing Lucy and her brother Roy when they show interest: "Who called you over here? Who be telling you to come see this snake?" (21). In contrast, the adults, with full understanding of racial conventions, draw the boundaries very strictly. Skippy's mother, Melvina, does not allow the white children inside her house, and Lucy and Roy's stepfather, Walter, has forbidden them to go to the black store. Because Skippy is a teenage black boy, he cannot go inside the white family's house, although his mother, his sister, and his baby brothers can.

Southern literary history is replete with childhood friendships across the color line, a plot line that allowed earlier southern white writers to whitewash race relations. By making her black and white buddies male and female, Kincaid is able to explore the sexual dynamic of adolescent race relations and to chart more complex territory for the well-worn cross-racial friendship plot. In *Crossing Blood,* Skippy is both a black boy and the boy next door, and Lucy finds herself captivated by his racial mystery and his individual flair. Lucy's goal is to make him like her before her breasts develop. The urgency she feels comes from the racial and sexual code that governs their relationship: "As soon as I got breasts then Skippy Williams could never look at me again, not out loud. . . . So if I was ever going to get him to like me I didn't have much time to do it in, because once I got golden—he was still going to be colored" (26). Kincaid begins the novel at the time in Lucy's racial awareness when she does not question authority: "It was not me that made up how things would be" (26). However, making up how things could be is just what she and Skippy do by the end of the novel.

Early on Lucy registers the limitations and confusions of racialized thinking. Her three categories for white people are based on class (white trash, regular, rich), while her categories for black people are based on how they relate to white people: "Colored was for people who did things closest to the regular white way"; a "nigger" lies, steals, and does not work or "cooperate with any white people"; "when someone talks about a Negro it means somebody they don't know at all" (30). She identifies Skippy's mother, who works for her mother, as "colored" and his more distant and therefore threatening father, Alfonso, as a "nigger." Lucy appears uncertain as to whether such designations are biologically or socially determined; she wonders what this parental difference means for their children, whom she is trying to befriend. After making such naive pronouncements about racial differences, Lucy frequently says, "Nobody told me this. I was just born knowing it" (27). But Kincaid shows that Lucy learns her misconceptions, if not directly, then indirectly, from her white friends and the adults in her life. Lucy has an advantage in that her mother, Sarah, teaches tolerance and practices it, too (she writes a letter to the *Talla-*

hassee Democrat supporting integration), but Lucy also has a potential problem because her stepfather, Walter, thinks in racial stereotypes and passes them on to Lucy and her brothers. Attempting to negotiate her parents' radically different racial ideologies adds to Lucy's confusion and makes for much of the novel's humor. Lucy assumes that any behavior she does not understand is "a colored-people thing" (158), but the daily proximity to a black family, which Lucy's new home provides, explodes Lucy's racial categories and tests her prejudices.

Before Lucy's move to California Street, racism and segregation have nurtured her two strongest feelings about black people—fear and curiosity. Despite the fact that *Crossing Blood* is narrated only from Lucy's perspective, Kincaid makes sure readers know that fear resides on both sides of the dividing line. She does this through such conversations as one Lucy has with Annie on the night Annie baby-sits for Lucy and her siblings. When a knock comes at the door, the frightened children end up hiding under the bed together. Lucy and Annie both fear strange men of the opposite race, whom they construct as sexually threatening. The children pass their time under the bed telling scary stories. Significantly, Annie's story sounds much more realistic than Lucy's. While Annie convincingly tells of a black girl who hitched a ride with a white man and subsequently disappeared, only to be found floating face down in Lake Jackson, Lucy's story comes across as made up: "I heard about this colored man that killed a white girl and didn't know what to do with her body. He didn't have time to dig a deep grave. So he got a saw and sawed off her arms and legs, sawed her up into manageable pieces and just scattered them out all over the place" (71).

When Annie's father, Old Alfonso, is around, Lucy's fears attach to him, because she first sees him drowning puppies, a sight that verifies the stories she has heard about bad black men. Kincaid signals the unreliability of Lucy's point of view by revealing that Lucy's stepfather, Walter, has killed a cat, which to Lucy is not as reprehensible as killing a dog. To further prevent readers' rush to judgment about Alfonso, Kincaid provides information about whites dumping unwanted cats and dogs at the edge of "colored town," which means in Alfonso's yard. In creating a black father who drinks and beats his wife and sires many children with little means of supporting them, Kincaid uses a familiar white stereotype of black men. Many readers might say Kincaid abuses Alfonso by using him this way, but Kincaid seems to have chosen such a characterization for two reasons: to suggest through Melvina that there are social causes for Alfonso's behavior and to depict a white man acting similarly. Walter drinks to drown his marital troubles and hits his wife when she refuses to support his racist views, and yet, ironically, Walter sees himself as morally superior to Alfonso and more civilized.

Because the novel is narrated by Lucy, readers see the mitigating factors of Walter's behavior and know how many times he acts reprehensibly, but we only vaguely know about Alfonso. Thus, one could argue that Alfonso seems more reprehensible than Walter and that his character could solidify white stereotypes. At the same time Kincaid clearly works to undermine even the most recalcitrant readers' thinking about Alfonso. Although Walter accuses Alfonso when his picture window is shot out and a pet rabbit killed, Kincaid makes sure readers know that Walter's racist white neighbors, angry at Lucy's mother's letter in the *Tallahassee Democrat,* are the more likely perpetrators. Ultimately, it is Walter, not Alfonso, who is a threat to the white children's safety. This reversal reminds readers that historically the white man has been responsible for cross-racial violence, not the black man, despite white fears. At the end of the novel Alfonso actually tries to protect Lucy and Roy by escorting them home from the black bar, not so much because he thinks black people will hurt them, but because he knows Walter and other white people do not want them mixing with black people.

Crossing Blood, like *Huckleberry Finn,* has many ironic moments, because Lucy's stereotyped notions about black people clash with the reality of the black individuals who live next door. Filled with curiosity, Lucy and Roy are preoccupied with penetrating the mysteries of the forbidden black world. As a result, near the end of the novel, the two decide that they must get inside Melvina's house before they move. They sneak in, only to face disappointment: "Old Alfonso was not drunk. He didn't smell of it or act it either. He made no move to burn the house down, get the wood ax after Melvina, or so much as strangle one of the yard dogs. Two of Melvina's dogs straggled over where he sat and lay down beside him. He didn't cuss, or swear, or sharpen his pocketknife to stab somebody with. No. Instead he cleaned his fingernails. And he hummed" (262). This scene is important for the development of Lucy's racial consciousness, if not for Roy's. She feels "ashamed," both for being a voyeur and for having feared Alfonso. But she follows Roy, who, undeterred, has decided to head up to the forbidden Blue Bird Café in his quest for "colored-people things." When Skippy joins their adventure, he finds their purpose surprising:

"Ain't you come way out of your way for that?"

"Not colored people like Melvina and y'all," Roy said. "Real colored people."

"Skippy looked Roy full in the face. "I'm gon try to pretend you ain't stupid."
(265)

While this scene is funny, it is sobering because it is indicative of what sociologists who study racial stereotyping have discovered. Ruth Frankenberg found
that even when the white women she interviewed lived in "racially marked
physical environments," many also inhabited "conceptual environments,"
which limited what they saw and remembered and thus how they interpreted
their physical world.[43]

In *Crossing Blood* Kincaid attempts to intervene in such conceptual patterns—of both characters and readers. She first undermines white stereotypes
by having white supremacist teenagers—not the black male strangers that Walter has taught her to fear—threaten Lucy when she goes to the Snack Shack in
"colored town." Extending the reversal, Kincaid makes Skippy Lucy's protector; he rescues her from the rough white teenagers who express concern about
a white girl being in a black store. Lucy is thrilled with Skippy's rescue because
for once she and Skippy are "on the same side" (48). In eluding the white boys,
they flee into what Lucy calls the "possibility" (51) of the woods. There, away
from their segregated world of racial inequality, they create another world,
where they interact equally, similar to Huck and Jim's alternate world on the
raft. While early on in their relationship Lucy sees Skippy as an exotic other
because of his race, by the time they begin to meet secretly, Skippy has become
the good-looking guy who lives next door. Lucy admits for the first time that
while she has been pretending "he was just another barefoot colored boy," the
truth is otherwise: "Of all the boys in the world, he was the one that I most
wanted to like me" (49). During this first meeting alone, Lucy never forgets
race, but away from California Street, she focuses on race as color, not character—noting how the bottoms of her feet are darker than the rest of her and the
bottoms of Skippy's feet are lighter. Lucy is ready for intimacy, but Skippy holds
back, unwilling or unable to verbalize the feelings he has enacted by rescuing
her. When they are back on California Street with Skippy's sister as an observer,
Skippy hides his feelings by making fun of Lucy and redraws the color line by
forbidding her to go back to the Snack Shack. Lucy's behavior is similarly contradictory: at first angry at Skippy for not returning her advances, she thinks
stereotypically about him; then she worries that Skippy will think she is prej-

udiced because she is white. When a white neighbor subsequently humiliates Skippy in front of the other children, Lucy experiences the same empathy that readers observe in her mother's relationships with black people.

When Lucy turns thirteen and develops those much-talked-about breasts, Kincaid alternates Lucy's socially sanctioned but boring dates with white boys with her clandestine, love-struck meetings with Skippy. One night he comes to her bedroom window to borrow her transistor radio, and she talks to him in her nightgown, well aware that her parents "would have . . . a fit" if they knew (191). The next time they meet in the woods again, armed with whiskey to loosen their inhibitions. There they alternate singing the lyrics of popular songs as a way to voice the romantic feelings they are not supposed to have. Skippy sings, "I know I done you wrong"; Lucy answers with, "Lipstick on your collar gonna tell on you" (204). Both white girl and black boy eventually find alternative social scripts that sanction their transgressive behavior. Because her mother has been paying her to read the Bible, Lucy looks there for guidance, finding that Moses offers a model of leadership and daring: "I hated the way the world bent me into shape. It was not the shape I wanted. It was not the shape my heart desired. I wanted to be like Moses, not like that herd of people wandering around lost" (199). Deep in the woods of possibility, Lucy has an epiphany. She realizes that she is an individual, distinctly "different" from her parents—a distinction that means Lucy can "taste whiskey even if [her mother] never did, waste money on movie magazines, smoke cigarettes, wrap a stolen quilt around a colored boy in the woods." Because of this realization Lucy has a daydream of taking Skippy to the white beach: she would feast her eyes on his gorgeous body, "his muscles tight and dark, his body like it had been carved from hard, polished wood"; he would watch her make a perfect high dive (205–6). In her fantasy they both "glowed" in the sun, a revision of her earlier racist thought that she would become "golden" and he would just be "colored." Lucy imagines kissing Skippy and touches her fingers to his lips while he sleeps off the whiskey's effects in their hideout. When he wakes, they prick their thumbs and mingle their blood, as a pledge to keep their drinking a secret, but the blood mixing of their ritual suggests their clandestine race mixing. The next time they meet, Skippy provides a transgressive script for future behavior, telling Lucy, "White and colored can go around together in New York if they want to" (218), a fact she did not know. In a scene that should be so innocent but that is taboo—Skippy and Lucy eating tuna salad sandwiches and potato chips at her kitchen table—they fantasize together about going north.

Their dynamic of interacting through fantasy changes when Skippy finds out that Lucy's family is moving and that they may never see each other again. This time when they meet, at night in Lucy's bedroom, they interact honestly and directly, with no assistance from song lyrics or whiskey or fantasies. With nothing to lose, Skippy drops the tough-guy act that he uses to deflect racism and the sarcasm he employs to mask his vulnerability. Then together they chip away at racial mistrust by asking the difficult questions about the friction between their fathers and the fears each has about their relationship, confessing the strong feelings that have been pulsing under the surface of their daily life. Lucy admits her worry that Skippy sees her as a "cracker"; Skippy confesses his concern that she wants to move away because he is black. Such honesty propels them into each other's arms, and they dance together to the music from Lucy's transistor radio—although not without admitting their fears of getting caught as they break the South's strongest taboo. The next time they get together, Skippy and Lucy make their emotional connection public, albeit in front of Roy, someone unlikely to do anything about their transgression. They hold hands and dance in the moonlight outside the Blue Bird, but even Roy is appalled by their behavior. He tries but fails to prevent their intimacy. For a few magic moments, Lucy and Skippy are simply two teenagers in love: "He was handsome—and for a moment I was beautiful. The world was good. It's possible to fly with your feet off the ground. It's possible for two things to stir into one, the blur so excellent, the blending so easy" (267).

Kincaid suggests that a place where blacks and whites can be open and honest and equal can be found, but that it must be constructed somewhere other than the separate worlds society has defined as black and white. By using a child narrator, Kincaid asserts that such a space will be found only when people drop their guard and open themselves up to imaginative acts such as children experience when they play. Although Lucy's imagination allows her to transcend her society's racial boundaries, the conclusion of the novel suggests that such imaginative individual flights make for only a temporary progression in race relations, because society's racial code impinges on the alternative world that she and Skippy create. If *Bombingham* shows the limitations of the human consciousness in forgetting the past, *Crossing Blood* shows the strength of society's structures to crush individual fantasies. Lucy and Skippy's desperate desire to be together causes them to take chances, meeting in her house or his yard, rather than going deep into the woods. Each of these meetings on California Street ends with a parent forcing them apart, reminding them of what

Lucy has tried to forget—"this is America. Skippy is not one of my choices" (216). The day that Lucy invites Skippy to lunch when her parents are away, Skippy's mother arrives for work unexpectedly and, frightened for her son's safety, sends him home. Right after Skippy leaves Lucy's bedroom the night they dance together, Walter comes in, saying he has seen a man running across the backyard. The gun in his hand and Lucy's realization that he might have shot Skippy foreshadows the end of Lucy and Skippy's summer idyll. The night they dance together outside the Blue Bird Café, Alfonso separates them and attempts to take all the children safely home, but Walter cocks his gun when he hears the car enter the driveway. Riled by the violent incidents on his property, Walter shoots at the car, only to discover after he has pulled the trigger that he has wounded his own son Roy and "accidentally" killed Alfonso.

Kincaid's message is not that children are harmed when they stray out of the protected worlds their parents have created, but that parents harm children when they create inhuman boundaries for them, when they preach prejudice as Walter has done. In their last meeting in the woods, Lucy and Skippy share a passionate kiss, and she gives him Walter's gun, an act that represents, as Paula Gallant Eckard says, "an attempt to equalize the power differences between black and white."[44] This is true, but it is also an act that passes the wrong tools to the next generation and a scene that reverberates differently when read alongside Audre Lorde's argument that "*the master's tools will never dismantle the master's house.* They may allow us temporarily to beat him at his own game, but they will never enable us to bring about genuine change."[45]

At the soft heart of *Crossing Blood* is Lucy's nostalgia for the "safe places" of her childhood (72), but this childish wish parallels an equally strong adolescent desire for a safe place where she and her black boyfriend Skippy can be together. *Crossing Blood* is filled with palpable desire for improved black-white relationships, and in her friendship with Skippy, Lucy moves beyond the sixties-style paternalistic relationship that her mother has with Skippy's mother, which makes black people beneficiaries of white virtue. However, because Kincaid has placed her story during a time with little possibility for the survival of a love affair between a southern white girl and a black boy, the novel's historical form finally thwarts readers' desires for this budding romance to flower. Although readers do not get a comfortable solution to racial tensions in *Crossing Blood,* they do glimpse the possibility in Lucy and Skippy's attempt. Martin Swales has noted that the bildungsroman is a novel form that "esteems possibilities as much as actualities,"[46] but the scale clearly tips more one way than the other, depending on the young protagonist's distance from the sixties. In Dori Sanders's *Clover* (1990) a youthful interracial flirtation in the 1960s, forgotten until a chance meeting in the 1980s, becomes the catalyst for a change in race relations.

In the scene in which Lucy and Skippy dance in the streets, they are the same color, "black as night" (266), "black" because the white girl has put fear aside and dared to enter Skippy's world. So often in literature and in life, however, when the setting is integrated, African Americans dwell in the white world; only rarely do whites dwell in the private spaces of African Americans, and when they do, interracial intimacy is the cause. In *Clover* Dori Sanders creates such a scenario and also reverses the well-worn southern white plot about loving relationships between white children and their black caretakers. Clover, a ten-year-old black girl, narrates the story of her relationship with Sara Kate, the white woman her father, Gaten, marries after her mother's death. When Gaten is killed in a car accident the day of the wedding, his family is surprised that Sara Kate decides to stay and take care of Clover, her stepdaughter of only one day. The relationship between stepmother and stepchild proves to be an especially appropriate vehicle for examining reluctant or forced integration. Sara Kate and Clover are living together, but Clover does not want to live with Sara Kate: "Even if I got a purple bike, I didn't want a stepmother. Even if I had to have one, I sure wouldn't pick one like Sara Kate."[47] Clover's question—"How could I know her? It takes time to learn a person" (13)—is the very question that Sanders attempts to answer with her novel. That the two must not only work and play together but also live together provides the answer.

Like Kincaid, Sanders depicts a social geography that allows Clover and Sara Kate to overcome racial misunderstandings, but unlike *Crossing Blood, Clover* leaves readers with the possibility of sustaining a cross-racial relationship, all because Sanders's characters have the support of the larger community. Not only does an antiracist public context prevail in the 1980s setting, but integration is no longer assumed to be assimilation to white culture, which humiliated the adult black male characters in *1959* and drove their male children especially toward separatism. In *Clover* successful integration proceeds by valuing cultural diversity, an idea that was gaining currency during the time Sanders was writing the novel.[48] Embedded in *Clover* is a paradigm of reading or interpreting race, which suggests that some of the difficulties in black-white relationships are caused by misreading cultural differences. A reviewer for the

San Francisco Chronicle heralded the novel as revealing "more about contemporary black-white relationships than any sociological study."[49] The *School Library Journal* chose *Clover* as one of their twenty-five best 1990 adult books for young adults mainly because of its treatment of rapprochement between the races.

In *Clover* Sanders illuminates the ways in which "racial" differences are social constructions, not irreducible natural differences. She makes this point easier to understand by situating the main characters, both black and white, in the middle class. The conflicts in the story turn on misunderstandings about food and clothing, funerals and jobs. In interviews Sanders has said that the differences between people in *Clover* are not so much "a matter of color but cultural and culinary."[50] Filling her novel with the objects and rituals of everyday life in the rural South, she focuses on the clash of manners and customs between the northern, urban white woman Sara Kate and the rural southern black family she has married into. *Strange* is the word Clover most frequently uses to describe Sara Kate. Unlike the child protagonists in *1959, Bombingham,* and *Crazy in Alabama,* Clover has never known segregation, although, like them, she struggles to make sense of what she has been taught to think of as "racial" difference. Sanders is primarily concerned with blacks' assumptions about whites, and she uses her novel to show that some black assumptions about white people are based on preconceived and unsubstantiated beliefs, the converse of Kincaid's point about white assumptions. Sociologists Michael Omi and Harold Winant have explained that "[e]verybody learns some combination, some version, of the rules of racial classification, and of their own racial identity, often without obvious teaching or conscious inculcation. 'Race' becomes 'common sense'—a way of comprehending, explaining and acting in the world."[51] The belief that your way is the right way is evident from the first page of *Clover.*

Throughout the early chapters, Clover frequently lets readers know what Sara Kate does not know. She doesn't know about wearing black to a funeral or what mountain oysters are or how to cook turnips in bacon grease or how to make fried pies and carrot cake with confectioners' sugar icing. The culinary differences are more regional than racial, more a clash of rural and urban than of black and white, but under the tutelage of her Aunt Everleen, Clover interprets Sara Kate's strangeness as a product of her whiteness. Clover's extended family, who own a peach orchard, believe that Sara Kate, like other white women they know, will just "sit around, and play tennis or golf" and depend on them to take care of her (6). When Sara Kate does not work in the peach orchard, they judge her lazy, not realizing that every day she puts in long hours drawing textile designs. When Sara Kate tells Clover that she has been working really hard all morning, Clover cannot understand what she means, because Clover associates hard work with the physical labor of the family peach orchard.

Similarly, by the only interpretative code that the black community knows, their own, they determine that Sara Kate never truly loved Gaten, based on observations that involve the cultural rituals of expressing emotion. For example, Sara Kate does not want to bring Gaten's body home for the wake, she does not cry openly at his funeral, and she later removes the mayonnaise jars full of plastic flowers from his grave. Exercising the authority of her age and experience, Aunt Everleen interprets Sara Kate's "strange" behavior for Clover, explaining that "white folks don't cry and carry on like we do when somebody dies" because "[t]hey don't love as hard as we do" (67). As the plot develops, Sanders makes it clear to her readers that any assessment of people that is made without close observation, cultural understanding, and dialogue is most likely to be wrong, because it is based on one's own cultural code, not theirs. Over time as Clover lives with Sara Kate and hears her crying in her bedroom, the girl comes to realize that her stepmother does mourn Gaten's death. Clover does not tell anyone that Sara Kate sits alone with a single candle burning, for fear her relatives will think Sara Kate even stranger than they already do, but Clover herself tries to make sense of this behavior. Reluctant to ask Sara Kate what she is doing, Clover observes her closely and eventually sees that there are different ways of expressing grief. This realization causes Clover to reinterpret Sara Kate's behavior at Gaten's funeral and allows Sanders to link Clover and Sara Kate (one of several times), since neither one cries during the service.

Sanders makes clear in this novel that true understanding does not come without dialogue. Long before Clover and Sara Kate actually have a frank discussion about anything, Clover knows they should: "I think of all the things I'd like to say to her. Think of all the things I think she'd like to say to me. I do believe if we could bring ourselves to say those things it would close the wide gap between us and draw us closer together. Yet the thoughts stay in my head—stay tied up on my tongue. Maybe my stepmother has the same fear I have, a fear of not being accepted" (100). While the conversations between Clover and Sara Kate about their differences do not begin until near the end of the novel, Sanders creates unspoken debates about racial difference for her readers early on, as Clover mentally weighs Aunt Everleen's and Uncle Jim Ed's comments about white people against what she observes living with Sara Kate.

Conversations about three significant subjects occur before Clover trusts Sara Kate enough to ask questions about her "strange" behavior. Each conversation concerns contemporary racial issues much talked about in segregated conversations but rarely in integrated ones. Several conversations in the present and in flashbacks deal with why a white woman would marry a black man. In other words, Sanders must prove to her readers that Sara Kate's motives are pure. The black women assume Sara Kate must have something wrong with her "to be rejected by her own men" (42). Clover overhears this conversation and silently answers it to her own satisfaction, and probably to most readers' satisfaction as well, with proof of Sara Kate's normalcy and evidence of why any woman, white or black, might fall in love with her dad, who is smart, handsome, and kind. Another conversation about motives occurs as a flashback between Gaten and his brother Jim Ed and engages popular notions about why white women marry black men. Jim Ed believes that Sara Kate's attraction to Gaten must be rooted in exoticism or materialism or exceptionalism, or all three. Gaten corrects Jim Ed's misconception with two crucial pieces of information: Sara Kate has a lucrative career as a textile designer, and Sara Kate and Gaten have a personal history as friends at Clemson University in the 1960s. Gaten says he "consciously avoided the possibility" of romance with her, because when they were younger "the time" was not right in South Carolina, and he was "hopelessly in love" with the woman who would become Clover's mother (92). This response works to prove that Gaten would not give up a black woman simply for a woman who is white and that his current attraction is not simply the stereotypical attraction to an exotic other but is based on a friendship and a shared history.

The second subject, which comes up in a conversation among Clover and her black aunt and uncle, tackles the sensitive issue of racial loyalty and highlights the role of mediator that a child might be forced to play in interracial families. The closer the relationship between Clover and Sara Kate becomes, the more Everleen and Jim Ed denigrate Sara Kate and her "white" ways. For example, when Clover praises Sara Kate for taking good care of the house, Everleen faults her for "sitting around drawing those flower designs," which she terms "piddling" work (132). Sanders encourages her readers to see that befriending a member of another race does not mean you have forsaken your own race. In imagining how she will explain Sara Kate's side of the story to her aunt and uncle, Clover expresses for readers what she does not have the courage to say to her relatives: "Yes, I am taking Sara Kate's side right now. But they can't seem to understand that just because I am, it still doesn't mean I am turning against them. Why can't they see that when you live with someone and they aren't mean or nothing they kind of grow on you?" (139–40).

The third subject, and the first interracial conversation about a controversial issue, deals with the suitability of a white parent for a black child.[52] Earlier in the novel, a related exchange between black women, which Clover overhears, reveals that Miss Kenyon, a black woman who is interested in Gaten, wishes he did not have a daughter. Thus Sanders first introduces readers to the question of race and parenting and leaves them with an easy choice. Even Clover recognizes that Sara Kate likes her and shows interest in her, whereas Miss Kenyon does not. But Sanders increases the stakes of the debate about cross-racial parenting when she presents the choice as one between two women who love Clover: one black, Clover's aunt, and the other white, Clover's new stepmother, who no longer has the significant qualification of being Gaten's wife, only his widow. Sanders initiates the confrontation between the two women as a showdown about Clover's health. In the heated conversation that ensues, Everleen denigrates Sara Kate as a mother and a white woman. Sara Kate defends herself against Everleen's prejudices, and in their frank exchange, Sara Kate finally emerges for Everleen as both a person whose feelings she has hurt and a caring mother, not simply a white woman. Sanders makes sure readers have seen evidence of Sara Kate's care and concern before she presents this argument, but she does not raise the issue either subtly or complexly, in part because her narrator is so young.

Not long after this heated disagreement, Everleen sides with Sara Kate against Clover, when Clover is rude to her stepmother—an important shift in the alignment of relationships, which here occurs along the generational line and across the color line. At first Clover cannot believe that her aunt, a black woman and a family member, is taking the side of Sara Kate, a white woman and an outsider, the very person Everleen has incessantly criticized. Although Sanders reconciles all disagreements, she does not suggest that creating an interracial family is easy, and she shows that the most difficult position is the child's, caught between her black extended family and her new white stepmother. Clover must frequently act as a mediator, reassuring Everleen that Sara Kate is a good mother and encouraging Sara Kate to visit the older family members and the peach shed so that the black family will not think her a snob. The peach shed is the site of misunderstanding on both sides, as Sara Kate has held back not because of lack of interest but because she had no invitation, and Jim Ed and Everleen did not think she needed one.

In the last few chapters of the novel, Sanders creates new possibilities for both Clover and Sara Kate as she shows that people of diverse backgrounds influence each other when their lives intersect for extended periods of time.[53] Clover says, "They say when two people live together, they start to look alike. Well, Sara Kate and I have been living together for a long time and there is no way we will ever look alike. But in strange little ways, we are starting to kind of act alike" (130). By the end of the novel, instead of seeing Sara Kate as a strange white woman, Clover realizes that Sara Kate does not understand the ways of Round Hill. Clover is beginning to comprehend that "racial" differences are not immutable but socially conditioned, and her growing ability to ask Sara Kate about these differences rather than to make assumptions about her because of them goes a long way in helping to clear up misunderstandings. For example, one morning at breakfast when Clover notices that Sara Kate never says a blessing before she eats, she assumes that Sara Kate has strayed from the way her family raised her; but when she asks, she learns that Sara Kate's family never asked a blessing and so Sara Kate does not know one. After their breakfast conversation, Sara Kate shows respect for Clover's religious values by asking her to say a blessing before they eat. The meals they concoct together late in the novel are only one example of the enrichment that occurs when different cultures encounter each other in a spirit of open-mindedness. Toward the end of the novel, Clover admits, "[T]hat woman can't fix my kind of hair" (173), but she does not judge Sara Kate as deficient or strange or unworthy of her love because she cannot. Clover and Sara Kate come to love each other not because they realize that they have no differences, but because they discover the nature of their differences and treat them with respect.

Clover and Sara Kate work out their differences in the privacy of their home and within the extended black family, but Sanders shows that the stepchild needs public recognition of the mother's love to validate the relationship. This need might be especially strong for the black child whose stepmother is white in a society with lingering racism. Sanders orchestrates three forays into white society, each of increasing significance—the grocery store, a doctor's office, and a cookout with the family of Sara Kate's white suitor Chase. In each location, Sara Kate proves that her primary concern is Clover's feelings, never what other white people might think of her. In the grocery store she indulges Clover with her favorite ice cream and calls her "honey" in front of the manager (113). In the doctor's office, she refers to Clover as her "daughter," not her stepdaughter, which is a momentous occasion for Clover, who thinks, "Now that was really something" (160). The cookout brings final proof of Sara Kate's sincerity, because in front of Clover she turns down Chase's marriage proposal, saying, "[L]oving each other is all Clover and I can handle" (175). While Chase's attention indicates that Sara Kate is being accepted by at least some white people in the community, Sanders does not explore what Clover's black friends will have to say about her white stepmother when she starts back to school. The struggle that Clover and her extended family have in overcoming racial stereotypes reflects the struggle that Sanders imagines is the current experience of some black readers. Despite the uniformly glowing reviews and popular success of *Clover,* some black writers have privately upbraided Sanders for giving white power and privilege a back seat in *Clover;* and some readers, perhaps used to plots about white people who need to better understand black culture and white racism, resist Sanders's belief that some black people need to make sure they are not misunderstanding white people.[54]

Novels like Dori Sanders's *Clover,* which take up vexing contemporary issues like blended families and interracial adoption, and novels with mixed-race protagonists, like *Half a Heart* and *Decorations in a Ruined Cemetery,* which I discuss in chapter 5, forecast a continued role for the child in fiction about social change and contemporary race relations. Faced with changing interracial social customs in the sixties, now the child protagonist is challenged with forging interracial family ties as well. All of the novelists I discuss in this chapter portray black and white children as both agents for social change and victims of social forces, sometimes caught in a cycle that seems to have no end. In so frequently framing their protagonists' childhood experiences from an adult perspective or so often having their young protagonists revise their interpretations of people and incidents, these writers remind readers of how difficult it is to know and understand one's own experience, as well as to narrate it. As Louis Althusser has argued, "experience is a product of ideology."[55] And yet, the very fact of not quite understanding can also open up the possibility for change, as readers are made aware, in the way these young characters puzzle things out, not only for themselves, but for readers as well. These novels about race and childhood remind readers that fiction written from a child's perspective can be surprisingly subversive.

CHAPTER 2

Dismantling Stereotypes

Feminist Connections, Womanist Corrections

> Too often, we pour the energy needed for recognizing and exploring
> difference into pretending those differences are insurmountable barriers,
> or that they do not exist at all. This results in a voluntary isolation, or
> false and treacherous connections. Either way, we do not develop tools
> for using human difference as a springboard for creative change within
> our lives. —AUDRE LORDE, *SISTER OUTSIDER*

When Audre Lorde spoke at Amherst College in 1980, she argued that "we have
all been programmed to respond to the human differences between us with
fear and loathing," and thus "we have no patterns for relating across our
human differences as equals." She ended her talk with a poem, the final lines
of which constitute a powerful plea for new patterns of relating across differences: "we seek beyond history / for a new and more possible meeting."[1] Her
unheralded move from prose to poetry suggests an unstated belief that imaginative literature might provide a space to draft these new relationships. Since
then, women novelists have been imagining new relationships for black and
white women and constructing new patterns of relating across differences as
equals, as if responding to Audre Lorde's call. More white writers than African
American writers have engaged in this project, for at least two reasons. In the
1970s and early 1980s white feminists were eager to claim gender solidarity
across racial and ethnic lines and so constructed theories and narratives of
sameness. At first their attempts to dismantle stereotypes did not give enough
attention to the diversity of women's experiences, with the result that differences among women were overlooked or downplayed. To make up for their
theoretical mistakes and political missteps, white feminists had to rethink their
grand narratives about women's shared experiences, perceptions, and oppres-
sions. In contrast, in the last two decades African American women writers
have been more engaged in understanding themselves and the African Ameri-

can community. They have created their own critical discourse, starting on a fundamental level with Alice Walker's term *womanist* to distinguish black feminists who called attention to gender issues without neglecting racism.[2] Rather than thinking about how to forge bonds with white women, African American writers have been using fiction to question the master narratives written by white writers and to examine their own connections to Africa and the African diaspora.[3] And yet, upset by the 1980s impasse between black and white feminists, some African American women writers, like Sherley Anne Williams and Dori Sanders, have used their fiction to build bridges between black and white women. The southern setting has proved a fertile ground for exploring racial self-deception and for locating interracial connections.

For years the history of slavery and segregation in the South rendered difficult black and white women's recognition of mutual humanity and individuality. White plantation society, because of its economic and social dominance, established conventions of behavior for women, both white and black.[4] The white woman was expected to be a "lady"—physically pure, socially correct, culturally refined, and dutiful to family. Lower-class white women were to aspire to be more hardworking versions of the dutiful wife. In contrast, black women were expected to be hardworking mules and nurturing mammies, and they were thought to be promiscuous wenches and prolific breeders. As Irving Bartlett and Glenn Cambor have pointed out, "each image was paradoxical and something far less than that of a mature, autonomous, and well-integrated woman."[5] The white "lady" was deprived of her full sexual and maternal identity, while the black woman was deprived of her equality and her humanity. Minrose Gwin argues that "just as black women were forced to be strong, white southern women often were compelled to appear weak."[6] Even though these racial stereotypes were inaccurate, as Catherine Clinton, Paula Giddings, Anne Firor Scott, Michelle Wallace, and others have shown, they have affected black and white women's images of themselves as well as their ideas about each other. Psychologist Mark Snyder argues that when people adopt stereotypical ways of thinking, they "tend to notice and remember the ways in which . . . [a] person seems to fit the stereotype while resisting evidence that contradicts the stereotype." He has also observed the power of stereotypes to become self-fulfilling in interracial encounters, stating that "racial stereotypes may constrain behavior in ways to cause both blacks and whites to behave in accordance with those stereotypes."[7]

A famous passage of Mary Chesnut's Civil War diary makes clear the difficulty of realizing that racial differences are socially constructed rather than biologically determined. Chesnut sees the inhumanity of slavery, but from her own narrow perspective as an upper-class white woman: "God forgive us, but ours is a monstrous system, a wrong and an iniquity! Like the patriarchs of old, our men live all in one house with their wives and their concubines; and the mulattoes one sees in every family partly resemble the white children. . . . My disgust sometimes is boiling over. Thank God for my country women, but alas for the men! They are probably no worse than men everywhere, but the lower their mistresses the more degraded they must be."[8] The racial ideology of the plantation society in which Chesnut lives blinds her to the fact that it is the social system that degrades the female slave, rather than the female slave who degrades white men. Such reasoning, Hazel Carby points out, was part of the nineteenth-century ideology of southern womanhood, which held that the white man was "merely prey to the rampant sexuality of his female slaves."[9] The stereotype functioned to simultaneously elevate the white woman and degrade the black woman.

For years white women defined themselves in opposition to black women, but black women have done the same. In a 1971 article for the *New York Times Magazine,* Toni Morrison rightly questioned the relevance of the white women's liberation movement for black women. She proudly affirmed her identity as a black woman by reminiscing about a trip to Charlotte, North Carolina, where she was struck by the "accuracy and fine distinctions" of the labels "White Ladies" and "Colored Women" on bathroom doors: "The difference between white and black females seemed to me an eminently satisfactory one. White females were ladies, said the sign maker, worthy of respect. And the quality that made ladyhood worthy? Softness, willingness to let others do their labor and their thinking. Colored females, on the other hand, were women unworthy of respect because they were tough, capable, independent and immodest."[10] Morrison does not point out that working-class white women did not find Betty Friedan's "problem that has no name" relevant to their condition either. Like black women, they could not identify with the angst suffered by upper-middle-class women who had everything (husband, children, nice home, economic well-being without working) but who felt unsatisfied with their lives.[11] While Morrison emphasizes significant differences in the experiences of black and white southern women, her analysis makes plain that black women have not always taken into account the differences between white individuals:

> Black women have always considered themselves superior to white women. Not racially superior, just superior in terms of their ability to function healthily in the world. . . . Whether vying with them for the few professional slots available to women in general, or moving their dirt from one place to another, they regarded them as willful children, pretty children, but never as real adults capable of handling the real problems of the world. . . . They were totally dependent on marriage for male support (emotionally or economically). They confronted their sexuality with furtiveness, complete abandon or repression.[12]

Later, in novels like *Beloved* (1987) and *Paradise* (1997), Morrison created interracial bonds between women victimized by the conditions of patriarchy.

Paradoxically, building bridges across the racial divide seems to require a situation that allows people to see beyond difference to some similarity; yet focusing on similarities carries the risk of overlooking crucial social inequities, power imbalances, cultural variations, and different perceptions of the same circumstances. Since the nineteenth century, white southern novelists have employed women's traditional nurturing roles to undermine racial stereotypes and to draw women together across the color line. Early efforts were facile, as Minrose Gwin, in *Black and White Women of the Old South: The Peculiar Sisterhood,* and Diane Roberts, in *The Myth of Aunt Jemima: Representations of Race and Region,* have pointed out, because these relationships involved a white racial power imbalance. Since the civil rights era, black and white women writers have begun to shift their focus to equality in interracial female friendships, thereby demonstrating that only equal-status relationships can produce true friendship. None of the contemporary writers whom I discuss here suggest that interracial friendships will eliminate prejudice between groups. Nor do they subscribe to "the mystical belief that the category 'woman' is the most natural and basic of all human groupings and can therefore transcend race division," a fallacy that Gloria Joseph and Jill Lewis warn against in *Common Differences.*[13]

For the most part, the struggle that each main character undergoes in overcoming racial stereotypes reflects the struggle that each writer imagines is the experience of readers of her own race. For example, in Alice Walker's *Meridian* (1976), a southern black civil rights worker, Meridian Hill, discovers that a northern white co-worker, Lynne Rabinowitz, is not simply a superficial white girl looking for adventure but a hard worker, just as committed to the movement as Meridian is. In Gail Godwin's *A Mother and Two Daughters* (1982), Lydia, a genteel young white "lady," enrolls in a women's studies class at the University of North Carolina at Greensboro, never expecting that her Harvard-educated professor would be a black woman or that they would share similar tastes and interests. Some writers, more often African American, clearly address two audiences, using a second major character of another race for complementary revelations. This is especially true in novels like *Meridian* and *Dessa Rose* (1986), by Sherley Anne Williams, in which both white and black women are filter characters. But even a first-person narrative from a single perspective can serve a dual audience. In Dori Sanders's *Clover* (1990), Clover and her Aunt Everleen learn not to make assumptions about Clover's new stepmother, Sara Kate, just because she is white, and Clover teaches Sara Kate that she could boost her standing in the black community by getting to know her black neighbors and joining in their activities.

In the South, the civil rights movement brought black and white women together as equals for the first time. In *Meridian*, Alice Walker spotlights the volatility of such racial mixing, even though the women were united in a common political cause. She sets the stage for Lynne and Meridian to meet in 1964 when Freedom Summer brought hundreds of college students from the North to the South to help with voter registration drives. Despite their liberal racial politics, the women have some difficulty relating to each other as individuals because both are doubly preoccupied with racial difference. Meridian, fighting against the limitations imposed on her by white society, has no experience with liberal-minded white people. Lynne does not think of blacks as inferior to whites, but she is overcome by white racial guilt and fascinated by black people as exotic others:

> To her eyes, used to Northern suburbs where every house looked sterile and identical even before it was built, where even the flowers were uniform and their nicknames were already in dictionaries, the shrubs incapable of strong odor or surprise of shape, and the people usually stamped with the seals of their professions; to her nestled in a big chair made of white oak strips, under a quilt called The Turkey Walk, from Attapulsa, Georgia, in a little wooden Mississippi sharecropper bungalow that had never known paint, the South—and the black people living there—was Art.[14]

Captivated by the differences she perceives between the races and blinded by her belief that all black people are passive sufferers, Lynne fails to recognize the differences between black individuals: "She had insisted on viewing them all as people who suffered without hatred; this was what intrigued her, made her like a child in awe of them" (162). Consequently, at first Lynne fails to discern the rage of black men like Tommy Odds, who feels powerless under white oppression and eventually rapes her in retaliation, or the anger of black women like Meridian, who loses her lover to Lynne.[15] Penny Patch, a white civil rights activist from New York, recently reflected on her own interracial affair during Freedom Summer and admitted how "abysmally ignorant" she was of black women's feelings about her affair, which she now perceives as "accumulated anger—anger they had borne for hundreds of years." In retrospect, she wishes she had "acted with greater sensitivity and discretion" but doubts whether she would have forgone the affair, because both blacks and whites were ready "to break all the taboos," and she was in love. As a result, Patch lays the blame for interracial misunderstanding during the civil rights era at history's door: "if we hurt each other, it was not my fault, not theirs. It is slavery and oppression that created the distance between black women and white women, not the fact that white women slept with black men during the Civil Rights Movement."[16]

In *Meridian* misunderstandings arise on both sides of the color line because of racial stereotyping. Although Meridian originally liked Lynne and appreciated her hard work for the movement, she is bewildered when Truman, the handsome black man whom she has been dating, shows an interest in Lynne. Walker suggests that Meridian's inability to understand the attraction her boyfriend feels for Lynne originates from Meridian's feeling of superiority over white women, the very feeling that Toni Morrison described in her *New York Times Magazine* article. Truman's interest forces Meridian to confront her prejudice against white women, which she realizes has been passed down from her mother and grandmother: "nobody wanted white girls except their emptyheaded, effeminate counterparts—white boys—whom her mother assured her smelled (in the mouth) of boiled corn and (in the body) of thirty-nine-cent glue. As far back as she could remember it seemed something *understood:* that while white men would climb on black women old enough to be their mothers—'for the experience'—white women were considered sexless, contemptible and ridiculous by all" (107). This stereotype breaks down, however, when Meridian applies it to Lynne. At first Meridian rationalizes Truman's interest in Lynne as a fascination with her color, but later she acknowledges that the attraction is more complex, although race in combination with class and region function together to create the complexities. Barbara Christian argues that "Because [Truman] is an intellectual as well as a man, he expects his mate to be worldly as well as virginal."[17] When Truman meets Meridian, she has neither qualification, although she is able to pose as a virgin by hiding information about her sexual history, her former husband, and her son. But Meridian cannot hide the fact that she does not read the *New York Times*—a sign to Truman of her provinciality, one he uses to distinguish her from the more cosmopolitan Lynne.

Meridian has been accustomed to thinking of white and black women as opposites in a very different way: black women as women who did "something unheard of" and white women as "frivolous, helpless creatures, lazy and without ingenuity . . . useless except as baby machines" (108). However, as Walker presents the facts of Lynne's and Meridian's young adult lives, she inverts the stereotypes. In her teenage marriage to Eddie, Meridian resembles the white women she derides: "she knew she had lacked courage, lacked initiative or a mind of her own" (109). And Lynne, rather than conforming to Meridian's narrow notion of the white woman's fate, more nearly fits Meridian's image of the black woman, who escapes from her family and hometown to do something adventurous, "to become something unheard of." Although Lynne's motives for joining the movement are far from pure, she does leave a nice home and loving parents to work for civil rights during a violent time in southern history. By marrying Truman and bearing a child by him, she effectively cuts herself off from her parents, who disown her for race mixing.

While Walker shows how racial stereotypes can separate women, she experiments with gender roles as a way to unite them. Several years later in the story, the brutal slaying of Lynne and Truman's daughter Camara on the streets of New York brings the two women together. As Lynne and Meridian mourn the death of Camara, whom they both loved, they begin to relate to one another as women: both have suffered the loss of a child and the loss of Truman, who by now has separated from Lynne. Walker suggests that Truman expresses his insecurity by breaking up with Meridian when the civil rights movement made white women more accessible and by leaving Lynne when the emerging black nationalism movement made black women more politically correct. Walker encourages readers to make the connections between Lynne and Meridian through her plotting parallels; she does not make readers privy to the conversations that knit the two women together. The narrator merely asserts that they talk "intimately, like sisters" and feel that they have "temporarily solved" the race problem through their connection as women. Meridian reads Margaret

Walker's poems to Lynne, and Lynne attempts to cornrow Meridian's hair, but they hunger "after more intricate and enduring patterns" (173). In *Meridian* gender similarities do not create these enduring patterns. Race gets in the way.

Meridian demonstrates Walker's concern with the long half-life of ubiquitous stereotypes in a racist society. She suggests that they lie latent but potent even in people who believe they are false, surfacing in times of anger or fear. A year after bonding with Meridian in New York, Lynne, separated from but still in love with Truman, tracks him to Meridian's house in Georgia. Although Meridian is no longer romantically interested in Truman and has told him so, he continues to visit her, almost as a masochistic penance for abandoning her for Lynne during Freedom Summer. Lynne, in an attempt to hurt Meridian and to boost her own self-esteem, falls back on racist clichés to explain their complex interactions: "Tell me, how does it feel to be a complete *flop* . . . at keeping your men? You know, I could—yes, fat ass 'n' all, walk up the street anywhere around here and Hey Presto! I'd have all y'all's men following after me, their little black tongues hanging out" (150). After Truman leaves, Lynne apologizes to Meridian for her racist remarks, admitting she has insulted her out of jealousy, but her motives seem more complicated. Judith Andre explains that when someone retains a stereotype in the face of contradictory evidence, it can function in many ways: "it may be relatively fundamental to our conceptual scheme; it may protect our self-esteem; it may help bring about some desirable situation; or it may shield us from facing an unchangeable, unpleasant fact."[18] Attempting to wound both Truman and Meridian with her barrage of hurtful remarks, Lynne succeeds only in harming her relationship with Meridian.

The aftermath of the "rape" scene between Tommy Odds and Lynne dramatizes Walker's preoccupation with the power that stereotypes have in times of fear. Consumed by white guilt, Lynne does not hold Tommy responsible for sexually assaulting her and so fails to cry out, a reaction that diminishes his expected feeling of power over her. When Tommy brings mutual male friends over to her house in hopes of avenging his emasculation, Lynne thinks in stereotypes, even though the men appear "horrified" by Tommy's innuendoes: "for the first time it seemed to her that black features were grossly different—more sullen and cruel—than white." Her experience with Tommy causes her to speculate wildly that "the sight of her naked" would turn the three men with Tommy "into savages" (161), even though they are her friends. Despite Lynne's initial ability to perceive black people without negative racial stereotypes, her switch to racist thinking in times of crisis implies that as a white

American she is unconsciously enmeshed in the conceptual framework of white racism.

In her representation of Lynne, Walker goes on to suggest that stereotypical thinking about the other eventually transforms Lynne into a stereotype herself, an example of Mark Snyder's "self-fulfilling stereotype." For when she moves back north after the rape, Lynne engages in indiscriminate sexual relationships with black men in order to reassure herself that black men do not hate her. These encounters make her think of herself stereotypically, as "irresistible" to black men, believing they "fucked her from love, not from hatred" (166). Lynne perversely enjoys black women's anger at her behavior as further "proof" of the power of her whiteness. The last time readers see Lynne (during that accusatory visit to Meridian in Georgia), Walker signals her reduction to type by physically exaggerating her whiteness—transforming her from a petite, olive-skinned woman with long dark hair into a stout, pasty-faced, gray-haired slob, who repels Truman because she reminds him of a "pig" (149). Lynne's racialized idealism ends in racism. Her union with Truman ends in separation, just as the civil rights movement, which began with whites and blacks working together, ended with blacks in SNCC demanding the ouster of whites. Since Lynne's parents have already disowned her, Truman's complete rejection leaves Lynne feeling very much alone. Thus, even though she unexpectedly insults Meridian because of her race, she just as unexpectedly demands her sympathy because of her gender, hoping to rekindle that feeling of closeness as women that they experienced in New York.

To bridge the distance Lynne has created, she tells Meridian that Tommy Odds raped her during their work in the movement. But the link that rape should create between women does not work. The intertwined history of race and gender in the South interferes. It is significant that Walker has the usually saintly Meridian react so insensitively here, telling Lynne that she cannot listen to such a story, much less believe it. Meridian's difficulty in listening to Lynne arises because Meridian believes that white women have always lied about black men raping them. Lynne's story resembles the lies white women told about being raped by black men in the decades following the Civil War. Although Meridian decides to take a nap, Lynne relates the incident with Tommy Odds anyway, and Alice Walker makes sure that both sides get told— the white woman's and the black man's—devoting a separate chapter to each viewpoint. For only in the telling of each side can readers, both black and white, understand that though the behavior may appear stereotypical, the motives are more complex. Tommy rapes Lynne not out of lust, as the old white stereotypes purport, but out of rage at white racism, at having his arm shot off by white bigots who are provoked when they see black men with a white woman. Lynne allows Tommy to rape her not because of the white woman's desire for the black man, as stereotypical thinking would have it, but because of white racial guilt. Lynne's recounting of the rape undermines conventional ways of thinking about the civil rights movement as well. Reading Lynne's acquiescence to rape according to a psychoanalytic model of moral masochism, Pamela Barnett argues that Walker's representation of both Lynne's and Meridian's politically motivated self-sacrifices asks readers to question the appeal of self-sacrificing resistance.[19] By including the rape in her novel, Alice Walker challenges the discourse of the black freedom movement that "equated freedom with manhood" and the discourse of the Black Power movement that bell hooks argues "forged a bond between oppressed black men and their white male oppressors" by using sexual metaphors when threatening retaliation.[20]

Lynne, by constructing her retrospective narrative for a black listener (whether Meridian is actually listening or not), seems to understand at least part of her problem in interacting with black people. In rejecting white racism, Lynne has created a simplistic ahistorical dichotomy of white oppressors and black victims. In attempting to reject her whiteness, Lynne has forgotten her Jewishness. Repressed memories of the white prejudice that a New York Jewish family encountered when they moved south surface and force Lynne to reflect on her own ethnicity, not just her race. Remembering that Jews as well as blacks have been victimized makes Lynne conclude that "black folks aren't so special." Thus she sees some of the other in herself, which positions her to move beyond thinking in racial binaries and glorifying black exoticism. Meridian conveniently wakes up at this point and draws the same parallel. Equating the oppression of blacks with that of Jews, she agrees that "maybe . . . the time for being special has passed" (181). Meridian's response is a bit surprising since she has said that she would not listen to a white woman accusing a black man of rape. Almost as if Walker wished to have it both ways, perhaps with an eye to two different sets of readers, she has Meridian speak "as if she had been wide awake all along" (181). Has Meridian listened to Lynne's story or not? Both black and white readers have interpreted this final exchange between the two women either positively or negatively, perhaps reflecting their own hopes or fears rather than accepting the novel's ambiguity.[21]

The humor with which Walker concludes Lynne's storytelling seems hopeful, because the women are able to poke fun at Lynne's lingering interest in Truman and at racial stereotypes:

"Good God, this [talk of oppression] is depressing," said Lynne. "It's even more depressing than knowing I want Truman back."

"That is depressing," said Meridian.

"Oh, I know he's not much," she said. "But he saved me from a fate worse than death. Because of him, I can never be as dumb as my mother was. . . . No, Truman isn't much, but he's instructional," said Lynne. "Besides," she continued, "nobody's perfect."

"Except white women," said Meridian, and winked.

"Yes," said Lynne, "but their time will come." (181)

But since this is their last scene together in the novel, their laughter may simply signal the release of tension at the end of a frustrating struggle rather than the beginning of a better friendship. The two women first tried bonding as comrades to fight racism, only to have Lynne's blindness alienate Meridian. Then they tried bonding as women, only to have Lynne's relapse into racial stereotyping prevent Meridian from fully listening to her. Although they finally bond by connecting as members of an oppressed group, Walker gives no clear indication that this bond, which has definitely cleared the air, will lead to a deeper friendship. Feminist critic Maureen Reddy sees shared victimization as a dead end for women's friendships unless the determination to fight for change is its outcome.[22] After Meridian's own period of introspection, which she does not share with Lynne, Meridian moves beyond moral masochism and out of the South, passing her activist baton on to Truman. Whether Lynne moves on or not is unclear; her desire for Truman undercuts the hope of her own introspective musings and promises more masochism. What is clear is that the two women do not meet again.

Walker's choice of oppression as the best basis for bonding between black and white women, rather than gender roles, may explain why she chose a northern Jewish woman to pair with her southern black woman, even though 19 percent of the white civil rights workers in 1964 were from the South and almost half of them were women.[23] In a 1983 anti-Semitism forum in *Ms.* magazine, Alice Walker described "a close, often unspoken bond between Jewish and black women that grows out of their awareness of oppression and injustice, an awareness many Gentile women simply do not have."[24] During the women's movement a rift occurred between black women and Jewish women that Barbara Smith believes was caused both by Jewish women's refusal to acknowledge white-skin privilege and the economic power that accrues from it and by black women's skepticism that white people can actually be oppressed.[25] In *Meridian* Walker moves Lynne and Meridian beyond these sticking points, but the psychological state in which she leaves Lynne is troubling. Some readers, particularly white readers, have deemed Lynne a caricature because of Walker's final portrait of her. Both *Deep in Our Hearts,* the memoirs of nine white women in the movement, and the autobiography of Mary King may help put Lynne's disillusionment and alienation, though not her racist remarks, in context. Twenty-three years after SNCC made white members feel unwelcome, Mary King wrote about the pain she felt: "I have never recovered from the loss of SNCC. I grieved for three years. It was even longer before I could talk without choking about what my experiences meant."[26] That Walker manifests Lynne's pain as a disfiguring whiteness brings to mind the black writer-narrator's sobering conclusion in Walker's "Advancing Luna—and Ida B. Wells": "Until such a society is created [in which an innocent black man's protestation of innocence of rape is unprejudicially heard], relationships of affection between black men and white women will be poisoned—from within as from without—by historical fear and the threat of violence, and solidarity among black and white women is only rarely likely to exist."[27]

Walker published "Advancing Luna—and Ida B. Wells" a year after *Meridian.* The story is a postmodern meditation on how to write about interracial rape—how to deal with all angles of the story when a writer knows only one perspective, her own. The black writer-narrator of this story is pulled between two parts of her identity, her race and her gender. Like Meridian, she is forced to confront her biases when her white roommate and friend, Luna, confesses that a black man raped her when she was working as a civil rights activist in the South. Anticipating an angry response from black readers if she is sympathetic to Luna, the writer-narrator begs to be forgiven for telling the truth by invoking the name of black researcher Ida B. Wells, who investigated many of the alleged rapes that led to lynchings after the Civil War. Wells became convinced that most had actually been affairs between consenting adults.[28] As a result of Wells's research, Walker's writer-narrator grew up believing black men did not rape white women. Thus, she says that "whenever interracial rape is mentioned, a black woman's first thought is to protect the lives of her brothers, her

father, her sons, her lover," because the "history of lynching has bred this reflex in her" (93). In her first draft of the story, the writer-narrator refuses to hear
Luna's story, in part because the writer-narrator refuses to imagine the white
woman's side of the story. In her second draft, she attempts to imagine what
Luna would say, much as Alice Walker enters Lynne's consciousness in *Meridian*. In "Advancing Luna—and Ida B. Wells" the writer-narrator begins to imagine a dialogue between the two "about the stumbling block of the rape, *which
they must remove themselves,* before proceeding" (101), but she stops short and
resorts to a summary of how she would rewrite the story. While Walker claims
that dialogue between black and white women is necessary to get to the next
stage in building a more just society, she does not get beyond alternating
monologues in either *Meridian* or "Advancing Luna—and Ida B. Wells." But the
self-consciousness of the short story makes clear the reasons for Walker's difficulty in writing about interracial rape, and the postmodern form reminds readers that representation is never transparent but always inflected with the
writer's politics; thus representation is, as narrative theorist Linda Hutcheon
points out, "a matter of construction, not reflection" of reality.[29]

If Walker shows race to be an almost "insurmountable barrier" to interracial
friendship between women, no matter their racial politics, Gail Godwin shows
class to be a very sturdy bridge, at least in the upper income bracket. Godwin
sets *A Mother and Two Daughters* in North Carolina about fifteen years after the
civil rights era, in an attempt to capture the changes that both the civil rights
movement and the women's movement have brought to the South. Lydia, one
of the two daughters of the title, is a contemporary version of the traditional
southern white lady, while her sister Cate is an unmarried, bohemian English
professor. Graceful, modest, refined, and well-mannered, Lydia has devoted her
life to her husband and children. When the novel opens, Lydia fits the stereotype that Godwin described in her 1975 *Ms.* article "The Southern Belle": "soft
hands and soft voices; first concern for others, not self; refusal to dwell on subjects of ugliness, unpleasantness, violence, tension, strife; suave short-circuiting
of all 'embarrassing questions'; cultivation and veneration of traditional and
beautiful things; impeccable manners; 'spotless reputation.'"[30] But in fulfilling
this role, Lydia has not been fulfilled, and as a result she behaves much like
Kate Chopin's Edna Pontellier, napping her way through life as an avoidance
strategy. Shocked on overhearing her son's friend ask if she is an invalid, Lydia
embarks on a quest to find a reason to stay awake. She leaves her passionless

marriage and returns to college at the University of North Carolina at Greensboro, where she enrolls in a women's studies class, discovers feminism, and begins a friendship with Renee Peverell-Watson, her young Harvard-educated women's studies professor. Although not as prominent as the interracial friendship in *Meridian*, Lydia's relationship with Renee plays a central role in Lydia's break with traditional southern notions about race and gender.

In contrast to the relationship between Lynne and Meridian, there is little conflict between Lydia and Renee or within either of them as they become friends. In part the ease of developing their friendship, despite Lydia's preconceptions, has to do with the social positions in which Godwin places them. Lydia, eager to prepare for a career and uncertain of her new status as a single woman, views Renee, who is single, attractive, and successful, as a role model. The details Godwin chooses to describe Renee not only suggest a cosmopolitan career woman dressed for success but also counter old southern stereotypes of black women as lower-class and undereducated: "[Renee] was sitting at her desk, reading an aerogram with an English stamp and smoking a little brown cigar. Framed by shelves full of glossy books and wearing a twill pantsuit with a low-necked cerise silk blouse, she was the advertiser's dream-image of the woman who has 'made it.'"[31] In her pairing of white and black women, Godwin inverts the traditional southern racial power hierarchy, with the result that Lydia acknowledges Renee's "superiority over her in many of the areas the world values" (158).

Godwin transforms their teacher-student relationship into a friendship through similarities in taste and values. When Renee invites Lydia to her house for lunch, Lydia immediately notices a similarity in their tastes: a gray frame house on a "genteel old street" (149), rooms filled with plants and antiques, the lunch table set with Japanese plates, soft damask napkins, silver, and fragile stemware. In Renee's conversation Lydia discovers, to their mutual delight, similar interests: French cuisine, the trials of mothering teenagers, the nature of love, the significance of social class. Race does not play a visible role in their emerging friendship. Lydia feels neither guilt, as Walker's Lynne does, nor a desire to confirm liberal views, either of which might cause a white woman to seek a friendship with Renee *because* she is black. To signal a generational shift in southern race relations, Godwin juxtaposes Lydia and Renee's friendship with the relationship between Lydia's mother's friend Theodora and her black maid, Azalea. Theodora hosts a luncheon on the same day that Lydia and Renee first have lunch together. Azalea eats in the kitchen while Theodora and her guests eat in the adjoining dining room, but Theodora spends most of her time talking with Azalea while her guests pick at their shrimp salad in silence. With this juxtaposition of scenes, Godwin enacts the conventional southern relationship between black maids and their white employers—physical closeness but social distance, companionship but inequality—and heralds the passing of an era in southern race relations.

Lydia is proud of the difference between her relationship with Renee and Theodora's relationship with Azalea. And yet for Lydia, the only awkward moments in her friendship with Renee come when she is reminded that Renee is black, a difference she does not like to think about. Godwin indicates that similarities in feminist politics and social class have made Lydia forget about the major differences between them: Renee's race and her mixed racial history. Renee's great-great-grandmother was a slave; her white great-great-grandfather owned the plantation. But Godwin has Renee remind Lydia of race when she uses the word *nigger* in class; Renee periodically drops her refined drawing-room drawl and turns on her down-home dialect. Lydia can only associate such language with Azalea and finds it disconcerting to link Renee with a maid. Renee's continued periodic use of Azalea's language makes Lydia momentarily conscious of race but never completely comfortable discussing it. Their most unselfconscious conversations are about social class.

In using class to cross the color line, Godwin seems aware that some readers may view her representation of Renee as "white." She employs Lydia's sister Cate to raise this objection so that she can counter it directly in the text. Godwin does not want readers to mistake Renee for a black woman trying to act white, Cate's assumption when Lydia first tells her about Renee. Godwin suggests that Cate too easily equates Renee's upward mobility with insensitivity to racism and to the plight of lower-class black people. Renee's teaching techniques and her later decision to become a civil rights lawyer are Godwin's attempts to prove Cate's view false. Lydia argues that Renee and her lover Calvin "want to claim their share of what Cate calls the 'dying world' because they haven't *had* their share yet" (491). Lydia (and I think Godwin) believes that Renee transcends stereotypical definitions of racial identity, as Lydia explains in analyzing Renee's dialect switches: "There was something wickedly arrogant about it, when Renee did it, as if she were showing her listeners that, though she was equally at home in both worlds, she was actually above both" (129). And yet Godwin makes Renee and Calvin so Anglophile in their tastes as to enable Lydia to think of Renee as "a person who is black but 'one of us'"

(321)—not quite the erasure of difference that Audre Lorde cautioned against but close enough to be problematic.

As Godwin assigns tastes to Renee which Cate thinks of as "white" but which Godwin clearly codes as class-based, she also assigns behaviors to Lydia that directly address the southern racial stereotypes she has inherited—much like the way Walker positions Meridian and Lynne to discover traits in each other that they assumed were racially exclusive. Lydia's marriage to Max has lacked sexual passion, a characteristic she stereotypically equates with blackness. On a vacation to New Orleans with Max the year before, she hoped they would be freed from their "tight, civilized" lives by "some Negro playing a saxophone" (274), but "not the faintest throb of the jungle drum beat in their veins" (275). After her separation from Max, Lydia finds sexual passion with a podiatrist named Stanley, but she has difficulty integrating this newly discovered part of her self into the old definition of the southern lady. To Lydia a lady is not a passionate lover; she is an "amiable bed partner" (268). For a while Lydia tries to compartmentalize her life (mother, student, respected friend of Max, secret lover of Stanley), deciding that if she is a lover in private, she can still be a lady in public. Eventually, though, the contents of one compartment of her life spill into another, and she is forced to come to terms with all parts of her self. She discovers that the passion she has attributed to the other is a repressed part of her self. In *Black and White Women of the Old South,* Minrose Gwin argues that in the nineteenth century women of both races were bound by dualistic thinking, with the result that they "often viewed one another as missing pieces of a female identity denied them by the patriarchal culture": "Female narrators of the slave narratives reveal their yearning for the chaste respectability of their white sisters, while the diaries and memoirs of the white women show their intense jealousy of the stereotypical sexuality of the slave woman. Each is only one half of a self."[32] In *A Mother and Two Daughters,* Gail Godwin brings together these two halves, with all their attendant virtues and flaws, in both Lydia and Renee.

At the conclusion of *A Mother and Two Daughters,* Lydia feels in some ways "closer to Renee than to her own sister" (397). Lydia and Renee are certainly much more alike than Lydia and Cate, but their "sisterhood," with its connotation of unconditional love, is never really tested as Lydia and Cate's is. As testament to the depth of Lydia and Renee's friendship, Godwin ends the novel with a symbolic marriage between Lydia's son Leo and Renee's daughter Camilla, which occurs between the final chapter and the 1984 epilogue. In that same white space, Lydia's new racial broadmindedness is tested, a situation that the narrator summarizes in the epilogue. Shocked by the prospect of an interracial marriage in her own family, Lydia forces herself, in the presence of her son, to think past Camilla's race to her quite acceptable class status and perfect manners—a move that enables her to pronounce Camilla "a perfect lady" (566) and accept her as a daughter-in-law. As Carolyn Rhodes points out, Godwin is clearly trying to detach the southern concept of the lady "from concern with color, although not from beauty and grace and demeanor."[33] But one might ask whether Godwin almost erases race in the process. In the 1970s white feminists were too quick to claim *sisterhood* with black women, a term that arose out of resistance to slavery and racism and which white women picked up when they worked side-by-side with black women in the civil rights movement. In transferring the term *sisterhood* to the women's movement, white feminists erased differences between women and in many cases ignored their own racism.[34] Both are reasons why Maureen Reddy has suggested that *comrades* is a better term for interracial friendships than *sisters*: "Thinking of each other as comrades might keep alive in us all the necessary understanding that comradeship, like friendship, can be withdrawn or lost and requires ongoing care to sustain, unlike sisterhood, which implies an unconditional love that is unrealistic to expect."[35] Gail Godwin does not make Lydia and Renee comrades, although her plot takes her to a point where she could have when bigots target Calvin and Renee.

The epilogue of *A Mother and Two Daughters* may be utopian with its interracial newlyweds and its happy family reunion high on a mountaintop above the fray, but it does not depart from reality altogether. In a traditional comedic resolution, the harmony between a man and a woman symbolizes a larger harmony within the society. However, in *A Mother and Two Daughters,* the harmony that exists between black and white individuals is not extended to racial groups. Racism still exists in North Carolina, although Godwin does not depict the racist acts. In the epilogue the narrator briefly summarizes a variety of troubling racist episodes that occur in the temporal break between the last chapter and the epilogue. A woman in a supermarket says she pities the children that Leo and Camilla will have, the Klan marches in Greensboro, Calvin's life is threatened and he moves to New York, and the prejudiced white father of a *D* student in Renee's class firebombs her house and kills her dog when she refuses to change the grade. This last incident pushes Renee to choose the legal profession as a more direct way of fighting racism than the undergraduate classroom. The epilogue with its exact date, 1984, roots Godwin's novel firmly in reality, but this date, which is two years after the actual publication of *A Mother and Two Daughters,* simultaneously reminds readers that she has created a fiction. Her intertextual play on George Orwell's dystopian novel *Nineteen Eighty-Four* (1949) suggests that North Carolina's future will be rosier than London's despite the scattered presence of the Klan, which periodically disrupts the emerging interracial community.

With its "faith in black-white mutuality and essential sameness," *A Mother and Two Daughters* borders on Benjamin DeMott's "friendship orthodoxy."[36] Godwin seems to sense as much and so gives readers this quick reality check in her epilogue, which is otherwise suffused with hope that upward mobility can dismantle racial stereotypes, foster interracial friendships, and produce interracial marriages in the next generation. And yet not all readers see hope in the ending. Elizabeth Schultz notes Renee's conspicuous absence from Cate's mountaintop gathering of family and friends and argues that when race becomes an issue between the two women, the friendship "wanes."[37] But Godwin makes clear that Lydia and Renee have just spoken on the phone before the party, and she gives Renee the excuse of having to study for the bar. Thus Renee's absence probably reveals less about Godwin's thinking on the viability of interracial friendships and more about her reluctance to tackle the big picture of race relations, even though she signals that she knows racism still exists.

In *A Mother and Two Daughters* Lydia and Renee indirectly acknowledge difference rather than directly confronting it as Meridian and Lynne do. Although Godwin certainly dismantles racial stereotypes in her characterization of both Lydia and Renee, she does so with such indirection and reserve that some readers have missed or quickly forgotten this important aspect of her novel.[38] There is a mannerliness about their relationship that does not exist in the relationship between Lydia and her sister Cate or between Meridian and Lynne. Lydia and Renee's friendship resembles the one Godwin imagines in her essay "The Southern Belle," between a black woman and her white friend who would probably hesitate to ask "embarrassing questions."[39] Because Godwin is ultimately responsible for the absence of such dialogue in the text, she remains the polite southern white lady herself. Although the narrator reassures readers that the conversations between Lydia and Renee make Lydia think about racial stereotypes, Godwin does not imagine a dialogue, an open exchange of questions and answers, between the two women about sensitive racial issues. Lydia and Renee do discuss black class hierarchy, but even in that conversation, the surprised Lydia does not reveal all she is thinking to her friend. One issue of racial misunderstanding that Renee and Lydia could have discussed is the problematic and simplistic identification of "black" culture with working-class black culture, which clearly troubles Godwin. However, Godwin reserves this heated discussion for Lydia and her sister Cate. Lydia's reluctance to ask difficult questions of Renee parallels her failure to ask difficult questions of herself about race, to examine how her own race and class privilege may continue to hamper her understanding of race relations in North Carolina, even as she herself moves beyond racial stereotyping. In discussing her progress with Cate, Lydia says she used to assume that all robbers and muggers were black and that all victims were white, but now she resents the "bad publicity" that an individual black criminal brings to the race (482). Her comment reveals that Lydia has yet to realize that the "bad publicity" comes not from black individuals who commit crimes but from whites who interpret such individual behavior as confirmation of racial inferiority.

In *Dessa Rose* (1986) Sherley Anne Williams complicates Godwin's easy cross-racial friendship by positioning a self-deceived white character so that she will have to view firsthand the scars of racial oppression, to acknowledge race privilege, and to work collaboratively with a black woman to fight both racism and sexism. Furthermore, Williams moves her black protagonist beyond *Meridian's* quick refusal to listen, and she uses dialogue between her black and white female characters more productively than Walker does. *Dessa Rose* is a historical novel based on two events almost lost to history because they do not fit the controlling narratives about race and gender relations in the South. Attempting to "seek beyond history" for the "new and more possible meeting" that Audre Lorde called for, Williams imagines the intersection of two unrelated historical incidents, thereby allowing the two real-life women to meet in fiction. In 1829 in Kentucky a pregnant black woman helped to lead an uprising on a slave coffle; about the same time in North Carolina, a white woman living on an isolated farm was giving sanctuary to runaway slaves. As is evident in the author's note to *Dessa Rose,* Williams conceived her historical novel out of three separate but interlocking desires. First, angered by William Styron's fictional portrayal of Nat Turner, she wanted to investigate the problem of understanding and writing about the other. Second, disappointed as a young lover of history "that there was no place in the American past that I could go and be free," she also wished to recover both acts of rebellion against slavery and precious moments of slave friendships and family relationships that slaves relied on to survive slavery's brutality.[40] Finally, upset by the 1980s impasse between black and white feminists in the wake of white feminists' preoccupation with universal definitions of womanhood, she longed to open up a space where black and white women could form an alliance. In an interview Williams said that she hoped the novel would "heal some wounds" caused by racism. Because she believed fiction is a means of "understanding the impossible," she hoped that by bringing these two historical women together, she "could come to understand something not only about their experience of slavery but about them as women, and imagine the basis for some kind of honest rapprochement between black and white women."[41] The relationship between Dessa Rose and Ruth Elizabeth (Rufel) Sutton begins by accident and continues out of self-interest and necessity—the only logical way Williams believes such an alliance could have occurred in the slave South.[42] With Rufel's husband away and most of their slaves escaped, Rufel needs help to run the farm, but she also needs companionship, because her personal slave, her mammy since childhood, has just died, and her farm is remote. Dessa needs care because of a complicated childbirth; she also needs a safe haven from the law.

When *Dessa Rose* was published, it garnered numerous favorable reviews and became an overnight popular and critical success, but although most critics praised its portrayal of slavery as "unflinchingly realistic," several critics pronounced its portrayal of nineteenth-century race relations "hard to believe."[43] On this basis, then, Boyd Tonkin dismissed the novel's importance, declaring that "since a piece of wishful thinking lies at its core, *Dessa Rose* finally shirks history in favour of romance." In her review Michele Wallace countered that *Dessa Rose* takes "the reader someplace we're not accustomed to going, someplace historical scholarship may never take us—into that world that black and white women shared in the antebellum South."[44] Williams has created a historical fiction of interracial collective struggle that is difficult to verify historically but which may have existed here and there, now and again, throughout the South. The historical accuracy of the relationship between Dessa and Rufel does not matter as much as its imaginative possibilities, its potential for creating the new "patterns of relating across our human differences as equals" for which Audre Lorde called. From both black and white perspectives, Williams examines why racial stereotypes persist, and she presents strategies for reconceptualizing difference, for correcting misconceptions, and for creating trust and respect. She transforms the ideological abstractions of southern race relations through her literal focus on skin color, and she dismantles racial stereotypes through analogies, the logic of which startles her characters (and, she must have hoped, her readers) out of accustomed ways of thinking.

Williams posits skin color as having absorbed all the negative characteristics that blacks and whites have projected onto each other and thus as reflecting so much accumulated fear and hate as to make understanding impossible. For Adam Nehemiah, the white man who is using Dessa's life story to write a book called *The Roots of Rebellion in the Slave Population,* black people are evil and stupid, characteristics he associates with their physical appearance: "The slave was a big, evil-visaged buck, black as sin, with great flaring nostrils, wide enough—or so it seemed to Nehemiah—to drive a team through, and dainty holes at the sides of his head where his outer ears had been cropped away. Whatever intelligence the nigra might once have possessed had long since fled, and Nehemiah had been unable to penetrate the smiling vacuity with which the darky now faced the world." For Dessa, the sight of white people, most of whom have been cruel to her, produces a similar revulsion. When Nehemiah fixes his blue-eyed gaze on her, she recoils, "thinking in that first instance of seeing that his eyes were covered by some film, milky and blank. . . . That's why we not supposed to look in white folks' eyes, she thought, with a shiver. There was only emptiness in them; the unwary would fall into the well of their eyes and drown" (45–46). Later, when another escaped slave, Harker, tells her that the French word for white is *blanc,* the word as she understands it (blank) operates not as an arbitrary sign for white skin but as a reflection of the essential white body. Through such ideologically laden references to color early in the novel, Williams makes physical revulsion an involuntary response to the unnatural interracial relationships created by slavery.

Then by focusing concretely on color rather than on the abstractions attributed to race, Williams momentarily strips skin color of its socially charged significance so that her readers, both white and black, can see color anew. Rufel's young son Timmy perceives the skin color of Dessa's baby quite literally in his attempt to understand "why they called them colored": "His color had been blotchy, pale patches of nut-shell brown, darker patches of chocolate, red, even green" (106). For Dessa, *darky,* the white word for black people, erases the incredible variety of skin color of African Americans, thereby masking their individuality and obscuring their beauty: "Wasn't no darky to it, [Dessa] would think indignantly. Kaine was the color of the cane syrup taffy they pulled and stretched to a glistening golden brown in winter" (58). With such statements, Williams must have hoped to open white readers' eyes to the beauty and variety of "black" skin tones. This technique is most evident in the bedroom scenes, where skin is bare and where interracial intimacy occurs behind closed doors.

Williams imagines her way across the racial divide by using familiar gender-role connections but combining them with the first of several unfamiliar race-role reversals—an attempt to reconceptualize difference creatively. In order to subvert the racial stereotype, Williams essentializes the gendered response of nursing mothers.[45] Thus, Rufel acts instinctively when she hears Dessa's hungry baby crying, and "without thought" she puts him to her breast, since Dessa cannot feed him. Nursing Dessa's baby produces a sensual pleasure that causes Rufel to notice the contrast in their skin color positively, "sleek black head, the nut-brown face flattened against the pearly paleness of her breast." Rufel finds this color contrast pleasurable until the social context overwhelms her physical response once the baby is fed and soothed. Then Rufel becomes "conscious" of her social position—serving as "a wet nurse for a darky." Williams makes plain the social construction of this position by having Rufel keep on nursing the baby when she realizes that no one will know. As the days pass and Rufel continues to nurse Dessa's baby, she takes regular aesthetic pleasure in the juxtaposition of black and white, a contrast that Williams presents as mutually enhancing: "She herself liked to watch the baby as he nursed, the way he screwed up his face and clenched his fist with the effort, the contrast between his mulberry colored mouth and the pink areola surrounding her nipple, between his caramel-colored fist and the rosy cream of her breast" (105–6). Recent psychological studies suggest that racial aversion can be minimized through prolonged contact if the contact undermines the stereotype,[46] and Williams fashions her plot to reinforce this idea. Rufel's experience with Dessa's baby complicates the way both Rufel and Dessa see race. While it shocks Dessa to see a white woman nursing her baby, it does not take long for her to realize that "where white peoples look at black and see something ugly, something hateful, she [Rufel] saw color" (184). Paradoxically, this turn of events upsets Dessa. Williams presents such unfamiliar white behavior as threatening Dessa's identity as a black woman, because she has constructed her sense of self in opposition to the white cruelty she has experienced in the past: "It went against everything she had been taught to think about white women but to inspect that fact too closely was almost to deny her own existence" (123).

Williams employs analogies to allow both Dessa and Rufel to rethink their relationship. Dessa's questions about Mammy cause Rufel to view her relationship with Mammy from a black perspective. In Dessa's delirium after childbirth, she momentarily thinks that the mammy whom Rufel talks about is Dessa's own mother, thereby leading her to believe that Rufel has robbed her of her mother as well as of her child. For readers, although not yet for Rufel, Dessa's thoughts reflect just one of the many injustices slavery caused black women and their families: the time spent caring for white children meant time away from their own children. The conversation provoked by Dessa's misunderstanding, however, forces Rufel to reconsider her relationship to Mammy. As a pampered white girl and spoiled young woman, Rufel has only thought about Mammy in relation to herself—that Mammy is like her mother, really a better mother than her biological mother, because Mammy has praised rather than criticized her, hugged rather than scolded her. Dessa's interest in Mammy's identity, her children, and her possible relationship to Dessa causes a flustered Rufel to say, "She just had me! I was like her child" (125). The simile spoken aloud to Dessa makes Rufel realize the implications of her comparison. If she is truly like a black woman's child, then she would be "a pickaninny" (132). Although Rufel shudders at the thought of being black, this new line of thinking causes her to take the analogy further: if she is a pickaninny, then Mammy is "a slave, a nigger." Rufel has repressed the economics, and therefore the inhumanity, of their relationship because she has spoken of Mammy as a maid or servant and thought of her as a "friend." But simply thinking this word makes Rufel realize that if she and Mammy had been friends, she could have easily answered Dessa's questions about Mammy's name, and she would have known whether Mammy had children or a sweetheart. Thus Rufel comes to understand that the relationship she had with Mammy was actually one of mistress and slave. This realization makes Rufel question whether Mammy loved her "freely" and leads her to feel "personally responsible for Mammy's pain, personally connected to it, not as the soother of hurt as Mammy has always been for her, but as the source of that pain" (147). For the first time, the horrors of slavery—whippings, brandings, children sold away—become vivid to Rufel when she imagines them happening to Mammy, someone she loved.

It is important to note that the contact between Rufel and Dessa that provokes these conceptual breakthroughs and others in the novel occurs because they are outside of their accustomed social roles and physical spaces and thus interacting with each other in new ways. But for both women new ideas coexist with old conceptual frameworks. While Alice Walker seems to view such contradictory thinking as proof of the inability to overcome old thought patterns, Williams depicts such contradictions as a stage in the process of dismantling stereotypes—an unsettling stage but an unavoidable one. For example, when Rufel returns to question Dessa about her alleged beatings and the scars, both Rufel's thoughts and her actions are contradictory. Although Rufel is finally ready to believe Dessa has been whipped, she wonders what Dessa did to provoke such punishment. Rufel's intrusion on Dessa's privacy underscores her power as a white woman even when she does not own the black people who live on her farm.[47] Williams represents Rufel's racism as being so ingrained as to be almost instinctive: her hand "almost of its own volition" reaches to draw back the bedcovers to see whether Dessa has been telling the truth about her scars. And yet, in this scene Rufel begins to think for the first time from Dessa's perspective as a slave. Perhaps because Dessa is in her bed, Rufel thinks "how humiliating she would find such an inspection" and tries to cover up her intrusive gesture as a concern about whether Dessa is healing from childbirth (149). But immediately after this, Rufel revels for the first time in her own power to make Dessa fearful at her intrusion. Reading Dessa and reading Dessa reading her, Rufel is in an interpersonal situation similar to the transformative one Diana Fuss describes between reader and text: "In reading . . . we bring (old) subject positions to the text at the same time the actual process of reading constructs (new) subject-positions for us. Consequently, we are always engaged in a 'double reading' . . . in the sense that we are continually caught within and between *at least* two constantly shifting subject-positions" that may be "in complete contradiction."[48] Rufel acts one minute as slave mistress, the next as fellow human being, because she is reading the same situation alternately, almost simultaneously, from her old perspective of slavery as a benevolent institution and from a new view of slavery as owning another human being. Later, when Rufel accidentally sees Dessa's heavily scarred buttocks, she feels "sympathy" and offers to pull the bedroom door closed so that Dessa can have "privacy" while she dresses (166–67). Realizing that Dessa has been telling the truth and imagining herself in Dessa's position finally allows Rufel to see her own power and privilege as a white woman. For the first time, Rufel treats Dessa as an equal, and Dessa accepts the olive branch.

Sherley Anne Williams must similarly position Dessa so that she can better understand Rufel in order to fulfill her goal of "imagining the basis for some kind of honest rapprochement between black and white women." While part 2 allows Rufel to see the world from a slave's perspective, part 3 contains scenes that afford Dessa a new vantage point. Because Rufel has never been mistreated by black people, Williams implies that it is easier for Rufel to see Dessa's humanity than for Dessa to see Rufel's. White people have whipped, branded, and sold Dessa and her family members, and they have killed her lover Kaine. As a result Dessa's thinking about interracial relationships has become deeply ingrained. Even though she knows Rufel is not her mistress, Dessa has difficulty getting beyond that habit of mind, which ultimately gives Rufel a certain measure of undeserved power. This power imbalance increases Dessa's fear of Rufel and consequently undermines the chance for trust to develop. However, their close proximity creates an opportunity for Williams to explore another important issue between the two women. Dessa walks into Rufel's bedroom when Rufel and the escaped slave Nathan are making love. Much like Walker's Lynne, Rufel is oblivious of the fact that a black woman might perceive their union as a betrayal by the black man and an assault on her own self-esteem. Williams, perhaps to increase the chances for her cross-racial female friendship to succeed, does not position Nathan as Dessa's lover, but as her comrade on the slave coffle, and she assigns Dessa another love interest, Harker.

Once again Williams uses an analogy to disrupt preconceptions; Harker employs Dessa's love of Kaine to explain the unfamiliar relationship between a black man and a white woman. In questioning the suitability of Dessa's asking Nathan to give up Rufel as a lover, Harker shifts the focus from race to heterosexual desire:

> "Who would you have gived Kaine up for if they had asked you?"
> My heart about turned over when he ask that. "It's like that, he feel like that for her?" (204)

Williams knows that analogies, though useful in making the unfamiliar more familiar, as they do for Dessa here, can be problematic when they mask differences. Certainly a black man's sexual relationship with a white woman in the antebellum South is not exactly the same as a black man's sexual relationship with a black woman. Thus Williams is careful to explore the possible motivations for Nathan's interest in Rufel in all of their complexity. Nathan desires Rufel for the beautiful woman she is; perhaps he even loves her. But other reasons may possibly heighten his pleasure, such as Rufel's symbolic value as forbidden fruit and her practical use as the linchpin in their money-making scheme. I discuss Williams's representation of their taboo affair in more detail in chapter 4.

All of these conversations—between Dessa and Rufel, Rufel and Nathan, Dessa and Harker—reveal misconceptions, contribute to increased under-standing, and therefore help to dismantle stereotypical thinking, but they do not create a bond between the women. Not until Dessa and Rufel develop a partnership out of necessity and mutual benefit—Dessa to escape to free terri-tory, Rufel to escape from her reprobate husband—do the two women form an alliance. The time spent together enacting Nathan's scheme (selling the black men as slaves who then escape to be sold again to fund their trip west) results in shared experiences, which mean, of course, time spent together talking and planning, but most importantly fostering trust and overcoming fear. As Dessa says, "[y]ou can't do something like this with someone and not develop some closeness, some trust" (225). The attempted rape that Williams employs to bring real camaraderie into their relationship seems contrived, but she uses it to further reinforce gender similarities across the color line. When a drunken white planter tries to rape Rufel, Dessa comes to her rescue, causing Dessa to realize for the first time the limits of the white woman's power: "The white woman was subject to the same ravishment as me; this the thought that kept me awake. I hadn't knowed white mens could use a white woman like that, just take her by force same as they could with us. . . . I never will forget the fear that come on me when Miz Lady called me on Mr. Oscar, that *knowing* that she was as helpless in this as I was, that our only protection was ourselves and each others" (220). In an essay published a few years before *Dessa Rose,* Barbara Smith pointed out that "a major problem for Black Women . . . is our profound skepticism that white people can actually be oppressed": "If white people as a group are our oppressors, and history and our individual experiences only ver-ify that in mass they are, how can we then perceive some of these same folks as being in trouble, sometimes as deep as our own?"[49] This scene in *Dessa Rose* seems designed to do just that—not to make this rape the equivalent of white men taking advantage of slave women, but simply to make the point that race privilege does not save the white woman from sexual oppression. By figuring the rapist as white, Williams makes her point and avoids the interracial rape that proved so thorny for Walker.

Once Williams has established Rufel and Dessa as comrades, she tests the possibility of interracial friendship. Rufel wants to take their camaraderie a step further and become friends, but Dessa believes interracial friendship impossible in a racist society, the same conclusion Alice Walker's protagonist comes to in "Advancing Luna—and Ida B. Wells." Dessa knows that Rufel has changed in her attitudes toward black people, but Dessa still cannot trust a white woman as she would her friend Martha or her sister Carrie. To move Dessa and Rufel toward friendship, Williams creates a situation in which Rufel can prove herself trustworthy. Dessa's escape hinges on Rufel's assistance in a climactic incident when Nehemiah turns up and identifies Dessa to the white sheriff as a runaway slave who has killed white people. When Rufel lies to protect Dessa, whom she has grown to like and respect, rather than agree with a white man whom she does not know, she wins Dessa's trust. That they finally acknowledge each other as individuals is clear from the way Williams ends this scene with a focus on their names. Rufel says, "My name, Ruth . . . I ain't your mistress," and Dessa says, "my name Dessa, Dessa Rose. Ain't no O to it." Refusing to allow the white woman to continue to call her something other than her name signals that Dessa is mentally no longer a slave. Using her given name, rather than the pet name Mammy bestowed on her as a child, signals Ruth's growth as a woman. Dessa's summary, which dismisses the contentious issues that have divided them previously, suggests the possibility of friendship in other circumstances: "I didn't hold nothing against her, not 'mistress,' not Nathan, not skin" (255–56).

Williams makes sure that her readers do not forget the differences between these women, even though she has highlighted certain similarities: raising children alone, being separated from their families, and living in a society that circumscribes both their lives. As Deborah McDowell has pointed out, "these commonalities are produced by radically different material circumstances and thus engender radically different effects."[50] The epilogue serves as a reminder to readers, particularly white readers, who may be tempted to forget about such differences and lapse into a simpler pattern of thinking only about women's similarities. Rufel and Dessa do not live happily ever after in an integrated community in California. Although their insulated personal relationship bears the signs of equality, they live in a society that does not view them that way, even outside the South. The black runaways have difficulty finding a wagon train that will take them west, even with Rufel's help. In contrast, Williams underlines Ruth's freedom of movement. She returns east and settles in a northern city, unwilling to live in the South once she has understood the inhumanity of its racial ideology. Despite the contemporary feminist sensibility of

Williams's female buddy plot, its antebellum setting forces racial separation. Thus, remembering Rufel fondly and missing her presence later in life, Dessa says, "Negro can't live in peace under protection of law, got to have some white person to stand protection for us. And who can you friend with, love with like that? Oh, Ruth would've tried it: no question in my mind about that" (259). The progress of Dessa and Ruth's friendship is finally undermined by the historical circumstances, not by any desire on Williams's part to focus solely on Dessa's growth as a woman, which seems to be the case in *Meridian*.

In her study of nineteenth-century women's writing, Minrose Gwin found that "color lines blinded white women to the humanity of their black sisters and built in black women massive layers of hatred for those fair ladies who would not, or could not, see their suffering."[51] African American novelists, such as Sherley Anne Williams, and African American theorists, such as Barbara Christian, bell hooks, and Audre Lorde, labored during the 1980s to make it clear that the centuries of stored anger would not dissipate if white women writers saw women's common humanity without seeing socially constructed differences. In *Can't Quit You, Baby* (1988), Ellen Douglas takes the next step by focusing on white self-deception in the familiar southern relationship between a white employer and her black maid.[52] By choosing metafiction as her vehicle, Douglas simultaneously invites readers to contemplate deception in the writer-reader relationship as well. Douglas says that over the years she has become "more and more interested in what's true and what isn't true and how impossible it is to recognize the truth or to tell the truth or to read a book and know it's true."[53]

In explaining the variety of narrative techniques she has employed throughout her career, Douglas emphasizes that "each project has its own reasons, so that the reason you do something is because it works in that project."[54] In *Can't Quit You, Baby*, Douglas uses a first-person writer-narrator who periodically breaks the spell of her fictional world to comment not only on the story, but on its construction as well. This strategy forces white readers, in particular, to reconsider their easy indulgence in illusions about interracial female friendships and race relations. By self-consciously exposing the way her novel is constructed, Douglas attempts to expose the way interracial relationships are constructed. From the opening of the novel to its conclusion, the writer-narrator raises questions about her own biases and perceptual limitations, about the story's very structure, and about the way to end the novel. *Can't Quit You, Baby* does not let its readers slide comfortably into an illusory fictional world in which well-meaning white people have thought (and sometimes still think), just as Cornelia does, that relationships between blacks and whites are better than they really are. Southern racial etiquette, which emphasized (and still emphasizes) politeness, helped (and still helps) disguise true feelings on both sides of the color line.

In Judith Rollins's research on black domestics and their employers in Boston, she learned that those who had also worked in the South preferred southern to northern white women as employers. One southern-born domestic explained this by referring to southern white and black women as "co-related": "I say 'co-related' meaning the Southern black and the Southern white understand each other—whether they like one another or not. You understand their goings and comings. And you feel a little easier with them. And they understand us more than northern whites do. And treat us better." If, as Rollins argues, "Southern black and white women developed a kind of mistress-servant relationship that was psychologically satisfying, to some degree, to both groups of women," it was because of three factors.[55] First, they were closer in culture, both being from the same region, but second, they were also closer in class, with its own experiential similarities. Because of the large cheap labor pool in the South, white southerners with fairly low incomes could afford domestic help until after the civil rights era. This fact led to a physical closeness of the women because of small houses, and it meant a more informal family interaction style, which in some cases carried over into their interactions with domestic help. Finally, because of southern racial segregation, white women and their black domestics were operating within a more clearly defined system of social and racial inequality with very precise conventions regarding racial interaction. Thus, paradoxically, because the social distance was unquestioned, and therefore individual intimacy did not affect the socially subordinate role of black women, southern white women could develop greater individual intimacy with their black domestics.[56]

However, even as southern racial etiquette created a script that allowed for a certain artificial ease in interracial relationships, it also allowed for white self-deception about the nature of race relations. This is revealed in oral histories and southern fictions in which white people call beloved black servants members of their families and praise the "mutual respect" between the races during the Jim Crow era.[57] Douglas points out that "this pervasive self-deception among white people about what their own behavior was and what its significance was, and the elaborate structure of beliefs about what black people were like—a structure meant to serve our own self-deception—created a sort of ghost world, a wholly unreal vision of the lives of the very black people we lived so intimately with."[58] From the beginning of *Can't Quit You, Baby,* Douglas's writer-narrator self-consciously insists on a more honest representation of a relationship that blacks remember differently from whites. Although Cornelia and Tweet daily work side by side in the kitchen, and although the black woman tells the white woman of being sexually harassed by a male employer, Douglas does not create a connection by privileging similarities based on gender roles. Instead, the writer-narrator seems more intent on pointedly reminding readers of facts that cannot be gotten around. For example, despite the temptation to hide behind euphemisms like "housekeeper and employer," the narrator forces the reader to see that "the black woman is the white woman's servant."[59]

Cornelia, whom Douglas marks as physically hard of hearing, politely listens to Tweet's stories about white injustice and black hardship, marital infidelity and familial competition over land. But Cornelia does not hear in these stories the evidence of institutionalized racism in the town's law offices and banks that Ellen Douglas makes sure her readers discern. Feminist theorist Jane Flax has pointed out that American white women have the "'privilege' of 'forgetting' or not noticing the operations of race and many socially sanctioned opportunities for doing so" because of their own relation to the privileges of racism, their own complicity in its maintenance, and/or their own guilt.[60] Certainly Cornelia falls into the first two categories, however unwittingly. In Tweet's stories Cornelia hears confirmation of her own unexamined stereotypes about black people as superstitious and immoral, because she attends to the details in Tweet's stories that fulfill her expectations about black people, much as psychologist Mark Snyder explains. Almost unconsciously Cornelia uses Tweet's stories to affirm herself as socially superior to the various white people who emerge as villains in them and as intellectually and morally superior to Tweet. But at the same time she consciously likes to focus on the special bond she thinks she has with Tweet. One of Cornelia's fondest memories is of helping Tweet nurse her stepfather Robert on his deathbed, proof, Cornelia thinks, of the two women's "intimacy and mutual understanding" (202). But Cornelia confuses the companionable hours they spend working together in intimate surroundings with the personal expressions of intimacy and vulnerability that characterize friendship and that come in a relationship between equals. Tweet tells Cornelia about her brother's deviousness regarding her grandfather's estate and about her husband's infidelities, but Cornelia does not share her personal life with Tweet. If she admitted the strains in her own marriage or family relationships, to herself or to Tweet, she could not feel superior. Because of the racial hierarchy in their relationship, Tweet does not tell Cornelia exactly what she thinks of her, although Tweet's stories reveal how unjust and untrustworthy she thinks many white people are. *Can't Quit You, Baby* shows how the inequality in their relationship makes it extremely difficult for Cornelia to hear the truth of Tweet's stories or for Tweet to express her true feelings.

The novel takes up the work of determining when a white woman will be able to understand a black woman's point of view and when a black woman will be able to tell the truth with impunity. For Douglas it seems that understanding can come only through experience, because it is when Cornelia leaves her sheltered life as a lady after her husband's death and travels to New York alone that she sees her common humanity with Tweet, whose life is filled with hardship. Although Cornelia has lectured Tweet about the futility of hating those who have been unjust to her and has self-righteously proclaimed that she herself has never hated anyone, Cornelia realizes in New York that she has always hated her mother for attempting to control her life. In a big city without her family to protect her, Cornelia is forced to stop "skimming over the surface of her life" (127). That is when she hears Tweet's voice, ignores her mother's, and mines Tweet's stories for advice about how to negotiate a difficult, indifferent, and sometimes hostile world. Tweet does not express her true feelings about Cornelia until late in the novel when she is no longer employed by her and has nothing to lose. Only when the white woman is put in a vulnerable position does she let go of her racial pride; only when the black woman is no longer dependent on the white woman for a job does she fully express her anger.

The postmodern form of the novel enacts the very difficulties in representing the other that Cornelia experiences in understanding Tweet's thoughts and feelings. Because readers inhabit Cornelia's consciousness, but not Tweet's, Douglas puts them in the position of sharing Cornelia's ignorance to some extent in order drive home her point. Postmodern theories about situated knowledge and positionality, the place from which one views and experiences the world, have spotlighted the difficulties both in understanding someone in a different position and in fully comprehending one's own experience. Douglas emphasizes this difficulty with the narrative strategy she chooses to tell the two women's stories. A third-person narrator tells Cornelia's story, which enables Douglas to reveal Cornelia's thoughts to readers, even though Cornelia will not tell Tweet her secrets. Tweet tells her own life stories from a first-person perspective. Readers hear her stories just as Cornelia does, but we do not enter Tweet's thoughts, a limitation the narrator readily acknowledges as a product of the "ghost world" that whites created. Douglas refuses to erase the presence of her writer-narrator and thus heightens the reader's awareness of the biased perspective from which this novel, or any novel, is written.

Most significantly, Douglas chooses not to posit her omniscient narrator in the conventional way as unraced. Instead she explores through her metafictional narrative technique the dangers of "positing one's writerly self . . . unraced and all others as raced" that Toni Morrison pointed out a few years later in *Playing in the Dark: Whiteness and the Literary Imagination*.[61] In *Can't Quit You, Baby* the writer-narrator reveals her identity as a white woman to her readers and calls attention both to her own biases in representing Cornelia's life and to her lack of knowledge about Tweet's thoughts. In so doing she emphasizes not just a social issue but a narrative problem as well. No matter who narrates a novel or how many narrative voices a reader hears, the author is the sole creator of all of them, as Douglas's writer-narrator explains: "Perhaps she [the narrator] can find someone more detached, more objective than she to tell us now about Cornelia. I call up faces and voices she may hide behind. A man, perhaps. An author who is a black lawyer with an extra Ph.D. in psychology. Or a soft-voiced, steely-eyed black grandmother. Or an elderly single aunt of Cornelia's who is wise and dispassionate. But I would still be there, wouldn't I?" (38). Instead, Douglas chooses to narrate *Can't Quit You, Baby* from the perspectives that replicate how a southern white woman writer would know the stories of a white employer and a black maid, "telling you [the reader] about Cornelia, letting Tweet speak for herself" (38). This is a position Douglas knew well, for she dedicated the novel to the memory of Mathelde Griffin, her longtime housekeeper, who according to Douglas could "assess who she could say what to and how uncomfortable she could make someone before she had to quit," much like Tweet.[62]

In telling Tweet's and Cornelia's stories asymmetrically, the writer-narrator points out that she has shied away from knowing Tweet other than in relation to Cornelia. She has omitted "how [Tweet] spoke at home, in bed at night with Nig, sitting in their crowded little house, the gas heater pulsing, with Robert and Rosa and their friends and neighbors" (240). Jan Shoemaker has asked if the resulting imbalance in narrative perspective might be "yet another way to silence Tweet."[63] This is an important and provocative question, but silencing would be the case only if Tweet never spoke her true feelings about Cornelia, and Tweet does reveal these unspoken feelings by the end of the novel. Douglas's asymmetrical narrative technique thus represents the problem, while her metafictional commentary on that choice exposes the imbalance in point of view for the very real problem that it is. To get outside of the illusory world of southern race relations, Douglas must give her characters another script, one that is not governed by politeness or guardedness, but first the white writer-narrator must make the imaginative leap into her black character's head and heart, the very leap that some reviewers and critics thought tripped up William Styron when writing about Nat Turner. Douglas's writer-narrator must go beyond relaying the stories that Tweet is willing to tell her white employer to revealing the hidden feelings about Cornelia that Tweet has had to suppress. However, when Cornelia is finally ready to listen carefully to Tweet, Tweet is not talking, having fallen victim to an aneurysm.

Ann Bomberger reads this plot development as a melodramatic ploy that provides an obvious way for Cornelia to demonstrate her newfound compassion for her old servant; but it is a choice, she feels, that "skirts more difficult issues that would have arisen had Cornelia decided to change her ways and deal with Tweet on a more equal footing."[64] True enough, but one could also interpret Douglas's choice to render Tweet speechless as a metaphoric parallel to Cornelia's deafness. In this reading Tweet's inability to speak becomes a second controlling metaphor in a novel that points both to the reasons for the impasse between black and white women and to a way out of the dilemma. If white women need to listen more carefully, then black women need to be able to speak their anger. Tweet's illness inverts the women's social positions, placing Cornelia in a position to take care of Tweet, instead of having Tweet take care of her, and to ask permission to visit Tweet in her home, rather than presume she is welcome, as she does on the day of Martin Luther King Jr.'s assassination. The white woman's desire to talk when the black woman falls silent reflects race relations in the late 1980s when Douglas was writing the novel— between white feminists who longed for dialogue with black woman about the problems in the women's movement and black feminists who, after decades of waiting for honest talk, were unimpressed with white feminists' self-centered approach. When Cornelia first begins visiting the incapacitated Tweet, she talks incessantly, saying everything she has suppressed or repressed for years, but she still does not listen as attentively to Tweet as she needs to in order to understand that the noises Tweet makes as she begins to recover actually have meaning. It takes a curious child, Cornelia's grandson, to notice that "Tweet can't talk, but she can sing" (247).

The writer-narrator makes readers aware of her quandary about how to end the stalemate between the women and thus the novel we are reading: "Can't someone else search for the end of this story? Discover where it is leading us? No. It has to be me" (250). She knows full well that the ending is crucial, because her ideology about race relations will reveal itself there. She worries that, much like Cornelia, she has skimmed over the surface of the narrative because of her limited perspective and wonders, "What tangle of snakes have I been skiing over?" (240). She points to two previous occasions in the text when Cornelia has been in Tweet's home: to pay a very awkward condolence call when King was assassinated and to help nurse Robert on his deathbed. The writer-narrator's self-conscious address to the reader—"Do you remember?"—is an invitation to readers to revisit these scenes and a reminder that we may have overlooked clues as well. In each scene there is a gold barrette and a tangle of Mardi Gras beads in a bowl, which the writer-narrator says she included "to give you a sense of the richness and poverty, the clutter and crowdedness and human closeness in Tweet's house" (240). In the final scenes these objects are still there, but Cornelia and readers see them differently because of the imaginative leap that the writer-narrator makes. Readers find out that the barrette is Cornelia's but that she has overlooked it in the other two scenes: in the first, after King's death, because she feels self-conscious and hurries out of the house to escape her discomfort; and in the second, when she helps nurse Robert, because she is preoccupied with how well she and Tweet understand each other. As Audre Lorde pointed out, in the first instance difference seems an "insurmountable barrier" and results in "voluntary isolation"; in the second difference is denied and "a false and treacherous connection" created.

Douglas's repetition of the word *tangle* makes the tangled beads and the gold barrette function symbolically in the story to represent not just Cornelia's blindness but the writer-narrator's and the reader's as well. In order to see beneath the surface, the writer-narrator moves the action to Tweet's house and positions Cornelia as a character in Tweet's story. The writer-narrator selects the stereotypical situation of a black servant having stolen from her white employer, but she reveals what the white employer and readers may not understand by ultimately allowing the servant to ascribe a meaning to the theft. The writer-narrator reveals that for Tweet the gold barrette is not significant because of its monetary value, as Cornelia suspects, but because of its symbolic value—as a object embodying Tweet's hatred of Cornelia's blindness to power and privilege. Cornelia has so many gold barrettes that she has not even noticed this one is missing until her grandchildren bring it home thoughtlessly after playing pirates at Tweet's house. Even after Cornelia realizes Tweet has taken the barrette, she remains too polite to confront Tweet directly, much like Godwin's Lydia, although she indirectly lets Tweet know that she knows about the theft.

But Douglas moves her characters beyond Godwin's polite interracial pas de deux. Tweet, who sees that Cornelia knows, cannot stand the artificiality of their relationship any longer. She finally breaks the silence caused by southern racial etiquette and symbolized by her illness, and she tells Cornelia that she took the barrette. When Cornelia asks why she stole the barrette, Tweet punctures Cornelia's illusion of mutual respect, speaking the unspoken stereotypes that she knows Cornelia holds about black people as immoral and superstitious and reminding Cornelia that the subordinate positions in which whites have held black people actually produce the stereotypes. The intensity of Tweet's outburst derives from years of suppressing her rage at the many white people who have discriminated against her—from the white neighbor who stole her land to the banker who helped him and the lawyer who failed her grandfather when her grandfather attempted to protect her. Tweet's inability to continue to suppress her emotions originates from her total frustration with Cornelia's blindness to Tweet's anger, with Cornelia's willful ignorance of white prejudice, and with Cornelia's inability to see their common humanity. The scene degenerates into a barrage of expletives they hurl at one another, much like the scene between Lynne and Meridian, but without the racial slurs. Karen Jacobsen points out that by expressing her anger, "Tweet does what bell hooks argues is necessary for black women to form authentic bonds with white women—to acknowledge the 'legacy of hostility and rage [black women] hold towards white women due to their complicity with white supremacy.'"[65] Their "I hate yous" and their "fuck yous" never evolve into real dialogue, however, because they are interrupted by the arrival of Tweet's husband. His presence makes for a rather abrupt and too-easy ending to their angry exchange.

The conclusion of the novel, which quickly follows, is open but holds a hint of promise that the relationship will continue. Tweet picks up the barrette and offers it to Cornelia, who returns it to the bowl on the table, as a gesture for Tweet to keep it, as both symbol and gift. The novel concludes with Cornelia's departure as Tweet sings the same blues lyrics to Cornelia that she has sung to her adulterous husband, "I love you, darlin, but I hate your treacherous low down ways" (256). Thus Douglas indicates that although Tweet and Cornelia may not be family, their daily life together has made them "co-related," and this will not be the last they see of each other—unlike Meridian and Lynne. Although they do not become friends, their angry curses signal that have finally put down the old script of southern racial etiquette. The novel's final words predict that they may create a new one: "Sing it, Tweet. Yeah. Sing it, Cornelia. Sing it" (256). Tweet's climactic outburst suggests that the self-conscious writer-narrator has risen above what she calls "her limitations" (39) as a white woman writer and succeeded in imagining how a black woman like Tweet might feel about her white employer. The writer-narrator's imaginative leap propels her out of the illusory world of southern race relations and thus enables her to end the fiction.

In *Night Talk* (1997), Elizabeth Cox picks up the subject of interracial relationships between women where Ellen Douglas and Sherley Anne Williams leave off. She is not so much concerned with dismantling stereotypes as the 1980s writers; she is more interested in opening white eyes to contemporary racism's subtleties and in testing the viability of interracial friendships among equals. A white writer who entered the University of Mississippi the same year that James Meredith desegregated that university, Cox joins black women writers in thinking that black and white women must be comrades in a struggle for equality that does not privilege gender over race.[66] To fulfill all these goals in her novel, she examines the lifelong friendship of a white girl, Evie, and a black girl, Janey Louise, who grew up together in Mercy, Georgia, in the 1950s and came of age in the turbulent 1960s. When Evie's father leaves his family to seek adventure and romance in Mexico, Evie's mother, Agnes, asks her black housekeeper Volusia to move into their small spare room. Volusia cannot do otherwise and keep her job, so she asks to bring her young daughter Janey Louise. The girls plot to share Evie's bedroom, and although at first their mothers object, they eventually share not only a room but also "night talk"—intimate secrets about their changing bodies and private dreams about boys and careers. In her review of the novel, Allison Miller calls attention to the schizophrenia of the girls' relationship: "Within the confines of the home, at least, segregation can be defied; in the dark, race and class differences can dissolve. But in public, racism strains their relationship." She points out that their relationship "mirrors that of their mothers, who, despite mutual dependence and emotional support, outwardly conform to expectations."[67] When Agnes Bell's white friends visit, Volusia's multifaceted relationship as Agnes's friend, adviser, business partner, and housekeeper is reduced to the single acceptable role of maid. When Evie and Janey Louise go to school, they attend separate segregated schools, and even when Evie's school is finally desegregated, they go their separate ways in public.

Positioning these women and girls in the same house allows Cox to point up similarities—the two women must raise their children without the help of husbands, the two girls both try to replace the loss of their fathers' love with early sexual experiences. But as in *Dessa Rose,* there are striking differences related to the material circumstances caused by race. For example, when Agnes and Volusia open a store to sell the specialty hats that Volusia makes, Agnes must make the arrangements with the real estate brokers and bankers, and everyone assumes it is Agnes's shop, although the business would not exist without Volusia's creativity. Both girls are abused by older men, but while Evie is duped into sex with a good-looking, fast-talking itinerant preacher, Janey Louise is raped by a white racist intent on sending a message to her older brother Albert. In the course of the novel, readers learn that Volusia and Janey Louise hide the identity of the perpetrator in order to protect Albert, who is a civil rights activist, and to preserve their relationship with Agnes and Evie. Mr. Turnbull, the man who raped Janey Louise, is one of the most prominent men in town and the husband of a woman with whom Agnes plays bridge. Volusia lies about a racist beating she received because she fears for Albert's life, a fear Cox proves legitimate when Mr. Turnbull and his friends finally beat Albert so badly that he dies. Readers learn that both Volusia's and Janey Louise's silences signify deep disappointment in and frustration with the white woman and her daughter, whom they hoped would be their allies.

Night Talk is a first-person narrative from Evie's perspective, covering both her years as a girl when she shared a bedroom with Janey Louise and her adult years in the late 1970s when she and Jane return to Georgia for Volusia's funeral. This juxtaposition of time periods allows Cox to assess the progress of a small southern town's race relations after the civil rights movement and to measure the long-term health of Evie and Janey Louise's relationship. Cox's decision not to use alternating first-person accounts means that the reader knows only as much as Evie understands about her relationship with Volusia and Janey Louise. Although readers, like Evie, are aware that the occasional silences of Janey Louise and her mother are potent with meaning, we do not know exactly what these silences signify, and we are not aware until the end of the novel who raped Janey Louise or that Volusia has been beaten by white supremacists. By withholding such information from readers, Cox certainly silences her black characters somewhat, even though they speak their minds plenty about other things. But limiting readers' knowledge of Janey Louise's and Volusia's private thoughts forces readers into a position of trying to read those silences and wishing they could ask questions—exactly the work that Cox believes white readers need to undertake. When Jane speaks very frankly to Evie at the novel's end, even the most racially sensitive white readers are made to realize just how much about a black woman's experience they may misunderstand or choose to overlook.

Night Talk reveals the sometimes hidden racial dimensions of mundane everyday experiences and the daily toll they take on African Americans and ultimately on race relations. Cox begins her novel with a prologue that functions as instruction in seeing beneath surface appearances. The prologue is really a primer on how to read *Night Talk*. Before Evie's biologist father, August, leaves his family, he enjoys teaching Evie and her brother about the natural world. One lesson, especially, is difficult to teach and harder to learn. August encourages Evie to observe the marine life hidden in the pond, but Evie is afraid to peer too closely and thus sees only the clouds and branches reflected on the pond's surface. One day when she is ten, she does look beyond her own reflection and beneath the surface; there she sees a crawdad devouring a baby bird that has fallen from its nest. Wanting his daughter to understand the food chain, August does not let Evie avert her eyes from the gruesome sight. Cox's novel provides readers with a similar learning experience. The novel is a study in what Evie did not see beneath the surface of her relationship with Janey Louise when they were growing up and what she fails to understand when they are adults.

Critical race theorist Patricia Williams's comments are particularly relevant to the way this novel works: "For white people . . . racial denial tends to engender a profoundly invested disingenuousness, an innocence that amounts to the transgressive refusal to know."[68] Evie admits as much when, as an adult, she remembers a crucial incident from which she averted her eyes as a child. One day after school, she notices that Volusia's face is bruised and swollen. Evie smells the presence of men in the house but accepts Volusia's story that she fell on the rickety back steps, and Evie does not tell her mother about the smell, even when her mother asks her what happened to Volusia. Reading the same signs as Evie, Agnes tells her daughter that it looks as if someone hit Volusia. But much like Douglas's Cornelia or Godwin's Lydia, rather than to risk an embarrassing scene by confronting Volusia or to face an unpleasant truth about her neighbors by contemplating white violence, Agnes takes a familiar, and ultimately prejudiced, route. When Evie asks her mother what she thinks happened, Agnes settles on a racist stereotype to make sense of the evidence:

> "Some man, I guess. They get like that sometimes."
> "Like what?"
> "Sometimes they hit their women."[69]

Just as quickly as that, with the use of the pronouns *they* and *their,* the budding interracial community of women is falsely divided by race, and Agnes, one of the town's most liberal white women, passes a racist stereotype on to her daughter.

Because Evie and Janey Louise grow up in the same house together and continue to see each other regularly as adults when they return to Mercy for holidays, Cox employs their relationship to probe the possibility of reviving early white feminists' hope for interracial sisterhood. Cox presents the sisterhood model as problematic because Evie and Janey Louise's relationship is not equal when they are girls and their love does not seem unconditional when readers meet them as adults, two characteristics that distinguish a strong kinship bond between sisters. When readers first encounter Jane and Evie as adults in chapter 2, they have not seen each other in three years, although previously they had gotten together annually. Evie attributes their break to external forces: "The politics of the seventies had pulled us apart. Her friends told her not to trust me, and mine were wary of us" (10). But through a flashback to their previous meeting, Cox guides readers to look beneath the surface, to see Evie's "innocence" as a large part of the problem.

A scene in which the two old friends shop in Neiman Marcus for sexy nightgowns as adults parallels an event in their childhood when a clerk humiliated Janey Louise by not allowing her to use the bathroom in a local department store. Evie still feels guilty that she did not leave the store with her friend that day. Cox shows that although much has changed in the South—the two women can now be friends in public—the legacy of racism lingers and continues to test their friendship. The Neiman Marcus saleslady keeps checking on the two women, counting the nightgowns they take into the dressing room. Jane believes the saleslady is racist and decides to leave without buying anything, even though she loves the lingerie. Evie, who has always stood by Jane since her failure in loyalty during childhood, is tired of having to leave stores on principle and insists to Jane that the saleslady is not racist but simply rude, and rude to both of them. Cox leaves the truth of the saleslady's motives ambiguous so that her readers will have to focus on the equally troubling facts of Jane's and Evie's different interpretations of the incident and the legacy of racism that makes the truth so difficult to discern. In retrospect Evie knows that their very different interpretations strained their friendship: "We didn't know how to be together anymore. I was afraid of saying something offensive, and no doubt she expected to be offended. We couldn't laugh at anything. I wished we could just be us again. I wished we could just be us" (13). Jane's remark that day, "All of a sudden it seems like you've been stupid all your life" (12), reveals the depth of her resentment and provides readers with an early clue to the anger that underlies the potent silences of Janey Louise's youth, which pile up as the novel unfolds. At the time of the Neiman Marcus incident, Jane is Evie's equal, thanks both to her family's financial independence from the Bells and to the civil rights movement. Volusia has married a kind and prosperous storeowner in Mercy, and Jane, a nurse, is happily married with two sons and living in Chicago. Weary of Evie's insouciance about race, Jane does not hesitate to end her relationship with her white "sister."

The remainder of the novel juxtaposes their early friendship with Evie's current attempts to forge a new intimacy when they meet again for Volusia's funeral. *Night Talk* demonstrates that for such intimacy to occur, the two women must be completely honest with each other about their past relationship as well as their present feelings. Cox calls on Evie and white readers to understand the burden of the subtle and not-so-subtle racism that black people encounter and the frustration they feel at white blindness to it and at the need to have to rely on white people to negotiate racism's land mines, even today. Such are the stumbling blocks to interracial friendship in *Night Talk*. Cox takes up an important contemporary concern about how differently white and black Americans understand and interpret interracial dynamics. According to a study that began the year before *Night Talk* was published, over 57 percent of African Americans said that "people of other races can't really understand the way my race sees things," whereas only 35 percent of whites agreed with this statement. When asked whether the quality of life of African Americans has improved in the last ten years, 34 percent of blacks thought life had improved for African Americans as compared with 62 percent of whites. Although blacks and whites overwhelmingly agree that achieving equality and eliminating racism are important American goals, they disagree about how far the United States has come in its efforts.[70]

Throughout the novel, Cox represents Evie and Agnes as feeling superior to their white neighbors because of their relationship with Volusia and Janey Louise. Their 1950s acts of racial kindness are sometimes offered in the spirit of largesse and often compromised by the hypocrisy of hiding the truth of their integrated domestic life behind the closed doors of their home. But when Jane is accused and indicted for the murder of Mr. Turnbull during her 1970s return to Mercy for Volusia's funeral, Evie openly comes to her aid. Their evening conversations through the bars of Jane's jail cell are oddly reminiscent of their night talks growing up, but with a very important difference: this time Jane holds nothing back and Evie finally becomes aware of her remaining racial blindness. During these conversations Jane reveals for Evie how the similarities that Evie perceived in their lives have really been materially different, including the present fact that she has been arrested in circumstances that would never have led to Evie's arrest. The brief summary not only puts Evie on notice, but it does the same for less alert readers. And while Evie's offer to post bail for Jane and to give her sanctuary in their home make Evie feel good, Jane points out that Evie does not seem to perceive the uncomfortably dependent position these favors put Jane in, once again having to be "saved by the Bells." "What you never got, Evie," Jane says, "was the fact that whenever we were together—walking in town or through the cemetery, anywhere—there was never any doubt in anybody's mind about who was servant and who wasn't. I was always there, because I was with you. I'd like the day to come when I exist for myself, the same as anyone. I'd like for the issue not to be a part of people's minds. I'd even like for it not to be very interesting" (213). Jane's combined feelings of powerlessness in her own social position and disappointment in Evie's blindness have previously occasioned the silences that Evie could not read. The feelings of frustration with Evie that Jane experiences as an adult make her weary with the effort of maintaining their friendship. When she is not with Evie, Jane can escape what Patricia Williams calls "the clanging symbolism of self."[71]

This frank talk between Jane and Evie concludes part 2 of the novel. Part 3 sends Evie back through her memories to revisit those times in the past when she looked away from the truth, such as the afternoon when she and her mother turned a blind eye to Volusia's troublesome bruises. Part 3 puts Jane on the witness stand during her trial to reveal to the entire town the secrets that she and her mother had guarded so closely in the 1950s—that it was Mr. Turnbull who raped her and beat her mother decades ago. The mere fact that Jane has been arrested in the 1970s just because a white woman saw her enter the Turnbulls' house the afternoon of Mr. Turnbull's murder makes Jane believe not much has changed in Mercy, Georgia, since the civil rights movement. Cox shows that racist violence still resides there and threatens to prevent Jane from finishing her testimony. White supremacists come to the Bells' house, where Jane is staying during the trial, and Agnes faces them down with an old shotgun. When Evie informs Jane the next morning, "My mother almost killed a man for you" (247), Jane meets her remark with the same stony silence she has exhibited in the past. Evie's choice of words seems worthy of past performances in "saved by the Bells," loaded as her sentence is with white desire for black gratitude. This small incident functions as a large test of white readers' racial sensitivity. Given Jane's jail cell revelations, the meaning of Jane's silence at this point in the novel should be clear. What is surprising and disappointing is that Cox did not have the two women work through this awkward moment together, as they do elsewhere in the novel.

The unexpected ending to the trial—Mrs. Turnbull coming to Jane's defense—could be read as yet another white woman saving Jane, but it does not function quite that way. Rather it is Jane's revelation that provokes Mrs. Turnbull to act, to admit that she too has been a victim of her husband's abuse. Thus, Mrs. Turnbull joins Evie and her mother and Jane in a female interracial alliance to fight white male violence. But unlike Sherley Anne Williams a decade before, Cox does not stop at interracial comradeship. She moves Jane and Evie from participation in a public struggle to combat racism and sexism back into their shared history of domestic intimacy. A year later the two women meet again in Mercy to celebrate their pregnancies. As they lie in the yard of their childhood home, which Agnes Bell has willed them jointly at her death, Cox restores their old intimacy, sealing it with the sweet scent of magnolia blossoms above their heads. Redolent with old South connotations, Cox reworks the symbol to crown an interracial southern friendship that has been nurtured in shared intimacy and shared struggle and that has survived a crucial and straining test. In the jail scene in which Jane makes Evie see both the privilege of whiteness and the differences between their racial experiences, Evie feels embarrassed at her ignorance and disappointed in her blindness; but mostly she is worried that Jane may never forgive her the way a sister might.

Evie explains her feelings for Jane in familial terms: "I do love you, you know? I love and hate you the way I love and hate Tucker [her brother], and Mama, and August, and Volusia. I want to change the whole world for you. I want to change myself" (216). Jane's hug is her answer.

But Evie is also concerned about whether Jane's troubling revelations mean that their shared past held no moments of joy for Jane. Evie asks, "Everything we did together—was it all wrong?" (214). Because Cox wants the reader to ponder this question, she leaves it hanging. But embedded in the intimate scene of the two pregnant friends is Evie's memory of another magical summer night when she and Jane were together. That night they awoke, went out in the moonlight in their long blue nightgowns, and made glittering jewelry from the lightning bugs they collected. This lovely memory and the intimate moment that follows it in the present as the two women feel each other's unborn daughters kick seems to be Cox's answer to Evie's question. Everything they did together was not "wrong." This scene shows a strong white need for reassurance that white blindness and misunderstanding has not extended to all past interracial interactions.

Cox does not conclude her novel with this poignant, rather sentimental 1979 scene between pregnant girlfriends. Her ending encapsulates the duality of so many contemporary southern novels about race relations. A brief epilogue follows, which strikes a more discordant note and creates a double ending for *Night Talk*. Set in 1991, this scene serves as a chilly and powerful warning—not about the future of Jane and Evie's friendship, which is no longer in doubt, but about race relations in general, and not only in the South, since Jane lives in Chicago. Evie contrasts her deep and abiding friendship with Jane to the shallow relationship of their twelve-year-old daughters, who see each other once a year at Thanksgiving and sometimes for a week each summer: "they know how to tolerate each other with politeness learned from schools and politicians. They speak guardedly about their feelings, because they have been told that words can start a riot. They do not yet believe that love can stop one" (265). Because Jane and Evie grew up sharing a room as sisters do, they laughed and cried together, they hurt and helped each other, and they argued but also confessed their most intimate secrets. Their daughters do not have the shared experiences that make for a close friendship because they do not experience daily life together as their mothers did—a cautionary comment on the dangers of desegregation without integration. But Elizabeth Cox does not seem to be able to let this story go until Jane and Evie put their daughters in at least one casual situation that takes them into a moment of mutual delight beyond the bounds of contemporary racial etiquette. Sharon Monteith has pointed out that white women's fictions about interracial friendship have always been more utopian than fictions by black women writers.[72] *Night Talk* holds to the pattern while making it more complex.

As Sherley Anne Williams and Ellen Douglas show, interracial friendship among unequals is impossible, since very often the person on top in the hierarchy simplifies the reality of the person of lower status. This is why Dessa Rose and Rufel cannot be friends but only comrades in a common political struggle. However, when black and white women are equals, Elizabeth Cox suggests that they can experience "the depth of emotional attachment, empathetic and sympathetic communication," that does not come with comradeship but which friendship requires.[73] Only because Evie attempts to see through Jane's eyes and only because Jane helps her by breaking her silence, do they move beyond the impasse between them. In Sanders's *Clover* the racial roles are reversed. Only because Everleen finally attempts to see through Sara Kate's eyes and only because Sara Kate helps her by breaking her silence, do they move beyond competing for Clover's affection to collaborating in her upbringing.

By spanning several decades in *Night Talk*, Cox demonstrates that maintaining an interracial friendship necessitates "a lifelong negotiation of endless subtlety"—Patricia Williams's prescription for building an integrated community.[74] Because of this negotiation Cox is able to create an interracial friendship that operates very much like the "pluralist friendship" that feminist critic María Lugones advocates: "a kind of practical love that commits one to perceptual changes in the knowledge of other persons." Lugones explains that "the commitment is there because understanding the other is central to the possibility of loving the other person practically." She describes "practical love" as "an emotion that involves a commitment to make decisions or act in ways that take the well-being of the other person into account."[75] But Elizabeth Cox goes a bit further. Living together and then inheriting a house together place Evie and Janey Louise in the intimate environment of sisters. Such situations enable these women to work and to play together but, perhaps most significantly, also to argue and to want to make up. In *Night Talk* Elizabeth Cox suggests that interracial friendship can become something like sisterhood when the color line is crossed within a family setting. The coming decades will test her hypothesis.

CHAPTER 3

Refighting Old Wars

Race, Masculinity, and the Sense of an Ending

> Just when do men that have different blood in them stop hating one
> another? —WILLIAM FAULKNER, *LIGHT IN AUGUST*

Long after the Civil War ended the pretense of genial southern race relations,
white male southern writers as different as Thomas Nelson Page and William
Faulkner created fond fictions about childhood friendships across the color
line. Given contemporary memoirs of men as different as Harry Crews and
Jimmy Carter, these interracial friendships had some basis in fact, but before
1970 most of them did not continue past childhood. Much of the poignancy
of Faulkner's *The Unvanquished* (1938) comes from Bayard Sartoris's description
of the close relationship he has with a black servant boy, Ringo, in the small
Mississippi town that separates them as they grow older and which from the
beginning marks them as different based on race. After their boyhood games
and real Civil War adventures together, Bayard and Ringo grow up to be not
close friends but master and faithful servant. Representations of interracial
male friendships between men beyond the period of childhood's innocence
have only recently begun to emerge in literature set in the South. Black writers like Ernest Gaines are more tentative in their portraits than such white writers as Larry Brown and Madison Smartt Bell. But all three novelists begin their
interracial buddy novels where earlier fictions about male friendships ended,
when innocent boys become racially self-conscious men, and none hold any
illusions about the ease of establishing such relationships.

In 1989 both Larry Brown and Madison Smartt Bell published novels that
explore the physical and psychological consequences of the Vietnam War. That
each novelist also selects two protagonists of different races suggests that the
representation of interracial friendships greatly concerns them as well. Their
novels examine the possibilities and limits of such friendships formed because
of shared experiences in Vietnam, but Bell's *Soldier's Joy* disrupts masculine con-

ventions of bonding in ways that Brown's *Dirty Work* does not. In *The Warriors,*
J. Glenn Gray argues that while combat settings are "unequaled in forging links
among people of unlike desire and temperament," these links can be fragile.[1]
Although such relationships are based on comradeship, which involves loyalty
to a group, dependence on group members for survival, and some knowledge
of individuals in the group, they are not based on reciprocal relationships of
mutual intimacy between individuals, which involve self-disclosure, genuine
understanding, and caring and comfortable emotional warmth. As a result, relationships based on comradeship may mean little outside the combat setting.[2]
Both Brown and Bell test the significance of their protagonists' similar combat experiences in Vietnam against their very different experiences back home.

Brown's protagonists, who occupy adjoining beds in a veterans' hospital in
Mississippi, are comrades; their male bonding is based on coping with their debilitating war injuries and their frustrated desires for more normal lives.
Braiden Chaney, who is black, has no legs or arms; Walter James, who is white,
has no face. For the first half of the novel, each man silently reminisces about
parallel subjects, an activity designed to show readers that, despite their racial
differences, they have significant similarities: both grew up poor in rural Mississippi, both came of age with loving mothers and distant or absent fathers,
and both saw Marine combat in Vietnam and sustained devastating war
wounds. Brown, however, reveals more to the reader than Braiden and Walter
disclose to each other. The alternating first-person narratives are related in dis-
tinctively individual voices. Their conversational styles seem to give some readers the mistaken impression that the two men are talking to each other more
than they really are; several reviewers single out for praise the "conversation"
these men of different races have and the "dialogue" they engage in.[3]

Even when Braiden and Walter begin to share their stories, they engage in
very little dialogue. One, then the other, tells his story, sometimes on different
topics altogether—an adult example of what sociologists call parallel play in
children,[4] or, to put it in a southern context, what Allen Tate termed the "traditional Southern mode of discourse," or "rhetorical" mode, which "presup-
poses somebody at the other end silently listening."[5] In "A Southern Mode of
the Imagination" Tate contrasted this nineteenth-century "rhetorical" mode
of discourse with the more modern "dialectical" mode, which involves the give
and take of two different minds. Although Walter frequently apologizes to
Braiden for going "off like that,"[6] he does not change his rhetorical mode of
communication, and Braiden does more listening than talking. Brown's nar-

rative technique, alternating first-person monologues in separate chapters, replicates the nature of the emerging relationship between Braiden Chaney and Walter James, which in all respects except one remains on a superficial level.

The only frank exchanges that occur in the novel concern the morality of suicide and assisted suicide in situations such as the one Braiden finds himself in—twenty-two years of living in a hospital bed with no legs or arms, totally dependent on others. While the heart-wrenching storytelling of both protagonists reveals the staggering toll on war's survivors, Braiden's story convinces Walter that assisted suicide, in cases like Braiden's, is not only a valid choice but a moral imperative. Before Walter is discharged from the hospital, he fulfills Braiden's wish and helps him die. Braiden's storytelling enables Walter to imagine himself in Braiden's situation, but the relationship that develops only passes for an intimate friendship. Before Walter finally decides to assist in Braiden's suicide, he promises himself, in order to ease his guilt, that he will come back and visit Braiden, "knowing all the time it was a damn lie" (148). Their emerging relationship is not rooted in a concern for the particularity of the individual other, which might create the basis of a friendship, but instead is based on a respect for and loyalty to a person of similar type, a comrade—in this case, a disabled Vietnam veteran living a death in life with no future. The men respond to each other's stories of woe as problem solvers, the role Deborah Tannen argues men have been socialized to play in conversation.[7] Although Walter solves Braiden's problem by agreeing to assist in his suicide, Braiden decides that he is unable to help Walter with his love life and family relationships and so tunes him out, thinking, "[S]urely didn't do me no good to hear all that" (214).

The way Larry Brown handles Walter's early resistance to Braiden's request for help suggests Brown's sensitivity to interracial dynamics but also his reluctance to directly confront topics of race that might deepen his characters' encounter. It is not clear from the text whether Braiden actually tells Walter how he thinks "all kinds of bad shit about white people" whenever a white person does not act as he expects (102), or whether Braiden simply thinks this because Larry Brown believes it is something white readers, especially, need to know. What is clear is that Walter behaves as if he is aware of this dynamic. For when Walter initially refuses to help Braiden commit suicide, Walter tells him stories that he hopes will show Braiden he is not refusing because of his race. Walter relates memories of his father's relationship with a black man, of his family defending a black family when both families were picking cotton for a corrupt white landowner, and of his own comradeship with a black soldier in Vietnam. But Walter does not directly respond to any of Braiden's comments about what it means to be black in America or how growing up poor in Mississippi may have been different for a black boy despite the class similarities. Because Brown marks Walter with a disfigurement that causes people to avoid him and thereby render him invisible, Brown creates a potential opportunity to allow a white character to better understand the discrimination black people experience, but Brown does not make use of this situation either directly or indirectly.

Although Brown successfully gives voice to individuals of both races, a narrative choice not always made in writing about race relations, he shies away from a real dialogue between men about racial issues. The contrast between their heated disagreements about the sensitive subject of assisted suicide and their anecdotes about the equally touchy subject of race relations is striking. Throughout the novel, there are times when each man has questions he does not ask the other, costly hesitations that invariably result in misunderstandings. For example, Braiden becomes emotional when talking about the waste of human lives caused by the war, and when Walter does not respond, Braiden assumes that his silence means he is "thinking about his woman." In actuality Walter is reflecting on war's horror but also on the injustice in the conscription for the Vietnam War that made its soldiers "young and black and poor" (187). While Walter's thoughts register important points for readers to ponder, such reluctance to speak about them limits not only the nature of the understanding between the two men but their self-understanding as well. Walter and Braiden remain comrades; they do not become real friends.

In contrast, Madison Smartt Bell's black and white protagonists, Rodney Redmon and Thomas Laidlaw, move beyond comradeship to a friendship of genuine intimacy. They knew each other as boys because Redmon's father was a laborer on the Laidlaw farm—a relationship commonly found in the older plots. But unlike an older generation of white writers, Bell portrays their relationship as distant because of this personal history. Redmon's father, Wat, took care of Laidlaw when he was a boy, and Redmon has always suspected that Laidlaw stole his father's love. While the two never had much of a relationship as boys, the Vietnam War makes them comrades: "we were both just so glad to see somebody from home. . . . So that's when we really got tight." Although Laidlaw and Redmon have depended on each other for their very lives in Vietnam, when the two men return to the Tennessee hills they both call home, they do nothing to seek each other out. Finally their paths cross by chance. But the way Laidlaw contrasts his relationship with Redmon in Vietnam with the uneasy tensions between them back home ("seems like he's got some things eating on him")[8] corresponds with J. Glenn Gray's belief that the strong bonds formed in combat can fray when the war is over. Thus, Bell may be questioning the depth of the interracial relationships forged in the military—the one institution that the United States likes to think of as a model of improved race relations.

The five books into which Bell divides *Soldier's Joy* mirror the evolution of Laidlaw and Redmon's friendship. In the first two books, the narration is filtered through alternating limited third-person viewpoints. Thus readers get a sense in book 1 of Laidlaw's thoughts and feelings and then in book 2 of Redmon's, as each tries to make a place for himself in the post–Vietnam War South. Laidlaw's task is easier because he is white and because his father has owned property. Even though fire has destroyed the family farmhouse, his father left him land, a small tenant house, and outbuildings. In contrast, Redmon, whose family owned no property, was hired as a real estate agent and then was betrayed by his white colleagues in a land-development scheme. Redmon ends up taking the rap for all of them and serving time in jail, although not in the jail customarily reserved for white white-collar criminals.

In books 3 and 4, where Laidlaw and Redmon finally become reacquainted, readers experience their tentative friendship first on Laidlaw's territory, at the bar where Laidlaw plays music and at Laidlaw's house, and then on Redmon's territory, at his father's house and at a Black Muslim friend's vegetarian restaurant. However, their emerging friendship is threatened from the beginning by prejudice on both sides of the color line. On Laidlaw's territory Redmon runs afoul of white racism: first, a mild form when white bigots vacate the bar as soon as he enters to hear Laidlaw's band, and then a more dangerous form in his warehouse job when a racist co-worker operates machinery irresponsibly, endangering his life. On Redmon's territory Laidlaw runs up against the belief of Redmon's friend Raschid that all whites are "blue-eyed devils." Although Raschid attempts to undermine the emerging interracial friendship, the Klan goes further, plotting to burn Laidlaw out of his home when they discover that he is socializing with a black man.

The relationship between Laidlaw and Redmon is superficial at first. They catch up over a six-pack, exchanging news of housing, work, women, and the after-effects of the Vietnam War—the kind of exchange that Larry Brown's characters engage in throughout *Dirty Work*. Bell suggests that although they know the facts of each other's lives, they do not fully understand one another. On the one hand, Laidlaw, who has no family, naively wants to think of Redmon as family because of their boyhood history. He desperately desires intimacy with Redmon without the hard work and time required to produce it. On the other hand, Redmon is too quick to suspect Laidlaw of being sympathetic to the racist Giles boys simply because their father, Laidlaw's neighbor, has helped him plant his garden. Laidlaw's naïveté about white racism, such as why the Klan targeted him, particularly infuriates Redmon, who does not have the luxury of being unaware of racial issues. Their second encounter ends acrimoniously, with Redmon declaring that the cost of their relationship is too high. But Laidlaw persists, and it pays off for both men.

Their relationship does not become a friendship until book 4, when they begin to speak suppressed thoughts and share feelings not usually expressed across the color line. Laidlaw and Redmon have the frank conversations about race that Larry Brown's characters never have. Because Laidlaw makes Redmon welcome in his home—sharing drinks, a bed, and a table of food, and thus breaking all the old southern customs for black-white interaction—Redmon comes to believe Laidlaw's professed liberal ideology about race relations. Finally Redmon trusts Laidlaw enough to disclose information about his white partners' betrayal and his resulting incarceration, facts he never divulges to anyone else. Similarly, Laidlaw confesses that on one of his insomnia-induced midnight prowls around the farm, he has impulsively knifed a deer poacher. He trusts Redmon to understand such behavior because of their guerrilla-warfare experiences together in the Vietnam jungle, experiences Redmon is still reliving in his dreams. This disclosure of vulnerabilities strengthens and deepens their relationship because it fosters understanding and trust.[9] Laidlaw begins to understand Redmon's racial sensitivity, and Redmon discerns Laidlaw's tendency to overreact in stressful situations. Bell mirrors their evolving intimacy with his mode of narration, mixing narrative perspectives within books 3 and 4 so that discrete chapters are filtered from alternating viewpoints. As their lives open up to each other and include each other, so the separate books of Bell's novel begin to include both perspectives.

The narration of the fifth and last book is at first limited to Laidlaw's perspective but becomes omniscient, which suggests the lowering of the psychic boundaries that enclose each individual male self. Western social and cultural patterns, which have made comradeship, not intimacy, the predominant model for male friendships, have also made some men reluctant to reveal their vulnerabilities. Susan Pollak and Carol Gilligan contend that the Western male social conventions of hiding and denying one's feelings have made it difficult for some men not only to share their feelings with others but even to be aware of them.[10] In book 5 Laidlaw and Redmon finally confront the particular history of their own relationship and articulate feelings they have been reluctant to voice. In one very painful interchange, Bell reminds readers of an important but neglected person in the black servant–white child relationship—the black servant's child. Readers of southern literature are familiar with the old black servant–white child story, but for a change they also hear in *Soldier's Joy* from the adult black child, who desperately needed some of the love and attention that his father showered on the white boy he was paid to care for. Redmon thinks his father loved Laidlaw not just because he was smart but mainly because he was white. As a result, Redmon has not told Laidlaw of his father's death or invited him to his funeral. Laidlaw feels hurt, because Wat was more of a father and mother to him than his own parents. He almost uses the word *father* to explain to Redmon how close he felt to Wat, but Redmon angrily cuts him off: *"Don't you say it. . . . Don't you never. He was my father. Mine"* (377). Although this scene reveals the truth of their present and their past feelings for each other, Bell emphasizes that they must work together to get at the more complex truth of Wat's feelings for each of them.

In *The Dialogic Imagination* Mikhail Bakhtin argues that we must know the other's language because understanding occurs "on the *boundary* between one's own and someone else's consciousness."[11] The activity Bakhtin calls "living hermeneutics" describes the high level of exchange that Laidlaw and Redmon work toward in the course of the novel. Unlike Brown's Braiden and Walter, they have real conversations and arguments about race in which they are not afraid to ask what the other means and to probe the truth of the stated meaning. Bakhtin points out how often in our speech we talk about what other people say, and he emphasizes "the psychological importance in our lives of what others say about us, and the importance, for us, of understanding and interpreting these words of others."[12] Laidlaw insists that Redmon's belief that Wat preferred him because of his race is "not the truth," and Redmon qualifies his statement by saying, "not the whole truth, anyway" (378). Bell uses several long dialogues between the two men in book 5 to work through the history of their tangled relationship, not only to better understand what each other is saying and to correct misunderstandings, but to better understand themselves.

Besides Wat Redmon, the other issue that has made a friendship back in the States more difficult than their comradeship in Vietnam is the economic difference in their families' relationship to the same land. Because Laidlaw's father owned the small farm in the Tennessee hills, Laidlaw can fall back on subsistence farming if his music does not earn him a living. Redmon, however, feels "stuck" "in a corner" in his dead-end warehouse job (390). Redmon reminds Laidlaw that his father, Wat, lived and worked on this land before Laidlaw's father bought it: "You all didn't do anything but buy it. And then you put him off it in the end" (378)—a perspective on land ownership that resembles the one Ernest Gaines advances in *A Gathering of Old Men*. For the first time, Laidlaw understands the power and privilege of his whiteness. Laidlaw immediately agrees with Redmon's point and generously, if impulsively, offers him half of the property, saying, "I'd do it for justice" (379).

The nature of co-owning this property, however, becomes a bone of contention that the two men chew on intermittently for the rest of the novel. Laidlaw desires a joint ownership that would follow the agrarian philosophy of his father, and of Madison Smartt Bell for that matter, who grew up with the Nashville Agrarians as guests in his parents' home.[13] Redmon pronounces such a deal, in which Laidlaw calls the shots, just as paternalistic as the one his father was engaged in with Laidlaw's father. But Bell is clearly on the side of Laidlaw as to the appropriate use of the land.[14] The half-built tract homes of the failed development scheme that landed Redmon in jail are depicted as a blight on the landscape. Bell even has Redmon, who admits he was "all for it at the time" (306), wish the land "back the way it was before" (154). Book 4 of the novel ends with an unexpected chapter from Wat's perspective, which Bell uses to ennoble Wat's close kinship with the land. This dreamlike sequence is printed in italics and written in the beautiful lyrical style that Bell takes up throughout the novel whenever he is describing the southern landscape, but especially when he is describing the reciprocal relationship between a man and the land, when the man is in tune with the earth's rhythms. In an interview with Mary Louise Weaks, Bell indirectly revealed his own approach to writing in a southern tradition when he distinguished contemporary writers of "small-town life," like Jill McCorkle, Mary Hood, and Lee Smith, from the earlier agrarian tradition of writers, like Andrew Lytle and Allen Tate, who wrote about "a culture of small farms" and who were concerned "about the destruction of the natural rhythms of life in connection to the land."[15] In *Soldier's Joy* some of Bell's most sympathetic characters have retained a traditional connection to the land: Laidlaw, Wat, Mr. Giles. Bell's least sympathetic characters, Vietnam veteran Earl Giles and real estate developer Goodbuddy, do not live in harmony with nature or with those around them.

In *Soldier's Joy* Bell harks back to his own southern agrarian roots, both emotionally and intellectually, but he goes beyond his agrarian predecessors' preoccupation with the machine invading the southern garden by acknowledging the evil of prejudice and discrimination that made that garden grow. Even as Bell would like to get back to agrarian relationships to the land, he knows they can never be the same as they were in his parents' day. Bell, like Laidlaw, "wanted to make up something new" (310) in *Soldier's Joy,* and indeed he almost succeeds. When Redmon and Laidlaw spend their first companionable night together in Laidlaw's mountain cabin, which is the tenant house Redmon grew up in, readers have great expectations that the two men will succeed in creating "something new." As the sunlight streams down from "a deep untrammeled blue sky" the next morning, Bell writes that Redmon looks "well at home there in the daylight" (304). The day that they spend together in harmony, in tune with nature and each other, is Edenic.

But the ending Bell chooses shatters the expectations of a new day dawning. *Soldier's Joy* is long and slow-moving, an attempt to represent the process of becoming aware of one's feelings and the difficulties involved in sharing them with a male friend of a different race, especially in the South. Interestingly, a number of reviewers, obviously used to the urban eccentricity and fast-paced plots of Bell's New York novels, faulted *Soldier's Joy* for its "somnolent pace"[16] and found his rural southern setting and introspective narrative technique boring; as Winston Groom put it, "The story's at its best when the action becomes fast paced, not when the writer lapses into his 'descriptive' mode: giving us the weather report or gaggles of complicated interior thoughts."[17] Such readers seem to resist Bell's disruption of masculine social conventions, a disruption that depends on "gaggles of complicated interior thoughts." Other reviewers, such as David Bradley and David Nicholson, find fresh and appealing just the characteristics that Groom and others criticize.[18] And since reviewers like Groom find the concluding violent confrontation between the Klan and Redmon and Laidlaw the most engaging part of the novel, it is perhaps not surprising that Bradley and Nicholson judge the ending contrived and clichéd or, as Bradley says, "degenerating into a gun-and-chase sequence à la 'Miami Vice.'"[19]

I think the ending works symbolically as a continuation of both the Vietnam War and the Civil War and as a statement that there are still unresolved issues of both. Bell, offended by the tactics of contemporary southern Klansmen who he felt were trying to speak for him as a white southerner, told an *Atlanta Journal-Constitution* reporter that the novel was a chance to speak for himself and advocate integration.[20] He suggests through his representation of Vietnam vets that neither the Civil War nor the Vietnam War have made the South safe for interracial friendships, despite the strong desires of some individuals of both races. The Klan targets Laidlaw as soon as he initiates a friendship with Redmon, and it tracks the activities of Brother Jacob, who, in the style of an evangelical preacher, advocates interracial friendships in open meetings throughout the South. From the subject matter of Bell's other novels, it is clear that he is fascinated by the causes of violence. He creates a plot in *Soldier's Joy* that allows him to speculate that the license to kill, which the Vietnam War granted, has become something almost instinctual in Vietnam veterans, and not just those who are racially prejudiced. Bell prepares readers for his explosive ending by the presence of violence not far below the surface throughout *Soldier's Joy*. Long before the novel's concluding bloody confrontation over improved race relations, racist Earl Giles draws his gun instinctively when his brother and some friends play a practical joke on him; Rodney Redmon tortures Goodbuddy in Laidlaw's barn; and Laidlaw, in the style of a guerrilla fighter, stalks and knifes the poacher. All three are Vietnam veterans. The narrator's explanation of the cause of the poaching incident is disturbing: "That taste in [Laidlaw's] mouth was certainly of blood, and vaguely he heard a familiar voice telling him that once acquired it was extremely hard to cure" (106). Bell uses Laidlaw's lover's first experience with a gun to solidify this position. Although Adrienne initially refuses to participate in the race war that ends the novel, she grows afraid that she may have to defend Laidlaw's life, so she has a change of heart and decides to learn how to shoot. When her first bullet hits the sign she is using for target practice, Bell writes that "she felt her face creasing into a weird smile" (457), a sign that she too has been captivated by the power of a gun. Until this point Adrienne's perspective has called the reader back from the precipice of coming to view Laidlaw's and Redmon's violent actions as somehow normal. In the middle of the novel, Bell briefly filters the action through Adrienne's consciousness, an unexpected technique that causes readers to distance themselves from Redmon's and Laidlaw's tendencies to escape through alcohol and violence and in so doing to endanger their own lives.

In contrast to the 1989 response to the novel's ending, skeptical readers just a few years later could view the violence as prophetic, given the proliferation of antigovernment militia groups during the Clinton presidency. Rather than "a contrived, unconvincing climactic explosion of melodrama,"[21] the ending could be seen as the inevitable lethal outcome of situations in the United States that combine rage and hatred with readily available guns. Although the western part of the United States takes a slight lead over the South in numbers of paramilitary groups, the South still leads the country in hate groups.[22] In *Warrior Dreams: Paramilitary Culture in Post-Vietnam America*, James William Gibson describes the personalities of men engaged in such activities as "deeply affected" by the Vietnam War (whether they fought in the war or not); he says the men were worried that "the white man's world was gone" and convinced that the "dark forces of chaos" that had been unleashed "made it not only permissible but morally imperative for them to take their personal battles far beyond the law." Gibson argues that "paramilitary mythology offered men the fantastic possibility of escaping their present lives, being reborn as warriors, and then remaking the world."[23] Certainly the weapons necessary are easily obtained. In a recent study, the South still emerges as the region where people are "more likely to own guns" and "more likely to view their guns as instruments of protection."[24] As soon as Laidlaw hears that he has been targeted by the Klan, he thinks first of the guns hidden beneath his house, not of the local sheriff. Laidlaw and Redmon succeed in thwarting the attempt on Brother Jacob's life and in saving each other's lives; however, men are killed on both sides, and the novel concludes with the possibility that Laidlaw may be dying in Redmon's arms.

But the ending hints at another, happier outcome and reminds readers of an ending that Bell seems to have abandoned, an ending that could perhaps have represented "something new" (310). Hit with submachine gun fire in the chest during the shoot-out with the Klan, Laidlaw is certain he is going to die, but Redmon refuses to give in to his pessimism, willing him to live with a reminder of the offer Laidlaw has made to split the land: "Hey, we still got a house to build. Are you taking back all you said?" (465). In a way this remark comes as a bit of a surprise to readers, because the two men have never resolved their differences about joint land ownership; indeed, the last time the subject comes up before this, it does not seem as if Redmon is interested in Laidlaw's gift unless Laidlaw will give him full rights to half of the property. Thus Bell tantalizes the reader with the possibility of a surprise happy ending, southern agrarian style—but racially integrated as befits the last years of the twentieth century. In many ways Bell's narrative (with its lyrical descriptions of the land, its dialogic working through of racial misunderstandings, its two filter characters providing both black and white perspectives, and its psychological realism in the first four books) does not seem to add up to the shoot-out with the Klan over Brother Jacob's promotion of a fully integrated South. Opting for violence, Bell chooses the more familiar masculine ending, only selecting the latest in firepower—submachine guns, instead of the aging shotguns that Ernest Gaines's old men arm themselves with. The ending can certainly be seen as a chilling reminder that not all white southerners are reconstructed. But it can also be seen as a capitulation to today's reading public, which cannot abide a "somnolent pace" and "gaggles of complicated interior thoughts." In "Literature and Pleasure: Bridging the Gap," Bell makes the case that the conventions of genre fiction should be "recovered for serious literature," arguing that "a little dabbling in genre does not necessarily corrupt the serious literary writer" and concluding that "as we take back some of that territory abandoned to genre fiction, we may get back some of the audience too."[25]

Once Vietnam veteran Ratman enters the novel to aid Laidlaw and Redmon with his military-style bunker and his arsenal of vintage Vietnam weapons, Bell's style changes from psychological realism to pulp fiction, and his subject changes from the struggle to forge adult male friendships across racial lines to the comradeship of warriors. Perhaps Bell saw interracial agrarianism as an "escapist fantasy" equal to the "New Age menu of magical solutions" that he disparages in his 1991 article,[26] and yet its presence in the novel cannot be dismissed so easily. For in the same article, Bell argues that for the novelist, "what the unconscious labors to discover is never a fact, but a vision." He goes on to say, "[W]hat maybe all my characters have always been after in all my books, is a visionary solution to the fatal problem which our collective consciousness is virtually unable to acknowledge."[27] Bell may have intended the violence in *Soldier's Joy* to be seductive to late-twentieth-century readers, particularly young male readers, brought up on *Lethal Weapon* and *Die Hard* movies. With just enough violence, perhaps Bell hoped "to soften the mind and render it receptive to all the more sophisticated pleasures that the finest literature can produce," as he says in "Literature and Pleasure."[28] As a reader, though, I feel, like David Bradley, that this "little dabbling in genre" in *Soldier's Joy* corrupts the integrity of the novel. With his choice of a violent ending, Bell abandons his agrarian "visionary solution" to the South's chronic racial problem—a problem that he, unlike Larry Brown, presents in its complexity. Bell's violent ending harks back to literary conventions that a previous generation of writers employed to resolve narratives about race. However, if readers believe Laidlaw will survive, Bell can have it both ways, both suggesting the possibility of interracial friendship and highlighting the obstacles.

With both *Dirty Work* and *Soldier's Joy* readers dwell momentarily in the tantalizing possibility of friendships between black and white men. Although the relationships they represent are different in their degrees of intimacy, they are similar in that they work only in cloistered settings: a veteran's hospital and a mountain cabin. Larry Brown does not test the relationship he creates in the larger context of southern society. Madison Smartt Bell does, but he cannot quite imagine how such a friendship will sustain itself in a society where hate still lurks in the shadows.

Like Bell, Ernest Gaines explores the same conjuncture of race, masculinity, and violence, but he focuses more intently on the burdensome southern history of white power and black humiliation. In *A Rage for Order: Black/White Relations in the American South since Emancipation,* historian Joel Williamson argues that for southern white men the traditional Victorian masculine role of provider and protector was directly linked with violence because of plantation society's "necessity of controlling a potentially explosive black population." As early as the seventeenth century, a patrol system, made up of masters and overseers, enforced the laws of slavery. By the nineteenth century, the duty of patrolling was extended to all white men, who had authority over all blacks (even free blacks) and over whites who conspired with blacks. Thus, a system for controlling slaves became a practice "of all whites controlling all blacks . . . a matter of race."[29] Whites created a complementary stereotype of black people as "simple, docile, and manageable"; if properly handled, they were like children, but if improperly cared for, they became animals. Williamson argues that this "Sambo" figure was a figment of white wishful thinking, which functioned "to build white egos" while masking whites' fears of black rebellion. Many black people played the Sambo role—"downcast eyes, shuffling feet, soft uncertain words, and a totally pliant manner"—in order to survive slavery and its aftermath.[30] The effects of this system lingered into the 1960s. In Gaines's *A Gathering of Old Men* (1983), which is set in rural Louisiana in the 1970s, the white characters are surprised when the black men do not act "like frightened little bedbugs."[31]

In both *A Gathering of Old Men* (1983) and *A Lesson before Dying* (1993), Gaines presents new models of manhood, for both black and white men. For his black characters, earning respect becomes a higher priority than friendship, because Gaines, much like Sherley Anne Williams in *Dessa Rose,* sees equality as the foundation for interracial friendship. The first step in gaining respect, though, is finding self-respect—a Catch-22 for black men in a racist society. Early in his career and in such works as *A Gathering of Old Men,* Gaines employed traditional Western definitions of manhood as his goal for black men, but the vision he sets forth in *A Lesson before Dying* resembles that of contemporary gender theorists, who believe that traditional notions of masculinity are "life-threatening," to use bell hooks's term. They argue that men in a modern world must accept vulnerability, express a range of emotions, ask for help and support, learn nonviolent means of resolving conflicts, and accept behaviors that have traditionally been labeled feminine (such as being nurturing, communicative, and cooperative) as necessary for full human development.[32]

Gaines's *A Gathering of Old Men* seems to have two definitions of manhood, one for white men and one for black men—a difference based on the social construction of race and masculinity and the history of race relations in the South. Gaines structures his novel with parallel maturation scenes that involve white and black men coming to terms with southern society's race and gender ideology. Gil Boutan, a young white man, exhibits maturity when he rejects his society's equation of masculinity with violence, while the old black men of the novel's title achieve manhood when they enact this definition. Gil attempts to break the cycle of racial violence that his father is notorious for by refusing to join his family in avenging his brother's death, allegedly at the hands of a black man. The old black men break a cycle of paralyzing fear by responding, first verbally but then violently, to the attempt of white men to wield power over them. These two definitions of what it means to be a man lead to an ideologically contradictory, though emotionally satisfying, double ending. As a result, *A Gathering of Old Men,* while reconstructing race relations and reversing historically southern social constructions of black and white manhood, does not go as far in questioning traditional definitions of masculinity and writing new masculine endings as does *A Lesson before Dying.* The model of manhood that Gaines confers on his young black protagonist Grant in *A Lesson before Dying* converges with Gil's. With these two portraits, Gaines suggests that in order to reconstruct the South, both black and white men must reject the traditional Western model of manhood that links masculinity and violence. Both novels enact Gaines's belief that the South needs new narratives of manhood before race relations can improve.

In *A Gathering of Old Men* Gaines focuses on a group of old black men in their seventies and eighties, who have been "boys" all their lives, not only in the eyes of the white men they have worked for but also in their own eyes. Born after Reconstruction failed in the South, they have grown up being beaten down by racial prejudice and boxed in by Jim Crow laws that have kept them in an inferior position socially and economically. The civil rights movement and its resulting laws promoting equality have had little effect on their lives, which continue to be shaped by de facto segregation and economic dependency on whites. These old black men, many of whom live gratis in the old slave quarters, once worked as sharecroppers or skilled artisans on the white-owned plantations. They find the prospects for their children's lives even less promising than their own, because their children are now working as laborers for Cajun farmers who are renting the land that the black men used to sharecrop. Social customs of deference to whites—looking down, going to the back door—remain unchanged. These conditions, which Gaines has termed "de facto slavery,"[33] give *A Gathering of Old Men* the feel of a historical novel rather than one set in the present.

The subordinate position of the old black men has lowered their self-esteem and caused doubts about their manhood, which they, like the white men they work for, define in traditional terms as providing for and protecting their families. Hazel Carby argues in *Reconstructing Womanhood* that manhood as traditionally defined by Western society could not be achieved or maintained by black men, "because of the inability of the slave to protect the black woman."[34] In this regard, Gaines's old black men have lived lives not very different from those of slaves. Each tells a story of a sister or brother, son or daughter, who was at the very least treated unfairly by whites, at the worst raped or killed by whites. Each knows that he did nothing to stop white injustice, both because he felt powerless to do so and because he feared for his life if he stood up for equal and just treatment. The old men's feelings of fear and powerlessness have created problems for their relationships with black women, for the men express their frustrations with white society and with themselves by verbally and physically abusing their wives.[35]

The question Gaines tackles involves determining what part the social construction of race, class, and masculinity plays in male violence on both sides of the color line. When Gandhi worked with the nonviolent struggle in South

Africa, he argued that passive violence (such as that practiced by racist whites in the American South) must be eliminated in order to rid society of physical violence: "Passive violence in the form of discrimination, oppression, exploitation, hate, anger and all the subtle ways in which it manifests itself gives rise to physical violence in society."[36] In *A Gathering of Old Men*, the mostly passive violence of white landowners and the mostly physical violence of the white working class eventually provokes retaliation by blacks, a classic case of Friedrich Nietzsche's *ressentiment*. Near the end of the novel, when the black laborer Charlie Biggs confesses to killing his Cajun employer Beau Boutan, he must go back forty-five years to explain his actions, to the time when he first ran from a white man who abused him. Beau's repeated verbal and physical abuse finally push Charlie over the edge: "It took fifty years. Half a hundred— and I said I been 'bused enough. He used to 'buse me. No matter if I did twice the work any other man could do, he 'bused me anyhow. . . . And long as I was Big Charlie, nigger boy, I took it. . . . But they comes a day! They comes a day when a man must be a man" (189). A similar day finally comes for the old men as well, a day when they will take no more abuse, when they are ready to take a stand. To explain their newfound courage to the white sheriff, they too return to the past, and they all tell stories of white injustice.

Previously only one man among them, Mathu, has stood up to the white men who demean him, and as a result Mathu is the only black man Sheriff Mapes has deemed a real man, worthy of going hunting and fishing with. As a result, before Charlie Biggs returns and confesses to the murder, everyone assumes that Mathu has killed Beau Boutan. Sheriff Mapes's easy equation of masculinity and the capacity for violence suggests the casual, often unconscious, way language is used to reinforce gender ideology: "But he killed him, all right. The only one with nuts enough to do it" (72). According to Mathu, a man is not afraid to do "what he thinks is right. . . . That's what part him from a boy" (85). The other old men have never done what they thought was right. They have never stood up to whites to protect themselves and their families and friends from rape and murder and discrimination—until the day in which this novel takes place. Responding to white plantation owner Candy Marshall's request to protect the old black man who has been influential in raising her, the old men rally around Mathu with their twelve-gauge shotguns. It is not surprising that the one black man Candy does not have power over, Clatoo, emerges as the leader of the old men, insisting on their right to congregate alone and to make decisions without Candy. Because Clatoo owns his own land and a gardening business, he does not depend on Candy for his home or livelihood, a fact she threatens the other men with: "'Y'all can go on and listen to Clatoo if y'all want,' she said. 'But remember this—Clatoo got a little piece of land to go back to. Y'all don't have nothing but this. You listen to him now, and you won't even have this'" (174). Sheriff Mapes's assessment of Candy's attempt to manipulate the old men—"you want to keep them slaves the rest of their lives" (175)—suggests that Candy's desire to help black people coexists with a desire to control them and to take responsibility for them that echoes the paternalistic role of her own male ancestors.

Standing up first to white injustice and then to Candy's paternalism is not enough to make the old black men feel like men; rather, it takes an act of physical force to certify their manhood and thus win respect. They have no doubt that Beau's father, Fix Boutan, who has allegedly fixed the fate of several black men and women in the past, will seek revenge for his son's death and give them the opportunity to stop him with force. Although some of them are afraid, they know that they have only their fear to lose and very much to gain. Facing death, the old men are determined to act like "men" before they die and protect Mathu, thereby winning self-respect and respect from the only man in their community thought to be "a real man" (84).

The novel turns on an interesting paradox in defining manhood as it relates to race. In order for Fix's youngest son Gil to be a man, he must refuse to kill the black man who has murdered his brother Beau; in order for each old black man to be a man, he must be ready to kill a white man. The old men only see themselves as men when they follow what Bob Connell has identified as the "hegemonic masculinity" in Western society, a model associated with aggressiveness and the capacity for violence.[37] The white man becomes a man when he rejects this model. The behavior that Gaines deems manly for each racial group is based on the history of race relations in the rural South. The old black men long, understandably, to get even for all the injustice their families have experienced at the hands of white people. Gil Boutan wants to put a stop to the misunderstanding, hatred, and violence that have characterized southern race relations and have come to epitomize his family's reputation in the community.

As a football player at Louisiana State University, Gil has grown to respect, like, and depend on Cal, a black player on his team. Together they are Salt and Pepper, destined to become All-Americans and win the conference title for their university. Together they have become a symbol of improved race relations in a new South. The "publicity people" (111) at the university have invented the nickname, encouraged the symbolism, and profited from the alliance: "It would be the first time this had ever happened, black and white in the same backfield—and in the Deep South, besides. LSU was fully aware of this, the black and white communities in Baton Rouge were aware of this, and so was the rest of the country. Wherever you went, people spoke of Salt and Pepper of LSU" (112). But for Gil and Cal the relationship goes beyond symbolism, and Gaines uses it to suggest that when diverse people live and work together for common goals, race relations improve. At the same time, though, Gaines shows the persistence of unconscious prejudice. Some readers have suggested that Gil's interest in Cal is purely self-serving and cite as evidence his coldness to Cal after hearing of his brother's murder by a black man. Psychologist Patricia Devine's research suggests that white people who appear unprejudiced may be consciously making an attempt to repress stereotypes that can potentially be activated by stereotypical situations,[38] such as the cross-racial murder. The scenes when Gil returns home after the murder reveal this complexity. There he is both shocked by the united stand of the old black men and dismayed by the prospect of more violence: "Won't it ever stop? I do all I can to stop it. Every day of my life, I do all I can to stop it. Won't it ever stop?" (122). In the discussion that follows between Gil and his family, Gaines makes it clear that Gil is no longer the bigoted young man his father raised him to be.

Gil's decision not to join his father in vengeful and violent behavior is seen by his father and the older men in his family as unmanly, and they impugn his manhood by calling Gil's restraint feminine: "He [Gil] says sit, weep with the women" (145). Gaines emphasizes the difficulty Gil has in opposing conventional masculine behavior by having Gil repeatedly ask the old white men gathered, "Haven't I been a good boy?" "Aren't I a good boy?" (147). The power of gender ideology makes Gil blur gender identity with obedience and family loyalty. While in some respects Gaines portrays this masculine role conflict between Gil and his father as generational and in doing so projects a more hopeful future, he also creates several young white "rednecks" who subscribe to the old conventions. The leader of the group, Luke Will, publicly tries to shame Gil and his brother Jean into avenging Beau's death by attacking their manhood and appealing to white racial solidarity. But Luke's attempt fails, because Gil and Jean have become members of a larger, racially integrated community and have left behind the violent practices of what southern historian Bertram Wyatt-Brown identifies as "primal honor."[39] That Gil is college educated is certainly significant. Gil's father thinks that an education at LSU should reinforce the old southern racial code, but Gaines suggests otherwise. Gil's college education has opened his mind to the racial oppression in the rural community in which he grew up. In Wyatt-Brown's terms, because Gil puts individual conscience before reputation, personal guilt before public shame,[40] he is able to take an unpopular stand in his family, which seeks to defend its honor, and in his parish, which seeks to keep black people in their customary place.

For Gaines, Gil becomes a man when he refuses to use or sanction violence, a reversal of the primal code of honor practiced by Gil's Cajun family and their working-class white friends. Because of Gil's compassion for the old black men, his father flippantly calls him "a regular Christ" and sarcastically quips, "Feels sorry for the entire world" (145). Gaines expects readers to take this comparison more seriously, as a new vision of southern white working-class manhood. This new vision includes the ability to express emotion other than anger (Gil cries in this scene), to articulate feelings, to empathize with black people, and to resolve conflict in nonaggressive ways.[41] Gil's and Jean's experiences indicate that solidarity is predicated not on race, or on class for that matter, but on community, whether on the football field at LSU or in the town of Bayonne, where Jean is a butcher.

With the scene in the bar between the professor of African American literature from the University of Southwestern Louisiana and Jack Marshall, who owns the plantation where Beau has been shot, Gaines advocates a reconstruction of masculine identity for upper-class southern white men as well. Such reconstructed men would try to ameliorate continuing racial tensions in their community, whether personally involved in them or not. While Jack Marshall escapes the conflict by leaving the plantation and drinking himself into oblivion at Tee Jack's bar, the professor suggests that in ignoring the situation, Marshall passively contributes to the violence. The professor asserts, "In the end, it's people like us, you and I, who pay for this," and "The debt is never finished as long as we stand for this" (165).

Whatever his accomplishments are in the classroom, this articulate, open-minded professor is unable to convince Luke and his cohorts to change their behavior by reasoning with them for a few minutes in a bar. The professor's call for restraint is met with Luke's physical intimidation, demanding that he leave the bar. When Tee Jack, the bar owner, protests that the professor is a white man, Luke responds, "If he's a white man, let him act like one" (165). The professor is beneath Luke's contempt because Luke defines his own manhood in terms of his ability to make life hard for "niggers" (159). His aggressive behav-

ior allows him to assert his power over both the black people whom he antag-
onizes and the educated white men of a higher social class (like the professor)
who have created new laws to end segregation and thus life in the South as
Luke knows it. As a result, Luke defines manliness only as fighting, not as refusing to fight. It is telling that during the shoot-out Luke's buddy Sharp sees
the old black men as "brave" (204) when they physically defend themselves,
behavior the white men do not expect from black men.

To help rationalize his decision to take the law into his own hands, Luke Will
asserts that the "next thing you know," black men will be "raping the women"
(149). The deputy sheriff's comment, "If they can't get you one way, they'll
bring in the women every time" (149), is Gaines's reminder that white men
have played the sex card in the past, both after the Civil War when they lost
political power to northern reconstructionists and after Reconstruction when
they lost economic power to an agricultural depression and to black male competition for jobs. Joel Williamson argues that because southern white men could
not play the role of "protector-as-breadwinner" for their women as well as they
expected during this time, they focused on another part of the traditional masculine role—"protector-as-defender of the purity of their women," a role that
Thomas Dixon Jr. popularized in his novels and plays and which D. W. Griffith
purveyed even more widely in the film *The Birth of a Nation* (1915).[42]

With *A Gathering of Old Men*, Gaines rewrites Dixon's narratives of courageous white masculinity. Although working-class Luke Will certainly thinks
of himself as a man because of his willingness to put blacks in "their place,"
Gaines represents Will and his cohorts as boys and portrays their bravery as
braggadocio. Big-talking Leroy, who can't wait to wield his gun against the old
black men, turns into a "sniveling" (202) little boy when he is grazed by a bullet in the shoot-out. His ineffectual pleas for mercy from the sheriff, "I'm a
white boy, Mapes," and "I ain't nothing but a child, Mapes" (203), are among
the funniest lines in the novel. The irony, of course, is heavy and twofold. First,
being white no longer automatically gives one protection in the eyes of the
law. Second, from the protected distance of Tee Jack's bar, this "child" was
"ready to kick me some ass" (166), but he crumples when he finds himself in
the cross fire of live ammunition. Charlie Biggs proves his maturity by returning and admitting to killing Beau, but Leroy will not admit that his cohorts
have shot Sheriff Mapes; he falsely accuses the old black men.

James Riener argues that manhood for the old black men in *A Gathering of*

Old Men is "to be found, not in wielding power over others, but in a man's response to the attempts to wield power over him." This is certainly true—the old men withstand Sheriff Mapes's slaps and Luke Will's bullets. Furthermore, they are willing, as Riener suggests, "to accept the consequences for the murder and for their defiance of the sheriff."[43] The willingness to accept responsibility for one's actions is especially evident in the case of Charlie, who shoots Beau in self-defense but initially allows his *parrain* Mathu to take the rap for the murder because he is afraid that, given past workings of the white-dominated legal system, he will never get a fair trial, a fear that reverberates in Gaines's fiction.[44] The scene in which Charlie returns and confesses in front of his relatives, the sheriff, and the old black men parallels the scene in which Gil changes the pattern of behavior expected of him and emerges as a man, willing to accept responsibility for his actions. The main differences, of course, are that Gil is white and thirty years younger than Charlie. Charlie declares before all gathered that at fifty years old, he is finally a man, "I want the world to know it. I ain't Big Charlie, nigger boy, no more, I'm a man. . . . A nigger boy run and run and run. But a man come back. I'm a man" (187). Referred to by whites as "Beau's nigger" and Beau's "boy" because he works for Beau, he demands to be called Mr. Biggs by the white men assembled, Sheriff Mapes and the reporter Lou Dimes. With Charlie's demand, Gaines once again underlines the power of language to construct identity. Sheriff Mapes's use of the appellation *Mr.,* which connotes respect and which has been reserved for adult white men, signifies Charlie's manhood.

While Riener is correct to point out that the old black men's defiance of the white establishment does not have to culminate in a fight, because they have proved their manhood to themselves,[45] most of them don't think so. Ironically, the manly behavior that the old black men are eager to exhibit comes in part from their capacity for violence and from a desire for revenge, which has the potential to threaten the emerging new relationship between the races that is symbolized in the cooperation of Gil and Cal on the football field. Indeed, Gaines originally titled the novel "The Revenge of Old Men" but says he changed it "because these guys don't get any revenge; they're just gathering."[46] After Charlie's confession, both Clatoo and Mathu suggest that the old men go home, pointing out that they have proved their manhood, just by standing up to Sheriff Mapes. They have gained self-respect and the respect of everyone there, black and white. But Rooster's reaction is typical of the majority: "No, that wasn't enough. Not after what I had put up with all these years. I wanted me a fight, even if I had to get killed" (181). At this point the old black men are ready to take their memories of injustice out on any white man, in a manner similar to how white men have treated them in the past. Earlier in the afternoon, Gable says he is ready to kill Fix because "he was just like them who throwed my boy in that 'lectric chair and pulled that switch. No, he wan't born yet, but the same blood run in all their vein" (102). The old men are very disappointed when Fix does not show up to avenge Beau's death, because they have projected onto him the responsibility for all past white injustice.

Blaming the old men for Fix's failure to arrive, Sheriff Mapes expresses the paradoxical nature of contemporary race relations: "Y'all the one—you cut your own throats. You told God you wanted Salt and Pepper to get together, and God did it for you. At the same time, you wanted God to keep Fix the way Fix was thirty years ago so one day you would get a chance to shoot him. Well, God couldn't do both. . . . Which do you want?" (171). But God can "do both," as Ernest Gaines illustrates. Although Fix does not show up, Luke Will does—giving the old men the chance not simply to stand up to attempts to wield power over them but to respond violently. To many readers, it seems only poetic justice, although it is hardly indicative of a new southern masculine order, that the old men get to fire their shotguns. Although they have proved their courage and Mathu's innocence before Luke's arrival, fighting seems necessary to prove their manhood, at least to them, if not to Gaines.

But it is Gaines, of course, who creates the fight and allows the men to do more than "gather." And Coot says he hasn't felt so good since World War I. Using slapstick humor, Gaines makes the fight more comic than tragic, even though two men are killed: Charlie, the black "boy" who becomes a man when he admits to shooting Beau, and Luke, the white man who remains a "boy" because he refuses to leave justice to the courts. When Luke Will wants to stop the fight and turn himself and his boys in, it is Charlie Biggs who encourages the old men to continue the fight, perhaps another reason Charlie must die in the end—because he encourages the black men to take justice into their own hands as the white men have done in the past. For Charlie, "standing up to Luke Will" (208) is equally as important as standing up for his rights. When Lou Dimes tells him that Luke Will wants to turn himself in and warns Charlie that if he continues to fight he will be charged with murder, not self-defense as with Beau, Charlie refuses to stop fighting, and he even enlists the old men to help him. One could argue that the old men lose some moral ground by following Charlie's lead rather than Mathu's and Clatoo's. While they do not provoke the racial conflict, they do not end it as soon as they could have. Perhaps Gaines allows the old men briefly to wield power over whites as revenge for having been at the mercy of whites in the past, perhaps as the only message racist white men, like Luke Will, who instigates the shoot-out, can understand.

Gaines's novel has two resolutions to the black-white conflict: first the shoot-out and then a trial banning guns for the next five years. This dual resolution allows readers to have it "both ways," because they get an emotional catharsis through the traditional masculine behavior in the shoot-out, plus a resolution through talk rather than aggression, in the form of the trial. This double ending seems to have been determined more by literary convention than by ideological considerations. Gaines thought the shoot-out necessary to fulfill readers' expectations. In an interview he said, "They brought guns, and I still believe in the old Chekhovian idea that if the gun is over the mantel at the beginning of the play, the gun must go off by the time the curtain comes down. And I thought that the only way the gun could go off in my book was Charlie and Luke Will out on the street shooting at each other."[47] Gaines's reply when asked to compare the novel's ending with that of the television movie is significant. The movie ends with Luke Will backing down once he sees that the old men have guns. When asked whether the ending of the television movie made a different point from that of the novel, Gaines replied, "I don't know if there's any difference at all. I think what I was trying to do in that entire book was show a group of old men standing."[48] It is interesting that when Gaines thinks of the novel's impact, he focuses on the old men gathering to support Mathu, finally taking a stand against white injustice and discrimination—not on the shoot-out that follows. Indeed, in the novel Gaines states that most of the old men are not very good shots, and he gives them comic roles in the fight as if to distance them from the deaths caused by this tragic encounter. While Gaines refers only to Charlie and Luke Will when he talks about the shoot-out, the old men are certainly emotionally as well as actively, if ineptly, involved in this event.

Unlike Gaines, I think the double ending does make a difference, because the two endings support contradictory themes about violence and masculinity. The first ending suggests that fighting is the only emotionally satisfying and manly way to resolve an argument; the second reaffirms what Gaines has already proved in the novel—that talking can produce results. Although Fix suggests that talking is the equivalent of doing "nothing" (144), Gaines proves otherwise in the gradual change that Sheriff Mapes undergoes as he listens to Charlie's and the old men's personal accounts of injustice and discrimination. Granted, Gaines does not suggest that talk always works. The conversation that the English professor has with Jack Marshall is disappointing, and his exchange with Luke Will is totally ineffective. Similarly, Gil struggles to make his father understand his new views about race relations. Begging his friend Sully to help him, Gil is still unable to move his father beyond football to civil rights, beyond Gil's chance at being an All-American to his heroic attempt to stop the cycle of violence. Gil's father views him as a coward rather than the brave young man Gaines presents him as. In contrast, the storytelling of the old black men is incredibly effective, particularly that of Tucker, Johnny Paul, and Charlie. They recreate scenes and situations so that the people listening, especially Sheriff Mapes, can see and feel the injustice they are talking about.

Gaines does have a point about readers' expectations and the convention of the gun. Many viewers of the television movie who had also read the book found the television ending disappointing; they preferred the shoot-out to the gathering.[49] Perhaps their disappointment is the natural reaction to viewing a movie ending that departs so radically from the novel. But perhaps these readers, like Gaines, expect guns to go off if they appear. Or perhaps they are used to violence as a tool to settle men's disputes and to conclude men's plots. In *Before Reading,* Peter Rabinowitz explains that "in a given literary context, when certain elements appear, rules of configuration activate certain expectations."[50] He goes on to explain, however, that the writer can make use of readers' expectations in a variety of ways: "not only to create a sense of resolution (that is, by completing the patterns that the rules lead readers to expect, either with or without detours) but also to create surprise (by reversing them, for instance, or by deflecting them, or by fulfilling them in some unanticipated way)." Gaines could have had Luke back down when faced with so many guns, which is what the television scriptwriter did, or he could have had Charlie heed Lou Dimes's advice and end the fight. Either ending would have been more in keeping with Gaines's stated focus on "a gathering of old men" rather than "the revenge of old men." Gaines speculated that television movie producers found his original resolution too sensitive for a large viewing audience, given the current racial climate: "maybe they just didn't want a black and white shoot-out, killing each other off."[51] To me, the ending of the novel sends an ambivalent message about violence. Gaines clearly is more interested in talk than in violence, in the power of storytelling rather than the power of guns. If he had banned the guns before the courtroom, thereby using the guns in a surprising way rather than the expected way, his novel would not have required two endings to get his point across.

While five years may be enough time in Gaines's fictional parish for blacks and whites to lay down their guns and to learn to solve disagreements without violence, it took Gaines a bit longer to write beyond the conventional endings about race and masculinity and to create a real friendship across the color line.[52] In *A Lesson before Dying* Gaines reconstructs black manhood in a very different way. Although set in 1948 in rural Louisiana, *A Lesson before Dying* speaks to several important contemporary issues—the racially unbalanced use of the death penalty, the responsibility of middle-class blacks to those less fortunate in the larger black community, questions of gender-role egalitarianism—in addition to the possibilities of cross-racial friendship and new definitions of manhood. In "A New Vision of Masculinity," Cooper Thompson delineates attitudes and behaviors that boys do not often learn but that he thinks boys should be taught: "being supportive and nurturant, accepting one's vulnerability and being able to ask for help, valuing women and 'women's work,' understanding and expressing emotions (except for anger), the ability to empathize with and empower other people, and learning to resolve conflict in non-aggressive, non-competitive ways."[53] These are the behaviors that Gil exhibits in *A Gathering of Old Men* and that Gaines's protagonist Grant Wiggins learns in *A Lesson before Dying*. But before Grant can grasp these new notions of masculinity, he must understand how the white power structure has defined and therefore confined black people and discover how to break the vicious circle. Grant, an elementary schoolteacher, has learned the first lesson in college. His aunt enlists him to teach it to Jefferson, who is on death row for a crime he did not commit, thereby enabling him to be something other than the "animal" white society has said he is. Although this lesson cannot commute Jefferson's death sentence, it frees him mentally and emotionally to construct another self within white society's prison in the days before he is electrocuted. Grant must learn the second lesson in order to escape the morass of his own bitterness.

To emphasize the white construction of black social reality, Gaines opens his novel with three versions of what happened the night when Jefferson, in the wrong place at the wrong time, entered a store with two black friends. First Gaines gives readers just the facts. The robbery attempt results in the white store owner and Jefferson's friends fatally shooting each other. Jefferson, who is a bit slow-witted, is unable to process what has happened before his eyes, so he takes a drink to calm his nerves and then steals from the open cash register, because he has no money and there are no witnesses. But to explain his actions, the prosecuting attorney and the defense attorney each tell their own version of the story. In doing so, both reveal their common assumptions of biological differences between the races, the kinds of assumptions that white southerners used first to defend slavery and then to justify segregation. The prosecuting attorney argues that Jefferson is an "animal" who "celebrated the event by drinking over their still-bleeding bodies."[54] The defense attorney, trying to prove that Jefferson is not capable of planning a robbery, also argues that he is not a "man" who could plan anything, but an animal with traits "inherited from his ancestors in the deepest jungle of blackest Africa": "What you see here is a thing that acts on command. . . . Why I would just as soon put a hog in the electric chair as this" (7–8). After the trial, Gaines underlines the power of the white man's words when Jefferson becomes the "hog" that his own lawyer has named him—dirty, unkempt, and rude. He acts this way both in reaction to and as a result of being called "a hog" at the trial—a complex cause-and-effect sequence of scenes that is emblematic of the social construction of black manhood in southern society.

Grant's first sessions with Jefferson have no effect, because his strategies to change Jefferson's attitude about himself and his life center on other people: trying to make Jefferson feel guilty for hurting his godmother's feelings and telling Jefferson that the white sheriff and his cronies are betting against Grant's project with him. At first Grant fails with Jefferson for the same reason he is failing with his elementary school students. He is not interested in them, he is cynical about the prospect of making a difference, and thus he is angry about being put in a position to fail. Grant does not reach Jefferson until he changes his tactics. Only when Grant shifts the focus from himself and others to Jefferson does Grant begin to have a positive effect. He allows Jefferson to talk about what is most important to him—dying—rather than what is most important to Grant, making Jefferson's godmother, Miss Emma, feel better. Also, Grant becomes more patient and empathetic, focusing on the reasons for Jefferson's rude behavior rather than on the behavior itself. When the date is scheduled for Jefferson's execution, Grant instinctively adds another strategy to his plan, asking Jefferson if there is anything he wants. He buys him a radio, comic books, and a pad and pencil. Grant's students send pecans and peanuts. Finally, Grant tells Jefferson he would like to be his friend. The care and respect that Grant shows Jefferson has an effect. Jefferson begins to care for and respect Grant and to show concern for those who have shown kindness to him. When Jefferson begins to think of others as well as himself, telling Grant to thank the children for the pecans they sent, Grant feels that he has made a breakthrough.

But Gaines shows that self-respect depends on self-understanding. Grant asks Jefferson philosophical questions that make him think about the meaning of life and ultimately how to live. He defines four crucial words for him: *friend* ("a friend would do anything to please a friend"), *hero* ("a hero does for others"), *scapegoat* ("someone else to blame"), and *myth* ("a myth is an old lie that people believe in. White people believe that they're better than anyone else on earth—and that's a myth") (190–92). With the first two words, Grant challenges Jefferson to fulfill his potential, to become both friend and hero. Grant's definition of *hero* matches Gaines's: "It occurred to me one day that the only black people I knew as a child *were* heroes. . . . My hero is a person who will get up and go to work every damn day, and see himself not accomplishing much that day or maybe the next day, but will get up anyway and try it again, against the odds, to make life a little bit better."[55] With the final two words, *scapegoat* and *myth,* Grant enables Jefferson to see how white people have shaped his identity: "To them, you're nothing but another nigger—no dignity, no heart, no love for your people" (191). It is this knowledge of the social construction of black masculinity that frees Jefferson to be a man in his own mind and a hero in his community. Gaines suggests that because Jefferson has internalized white racism, he has limited what he expects of himself, and he has accepted mistreatment and disrespect as his due. Jefferson tells Grant, "Yes, I'm youman, Mr. Wiggins. But nobody didn't know that 'fore now. Cuss for nothing. Beat for nothing. Work for nothing. Grinned to get by. Everybody thought that's how it was s'pose to be. You too, Mr. Wiggins. You never thought I was nothing else. I didn't neither" (224).

Gaines shows that while language can be used to construct reality, it can also be used to deconstruct and redefine it. It is significant that at Jefferson's trial he does not speak for himself; white lawyers speak for and about him. Grant gives Jefferson the encouragement to voice his thoughts and emotions and the words to understand and articulate what has happened to him. Gaines uses language, the diary that Jefferson has kept, as moving proof of Jefferson's dignity, integrity, and humanity, despite the bad grammar, poor spelling, and punctuation mistakes. Jefferson writes that until Grant showed interest in him, "nobody aint never been that good to me an make me think im sombody"

(232). Abandoned by his parents, he says no one had ever shown him affection, or complimented him, or asked him what he wanted. One of the most poignant passages in Jefferson's diary regards the effects of this emotional deprivation: "mr wigin i just feel like tellin you i like you but i dont kno how to say this cause i aint never say it to nobody before an nobody aint never say it to me" (228). Grant dismantles white notions of black masculinity and reconstructs Jefferson's manhood by nurturing him. Before his death Jefferson exhibits the daily "grace under pressure" of black people that Gaines so much admires and links to the extraordinary moments in the lives of Ernest Hemingway's heroes.[56]

But it is in his depiction of Grant's coming to manhood that Gaines moves beyond Hemingway's model of manhood, for Gaines is ultimately more interested in how to live than in how to die, in the creation of new worlds than in the death of old ones. That Jefferson learns the lessons that Grant teaches, that he makes something of himself even within the confines of a jail cell and in the course of a few weeks, becomes a lesson for Grant, who by succeeding with Jefferson learns that he can make a difference by teaching in the rural South. In becoming a teacher, Grant has thought that whites have controlled his fate as much as they have controlled Jefferson's, because teaching is one of the few careers that educated blacks are allowed to have in the 1940s South. Gaines shows that although this may be true, Grant can control how and what he teaches. Gaines also suggests that Grant's teaching is necessary to deconstruct white definitions of black manhood. But when the novel opens, Grant is pessimistic about the chances of making a difference in his students' lives: "I teach what the white folks around here tell me to teach—reading, writing, and 'rithmetic. They never told me how to keep a black boy out of a liquor store" (13). Gaines juxtaposes Grant's thoughts of Jefferson's execution with the illegible papers that he is grading, with the memories of boys he went to school with who have been killed or sent to prison for killing someone else, and with the sight of his young male students who act exactly like the illiterate black men who bring firewood to the school. Grant's thoughts depress him: "Am I reaching them at all? . . . Is it just a vicious circle? Am I doing anything?" (62). But when he is teaching Jefferson about the social construction of identity, Grant realizes how he has short-changed his own students for six years: "I have always done what they [the white school board] wanted me to do, teach reading, writing, and arithmetic. Nothing else—nothing about dignity, nothing about identity, nothing about loving and caring" (192). Given the effect Grant has on Jefferson by teaching him just such lessons, Gaines suggests that these other subjects are as important as the three R's.

When the novel opens, Grant cynically asks how he is supposed to teach a man how to die when he himself is "still trying to find out how a man should live" (31). His most influential childhood teacher, Matthew Antoine, has taught him a lesson that he cannot forget: "He told us then that most of us would die violently, and those who did not would be brought down to the level of beasts. Told us that there was no other choice but to run and run. . . . He could teach any of us only one thing, and that one thing was flight. Because there was no freedom here. He said it, and he didn't say it. But we felt it" (62–63).[57] When Grant decides to return to rural Louisiana after college, Matthew Antoine discourages him: "You'll see that it'll take more than five and a half months to wipe away—peel—scrape away the blanket of ignorance that has been plastered and replastered over those brains in the past three hundred years" (64).

Grant learns Antoine's lessons well. Although he stays in the South, he is bitter about white racism and cynical about whether he is having any effect on his students. These factors combine to keep him alienated and on the verge of leaving. That his aunt should ask him to help Jefferson die with dignity presents a special problem for Grant. He himself has gained dignity and self-respect by leaving the plantation, and he worries that the humiliating encounters he must have with the white power structure in order to help Jefferson—going through the plantation owner's back door, being made to wait by whites, and having his body searched at the jail—will slowly strip him of his hard-earned self-respect: "Professor Antoine told me that if I stayed here, they were going to break me down to the nigger I was born to be" (79). Grant's fears about remaining in the South resemble Richard Wright's in his memoir *Black Boy* (1945). Both protagonists resist white definitions of black inferiority, both recognize the power of these constructions of black identity, and both feel it is chance that has kept them from becoming the "nigger" they were supposed to be. But Wright ends his autobiographical narrative with departure from the South so that he can understand it, while Grant stays to try to change it. Thus, in some respects, Gaines rewrites Wright's ending and revises Wright's vision of black manhood, which is premised on solitude and repudiation of community and region.

In the course of this novel, Gaines gives Grant some new teachers. Most remarkable is his own pupil Jefferson, who instructs Grant in Gaines's belief that a hero is one who perseveres "against the odds." The most unlikely one may be the young white deputy Paul. Open-minded and compassionate, he keeps Grant informed about Jefferson's state of mind. Paul's politeness to Grant and Jefferson and Miss Emma reminds Grant of an informal lesson his black English professor taught him after a white professor checked out a book for him because the black library did not have it: "He's a pretty decent fellow. . . . Some of them are, you know. And always remember that" (89). The daily racial humiliation of once again going to Mr. Pichot's back door, of being searched at the jail every time he visits Jefferson, of constant discrimination wherever he turns have made Grant forget this lesson, since he has not seen decency from a white man after returning home. Gaines charts the slow evolution of Grant and Paul's emerging friendship with the brief but increasingly significant interactions that Grant has with Paul throughout the novel. From the first day Grant goes to the jail, Paul stands out as "pretty decent" when compared with the white men he works with—a surly senior deputy and the condescending Sheriff Guidry. But Grant is not disposed to see Paul's genuine politeness as anything more than superficial good manners, so Gaines's initial individuation of Paul for readers is lost on Grant. After the first encounter, Paul becomes simply "the deputy" to Grant, until he loses enough of his anger and cynicism to look past his own racial expectations and discern Paul's friendliness, his youth, his educational background, and the "good stock" he comes from (124). Gaines presents their first real conversation as guarded on Grant's side—not so much opening up to Paul as testing him for racial sensitivity. Paul passes Grant's test by admitting his concern for Jefferson and his apprehension about the execution, feelings Grant shares. Paul follows up Grant's overture with a formal introduction—signaling a desire to relate as individuals rather than interact according to social roles, either racial or professional. Paul's break in the southern racial script during such private moments causes Grant to reciprocate by letting down the guard he uses to shield himself from white treachery. Paul's subsequent kindness and concern for both Jefferson and Grant bring to life Grant's forgotten university lesson: don't generalize about white people. The care and respect that Paul shows Grant parallels the care and respect Grant shows Jefferson and produces similar results. The frequency of the brief scenes between the two men allows Gaines to demonstrate the patience needed to overcome a history of racial mistrust and misunderstanding. Gaines shows that what might look like black disinterest or even hostility to white people may be simple caution, and what might seem like superficial white politeness to black people may well be genuine concern.

Perhaps the most influential teacher in guiding Grant to a new vision of black manhood is his lady friend Vivian, who is also a teacher. More than a love interest, she provides the role model for Grant that Mathu provides for the old men in *A Gathering of Old Men*. But unlike Mathu, Vivian teaches Grant the lessons that boys traditionally have not learned. When Vivian visits Grant at the house he shares with his aunt, she gets him to help her wash the dishes rather than leaving them for his aunt to do, thus teaching him that domestic work is not by definition woman's work. Because Vivian must be prudent in her relationship with Grant so that she will not lose her children before her divorce is final, she teaches him that in family relationships the individual cannot always fulfill his or her desires first. Also, since Vivian is a committed elementary school teacher, she shows Grant that individual fulfillment involves commitment to others.

Whereas Grant's most important lesson for Jefferson is about the social construction of race and masculinity, Vivian's most important lesson for Grant is about violence and manhood. She teaches him this lesson after dragging him out of a barroom brawl. Grant has started a fight with two mulatto bricklayers whom he overhears maligning Jefferson as a discredit to men of color. This fight is very different in length and function from the violence in *A Gathering of Old Men*. The fight in *A Lesson before Dying* functions as a key scene representing the necessity of redefining masculinity. Gaines devotes much more narrative time to a discussion between Vivian and Grant about the violence he has provoked than to the fight itself. With Vivian's lesson ("That's how you all get yourselves killed" [206]), Gaines promotes talking through or walking away from potentially violent confrontations, thereby seconding bell hooks's contention that the Western "myth of masculinity" is "life-threatening." She argues that "the most visionary task of all remains that of re-conceptualizing masculinity so that alternative, transformative models are there in the culture."[58]

The placement of this scene involving Vivian and Grant is crucial. It comes right after the pivotal scene in which Grant has succeeded in making Jefferson understand that he is as much a man as any other man, white or black. At this precarious time when Vivian is awaiting a divorce from her first husband and trying to keep custody of her children, she must be the model of propriety. Thus Vivian feels "disgusted" (209) not only by Grant's failure to control his behavior but also by his failure to think about the consequences of his fighting, both for himself and for her and her children. Just as Grant asks Jefferson difficult questions about friendship, love, and family, Vivian asks Grant hard questions about meaningful relationships between men and women, about sex and love, and about marriage. Grant's first emotion is anger, and his first inclination is to run out on her, but he thinks better of both. This chapter ends with the sentence, "I knelt down and buried my face in her lap" (210)—a striking contrast to the ending of the previous chapter, where Grant is "standing up" after the fight (203). Gaines makes Grant's kneeling courageous, more an act of manhood than his ability to win the fight with the bricklayers. Kneeling before the woman he loves suggests an ability to learn from her and to commit himself fully to their relationship. Throughout his fiction Gaines uses the physical act of standing as a symbolic representation of coming to manhood. In this novel, though, he adds kneeling and broadens the definition of manhood to include behaviors traditionally associated with women.

In the very next scene, Reverend Ambrose visits a rude, unkempt, and cynical Grant in his bedroom, much as Grant has visited Jefferson in the same state in his cell. This parallel suggests that Reverend Ambrose will teach Grant a lesson, despite Grant's aversion to a faith that keeps black people docile. Reverend Ambrose argues that although Grant is college educated, he does not know himself or his own community very well. He questions Grant's manhood, in part because of the rivalry between them over whose services Jefferson needs most and because Grant refuses to cooperate with Reverend Ambrose, but also in part because Grant does not understand the role that the black church and the black community have played in creating traditions that have sustained black people in a racist society. In a scene with echoes from the one in *A Gathering of Old Men* in which Charlie asks to be called Mr. Biggs, Reverend Ambrose tells Grant, "When you act educated, I'll call you Grant. I'll even call you Mr. Grant when you act like a man" (216). Because Reverend Ambrose knows of Grant's success with Jefferson, he wants Grant to ask Jefferson to kneel and pray for forgiveness in front of his godmother. But Grant does not believe in heaven or in the black church's placation of oppressed people, which he thinks has had the effect of bolstering the white power structure.[59] Although Reverend Ambrose's remark, "You think a man can't kneel and stand" (216), makes Grant dig in his heels in their argument about institutionalized religion, it reverberates powerfully for the reader as regards issues of masculinity, because it echoes the previous scene in which Grant kneels with his head in Vivian's lap.

A Lesson before Dying ends with Gaines's vision that coming to manhood involves more than "standing." On the day that a transformed Jefferson is to be executed, a transformed Grant awaits word of the execution at his school.

Grant admits to himself that Reverend Ambrose is "brave" because he has chosen to be with Jefferson the day of his execution, and Grant fervently hopes that he has not done anything to weaken Jefferson's belief in God (249). He also opens himself up to a friendship with Paul. When Paul brings Grant the news the Jefferson has died with dignity, Paul congratulates Grant for transforming Jefferson: "You're one great teacher, Grant Wiggins" (254), and he asks Grant to allow him to be "his friend" (255). Grant responds by asking Paul to return to tell his students about Jefferson's last day. In his portrait of an emerging cross-racial friendship, Gaines suggests that the white man's humility encourages the black man's magnanimity.

The story that Paul promises to recount of Jefferson's bravery will be very different from the reading, writing, 'rithmetic, and rote memorization Grant has employed in the past. This pedagogical change echoes the introduction of Gaines's *The Autobiography of Miss Jane Pittman,* in which the history teacher explains that he needs to record Miss Jane's life story not simply because it has been left out of the history books but because it can help him "explain things" to his students.[60] But the pedagogical method differs from Miss Jane's in that it will involve a team-teaching effort with a white man. While Michael Kreyling is right to say that Grant's development affirms "the black man's membership in a traditional black community,"[61] the presence of Paul in the last scene makes the novel something more than simply a reaffirmation of the traditional black community. Surely their final meeting, coming as it does at the end of the novel, projects some hope for a more inclusive southern community, even if the community has to be built incrementally. That word of Jefferson's execution comes from Paul (a source unexpected by both Grant and the reader), that Paul gets out of his car to approach Grant rather than expecting Grant to approach him, and that Paul admires both Jefferson and Grant are all signs of small but significant changes between black and white individuals. But Gaines does not let readers succumb to "the integration illusion" that Steinhorn and Diggs-Brown warn against. Readers cannot forget the overall racial climate of Louisiana, because before this final scene, Gaines inserts a surprising, yet fitting, omniscient overview of what blacks and whites are doing and thinking on the day Jefferson is executed for a crime he did not commit. This bleak picture of white blindness and black stoicism serves as a reminder that although Grant and Jefferson have changed, white people in general have not, that although Paul is enlightened and supportive, he is the only white person who is.

The conclusion of *A Lesson before Dying* holds one more surprise for readers. Up to the final scene with Paul, Grant internalizes most of his emotions except for anger. He has repeatedly held back tears for Jefferson, both tears of joy at his progress and tears of sadness at his fate. While Grant waits to hear word of the execution, he thinks, "I felt like crying, but I refused to cry. No, I would not cry. There were too many more who would end up as he did. I could not cry for all of them, could I?" (249). Grant's last action in *A Lesson before Dying*, standing before his class and crying while telling his students of Jefferson's execution, removes the shame from male tears. With this act, Gaines signals that Grant has finally become a man, both because he knows who he is and what he can do for his community and because he is not afraid to express his emotions. That Gaines's final portrait of Grant is similar to his portrait of Gil in *A Gathering of Old Men* suggests that Gaines thinks both black and white men must reject traditional models of manhood that link masculinity with the capacity for violence. They must embrace a new model of manhood that includes empathizing with others, resolving conflict in nonaggressive ways, and expressing a wide range of emotions. By choosing as the final words of the novel "I was crying" (256), Gaines has expanded the possibilities of masculine endings.

Sadly, the 1999 Hollywood film of *A Lesson before Dying* mostly fails to reveal Gaines's new interventions in old notions of masculinity and his hope for improved southern race relations. In the made-for-TV movie, Vivian does not stop Grant from fighting, Grant does not cry in front of his students, and the white deputy Paul never makes an appearance. This latter omission not only excises the only interracial friendship in the novel but undermines the hope for cross-racial cooperation that Gaines has embedded so prominently in his ending. Was *A Lesson before Dying* too complex to prune into a two-hour movie, or were the popular templates for portraying race relations in a southern setting too ubiquitous for filmmakers to look beyond?

Unlike the white protagonists in Brown's *Dirty Work* and Bell's *Soldier's Joy*, who assume respect and a desire for friendship from the black men they seek to befriend, Gaines's black protagonists demonstrate that respect and trust are freighted expectations in cross-racial relationships and that both must be earned before friendships can evolve. For Gaines's black men, earning self-respect and being shown respect by white people come before cross-racial friendship. A comparison of *A Gathering of Old Men* and *A Lesson before Dying* suggests that the potential for cross-racial friendship varies depending on how the respect is won. Relationships between black and white men in *A Gathering of Old Men* are presented as an agonistic drama, resulting in a balance of power and an emerging white respect for black men but no new cross-racial male friendships. In contrast, in *A Lesson before Dying* an interracial relationship of respect emerges from a cooperative venture that results in continued collaboration, a new model of relating that holds the promise of real friendship. Similarities among the four novels involve moments of illumination when characters not only see the humanity in the other but also realize how their own hidden cultural practices, whether white or black, are implicated in continued racial tensions. Anthropologist Renato Rosaldo terms such understanding "relational knowledge." Questions like "How do 'they' see 'us'?" and "Who are 'we' looking at 'them'?"[62] are crucial for improved race relations. But of these three novelists, Ernest Gaines best demonstrates how old notions of masculinity compound the problem.

CHAPTER 4

Tabooed Romance

Love, Lies, and the Burden of Southern History

> Love does not accept barriers of any kind.
> —ALICE WALKER, *THE WAY FORWARD IS WITH A BROKEN HEART*

The Old South's taboo against love between blacks and whites has cast a long shadow. No other cross-racial relationship has been so pathologized by American society. Even in 1967, when the Supreme Court finally declared antimiscegenation laws unconstitutional in the case of *Loving v. Virginia,* sixteen states still prohibited interracial marriage, down from forty states at one time.[1] Not until 1998 and 2000 did ballot initiatives in South Carolina and Alabama finally remove moribund antimiscegenation laws, although no one had tried to enforce them for years. Recent U.S. census figures show that interracial unions are increasing—up from 3 percent in 1980 to 5 percent in 2000, or just over 3 million couples. However, American inhibitions about black-white marriages still remain comparatively strong: the United States has the lowest black-white intermarriage rate among Western nations, and the 450,000 black-white couples make up only 14 percent of all interracial marriages. But the numbers are increasing among young people; young blacks are marrying across the color line at double the overall average, with 11 percent marrying outside their race. Although 40.1 percent of black interracial marriages occur in the South (as compared to 19.3% in the Northeast, 21.3% in the Midwest, and 19.3% in the West), a 1997 survey by *Interrace* magazine does not include a single southern city in its list of the ten cities most hospitable to interracial couples.[2] Contemporary fiction set in the South is only somewhat more hospitable, in large part because this fiction is almost always set in the past.

In *Neither Black nor White Yet Both,* Werner Sollors notes that *how* an American interracial love story ends has been "tied up with *where* a story ends."[3] In his discussion of mostly nineteenth- and early-twentieth-century fiction, Sollors delineates two basic modes of plotting interracial American literature: either as a tragic impossibility with an irresolvable conflict, often ending in death, or as a comic possibility with a marriage, usually ending in Europe. In popular fiction published by the New York trade presses, New York and California have recently been added as congenial places for interracial and interethnic couples. For example, such popular black-white romances as Sandra Kitt's *The Color of Love* (1995) and Eric Jerome Dickey's bestseller *Milk in My Coffee* (1998) are set in New York and conclude happily. Interestingly, Dickey, like his black male protagonist Jordan Greene, is from Tennessee, but he positions Jordan in New York for his interracial affair. Although the narrator repeatedly extols the South's less stressful "lifestyle" and praises Jordan's easy, casual manner, which makes him attractive to women, no matter their race or ethnicity, the narrator states that Jordan's southern past can even render a brief friendly encounter with a white woman "awkward." A white woman he meets in a taxi helps Jordan over that initial awkward hurdle, though, and they become lovers. But Dickey's concluding surprise revelation that Kimberly is "part black" detracts from what seems to be the novel's attempt to dismantle stereotypes about interracial love. The fact that Kimberly is a "sistah" belies the progress Jordan Greene has made in crossing racial boundaries and in overcoming narrow notions about racial identity.[4] It reproduces the notion that it is better to marry within "the race," and it explains everything from Kimberly's full, sensuous lips to her feistiness and her interest in jazz as products of her hidden blackness.

Blacks and whites working together in the civil rights movement opened the door to interracial sexual encounters in the South and increased the number of interracial marriages,[5] although the number of white men marrying black women declined, even as the number of white women marrying black men increased dramatically. Accompanying this shift, psychologists noted "a corresponding shift in blame away from African American women and toward African American men for ostensibly 'selling out.'"[6] Questions about motivation arose as quickly as the interracial couples appeared in public. Was the increase in interracial couples explained by structural changes, such as the desegregation of neighborhoods, schools, and the work place, which facilitated the opportunity for people of different races to get to know each other as equals and as individuals? Or did mixed couples increase because of racial difference itself: curiosity creating heightened sexual interest, rage about past injustice fueling sexual revenge, youthful rebellion or self-doubt playing itself out in cross-racial love affairs? The South's long history of slavery and racial injustice, entrenched customs of racial segregation, and the black separatist movement of the 1960s and 1970s combined to retain the taboo at some level for both white and black Americans. Today the barriers to interracial love have been redefined to some extent in terms of cultural affinity, rather than simply race, but in many ways the new definitions reinforce the old taboos. While about half of all American marriages fail, two out of three interracial marriages end in divorce, suggesting additional social and psychological pressures on interracial couples, although not necessarily pathological motives in getting married.[7]

So pervasive are contemporary beliefs about the ulterior motives for love across the color line (desire for the exotic other, revenge) and the stereotypes about the psychology of individuals in mixed couples (self-hate, rebellious nature) that psychologists recently conducted a study to determine whether interracial couples are dysfunctional. Not surprisingly, they found no evidence of dysfunction in interracial couples who were still living together and thus concluded that individuals' "ability to attend to their partners' (and their own) needs for love and esteem may allow them to weather the psychological storms that frequently accompany the decision to enter and remain in interracial relationships." These psychologists speculate that social scientists' failure to address interracial taboos may contribute to their persistence, but they also contend that popular culture, "which all too often exploits fear, hate, and ignorance among large segments of the American population," is reinforcing stereotypes.[8] The mixed messages about the possibilities of interracial love in Spike Lee's film *Jungle Fever* (1991), Bebe Moore Campbell's novel *Brothers and Sisters* (1995), and Dickey's *Milk in My Coffee* are examples. In some respects, these works serve to reproduce the notion that interracial sexual relationships are the result of racialized passion or rebellious transgression. But this trend may be changing.

Very recently interracial romance novels have turned south, and it has taken a southern publisher to make this happen. In 1998 Genesis Press in Columbus, Mississippi, added the Love Spectrum imprint to its fledgling African American romance line. Its first interracial novel, *Forbidden Quest* (1998), by Dar Tomlinson, is a steamy love story about the daughter of a rich white senator and a Jamaican artist whom she meets while working as an interior designer in Savannah. Tomlinson tells a distressing tale of struggling to find a publisher for her southern interethnic and interracial romances, even though her first novel won the 1994 Hemingway Award. She has said that New York publishers found her interracial and interethnic subject matter "too sensitive" and "too controversial."[9] Of course, one might assume that none of the Genesis Press novels are as well written as Signet's *Milk in My Coffee* and *The Color of Love,* and some of them are not. But *Forbidden Quest* compares favorably with *Milk in My Coffee,* although the small-press novel is certainly not as well known. Does the southern setting for a contemporary interracial love story seem unrealistic to New York publishers? Are the southern interracial love stories simply not urban-edgy enough? Or are they not southern gothic enough, in the manner of Jay McInerny's *The Last of the Savages,* which Knopf published in 1996? Whatever the case, a majority of the Internet reader reviews for interracial romances are written by southern readers—not surprising, given that so many black-white couples live in the South.

In contrast to best-selling popular romances, which are usually set outside the South, most of the serious contemporary literature focusing on interracial love has a southern setting, but these works most often take place in the past or, if set in the present, disclose forbidden love affairs that occurred in the past. Although the burden of southern racial history automatically precludes happy endings, these contemporary historical novels do complicate the regional story of race and sex as it has been told. Contemporary writers are interested in the very stories that bell hooks argues have not been told: stories that examine the conditions under which interracial sexuality served "as a force subverting and disrupting power relations, unsettling the oppressor/oppressed paradigm."[10] These recent fictions, even though set in the past, explore interracial relationships of mutual desire and examine contemporary social concerns without neglecting the exploitation of black women or the demonization of black men that white prejudice both produced and denied. This recent outpouring of historical fiction set in the South expresses a deep need to recover repressed truths about past interracial intimacy that too many people, white southerners especially, have refused to acknowledge. Perhaps the output also reflects a need to better understand the past before turning to the present or imagining the future. Whether this focus on the past also betrays a reticence to represent interracial love in the present is difficult to determine. What is clearer, and perhaps more significant, is that readers of these historical southern fictions—which invariably end in thwarted interracial love, no matter the hope embedded in their plots—may find it surprising that today twice as many interracial couples in which one partner is African American live in the South as in any other region of the country.

Werner Sollors points to "the structural ambivalence in plot lines that are brought to a forced closure at a price: each resolution rests on the denial of another possibility that is being eliminated by the choice made." To encourage telling the interracial love story in its complexity, he calls for a "relativization" of tragedy and comedy in interracial love plots, for "imagining a world of neither, nor, and yet both."[11] However, because of his focus on the nineteenth century, Sollors does not write about the contemporary novels that do just that, although he does cite Faulkner's *Absalom, Absalom!* as a prototype. In this chapter I suggest some broad trends in the representation of interracial love stories set in the South. But I examine most closely those works by contemporary writers who are writing beyond the customary endings—the either/or trajectories of interracial love plots—even when they are set in the past. Contemporary writers like Ernest Gaines, Ellen Douglas, Reynolds Price, and Sherley Anne Williams shy away from the reductive patterns that bell hooks and Anuradha Dingwaney call attention to in their review of the film *Mississippi Masala* (1991): "love conquers all" or "difference is always the site of chaos and conflict, not of constructive contestation and solidarity."[12] The endings of these new historical novels are more nuanced, showing both that love does not accept any barriers and that the ubiquitousness of society's barriers often overwhelms the love that leaps over them.

Black Men, White Women, and Forbidden Love

In 1967, the year the Supreme Court decided *Loving v. Virginia,* Ernest Gaines published *Of Love and Dust,* a novel about interracial love that questioned prevailing opinions. Gaines wrote this novel during a time of growing militancy in the civil rights movement, especially from urban and northern blacks. But he set the novel in 1948, when African American veterans, recently returned from World War II to the rural South, brought home a more cosmopolitan perspective, which historians believe "laid the foundation for a change in race relations."[13] The novel is resonant with the apprehension and dynamism of both of these periods of change. Told from the first-person perspective of black farm laborer Jim Kelly, *Of Love and Dust* tracks his transformation in thinking not just about the degradation of southern blacks but about his own behavior of accommodation as well.[14] The events that Gaines chooses to broaden Jim's consciousness involve two interracial couples. Sidney Bonbon, a Cajun overseer, is involved in a long-term affair with Pauline, the plantation owner's black cook. In the course of the novel, Bonbon's wife, Louise, avenges this betrayal by having an affair with Marcus, a black man from Baton Rouge who has been bonded to work on the plantation while awaiting trial for murder. Their affair begins as a seductive dance of mutual revenge: Marcus is enraged by Bonbon's harsh treatment in the cane fields and by Pauline's cold shoulder in the quarters. The different configurations of these two couples allow Gaines to probe the complexities of how the interracial sexual taboo functioned in relation to both gender and race in the segregated South. Bonbon and Pauline are the interracial pair most readers of southern fiction would have been familiar with when Gaines published *Of Love and Dust.* Bonbon is the abusive white overseer who lords it over his black laborers and who takes sexual advantage of the women he desires, Pauline being only the most recent.

But Gaines undermines readers' expectations about the pathology of their interracial relationship by revealing that Bonbon has fallen in love with Pauline, fathered twins with her, and remained faithful to her, even though he is married to Louise. Nor does Gaines portray Pauline as completely a victim. She uses Bonbon's growing affection for her to improve her working conditions and purchasing power. She moves from the fields to the kitchen, from coarse gingham dresses to lovely flowered frocks and big white hats—thus increasing her status, a popular explanation in the 1960s for why a black person might become sexually involved with a white person.[15] When Bonbon becomes affectionate, Pauline does not allow herself to care for him, because she expects his sexual desire for her will fade, just as it has for other black women he has raped. But over the years Pauline's compliant wariness evolves into something resembling wifely affection. In the only scene in which readers see them together, the narrator, Jim, notices that Pauline's occasional smart remark to Bonbon sounds "just like a wife."[16]

Gaines uses their relationship to demonstrate that for the white man transgression of the southern interracial taboo is not sex with a black woman, but love. Jim says, "Everybody expected the white overseer to have a black woman—even his wife expected that. But when he started neglecting his wife for this black woman, then that was a different thing" (147). Because of his emotional attachment to Pauline, Bonbon is marginalized by the Cajun community and by his family, although he still goes hunting and fishing with his brothers. As a result, he turns to black people on the plantation for help and support, using the fear that his position as overseer garners to create a human screen for his private life with Pauline and their twin sons. A black teacher quits his job to avoid being accused of "allowing Billy and Willy to go around school calling [Bonbon] 'father'" (71). Aunt Ca'line and Pa Bully, who live next to Pauline, pretend not to hear the sounds of lovemaking when Bonbon visits. Bishop, Marshall Hebert's butler, stands guard on the gallery when Bonbon visits Pauline during the day at the big house. Needy for emotional support as well, Bonbon turns to the novel's narrator, Jim Kelly, a relative newcomer whom Bonbon respects for his expertise with farm equipment. Shop talk about trucks and tractors evolves into casual exchanges about leisure-time activities like hunting and fishing and finally into personal disclosures about Bonbon's background—growing up poor and uneducated. Although Bonbon never talks directly to Jim about Louise or Pauline, his need to confide in someone leads him to talk about subjects that explain his inability to leave Louise (he hates and fears her brothers) and that reveal his pride in his biracial sons, although he never admits he is their father. Gaines uses Jim's sympathy for Bonbon to help naturalize the relationship between Bonbon and Pauline.

Bonbon's dependence on the black community's tacit involvement in his "marriage" to Pauline is especially evident in a scene in which he must ask Jim to accompany him and Pauline when they want to have a casual afternoon together in Baton Rouge. Jim functions as Pauline's surrogate husband when Bonbon and Pauline appear in public. Jim sits between them in the car, and Jim plays the role of husband when Pauline shops, telling her what he thinks Bonbon would say about a scarf she likes, admiring her legs when she buys stockings, helping her choose presents for the children. The only time that Pauline and Bonbon are able to forget about race in a public place is in a mulatto bar where Jim "supposed they took Bonbon for a mulatto, too," because his tan makes him "darker than many of them" (144). As a "white" man in the Jim Crow South, Bonbon can have illicit sex with Pauline or any other black woman without degrading himself, but he cannot show the world how much he loves and respects Pauline unless he is "black." While this scene highlights the social construction of interracial sexuality, it is interesting for another reason. Playing pimp for Bonbon forces Jim to take a long hard look at how he is implicated in maintaining the status quo for black people when he facilitates the southern racial customs that discriminate against them.[17]

Concern with family reputation means that Bonbon's relatives do not publicly discuss Bonbon's transgression either. Because of the reticence of both blacks and whites to talk publicly about interracial romance, Bonbon is privately, although not publicly or legally, able to have two wives and two sets of children. He has no practical reason for further transgression, such as divorcing Louise and living openly with Pauline—both his family and Louise's would need to retaliate against him to defend family honor—and he has every reason to continue the status quo. Although the white community represses its suspicions about interracial love, the black people in the quarter whisper about it. Gaines depicts them as having two reactions: either Pauline was taking advantage of a bad situation that she could not control, or she was sinning.

When Marcus meets Pauline, Gaines suggests that his reaction resembles Bonbon's first feelings for Pauline: a mixture of lust and proprietorship. Given Marcus's high opinion of his own sex appeal, he expects Pauline to be eager for the attention of a self-confident black man. He also believes that he has a "right" to her because she is black. That he does not succeed in his suit underlines both the racial motivation for Marcus's attraction and the fact that Bonbon's relationship with Pauline has moved beyond its origins. Gaines disrupts a popular equation between sexual prowess and black masculinity not only by having Pauline refuse Marcus's advances but also by having Jim interrupt the story of Marcus's pursuit of Pauline with the story of Pauline's love for Bonbon—a fact that Marcus finds incomprehensible. Marcus assumes not only his sexual superiority over the white man, especially the ethnic Cajun, but also the black woman's solidarity with her black brother against the white man who is his boss. Marcus is furious that Pauline would prefer "a white man—no, not even a solid white man, but a bayou, catfish-eating Cajun" (57), when she could have a black man who has the pride and courage to stand up to the white man who has raped black women and abused black men in the fields.

Racial inequality determines how Marcus expresses his rage. He punishes Pauline directly for her indifference by slapping her, but he indirectly gets even with Bonbon by pursuing his wife, Louise. Thus Gaines employs a notion popular in the 1960s that black men have sex with white women as revenge for past racial wrongs,[18] but he complicates it by making revenge Louise's motivation in welcoming Marcus's advances. Gaines links the white woman and the black man in two other ways: their courage in breaking the sexual taboo, which can endanger their lives, and their subsequent fanciful notion that they will be able to flee the plantation together and live happily ever after. As David Lionel Smith has argued, in contrast to Faulkner's characters, who "look constantly backward, overwhelmed by past events and trapped by their tragic inability to make meaningful change," Gaines's characters are "deeply bound by the past, yet they recognize that change is possible if one is willing to pay the price."[19]

Gaines suggests that it does not take perfect heroes to effect social change or extraordinary events to occasion individual transformation. A key ingredient for Gaines is moving his characters out of the box in which southern race relations has confined them. Marcus's courage comes from arrogance as much as self-respect, socially conditioned thinking as much as bold ideas: in planning his revenge by seducing the overseer's wife, Marcus has no doubts about his ability to charm a white woman. Louise's courage to defy southern racial customs arises more from stereotypical thinking than from broad-mindedness, more from desperation than from self-assertion: "She wanted a mark on her flesh. She had to have proof, she had to have a mark. . . . Because she wasn't sure she had anything worthwhile, and she was afraid if she hollered rape everybody might laugh at her. But with a mark, Bonbon would definitely have to kill the nigger. Marshall Hebert would definitely get rid of Bonbon for the stealing that he had been doing—and she would be free to leave" (165). Ironically, the vengeful sexual encounters that each separately engineers metamorphose into a mutually satisfying emotional relationship, transformative for them as individuals. Gaines bases the possibility of the unconventional interracial love affair on the conventionality of the gender roles they assume. Marcus's smooth talk and lengthy foreplay make Louise feel sexy. Because Marcus gives her the attention Bonbon has denied her, Louise grows attached him, and her admiration transforms him into the man who will protect her and share her freedom rather than simply the black male who was to be the unwitting instrument of her escape. For once in Marcus's life, someone loves and depends on him—a situation that makes his desire to take care of Louise take precedence over his single-minded concern for himself. Ultimately, Marcus gives his life for her. When Bonbon discovers them together, Marcus's concern for Louise prevents him from running, the only chance he has to save himself.

Thus, *Of Love and Dust* counters in a very nuanced way simplistic 1960s notions about the pathology of interracial love and discloses truths about interracial love that late-twentieth-century white southerners had repressed. And yet at the same time, reticence in depicting interracial lovemaking is embedded in the novel's structure. Because Gaines tells his story from the first-person perspective of Jim Kelly, what we know about Bonbon and Pauline's lovemaking is limited to the sounds Pauline's neighbors overhear and then gossip to Jim about. Readers do not know how mutual love evolved from Bonbon's first unwanted advances. A similar narrative reticence holds for Marcus and Louise's love affair. Margaret overhears Marcus's appreciative remarks about Louise's "sweet little pears" (169) and "the deep moan" Louise makes as she climaxes—all of which she reports to Jim Kelly. But great gaps exist between their first revenge-filled encounter and the love that leads to their mutual plan to escape north.

By creating parallels between the two interracial couples,[20] Gaines succeeds in pointing up crucial differences: how black and white reactions to interracial love affairs differ and how reactions differ further depending on the race and gender configuration of each couple. The black characters know more than the white characters about each relationship. The white character must in some way pass as "black" to facilitate the affair: Bonbon takes Pauline to a mulatto bar, and Louise blackens her skin with coal for the planned escape with Marcus. Long after slavery was outlawed, the black woman remained vulnerable to the white man, but the white woman continued to be off-limits to the black man. Bonbon takes Pauline in a moment in the field one afternoon, while Marcus takes days to work up from distant eye contact to an accidental touching across the fence separating him from Louise. Gaines represents the extent of Marcus's transgression with the elaborate obstacle course that he must negotiate: watchful eyes, the fence, a protective dog, and two guards (Aunt Margaret for Louise and Jim Kelly for Marcus). While the white man worries about his reputation in the white community, the black man fears for his life because of white retaliation.

When the truth of both interracial affairs is publicly told, the consequences are dramatic, but the outcome for individuals is very different, depending on their race and gender. When Marcus and Louise finally have sex and subsequently fall in love, the tragic outcome of their affair is never in doubt to anyone except them, as Gaines's repeated use of foreshadowing demonstrates. In the end, Marcus lies dead, just as the black people feared, and Louise's family carts her off to an insane asylum, convinced that her affair with a black man is proof of her insanity. At the same time that Gaines depicts Marcus, an alleged felon, as the courageous defender of the woman he loves and the transgressor of the South's strictest taboo, he portrays Bonbon as a coward, the victim of a southern racial code that paradoxically obligates him to either kill the black man who has slept with the wife he does not love or be killed himself by Louise's family for not defending her honor. Bonbon kills Marcus, not to avenge his wife's honor, but to protect his own, once the facts of his wife's affair are public knowledge. Bonbon must leave the plantation, not for killing Marcus, which is officially recorded as "justifiable homicide" (277), but for knowing too much about a murder that Marshall Hebert ordered years ago. Ironically, Bonbon and Pauline are free to begin the new life up north that Marcus and Louise dreamed of, to live publicly as a family with their twin sons. Gaines's conclusion, then, is both happy and sad: happy for the white man and the black woman and tragic for the black man and the white woman. But his story is a tragedy on both counts for the segregated South, which only repressed the interracial love that actually occurred there. The fact that both couples should have lived happily ever after makes painfully obvious the absurdity of the society's conventions about interracial love. That Bonbon and Pauline did live a sort of shadow marriage for years highlights the gender asymmetry in the racial code.[21]

Since 1967, when Gaines published *Of Love and Dust,* tragic endings have predominated in black men's fiction about black male–white female love in the South, even though the number of such real-life unions has by now far surpassed those between white men and black women. The memory of black men being beaten, hanged, drowned, and dragged to death in the South cannot recede when incidents such as the 1998 lynching of James Byrd in Jasper, Texas, still occur. As Martin Luther King Jr. pointed out, "no society can repress an ugly past when the ravages persist in the present."[22] This ugly past looms in the present when black men write about interracial love. For example, in *Holly* (1995), Albert French selects the same 1940s time period as that found in *Of Love and Dust,* and once again the black lover of the white woman lies dead at the end of the novel.[23] But French's protagonist, Elias, exerts some control over his fate by committing suicide in his jail cell, rather than being killed by the white men who put him there. Although the tragic trajectory of this plot as black men write it has not changed in three decades, a strong revisionist impulse is evident, because French inverts the social positions of the interracial couple. Elias is a well-educated artist from a prominent Washington, D.C., family, who has lost his arm in World War II; Holly is a poor rural teenager looking for a man who will appreciate her inner beauty and sensitivity rather than simply her good looks. Both characters are on the margins of their provincial North Carolina community: Elias is an artist, better educated than the rural relatives he is staying with; Holly is open-minded and more introspective than her white friends and family. They meet near a shaded brook where Elias likes to paint and Holly goes to think, but the love nurtured in this private place cannot be sustained in 1940s North Carolina. French has created something of an escape hatch for the couple that provides hope for readers as well. The train carries the pregnant Holly safely to Elias's accepting parents in Washington, a place that functions as a liminal space—southern in culture, but northern in racial politics. The novel seems to be plotted with what Sollors calls "an initial ambivalence in the creative process,"[24] for Elias, who is traveling separately for safety, is captured and jailed by a group of angry white men before he leaves North Carolina. Thus the plot presents the possibility of a change in interracial relationships in the South, but the conclusion denies a change in race relations, making the black man as vulnerable as he was during Reconstruction and its aftermath.

In Randall Kenan's collection of stories *Let the Dead Bury Their Dead* (1992), interracial gay couples are not safe either—even in contemporary North Carolina. In "Run Mourner, Run," Percy Terrell, a white landowner, bribes Dean Williams, a poor white gay man, into having sex with Ray Brown, a prominent black landowner, so that Percy can shame Ray into having to sell his family farm. The threat of public humiliation results not from the old taboo against interracial love so much as from the stronger contemporary taboo against homosexual love. Eager for the promised promotion and raise, Dean accepts the bribe, only to find himself falling in love with Ray. But when Percy follows up with photos of their lovemaking, Ray is forced to sell some of his land in order to protect his reputation in the community and to hide his sexual orientation from his wife and daughters. Months later, when Dean begs Percy for the promised promotion and raise, Percy's sons taunt him because of his sexual orientation and then beat him mercilessly. Kenan structures this story so that readers will be aware that times have changed the black man's status in rural North Carolina if he is wealthy, but that a nasty strain of hate-filled provincialism has found other targets. Confident and well educated, Ray does not capitulate immediately to Percy's demands: "You got to be kidding, Terrell. You come in here with your boys and your dogs and pull this bullshit TV-movie camera stunt and expect me to whimper like some snot-nosed pickaninny, 'Yassuh, Mr. Terrell, suh, I'll give you anything, suh. Take my land. Take my wife. I sho is scared of you, suh.' Come off it." Nor will Ray later give in fully to Percy's demands that he sell his entire farm or see his reputation ruined. Eventually Ray does lose "a tiny piece of property." In contrast, Dean loses his livelihood, because Percy and his ilk consider him "a pathetic white-trash faggot whore," an identity that affords him no power at all in this small rural community.[25] Kenan depicts the poverty-stricken Dean as the "pickaninny" in this story, a grown man dragging his bare feet in the red-clay trough under his childhood rope swing—manipulated by a powerful white man, rejected by his rich black lover, and as dependent on his mother at twenty-three as he was at five, when his father hung the swing. This contemporary image of strange fruit hanging from a southern tree conjures up, even as it reverses in a way, old images of black men lynched after rumored offenses to white women. Only in Kenan's "The Foundations of the Earth" does a southern black man find happiness in an interracial homosexual affair, and then it occurs in Boston.[26]

Some African American women writers have been especially concerned with the motivations for interracial romance between black men and white women. Until very recently, they have treated the black male–white female couple in fiction more often than the black female–white male configuration. These portraits vary from Alice Walker's pathology in *Meridian* (1976) to Sherley Anne Williams's ambiguity in *Dessa Rose* (1986) to Dori Sanders's acceptance under erasure in *Clover* (1990) when the black man is killed on his wedding day. Alice Walker's *Meridian* is an early portrait of the pressures on interracial love between a white woman and a black man during the civil rights movement. Lynne is an idealistic white civil rights activist, rebelling against her Jewish parents' bourgeois life and the homogeneity of the northern suburb where she grew up. Truman is more cosmopolitan and more self-confident and also less idealistic about the movement. But he is eager to take advantage of its opportunities for new experiences, which include the white coeds who come south during Freedom Summer. Although both Truman and Lynne are northerners, they meet in Georgia and live out their brief marriage in Mississippi. Lynne's parents disown her for becoming involved with a black man, but Truman's black nationalist friends prove to be an even more destructive force on their marriage than family disapproval. Meridian, the black civil rights activist who loved Truman before Lynne came on the scene, is shocked and saddened by their strong attraction and assumes that simple exoticism has drawn them together. Walker hints that the reasons for their attraction are not so superficial. Since Lynne's life and her prospects have not been constricted by race, poverty, and provincialism, Lynne is better educated, more cosmopolitan, and more confident than Meridian the summer that Truman dates both of them. Walker combines these characteristics with Lynne's desire "to put her body on the line for his freedom" and depicts Truman as irresistibly and fatally drawn to her. Lynn has dark, curly hair, and Walker, like many African American writers, uses blond hair and blue eyes to code the otherness of white people. Thus she makes Truman's objectification of white women more evident in his infatuation with the northern blond coed during Freedom Summer and in his affair with the southern blond airhead he meets in New York after he and Lynne separate. When black nationalism changes the dynamic of race relations within the movement, Truman's friend Tommy Odds wants him to divorce Lynne, but earlier even Tommy judges them compatible and "content" in their marriage because of their shared interests.[27]

But Walker does not make her readers privy to the happy times in Truman and Lynne's courtship and marriage. She gives readers glimpses of their love in faded photographs and in fleeting moments of togetherness that actually illustrate their isolation as a couple and that foreshadow their troubled marriage: riding a motorcycle at dusk rather than at night so that her white face would not be so obvious, celebrating a successful voter registration drive, only to be stalked by white racists when they leave the bar. Instead Walker draws readers' attention to the social pressures that force the couple apart. Rejected by her parents and the white community because of her interracial relationship, Lynne is never fully accepted by the black community, either. As black nationalism gains force, Truman faces increasing pressure from his black friends to prove both his own blackness and his allegiance to the black community by leaving his white wife.[28] Truman and Lynne's marriage does not withstand the social and psychological pressures brought to bear on it. Nor did Alice Walker's own interracial marriage to Jewish civil rights lawyer Mel Leventhal; their divorce became final in 1976, the same year *Meridian* was published. But not until 2000 did Walker write about the unexpected wonder of their love and the failure of their marriage. In retrospect she views herself and Mel as "kindred spirits" drawn together by the civil rights movement and driven apart by the stress that everyday life in Mississippi left in its wake: "living interracially, attempting to raise a child, attempting to have a normal life, wore us out. I think we were exhausted. In our tiredness we turned away from each other."[29]

Meridian's division into three parts—"Meridian," "Truman," and "Ending"—indicates that Walker saw the novel as the story of Meridian's and Truman's personal growth and their encounters with Lynne as playing a central role in their development. Because of Walker's interest in criticizing traditional gender roles and expectations for women, Meridian and Truman must grow in different directions. As suits her womanist politics, Walker self-consciously does not end the novel with either marriage or death,[30] the traditional endings for women, although death seems the more likely of the two. Meridian's work as an activist takes a toll on her health and results in her preoccupation with death: "She dreamed she was a character in a novel and that her existence presented an insoluble problem, one that would be solved only by her death at the end" (117). The womanist politics of the novel make the conclusion dependent on Meridian's liberation from both traditional female selflessness and black female guilt and on Truman's reeducation as a nurturing male, willing to interrupt his career as an artist in New York, to take Meridian's place as community activist in the Deep South, and to allow Meridian to fulfill her potential. The racial politics of the novel demand that Truman see his desires for both Meridian and Lynne as products of the social construction of race and gender. At the end of the novel, Truman's reeducation is complete when he frees Meridian from his inappropriate desire to possess her and direct her life because she is black. The last chapter of the novel is entitled "Release." In the penultimate chapter, "Settling Accounts," Meridian releases Truman as well: "You are free to be whichever way you like, to be with whoever, of whatever color or sex you like" (216). Thus Walker's message seems to be that interracial sexual relationships should be accepted, or at least tolerated, and that race does not give black women the right to control black men's lives any more than it gives black men the right to control black women's lives.

But it could be argued that the trajectory of Lynne and Truman's plot reinforces the notion, particularly prevalent in the 1960s and 1970s, that interracial sexual relationships are inherently dysfunctional, even though Walker posits the causes as socially constructed and has Truman and Meridian release each other to love freely. Not a single interracial love affair survives in this novel, and there are several. The relationship between Truman and Lynne not only proves hurtful to them as individuals and as a couple, but it creates intraracial misunderstanding between Truman and Meridian and disrupts the emerging cross-racial friendship between Lynne and Meridian, which I discuss in chapter 2.

A decade after the publication of *Meridian*, the use of a subplot involving interracial love in Sherley Anne Williams's historical novel *Dessa Rose* (1985) seems directed at readers who continue to question the legitimacy of romantic relationships between black men and white women. *Dessa Rose*, like *Meridian*, is primarily about a black woman's quest for self-definition. Williams interrogates the role that interracial love plays in this quest when the interracial affair is not part of a love triangle as in *Meridian*. At first Dessa's knowledge of the interracial affair between a black friend, Nathan, and the white woman Rufel undermines Dessa's growing sense of self-worth. While Walker suggests that the interracial love affair itself is problematic because rooted in the wrong motives, Williams represents Dessa's perspective on the interracial affair as somewhat problematic. Whereas Walker withholds the scenes of love between Truman and Lynne, Williams portrays the evolving interracial romance between the plantation mistress and the escaped slave, even if only in three brief scenes.

When Rufel first encounters Nathan by the fishing hole, she initially sees him as just another darky who has invaded her private space: "It was *her* place, she thought indignantly. . . . Everywhere; they were everywhere, her house, her bed."[31] Very upset by Dessa's accusations that she did not really know her black Mammy, Rufel needs comfort and reassurance. As a result she responds to Nathan's dark body near her as she has habitually responded to Mammy, "her head seeking that spot where the frayed collar lay open against the black neck" (130). For the distraught white woman, accustomed to comfort on demand from her personal slave, Nathan's dark skin momentarily becomes interchangeable with Mammy's. The long hug she receives from him gives her a measure of security, which allows her to recall Mammy's real name and their relationship. Because these memories act to counter Dessa's accusations, Nathan is able to soothe Rufel at his breast, much as Mammy once did. Physical and emotional needs sated, Rufel recalls the social context of their encounter, much as she did after nursing Dessa's baby. Looking up, she expects to see popular culture's image of a black man, "the bulbous lips and bulging eyes of a burnt-cork minstrel," but is surprised to look "into a pair of rather shadowy eyes and strongly defined features that were—handsome!" (132). Because Rufel is lonely and because Nathan treats her "like a person" (160) even though she at first treats him like her slave, Rufel sees Nathan as an individual, and they continue to meet.

When Nathan and Rufel make love for the first time, the impersonal narrator presents the potentially shocking scene from a purely aesthetic angle, as if through a camera lens: "Nathan was the color of eggplant, a rich, velvety blue-black; beside him, Rufel's skin took on a pearly glow. They sweated and rested, his face buried in her bosom, one leg caught between hers. She stroked his back; his fingers played purposefully in matted pubic hair, teasing the slick lips of her vagina. Supine, she waited for him to enter her again" (171). And yet this taboo act, unlike the scene in which Rufel nurses Dessa's baby, is prefaced with a politically charged reminder of its social context that racializes the sexual act. For in the preceding scene Nathan tells the men in the quarters about the mixed motives of his previous interracial sexual exploits: "It was the terror, he knew, that made it so sweet. If climax, as some men said, was like death, then a nigger died a double death in a white woman's arms. And he had survived it. He walked a little taller, aware of the power hanging secret and heavy between his legs" (171). Williams ends the brief scene of Nathan and Rufel's lovemaking with Dessa's unwitting interruption and reaction, thereby totally enveloping the interracial sexual act in ideological overtones, despite the aesthetic, impersonal presentation of the act itself. Dessa's surprised response combines white-inflected derision at Rufel's comedown with black female shock at Nathan's betrayal. Calling Rufel "Miz Ruint" (172), Dessa feels overwhelmed to the point of obliteration by whiteness: "All I seed as I listened was Nathan sprawled in whiteness, white sheets, white pillows, white bosom. All he did was make them look whiter. He wasn't nothing but a mark on them. That's what we was in white folks' eyes, nothing but marks to be used, wiped out. . . . I couldn't trust all we had to something could swallow us like so many drops; I made up my mind not to put my freedom in no white woman's hand" (185).

Williams spends almost as much time on the interracial relationship's defense as its development—in two different scenes in which first Nathan and then his friend Harker, another escaped slave, try to convince Dessa that the love affair is not unnatural and really none of her business since she is not romantically interested in Nathan. The ways in which the men try to get Dessa to reconsider the interracial affair involve both changing her perspective and making her aware that there are multiple perspectives, a narrative structure that Julius Lester built on a decade later when presenting the same subject in *And All Our Wounds Forgiven* (1994). Nathan uses wordplay, attempting to prove that words are mere signs, given signification by their context. He redefines skin color as a matter not just of the social construction of race in the South but of the aesthetics of color. When Dessa accuses Nathan of "liking [Rufel] cause she white," he answers, "I likes her cause she white; I likes you cause you got that old pretty red color under your skin. Now what of that?" (187). Nathan also emphasizes that interracial relationships are interactions between people who are individuals as well as members of racial groups. Thus, when Dessa asks, "Why you doing something you know can't mean you no good?" he replies, "Felt plenty good to me" (187). Nathan's playful remarks, which reduce the affair to a personal matter, prove ineffective in altering her thinking in part because she fears for his safety.

Only when Harker reminds Dessa that love accepts no barriers and makes her understand how emotion affects perception does she understand that the relationship between Rufel and Nathan, as well as the impasse between Nathan and herself, might be perceived differently depending on the perspective. Williams characterizes Dessa as emotionally enmeshed in an almost possessive relationship with Nathan, but this is understandable because of the strong bond forged during their escape from the slave coffle and because of slavery's construction of whiteness and race relations. For Dessa, who has never known a kind or trustworthy white person, Nathan is very simply sleeping with the enemy. Because of his friendship with her, Dessa wants Nathan to give up his love affair with Rufel; but she does not see the price she is asking him to pay, until Harker equates Nathan's feelings for Rufel with Dessa's for her husband, Kaine. His question "Who would you have gived Kaine up for if they had asked you?" (205) causes Dessa to see that the interracial love cannot be interpreted simply as race relations but must also be interpreted as human relations. Nathan also reminds her of the new bonds of trust formed across the color line since Rufel's husband decamped and the runaways set themselves up in the slave quarters on Rufel's plantation: "We *been* trusting her all along, just like *she* been trusting us" (206). Eventually Williams stops Dessa's protestations with Harker's kiss, thus diverting Dessa with a love affair of her own, and Williams leaves the interracial love affair behind closed doors for the rest of the novel.

Although Dessa assures Harker that her anger at Nathan has been provoked not by sexual jealousy but by racial solidarity, the kiss as conclusion to the discussion of interracial love injects into this historical fiction a contemporary concern, similar to Walker's. Dessa's first reaction after seeing Nathan and Rufel together in bed is a cry of loss, "Can't I have nothing?" (175). Her final thought as their wagon heads west is a surge of anger: "Setting up there between them that morning, seemed like I could feel them *wanting* at each other. Not with they hands, now; they didn't even hardly touch *me*. But it was something between them and it made me mad. I sat there hoping they'd feel *that*" (213). While Williams's novel, unlike Walker's, does much to naturalize the interracial love affair between a black man and a white women, the way the affair is treated after the lengthy discussions about its sincerity leaves little doubt about Dessa's difficulty accepting it, no matter how well she understands it. Its presentation also leaves some room for ambiguity as to Nathan's motives. In the epilogue, Dessa lets readers know that Nathan has never asked Rufel to marry him, although she was willing. At the end of the novel, readers are left with an important question: has Nathan bedded Rufel mainly to entice her into helping the runaways in their scheme to go west? An exchange in the slave quarters right after Dessa discloses that she has seen them making love suggests that Nathan may have purposefully toyed with Rufel's affections so as to manipulate her into helping the runaways escape west:

> Finally Harker slap his thigh and laugh, "Doggone it, Cully," he say, "I didn't believe old Nathan'd do it!"
> Cully let out a big whoop. "Miz Lady bound to come in on the deal now!" (179)

Readers can never be sure of Nathan's true motives, in either beginning or ending the relationship, because Williams does not give us access to his thoughts or create a farewell scene between Nathan and Rufel.

Like her early-twentieth-century predecessor Oscar Micheaux (*The Conquest,* 1913), Sherley Anne Williams brings up but avoids interracial marriage, even in the West, although she does not directly oppose it. In *Dessa Rose,* as in *Meridian,* the white woman who loves across the color line must cut herself off from her white community and never finds full acceptance in the black community.[32] Rather than return to the South and the inhumanity of slavery, Rufel goes north to Philadelphia. Perhaps Williams makes this narrative choice to protect her fledgling black community from white prejudice in the West and to promote group solidarity, for when Rufel brings up the possibility of continuing west with the runaways, Dessa stops listening, overcome by feelings "of danger, of fear" (239). But perhaps Williams makes this choice to maintain goodwill in the relationship she has created between Dessa and Rufel, which is more centrally her concern than the interracial romance. While Williams does not depict interracial love as dysfunctional, she definitely suggests that racial inequality prevents true intimacy in interracial love or interracial friendship, which I discuss in chapter 2. Thus Williams withholds from Nathan and Rufel the happy outcome for which she so carefully prepares her readers.

Given the disparity in the configurations of interracial couples after the civil rights era—many more black men with white women than white men with black women—some black women understandably became increasingly critical of black men and the white women they dated and lived with or married. Thirty years later, their criticism of such interracial unions has not totally abated. Perhaps American racial history, combined with the continued disproportionately high rate at which black men are incarcerated, the lower number of black men with college degrees compared to black women,[33] and the much lower percentage of white men marrying black women than black men marrying white women still fuels resentment among black women. As recently as 1997, a survey found that while the primary cause for stress for both black and white women is "not enough time for myself," the second leading cause for stress among black women is "seeing an interracial couple."[34] Thus it is not surprising to find that some black women writers, especially in the two decades following the civil rights era, would not only question the motives of such matches but would link the fact of interracial union between black men and white women with the problem of black women finding a suitable black partner, with tensions between black and white women, and with white beauty as the prevailing standard in the United States. Popular novelist Bebe Moore Campbell is convinced that "[i]n the land where Marilyn Monroe's beauty still reigns supreme, few black women emerge unscathed . . . and few black men."[35] In the essay "Black Men, White Women," she relinquishes her anger, but not her suspicion that the motive for interracial liaisons between black men and white women is rarely true love.

In 1994 Julius Lester revisited this volatile issue in *And All Our Wounds Forgiven*, a novel about the "unanticipated consequences" of the civil rights movement.[36] One of the novel's four voices is that of a slain civil rights leader, John Calvin Marshall, who speaks from the grave. He resembles Martin Luther King Jr. in both his passive resistance and his adulterous affairs. Lester depicts Marshall as wounded by the movement's past history in turning from him to Malcolm X, but also by its present unfinished business. Wounded veterans of the movement provide the novel's three other voices. Marshall's widow, Andrea, lives with two especially painful facts: that she has devoted more time and money to the cause after Marshall's death than during the sixties and that her husband loved a white woman, Lisa, as much as he loved her, if not more. Lisa, a former civil rights activist, feels betrayed by the black people who forced whites from integrated organizations such as SNCC, and she feels misunderstood by those black women who continue to criticize interracial love. Bobby Card, a black movement organizer, feels bereft and adrift. He dropped out of college to follow Marshall, only to see his friends and co-workers murdered and the promise of the civil rights movement unfulfilled—losses that he has tried to escape from through drugs, alcohol, and misguided relationships with women, both black and white.

Like Alice Walker, Julius Lester, who also worked in the movement, represents the attraction between a black man and a white woman as predestined by southern history's strongest racial taboo, but with a twist. Marshall certainly seems fated to have an affair with Lisa. He is drawn to her picture in the newspaper, the lone white woman at a sit-in. When their eyes meet across a crowded room at Fisk University, which she attends as an exchange student from California, Lisa becomes enthralled by his magnetic power. But *And All Our Wounds Forgiven* complicates the simple cross-racial "sexual attraction" to the exotic other (74) that Marshall's wife assumes. Instead, in this imaginative reworking of history, Lester portrays Marshall and Andrea's relationship as the one more rooted in race than love. They met when attending a predominately white college in Boston and fell into a relationship because there were so few black students. The novel returns again and again to the statement that, unlike Marshall and Lisa, who are repeatedly referred to as "kindred spirits," he and Andrea are romantically ill suited. Andrea is more traditional and conventional than Marshall—desiring not the dangerous life of activism in the South, to which he gravitates after their marriage, but a safer academic life in the Northeast, which she assumed she would have if she married a graduate student. Lester constructs the plot so that because of Marshall's physically and psychically demanding public role, he turns for respite to Lisa. With her, Lester suggests, Marshall can more simply be Cal, a man, rather than the messiah for his people that John Calvin Marshall must always be. Although Lisa understands his important political role as a black leader, she does not rely on him to save her. When they are alone in her small cabin or in tiny rooms in black motels, Lisa is able to forget, at least briefly, the fact that Andrea and Marshall can never forget: death stalks black men in the South, especially those in leadership positions. Ironically, her forgetfulness allows Marshall periodic and much-needed rest from Andrea's anxiety about his safety. This is not to say that Lisa is not aware of what their sexual relationship means historically. As Marshall says, "the first time elizabeth and i were together, we were both nervous. more, we were frightened. . . . what we were about to do had been forbidden for centuries. black man, white woman. it was a social taboo with almost as much force as the one against incest. black men were killed if a white man thought they might be thinking about white women." They do not simply defy history; they attempt "to heal history with their bodies" (73). By adding an interracial affair to John Calvin Marshall's hidden history of adultery, Lester creates one more strike against him in the FBI's secret files and one more wound that must be forgiven by the black community after his death. Marshall addresses their concern: "i am not naïve. i know many of those black men and white women abused each other [in the sixties]. i know many black women were made to feel worthless as they saw black men walk past them to get to the nearest white woman. history extracts its price, regardless. i also know that some of history's wounds could not have been tended any other way" (73).

This statement reverses Lester's 1968 ridicule in *Look Out, Whitey! Black Power's Gon' Get Your Mama!* of King's nonviolent message: "What is love supposed to do? Wrap the bullet in a warm embrace? Caress the cattle prod?"[37] Even as *And All Our Wounds Forgiven* acknowledges the troubled history of interracial love, Lester seems to seize it as the best metaphor for King's dream of integration and the best symbol of the risks blacks and whites took during the civil rights movement. Marshall muses, "i have wondered if the real work of the civil rights movement was not interracial sex. do not misunderstand. i am not deriding the passage of the 1964 civil rights act or the 1965 voting right act. i am not dishonoring the memories of all of us who died. but if social change is the transformation of values, then the civil rights movement did not fulfill itself" (71). Knowing the danger of using such a freighted metaphor to stand in for the political and economic goals of the movement, Lester takes that risk to focus readers' attention on contemporary race relations. As Sharon Monteith has pointed out, "[t]he slippage between imagination and the facts that historical commentators work so assiduously to retrieve becomes the creative wellspring for writers of fiction for whom strict allegiance to the facts may limit what they can do with them."[38]

And All Our Wounds Forgiven probes not the civil rights movement so much as the consequences that occurred when the Black Power movement and black nationalism overwhelmed Marshall's/King's model of passive resistance and integration. Marshall believes that when the Black Power movement ousted whites from such organizations as SNCC, "blacks placed racial exaltation above a love of humanity" (8), with the result that "racism has added legions of *black* adherents, making america an integrated society in a way i never dreamed. our racial suspicions and hatreds have made us one nation" (71). *And All Our Wounds Forgiven* is Lester's attempt to examine this legacy, to reveal the wounds, and to start the process of healing through forgiveness. As a result he constructs the novel as a series of confessions, both of wounds received and wounds inflicted, of the desire to be forgiven and the need to forgive. John Calvin Marshall, seeing how the movement wounded young people far beyond the sixties, wants forgiveness from former activists like Bobby Card for the great sacrifices he asked of black youth, and from America for the backlash, on both sides, that still tugs at the country's heartstrings. He seeks understanding from his wife for his love affair with a white woman. Lisa seeks forgiveness from Marshall's widow for not acting with more sensitivity to black women during the sixties and for refusing Marshall's final wish that Lisa tell Andrea how much he loved Andrea. Andrea mentally seeks forgiveness from Marshall for not understanding him as well as Lisa did and from Lisa for writing her out of the memoir of Marshall's life. Bobby seeks forgiveness from Marshall for not killing a racist white sheriff when he could have, but also from the white woman he loved most and from the black woman who bore his child, both of whom he abandoned in his psychic misery.

While taking an unflinching backward glance at the racial violence and cross-racial hate that consumed the 1960s, *And All Our Wounds Forgiven* also enshrines the decade as a time when "blacks and whites lived and worked and slept with each other," positing that by doing so they were "forever changed" (71). And it replaces the beloved photograph of John F. Kennedy with a portrait of his southern successor, Lyndon Baines Johnson, whom Lester depicts as the president who really understood the goals of the civil rights movement and who did more than any other white leader during that time to codify them into law. Reviewer Arnold Rampersad believes that Lester links Johnson and his King figure, John Calvin Marshall, as "victims of history in that they set in motion forces that led to their repudiation."[39]

As provocative, even hopeful, as this novel is with its message of forgiveness, as poignant as it is with its long list of wounds that need to be forgiven, Lester's vision seems compromised by his portrayal of Lisa as a sexual saint ministering almost exclusively to Cal's sexual needs, even though she is supposedly his perfect soul mate. Their special bond seems oddly reduced to the old stereotypical images of black male lust and white female desire.[40] The lengthy, explicit sex scenes overwhelm the supposed complexity and richness of their relationship. Lisa's final attempt to be "open and honest" about her interracial affair in an e-mail to her husband seems cowardly, an example of confession without real dialogue, and her e-mail message—a paean to Cal's large penis, "his stallion, his eagle"—might come across to some readers as an ill-conceived attempt to wound a white man in a novel purporting that all wounds be forgiven (180–81). By having blacks and whites confess their in-nermost secrets as well as recognize their failings, the novel works as a fictional version of South Africa's Truth and Reconciliation Commission, but in *And All Our Wounds Forgiven* little real racial reconciliation occurs, because the charac-ters who most need to talk are not in dialogue. Marshall is dead, and since An-drea is on her deathbed, she is unable to speak when Bobby and Lisa seek her out. Thus, although the confessions by her bedside relieve internal pain, they do little else within the world of the novel. However, the novel's cross-racial confessional form suggests to readers that acknowledging old wounds, under-standing why they were inflicted, and seeking forgiveness are necessary steps toward racial healing that Americans have yet to take. The novel's strength lies in the number of its voices and the fact that none silences any other out of anger. Lester's fiction presaged a deep need among aging civil rights activists to talk about the movement's repressed wounds, as evidenced by recent mem-oirs, such as *Deep in Our Hearts: Nine White Women in the Freedom Movement* (2000) and Alice Walker's *The Way Forward Is with a Broken Heart* (2000).

With a few exceptions, love affairs between black men and white women have remained the province of black authors—until very recently. In the 1980s and especially the 1990s, white women writers have become increasingly interested in this subject. Because the black male–white female sexual relationship was the old South's strongest taboo, many white people have assumed such love affairs never happened, though historians like Martha Hodes have begun to document that they occurred as early as the seventeenth century.[41] Recently southern white women have been intent on setting the record straight in their fiction, crafting plots of secret interracial love that surprise both characters and readers—stories so long suppressed that the truth has virtually disappeared in the white South's collective memory. Novels by Rita Mae Brown, Myra McLarey, and Ellen Douglas, for example, focus not so much on the interracial sexual relationships as on the effects of keeping such love affairs secret. Thus these novelists reveal to their readers the possibility of interracial love, even as they withhold the happily-ever-after ending. These narratives are shaped by secrets of interracial sex, even though the relationships for the most part occur offstage.

   In *Southern Discomfort* (1982) Rita Mae Brown writes about such an affair, but as only one in a series of taboo loves, which occurred in a society that pre-tended they did not: white women desire black men, sons desire mothers, aristocrats desire prostitutes, and women desire women. Hortensia Banastre's young black lover, Hercules Jinks, dies in a freak railroad accident early in the story, perhaps so that Brown can move on to other taboo relationships that supposedly do not exist in the South. Brown's prologue sets the light tone of the novel and introduces the nature of the secrets to be revealed: "The town resembled a stud farm, although everybody lied through their teeth about fucking."[42] In *Southern Discomfort* Brown dismantles southern honor, unmasks southern manners, and sends racial and sexual mores packing. A systematic revelation of secrets drives the plot and startles both characters and readers—right down to the last page, when the burial preparations for the prostitute Blue Rhonda Latrec reveal that she is a man. The discomfort referred to in the title results from both the psychological pain of repressed desires and the social costs to reputations if desires are fulfilled. Proof exists of Hortensia and Hercules' interracial affair in the form of a child she secretly bears and whom her black maid cares for as her own. When the child finally discovers her paternity, she confronts her biological mother but chooses to protect her reputation at the same time by basing their special bond on the shared secret. This choice means that in 1982 Rita Mae Brown did not fully tackle the subject of biracial identity that writers in the 1990s have found so fascinating.

Unlike Rebecca Harding Davis's nineteenth-century prototype, the black men in these recent novels by white women are not tragic mulattos who could pass for white. In Davis's 1867 novel *Waiting for the Verdict,* a white woman rejects a mulatto doctor as a suitor when he reveals his true ancestry. In recent novels it is the beauty of a black man's body that attracts a white woman's attention—not so much as an exotic erotic object, but as a handsome human figure. Early in *Water from the Well* (1995), Myra McLarey shows her readers how she wants them to read skin color by having an older white woman stare at two men's bodies during a baseball game, thankful the night is warm and thus clothing scanty: one of them is white, David Ben Sugars, "naked to the waist at the game that day, his skin a rich and glowing bronze," and the other black, Samuel Daniel McElroy, "with skin the color of walnuts or molasses."[43] In *The Rock Cried Out* (1979), Douglas similarly has her white female character, Lelia, call attention to her black lover's body, rather than his race. Douglas, however, is careful to show how racial discrimination can be written on the body when Delia sees Sam many years later, after he has been released from Parchman

Prison Farm a physically "damaged" man. She cannot hold back the tears as she remembers how his physical beauty mesmerized her when she first saw him taming a colt: "I stood a long time watching him work. . . . He had taken off his shirt and hung it on the fence and I watched the muscles in his back and shoulders move as he stroked the colt and talked to him . . . watched as if I were in a trance, feeling the heat of the sun on my arms and face and the movement of the air, like breath, heavy with the smell of the chinaberry blooms that hung everywhere in the woods like a sweet lavender mist. I hadn't thought of a man for almost a year—hadn't thought of wanting sex."[44] Such scenes work not to negate race but to discount the notion that the interracial attraction is motivated only by race, that curiosity about racial difference heightens sexual interest. In these novels, as in Albert French's *Holly,* white women initiate the interracial relationship, a move that undermines the white racist myth of the black man's sexual aggression.

In *Water from the Well* McLarey questions a contemporary notion that southerners were completely socially segregated before court-ordered desegregation; throughout the novel she presents readers with clandestine interracial encounters at unexpected moments. Beginning with a baseball game between segregated teams on a hot day in 1919, McLarey quickly lets readers in on her characters' secret desires, as players and fans survey each other's partially clothed bodies across the color line on the playing field and in the stands. For example, the white third baseman, who should be focusing on the black power hitter at the plate, is thinking about his lover, "Delie Turner the colored woman with glossy hair and skin the color of pecans" (10). Through several filter characters, McLarey reveals a variety of interracial encounters, typically at night and behind closed doors. She positions her readers variously as eavesdroppers and voyeurs, thereby allowing them to penetrate the southern white cover-up not only of interracial rape but also of interracial love.

At one point, readers look over the shoulder of David Ben Sugars, the town's most handsome white man, as he peeps through the window and discovers Isannah Sanders, the town's most beautiful white woman, making love with Samuel Daniel McElroy, the town's most handsome black man. David Ben has desired Isannah for years but has never approached her. Because he also respects Samuel Daniel, David Ben's first response to their lovemaking is to be awestruck at their "audacity" and thankful that other white townspeople who would not admire their courage have not seen what he has. His second response is to repress the memory of the transgression he has observed: "That was before he came to his senses and realized it was his imagination, that it was the way the shadows fell, and his tired eyes from being up all night, and all the talk that his card-playing friends were given to, that what he saw had been a colored man at all. It was the shadows that made him look so dark, that made it look like anyone at all. After all Isannah Sanders, everyone knew, was beyond reproach" (174). As readers we never know for sure whether we have witnessed a black man and a white woman making love, but the text's circumstantial evidence points heavily in that direction. We know that David Ben makes some noise as he steps back in shock and that Isannah Sanders immediately leaves town, never to return. Furthermore, the first time we are privy to her thoughts, Isannah is remembering the rich "mahogany" of Samuel Daniel's skin at the baseball game. In writing *Water from the Well* in this mystifying way, McLarey demonstrates how the facts of interracial love were lost to posterity because of the enormity of the taboo.

In *The Rock Cried Out* Ellen Douglas shows how the revelation of such secrets changes individuals' lives and revises a region's myths. When Lelia offhandedly reveals to her nephew Alan that in the 1950s she had a passionate, stormy affair with Sam Daniels, their black tenant farmer, Alan, a college student who prides himself in being a liberal thinker about race relations, is stunned: "Wait! Wait! I'm too young to hear such things. And about my own aunt!" (131). Douglas drops this revelation like a bomb directly in the center of the novel so that readers will experience some of the same shock as Alan. The truth about Lelia and Sam's affair complicates Alan's relationship to the farm, to his family, and to Sam, who has been his mentor, and it propels him to uncover the hidden interracial history of his Mississippi community. Alan begins by collecting oral histories, which Douglas embeds in the text; he ends by revealing that the process of uncovering suppressed stories has enabled him to write the novel that we are reading. In addition to Lelia's sexual history, Alan discovers a story much like the one Reynolds Price tells in his novel *The Surface of Earth* (1975): a well-respected white man has taken a black woman as his common law wife but has allowed neighbors and extended family members to assume she is his housekeeper. Social roles allocated by gender and race made the logistics of clandestine interracial love easier for white men and black women than for white women and black men. The suppressed stories Alan uncovers complicate southern racial history in a variety of other ways—from the white union organizer who tries to unite blacks and whites along class lines to the light-skinned African American couple who want to adopt the organizer's daughter when he is killed and raise her as a person of color: "She could have passed as ours. . . . But of course that was out of the question" (220). Alan finds that encouraging people to tell the truth about the past is easier than getting the truths published: "None of these stories lent themselves to the needs of *The New York Times*—or *The Speckled Bird*. I doubt they would have borne out anybody's theories—economic, political, moral—or mythological" (145). But the very failure of the stories to live up to stereotyped expectations about southern race relations is precisely Douglas's point for making their revelation the central subject of *The Rock Cried Out*. If audience expectations determine publication, how will the suppressed truths get published? Alan finds that in the 1970s he must write these truths about the South into fiction, for they will not sell as facts.

Douglas uses an outsider to the South, Alan's girlfriend Miriam, to illustrate the difficulty in getting nonnatives to accept southern interracial love. Miriam predictably simplifies the unhappy outcome of Sam and Lelia's love affair by reducing the causes to race alone, missing the very human emotions of jealousy and lust and revenge and love of place. Douglas uses Miriam's reductive language to construct a parodic representation of the outsider's perception of southerners' behavior. As Alan's Aunt Lelia histrionically lists what she was willing to relinquish for her black lover, Sam—"friends, family, my country"— and bemoans Sam's refusal to leave the South, to go to Harlem or Paris with her, Miriam interrupts: "Weren't you, no matter what happened, an enemy? I mean, *white?* Wouldn't that enter into it?" (140). As readers get to know Sam, we see that the motivations for his refusal to leave are neither as simple as Miriam thinks (white racism), nor as simple as Lelia thinks (insatiable male sexual desire), nor as simple as Alan thinks (love of farming). Rather, the Sam whom Douglas slowly reveals is a complex man, motivated by many strong feelings. Paradoxically, he is emotionally tied to the rural landscape of a region that has discriminated against him; ironically, he is a tenant farmer on the very land that his white lover's family owns. And as he later tells Alan, sexually he likes to hang free. In the account of this interracial affair, Douglas makes sure that the black man, as well as the white woman, freely asserts sexual agency. Interestingly, when Lelia and Sam meet again in the 1970s during Alan's sojourn at the farm, they begin a mutually sustaining friendship. Douglas is coy about whether they once again become lovers; that fact does not seem nearly as important as their friendship.

It has taken a southern white romance novelist to bring into the present the story of white female–black male love that white writers of serious fiction have relegated to the past. In *Forbidden Quest* (1998), Dar Tomlinson brings this plot out from under its cloak of secrecy and its pall of neuroses, in order to examine the viability of interracial love in the contemporary South. Romance fiction is susceptible to problems created by its strict formal conventions, and *Forbidden Quest* is no exception. Invariably in the romance, conflict is produced through a love triangle, which can make for sexual rivals across the color line and lead to stereotyping. In *Forbidden Quest* Cally's upper-class white fiancé is traditional, uptight, and controlling, and her Jamaican suitor Paul Michael Quest is an artist—bohemian, laid-back and accepting. His lilting refrain, "Don' worry, girl. Every little t'ing going to be *awl* right,"[45] captures the sensibility that makes him the hands-down favorite. The black woman Ebony, who fancies Paul Michael, is especially problematic. She is uneducated, obnoxious, and violent. Given Paul Michael's character, it seems unlikely that he would be romantically interested in Ebony, and indeed he is not. But Tomlinson leaves the nature of his friendship with her mysterious in order to create the suspense and tension that readers of romance novels expect, going so far as to include a fight between Ebony and Cally.

At first glance it looks as if Tomlinson takes the easy way out for white readers with her male romantic lead by neutralizing his blackness. Paul Michael is the son of a black Jamaican father and a white American mother, whom he has never known. Tomlinson portrays him as simultaneously exotic and safe for both her white protagonist and her white readers—a foreign man of color with "lush" lips and corn-rowed hair but with selective "white" features, "deepwater blue" eyes and a slender nose. But Paul Michael is not even as exotic as he first appears because the cornrows are a sign of Caribbean blackness that he has assumed in Savannah to play in a Jamaican band. In Jamaica, he dresses like a model from *GQ:* "close-cropped curly hair . . . khakis and a pink polo shirt" (8–9, 209). Tomlinson's characterization of Paul Michael is difficult to pin down. Certainly it is his "foreign and engaging" manner that first catches the eye of interior designer Cally Sinclair and enables her to move "above and away from the prejudice" of her native Savannah (36). But as the novel progresses, their relationship grows more serious because of a shared interest in art and a similar philosophy of life. Cally's decision to let him cornrow her thick hair, unruly in Savannah's humidity, and his choice of a preppy pink polo shirt can both be read as "wannabe" racial signifiers. This is the way Tomlinson's least cosmopolitan characters and perhaps some of her readers interpret these signs. But Tomlinson seems to suggest that some, such as Cally's cornrows, are pragmatic cultural exchanges. For example, Cally loves the Jamaican food Paul Michael prepares for her because her white fiancé is a martinet about her weight. Thus, in characterizing Cally and Paul Michael as she does, Tomlinson could also be read as celebrating cultural hybridity between races and affirming diversity within racial groups. If interpreted this way, the novel would work to deconstruct notions of monolithic black identity, which bell hooks argues can type black people in two categories, as "black-identified and white-identified."[46] Despite this romance novel's shortcomings (and there are several),[47] *Forbidden Quest* does not totally neutralize racial difference in order to more easily enable interracial romance. Both Paul Michael and Cally know that white people in Savannah will see him quite simply as "black," no matter his nationality or biracial bloodlines, and it is that reality that they encounter as they continue their relationship. The interracial couple faces a difficult choice: to combat racism in the American South or sexism in Jamaica. The choice Tomlinson selects for her ending is the white woman's fantasy—to be treated like a Rastafarian queen and allowed to pursue her decorating career, while promoting interracial harmony in the southern city she loves. While Tomlinson puts realistic doubts in Paul Michael's mouth about whether he will be able to survive the racism directed at an interracial couple in the South, she leaves no doubt in readers' minds that love will conquer all, because the action-packed plot presents them with a variety of hurdles that *together* they clear with aplomb. The romance genre guarantees that.

White Men, Black Women, and Hidden Love

In the nineteenth century, both before and after the Civil War, white novelists, though rarely from the South, employed the love affair between a white man and a black woman as a vehicle for illustrating the common humanity of blacks and as a hope for racial reconciliation. But many African American novelists treated such affairs as a sad fact of life or a threat to black solidarity. While events of the 1960s released a flood of fiction examining black male–white female couples, treatment of white male–black female couples, so prominent in nineteenth-century fiction, ebbed. But this tide seems to have turned at the very end of the twentieth century. Intimacy between white men and black women has figured in several recent novels and even more nonfiction about the Old South. The nonfiction includes Carrie McCray's *Freedom's Child: The Life of a Confederate General's Black Daughter* (1998), Edward Ball's *Slaves in the Family* (1998), Henry Wiencek's *The Hairstons* (1999), and perhaps most notably, Annette Gordon-Reed's *Thomas Jefferson and Sally Hemings: An American Controversy* (1997), which ultimately argues that white male historians did a disservice not only to black Americans but to all Americans in refusing to see the truth of interracial intimacy. Twenty years after Fawn Brodie's speculations in *Thomas Jefferson: An Intimate History* (1974) and Barbara-Chase Riboud's fictional follow-up in *Sally Hemings* (1979), the United States appears more willing to accept a founding father's transgressions. As a result popular culture cannot get enough of the Jefferson-Hemings story, which many white historians thought they had laid to rest in the 1980s.[48] Lingering doubts about the story's veracity that helped make the Merchant-Ivory film *Jefferson in Paris* (1995) a flop at the box office were much less evident four years and several DNA tests later, when the television miniseries *Sally Hemings: An American Scandal* (1999) made its debut.

In the preface to her persuasive study about Jefferson and Hemings, Gordon-Reed argues that Chase-Riboud's novel *Sally Hemings* "has been the single greatest influence shaping the public's attitude about the Jefferson-Hemings story."[49] Intrigued by Brodie's argument and dismayed by other historians' dismissal of it, Chase-Riboud breathed life into fictional characters in order to explore the emotions that might have led to such an unlikely interracial affair in real life. She portrays Jefferson as not only the president of the United States and a gentleman who promised his dying wife Martha never to remarry, but also a healthy young widower and a southern slave owner of a light-skinned slave, who happened to be his dead wife's half sister. Sally Hemings was a slave, but Chase-Riboud reminds readers that she was also a beautiful woman, who came of age not at Monticello but in Jefferson's household in Paris and who, because she happened to be in France with Jefferson's daughters, acquired an education that she never would have received in Virginia. Chase-Riboud's novel allows readers to see Hemings's humanity, and it encourages readers to accept Jefferson's complexity. In *Yearning* (1990), bell hooks argues that "no one seems to know how to tell the story" of white men romantically involved with slave women because long ago another story supplanted it: "that story, invented by white men, is about the overwhelming desperate longing black men have to sexually violate the bodies of white women." She predicted that the suppressed story, if told, would explain how sexuality could serve as "a force subverting and disrupting power relations, unsettling the oppressor/oppressed paradigm."[50] In *Sally Hemings* Chase-Riboud does just that by attempting to answer the questions most often asked about the Jefferson-Hemings liaison: Could Jefferson love a slave? Could a slave love her enslaver? The extended conceit that Chase-Riboud develops to answer both questions is an emotional paradox—to be in love is to be enslaved.

The question of whether Jefferson could have loved a slave, Chase-Riboud tackles first by fashioning a fictional frame around her historical figures. In 1830 a young white man, Nathan Langdon, meets the infamous but reclusive Sally Hemings while taking the census in Albemarle County, Virginia. Even though Sally is fifty-six when they meet, Nathan finds himself "unnerved by her physical beauty" and startled to discover that she is "fair enough to be his mother."[51] He becomes the first in a series of characters—present and past, historical and fictional—that Chase-Riboud uses to verify Sally's extraordinary beauty and appearance of whiteness, even before she stages the first encounter between Jefferson and Sally. Nathan becomes so obsessed with her and the secrets she reveals to him that he makes repeated visits after his official one as a census taker. When she learns, however, that he has changed her race and that of her sons Madison and Eston to white on the census, she banishes him. Although he changes the historical record in order to protect Jefferson's reputation (miscegenation was illegal), Nathan tells her he has changed her identity in order to protect her from being banished from Virginia, now that she is free (Virginia law required all freed slaves to leave the state). Nathan argues that if one employs Jefferson's definitions of racial identity in *Notes on the State of Virginia*, Sally is technically white. With this presumptive act, Nathan becomes both the first in a long line of amateur and professional historians who distort the truth about Sally Hemings and a supersleuth determined to "unravel" the "mystery" of her attraction (91).

Chase-Riboud uses Nathan's subsequent meetings with the historical figures John Quincy Adams, Aaron Burr, and John Trumbull as much to verify that Jefferson actually loved Sally Hemings as to corroborate the truth of their liaison. Much as psychoanalytic reader-response critic Norman Holland argues that readers interpret texts through the context of their own identity themes,[52] each man reads Jefferson differently, based on his own psychology and ideology as well as his own personal relationship with Jefferson, but none doubts Jefferson's love for Sally. John Quincy Adams—with his "Yankee sense of thrift," his distrust of Jefferson's "affected simplicity," his own abolitionist principles, and the stories his parents John and Abigail have told him—bases his certainty of that love on Jefferson's "duplicity." Noting Jefferson's inexplicable turn away from abolition after he returned from Paris, Adams muses, "That such an unnatural love may have changed the course of history, undoubtedly preventing Jefferson from using his power and genius to turn the tide against slavery instead of being an accomplice to all its darkest and most passionate aspects, was tragic indeed" (164–65). While Adams decides that Jefferson's greatest weakness was self-deception, Aaron Burr casts his vote for hypocrisy, because he is furious with Jefferson for having him arrested for treason and thus denying him the presidency. Aware of Sally's great beauty and mindful of his own bastard children, Aaron Burr argues that Sally surely seduced Jefferson, whose "cold façade" hid uncontrolled sensuality (174). Indeed, at the same time that Burr hates Jefferson, Burr admires his courage in the Hemings affair: "If a man arrives at love, no matter how, when, or why—love beyond convention—then he has already lived well. Does not every man dream of some overwhelming, unfathomable love? But few have the courage to risk it, to keep it, or to honor it" (176). The painter John Trumbull, although an abolitionist and no admirer of Jefferson's "atheism, his want of credibility, his stupidities in military matters" (184), identifies with "the pain" Jefferson felt in loving a "forbidden woman" and in having illegitimate sons whom he could not acknowledge and who hated him because of it. Because the love of Trumbull's life was a socially unacceptable woman of the lower class, he knows the feelings "of not being able to protect her . . . of always being something of a coward in her eyes because of it" (183). Although no likeness of Sally Hemings survives, Chase-Riboud imagines that drawings existed, since Trumbull could have sketched Sally when he went to Paris to paint portraits for *The Surrender of Lord Cornwallis at Yorktown* and *The Declaration of Independence*. As Chase-Riboud represents it, Trumbull's self-protective belief that "the history of private passions has no place in public history" (184) leads him not only to deny Nathan's request for corroboration of the liaison but also to destroy his sketches of Sally.

Chase-Riboud's portrait of the complex duality of the love between Sally Hemings and Thomas Jefferson contains elements of all three stories, but the trajectory of her plot most resembles John Quincy Adams's analysis: "It was power that was the great deceiver, and those who wielded it were the first to be deceived. How well he knew. It was Jefferson himself who had been the first deceived. He had deceived himself into believing he could love a woman he held in slavery. He had deceived Sally Hemings into believing a man that held her in such servitude could love her. Adams wondered suddenly if she had realized this finally, or had she loved him to the end?" (168). Chase-Riboud answers Adams's question by imagining scenes of intimacy between Thomas and Sally throughout their life together. She envisions a love for Sally that begins in the innocence of youth and in a foreign country, with high expectations that the power of their love would naturally lead to life together in France, if not to freedom in America. But if Chase-Riboud begins their lifelong affair with Sally's belief in her power over Jefferson—to "part that beautiful mouth with desire" and "fill those eyes with agony or joy" (120)—she suggests that Sally quickly realized that her power to control Jefferson only extended so far. For Jefferson had an equally passionate and idealistic dedication to the young country he helped create and an undying love for Monticello. Although Chase-Riboud imagines that attending the trial of Nat Turner made Sally aware that her lover had also been her enemy, Chase-Riboud does not give an easy answer to questions about the nature of their love. Instead she suggests that the answer changes depending on the variables of place and time, public and private moments. The inception of Thomas Jefferson and Sally Hemings's mutual desire in Paris, combined with the race relations in Virginia, fuels the tragic ironies that underlie their liaison. If Jefferson had freed Sally when they returned to Monticello, he would have lost the love of his life because of Virginia's law that freed slaves had to leave the state. If Sally had chosen freedom by staying in France, she would have lost the love of her life as well. Chase-Riboud complicates the power dynamic in Adams's perception of the relationship by giving Sally the power to fulfill Jefferson's sexual and emotional needs and by portraying them both as enslaved first by their desire and finally by their love's history. By intertwining their love story with the young white census taker's power to control their story, Chase-Riboud, like Ellen Douglas, asks questions about history, memory, and truth. Like Ralph Ellison, she suggests that historical fiction must sometimes serve as the repository for historical truth when the collective historical memory has repressed the facts.[53]

Southern white male writers are also beginning to explore how sexual attraction across the color line can subvert and disrupt power relations. Their stories are driven by the ironies generated when southern honor intersects with cross-racial desire and when the conventions of a racially segregated society conflict with traditional chivalric gender roles. In their plots, white men transgress southern racial customs not by having interracial affairs, but by publicly acknowledging their love for black women. Both Donald McCaig's *Jacob's Ladder: A Story of Virginia during the War* (1998) and James Kilgo's *Daughter of My People* (1998) turn on conflicts generated when southern honor competes with cross-racial desire, when reputations of racial identity belie the truths of racial genealogy, and when chivalric gender roles conflict with southern racial codes.

Jacob's Ladder is a capacious novel that prods readers to rethink the Civil War and its aftermath, perhaps most surprisingly the social mobility that the war afforded a few poor whites and some African Americans. Duncan Gatewood, the son of a prominent landowner in the Shenandoah Valley, becomes intimately involved with the contradictions in southern society after he falls in love with Midge, a mulatto slave, and conceives a child with her. His father tries to erase this fact by marrying Midge off to a slave she does not love and by exiling Duncan to Virginia Military Institute. At the end of the college term, Duncan's father administers the ultimate final examination by forcing him to meet Midge's new husband and to accept his own son Jacob as his slave. McCaig employs a familiar nineteenth-century trope, making Jacob "as white as" Duncan and forcing Duncan to contemplate his son's future as "a field hand perhaps, a woods worker like Rufus or a house nigger like Pompey."[54] Still in love with Midge and falling in love with their child, Duncan angrily raises his hand to strike his father. However, equally determined to be the southern gentleman his father expects him to be, Duncan manages to check his rage, but only by biting his own hand so hard that blood spatters onto Midge and Jacob. Duncan's reflex reconsideration of his seemingly instinctual paternal response symbolizes both the contradictions inherent in the southern code of honor and the epistemological problems of racial and familial identity in the nineteenth-century South. In protecting his father from the blow, Duncan has protected the Gatewood family reputation but has harmed himself. By honoring his father's desire to keep the family's bloodlines pure, he dishonors the new family he has created with Midge—producing the very southern family fictions that have turned contemporary southern historians, both professional and amateur, into detectives.

When Duncan later fails to persuade his father to allow him to marry Midge and to recognize Jacob as his son, his father sells Midge and Jacob. In so doing,

Mr. Gatewood effectively banishes the muse who has provoked Duncan's preliminary but "imaginative" new thinking about southern race relations (70). Duncan's inchoate questions about his society's racial code are not powerful enough to throw off the heavy mantle of southern honor and the awful reality that the woman he loves is a slave. After a period of dissipation, in which Duncan attempts to forget his sorrow by drinking and gambling, he joins the Confederate Army, hoping that "[h]onor will be retrieved" (93). Although the war deprives Duncan of his youth, his good looks, and his right arm, he feels that courageous military service has restored his honor. He never once considers that a bolder move would have been to join the Union Army and fight for Midge's freedom. McCaig suggests that even a sensitive, thoughtful, rebellious Virginia gentleman's imagination could not make such an enormous leap in the nineteenth century.

McCaig employs the women who love Duncan, Midge and Sallie, to reveal how southern notions of both honor and racial identity have been deceptive. For Sallie, the white woman who nurses Duncan in a Richmond hospital, the war restores nothing; rather, it takes away life and limb, health and well-being, all for an ignominious cause. To Sallie, honor is an empty abstraction that keeps men tragically enthralled. She responds to Duncan's rhapsodies about Dixie, the Confederate battle flag, and General Lee's army by averting her face and declaring, "I have seen too much of honor" (305). For Midge, whom Duncan later meets by chance at a party in Richmond, "honor" is a commodity, which can be "preserved" only because "southern gentlemen . . . can sell their embarrassments" (335). For Donald McCaig, honor is a poignant metaphor for the charade that southern white men lived. What the war has really done for Duncan is to restore his public reputation as a gentleman by allowing him to fight honorably for the Confederacy. But privately he finds that he must come to terms with his own guilty conscience for allowing his father to sell his son Jacob into slavery and for giving up the woman he loved. Guilt continues to eat away at Duncan, because he has seen the beautiful southern lady Midge has become—a fact that produces the change in ideology his youthful imagining failed to provoke. Slowly Duncan realizes that the cause he has fought for was not just. Only then does Sallie consent to marry him.

In *Jacob's Ladder* McCaig exposes racial identity to be a charade as well. What the war has done for Midge is to establish her reputation as white. Eric Sundquist argues that under the southern taboo of miscegenation, racial identity became "a radical act of imagination," "either in an act of self-recognition or in the attribution of identity to another."[55] McCaig employs this idea when Midge and Duncan meet in Richmond. Midge tells Duncan how she let her imagination run wild during their youthful affair: "I pictured us married! Me: the mistress of Stratford! Ignorant pickaninny playing the lady. Imagine!" (336). Although Duncan never acts on his own radical act of "imaginative" thinking, Midge does, but it takes a poor white partner who is also a southern social climber to assist her. Silas Omohundru, the upwardly mobile slave trader who bought her from Mr. Gatewood, falls in love with her. Unlike Faulkner's Thomas Sutpen in *Absalom, Absalom!* Silas believes that what he can hide will not hurt either him or his design. Silas proposes to Midge once they have left Virginia and moved to the more cosmopolitan port city of Wilmington, North Carolina. There Silas abandons slave trading for the lucrative and glamorous job of blockade running. Midge seizes this opportunity to pass as white and easily becomes Marguerite, Silas's beautiful Bahamian wife. Although she does not love Silas, marriage to him ascribes to her son Jacob the racial identity that his biological father, Duncan, denied him. This marriage also unexpectedly allows her to prove to Duncan, when she encounters him again at that Richmond party, that her southern racial identity did not have to be her destiny. At first he does not recognize her, but then heartbreakingly he realizes that she has become "the lady" he once fleetingly imagined she could be. McCaig titles the chapter in which they meet "Charades" after the parlor game played that evening, but also to signify the racial masquerade that Marguerite has embarked on and that Duncan kindly pledges he will not divulge—an illusion of white racial purity that many white southerners still believe in, the southern family fiction that they have been reluctant to confront.

Although Marguerite cannot give Jacob the Gatewood family name, her choice to pass as white eventually makes Jacob the son of a Confederate war hero, if not a descendant of one of the First Families of Virginia. While Silas's blockade running in Wilmington makes him rich during the war, he cannot buy his way into southern high society, because he is a bastard, so he enlists in the Confederate Army to enhance his status. Eventually Silas posthumously earns his reputation as a southern gentleman by dying for the lost cause—with the result that Marguerite's position in Richmond society is also secured. She becomes a wealthy, well-respected Confederate widow, and as a result she succeeds in making Jacob both a gentleman and a graduate of Harvard Law School. By the 1930s, when she chooses to end her masquerade, Marguerite Omohundru is the aging matriarch of a prominent "white" family, who lives in "one of the grandest homes" in Richmond (247) and who belongs to the Virginia Historical Society—not quite First Family of Virginia, but not bad for a slave named Midge. Or so Donald McCaig seems to want his readers to think. And yet the narrative frame around his Civil War story suggests that he is striving for much more.

Unlike most African American novelists on the subject of passing, McCaig does not ascribe guilt to Marguerite's masquerade, but he does register her anger at not having been able to fulfill her own potential without the white mask. As recompense he gives her pride of accomplishment in having given her child a better life and no small amount of pleasure at having deceived the Richmond aristocracy. The way McCaig frames Marguerite's story suggests that his ultimate target is really the contemporary white myth of racial purity, not the older story of blacks passing as white. McCaig registers the shock of realization that he must have hoped many white readers would experience through the perspective of his unnamed young white WPA worker, herself a member of Richmond high society. Expecting to talk with Marguerite's black servant Kizzy about her life as a slave, the young white woman is speechless when she learns that it is Marguerite whose oral history she will be collecting. But she is willing to listen. The interviewer's family, however, pronounces Marguerite Omohundru "not herself" (247), and her father urges her to read Thomas Nelson Page's stories in order "to know" what Virginia's past was really like (295). The attempts by the young woman's family to deter her from taking Marguerite's story seriously call attention to southern white power in ascribing meaning to race and in controlling the South's interracial history (247).

Donald McCaig is a transplanted New Yorker who considers himself a Virginian after living twenty-five years on a farm in the Allegheny Highlands. He clearly sees himself as telling a different "Story of Virginia during the War" than Virginia's nineteenth-century chronicler, Thomas Nelson Page, told.[56] In his collection *In Ole Virginia* (1887), Page blames southern problems on northern interference, rather than on slavery and the contradictions inherent in southern racial codes and social customs. McCaig assigns blame very differently. His Confederate veteran, Duncan Gatewood, eventually judges himself "a damned coward" (299) for allowing his son to be sold into slavery and subsequently views Virginia plantation society, the slavery that supported it, and the Confederacy that defended it as the causes of the South's demise. In his final reassessment, Duncan's position resembles Robert E. Lee's 1869 comment, which provides McCaig his afterword: "So far from engaging in a war to perpetuate slavery, I am rejoiced that slavery is abolished. I believe it will be greatly in the interests of the South" (527).

The difference between Page's and McCaig's choice of frame narrators for their Civil War stories is equally significant. In Page's "Marse Chan" a former slave tells a northern tourist a fanciful story of happy darkies and genteel southern families, a romanticized tale of southern honor and Confederate glory. A century later, in *Jacob's Ladder* a former slave who is passing as white tells a native Virginian a revisionary story of southern dishonor and Civil War horrors and a cautionary tale about the bloodlines of Virginia's finest white families. Page was trying to convince skeptical nonnatives that Virginia's way of life was honorable; McCaig is trying to convince skeptical Virginians that stories like Page's have deprived them of the truth. By having the WPA worker choose Marguerite's oral history over Page's published stories, McCaig unseats Page as Virginia's Civil War chronicler and suggests a hidden Virginia history that some white Virginians are ready to hear.

In *Daughter of My People* (1998), James Kilgo similarly foregrounds the continuing "charade" of southern honor and southern race relations two generations after the slaves have been freed. Although his conclusion is not as provocative as McCaig's, his psychological portrait of a conflicted white man in love with a black woman is probing and extremely ironic. Set in rural South Carolina in the early twentieth century, the novel opens with a family Christmas dinner that depicts Byzantine interracial intertwinings across generations. Jennie Grant, a light-skinned black woman, serves dinner to her white half sister Sallie's family. Seated at the table is Jennie's white lover, Hart Bonner, who is Sallie's brother-in-law. According to southern custom, no one acknowledges Jennie as a member of Sallie's family or as the woman Hart loves, although she is heartily recognized for her skills as a servant and her talents as a cook. Kilgo employs Sallie's brother Jim, who is a college professor and one of the novel's four filter characters, to explain this scene for contemporary readers who might not understand what they have just witnessed: "The keeping of Negro women by white men had been going on in Heyward County for so long as to have become almost a custom. . . . It was as though the community had tacitly agreed with the offending members to participate in a great charade: we will gladly pretend that you are not engaged in this abomination if you will have the decency not to confront us with it. As long as both sides played by the rules, life limped along."[57]

The conflict in Kilgo's novel occurs when Hart ceases to play by these rules.

Just as in McCaig's novel, the contradictions in the southern code of honor become painfully problematic when the rules about race relations conflict with those governing gender relations. Because Hart is a filter character, readers can witness his conflicted thinking. When lower-class white men taunt Jennie as "the nigger girl Hart Bonner was fucking" (23), Hart's internalized chivalric code prompts him to spring to the defense of the woman he loves. But because Jennie is not white, Hart, much like McCaig's Duncan, quickly defers to his racial code, which dictates that white men cannot publicly acknowledge a liaison with a black woman. A subsequent incident brings the two sets of rules into conflict in such a complicated way that Hart cannot simply ignore the insult. A sleazy white man named Coe offends Jennie by offering to allow her to pay her debts with sexual favors. Hart's sister-in-law Sallie overhears both Coe's remarks and Jennie's response that Hart Bonner pays her debts. Hart is caught in a double bind in his desires to protect both Jennie and Sallie. But he finds that he cannot protect both his lover and his sister-in-law, for to protect Jennie would be to reveal the unmentionable to Sallie—that he loves a black woman. He chooses to protect Sallie, but in doing so he knows he dishonors Jennie, because Sallie continues to think of her "as a kept woman no different from any other colored girl" (18).

Reverberations of this incident ripple through the family, because Hart's half brother Tison grows furious with Hart for humiliating family members with his interracial liaison, which has become fodder for public gossip. Acting out his anger at this threat to family honor, Tison tries to put Jennie in "her place" at the holiday dinner, and Hart is unable to suppress his desire to defend her (126). Tensions between the brothers over Jennie double in the days ahead: in spying on Jennie's activities, Tison becomes attracted to her himself and makes sexual advances, which she spurns. When Tison is murdered, Hart naturally becomes a suspect. Once again Kilgo places his protagonist in a double bind. Hart did not kill Tison, but in order to defend himself in court, he would have to reveal the truth of his and Jennie's relationship, which would humiliate not only his mother and the other women in his family but also Jennie, who would be treated by the racist prosecutor as "Hart Bonner's nigger whore" (244). To protect all the women in his life, Hart decides that his only solution is to kill himself, using the chivalric code as his guide: "Any man unwilling to lay down his life for the woman he loved lived a life not worth the effort" (252). Thus, like McCaig, Kilgo shows that the codes southern white men lived by not only ruined their emotional well-being but actually endangered their lives.

Kilgo gives Jennie the last word on Hart's sacrifice, much as McCaig privileges the female assessment in *Jacob's Ladder*. Hart's attempt to defend family honor by hiding his liaison with Jennie proves futile, because Jennie tells the sheriff the truth and the papers publish her story. Ironically, Hart's attempt to protect Jennie actually liberates her not only from the claustrophobic secrecy of their affair but also from the Creighton family members who claim to want to protect her but who are really protecting themselves. While Jim, ever the professor, likens the passionate Hart to heroic characters of *The Iliad*, Jennie undercuts this romantic response, calling Hart a "poor, dear fool" (278) in the penultimate chapter, the only one that is presented from her perspective. Both Kilgo and McCaig base their fictions on actual events from southern history,[58] and both seem intent on honoring the black women whom other southern white men dishonored.

Although Reynolds Price also sets his story of interracial love in the past—1940s North Carolina—he is less interested in exposing past masquerades than in probing present difficulties in interpretations based solely on race. In Ernest Gaines's *Of Love and Dust*, southern black collective memory makes it difficult for the black narrator to move beyond fear of white retaliation in interpreting the bold behavior of Marcus and Louise. In Price's "The Fare to the Moon" (1991), southern white collective memory makes it difficult to move beyond race in interpreting Kayes Paschal's motives for beginning and ending an interracial affair. Kayes walks away from his rich wife, his doting fourteen-year-old son, and social prominence in his rural community outside Raleigh, so that he can live with Leah Birch, a beautiful light-skinned black woman, in her great-aunt's ramshackle house. No one can understand Kayes's behavior, least of all his wife, who has "money to spare from her banker daddy and blood so blue it could pass for ink."[59] Much of her anguish is generated by her inability to come up with an appropriate "explanation to give the world" (25), a desperate attempt to save face. Conventional explanations that have comforted southern white women for years—of white men clandestinely using dark-skinned women merely for sexual pleasure—do not hold in this case. The only explanation Daphne Paschal can come up with is that Kayes is "crazy" (25), the same explanation Louise Bonbon's family uses to explain her love affair with Marcus in *Of Love and Dust*. Daphne and her son, Curtis, have not talked about Leah, nor has Kayes mentioned her to Curtis during their four meetings in the six months he has been with her. This reticence is oddly but directly linked to the old rule of southern honor that the practice of miscegenation remains "irrelevant as long as the fact of it could be denied."[60] Daphne operates in a fantasy world where the fact of her husband's interracial affair, even though it cannot be denied, can be written off as "nothing but a nightmare" (27) if Kayes returns to her soon.

Price's narrative technique makes readers confront both the difficulty in knowing the truth when race is involved and the importance of trying to discern it. By juxtaposing characters' actions with alternating speculations about motives, Price forces readers to discover the complex motives beneath the most clichéd behavior. For example, readers learn that Leah is far from the helpless Negro Daphne likes to think of her as, or that readers familiar with nineteenth-century fictions of miscegenation may assume her to be. Leah has rebuffed many suitors, both black and white, male and female, and she makes "the first step forward" to meet Kayes (12). Price continues to surprise "readers" both within and outside the story who presume to foresee Leah's future as simply the tragic mulatta once Kayes leaves. When Kayes's brother Riley drives him to Raleigh for his army physical, they discuss Leah's welfare and plan for her future. Fearing that white racist reprisals against the interracial affair will make it impossible for Leah to find work and unsafe for her to stay alone in her house, Riley offers to assist Leah in leaving North Carolina. Subsequently readers learn that after meeting with Kayes's son Curtis and hearing how much the love affair has hurt him, Leah has made her own plans, deciding to leave even if Kayes fails his physical and is unable to enlist. Thus Price makes her motivation a human one, a feeling of guilt she shares with Kayes for their adultery, rather than a motivation grounded in race relations—which is not to say that Leah is unaware of the problems their race mixing has caused. The following exchange between Leah and Curtis underscores this point:

> "Did me being colored make it worse on you?"
> Curtis knew at once and shook his head firmly. "It was you being in this world, out here." (31)

The scene with Curtis reminds readers that Leah is not simply a racialized body, even if the scene with Kayes and Riley has encouraged readers to think of her that way. Price's narrative strategy illustrates that misunderstandings will be inevitable if race is the only lens through which readers view human relationships.

In making the reasons for Leah's decision and Curtis's reaction more complex than race alone, Price aids his readers in reinterpreting Kayes's seemingly predictable behavior as well. This is more difficult, because Kayes is not as astute in understanding motivations as Leah is, nor are he and Leah as frank in discussing race as Curtis and Leah are. One of the most difficult tasks, but one of the most crucial, in reading "The Fare to the Moon" is determining what the two lovers feel for each other and why, the perennial question in interracial affairs. Price begins his novella, which opens with the morning Kayes has to report for his army physical, without identifying the race of the still unnamed woman and man. Readers only know that the man has talked about a way of beating the draft without acting on it—drinking vinegar and swallowing prune pits to mimic stomach ulcers—and that the woman has bought prunes and left them out on the kitchen counter without saying a word to him. As a result, readers experience Kayes's and Leah's uncertainty about their future as the normal doubts of any World War II–era couple who have been together six months and find themselves faced with the draft without having talked about marriage. However, when Kayes gives Leah two fifty-dollar bills, Price injects race and its ability to color interpretation. Primed by southern racial history, Leah immediately thinks, "Oh Jesus, now here it comes. Like every other white man God ever made, he thinks we can cross this out with money" (5). Her comment encourages readers to think of Kayes as the proverbial southern white hypocrite who has taken advantage of a defenseless black woman. But Price causes his readers to reevaluate Kayes's gesture when Leah revises her first response. She sees that Kayes "managed it altogether differently" (5) by telling her for the first time how good she has been to him and how much he loves her. In a subsequent scene, Kayes gives his son Curtis the same amount of money. This link suggests that he is treating Leah as either a family member or a dependent.

Just how different Kayes really is from "every other white man" is up for debate and provides much of the novella's ambiguity. The day he goes for his army physical, readers, like Leah, have difficulty interpreting his farewell to her. Although he gives her his watch, a symbolic object they have used on days when she doubted his return, he does not say that he will continue to live with her if he comes back alive. That Kayes has not used the prunes to avoid the draft takes on added significance. Is he being patriotic, or extricating himself passively from an affair with a black woman, or simply from an affair? Price forces his readers into constant reinterpretation of this incident. One such time occurs when Leah admits that her own patriotism is a reason she "couldn't tell Kayes to shirk, even with that box of prunes I bought" (10).

Although not a constant source of irritation, the pressure of southern racial history erupts on the first day of their six-month relationship as well as the last, and Price makes readers painfully aware of the layer of difficulty it adds to their ability to understand each other's words and gestures. By giving readers dual flashbacks of their reacquaintance as adults on the day of Leah's great-aunt's funeral, Price shows that although each is attracted to the other's good looks, each then fixates on race, which causes both to abruptly dismiss the possibility of friendship. Leah's thought, "I've never been partial to grown white people," is immediately complicated when she remembers that her mother and aunt have told her that white people you know can be trusted. Her next thought is that she has known Kayes since she was four. Her physical attraction to him is so powerful that it overwhelms her memory of "how hard his family had worked poor Red and for what slim pay" (12). As a result, she does not base her relationship with Kayes on his family's relationship with her great-aunt Red, who was their housekeeper. Juxtaposed with Leah's memory of that day is Kayes's interior monologue, which reveals an initial preoccupation with race that parallels Leah's: "The Negro part had concerned him at once. When he turned away from Red's graveside, and Leah there behind him, he told himself 'Forget her *now.*' And he nearly succeeded. Despite the fresh sight of Leah's good face and his older memory of tales his friends told, long years back about colored girls." But on encountering his wife, he thinks of Leah again, not as simply a "Negro," but as one of the most beautiful women "in the county" (15)—a woman who might respond to him with the affection and attention he does not get from Daphne. His next thought, like Leah's, is about how long they have known each other—a fact that trumps the fear of transgressive attraction across the color line.

Although "The Fare to the Moon" is set in the 1940s like *Of Love and Dust,* it was written decades later and thus reflects concerns of the 1990s rather than the 1960s. Price's interracial lovers are not attracted perversely because of race, as Gaines's characters initially are, but are drawn together by powerful forces that overcome the reluctance that an initial preoccupation with race causes. These forces are the same as those that draw any couple together: first and foremost mutual physical and personal attraction, but, second, shared experiences. Leah's great-aunt Red had been the Paschal family housekeeper. The price of their bliss is high, just as that of other adulterous couples, because their affair hurts other people. But this price—this "fare to the moon"—has brought Leah the only love affair of her life and Kayes the unconditional love of a beautiful, kind, and intelligent woman. Kayes's time with Leah has given him intimate knowledge of a black woman that takes him beyond his region's racially inflected thinking. That is why in each of his interior monologues he repeatedly seeks to be honest about the "truth" of their relationship, and that is why Price concludes his last monologue with this assessment of Leah: "This much was true—he had spent from eight to twenty-four hours a day, these six months, beside a kind intelligent person who fit against his mind and body, and *chose* to fit, in every way a sane human being would pray to find this side of death. She was one real woman named Leah Birch—whatever her color, or the size of her house—who had finally cared so deep and steady as to all but fill the gully cut in him by his beautiful mother when she heard his prayers one December night and kissed his cheek and then left him forever by morning" (58). This final restatement of the "truth" about his feelings for Leah, Kayes's fullest so far, is necessary at this point because he has been contemplating a return to Daphne and Curtis if he comes back from the war alive. The reason Kayes gives for making this preliminary choice—"starting over in decency" (57)—can be read in several ways, foregrounding once again Price's concern with interpretation. Does Kayes think of his previous behavior as "indecent" because he has been living with a black woman or because he has been committing adultery, or both?

The outcome of Price's plot could have been a happy one for the interracial couple, because Kayes has taken the step that McCaig's and Kilgo's protagonists do not take. He lives openly with Leah. He could continue to do that and even suggests to Curtis that he might. The strong emotions Kayes feels for both Curtis and Leah put him in limbo. When Riley drops Kayes off at the induction center, he asks how he will get "home" if he fails the physical. That he has not thought of this possibility makes it clear that he has come to think of war as an escape from his dilemma. At the same time that he chooses not to think about "the word *home* (where on Earth was that?)," his answer (he will get a bus back to Leah's house) reveals where his emotional home is at this point in the novella (20). Kayes is truly in a quandary about what to do, but Price lets chance tip the scales in his thinking while he waits to have his physical. Kayes unexpectedly encounters a childhood friend, Brutus Bitford, which reminds him of the embarrassment Mrs. Bitford's love affair caused her son. Then after his physical, when the reality of war's horror displaces his use of it as an escape, Kayes decides he wants to live and finds himself contemplating the future. His farewell call to Curtis leads to an unexpected conversation with Daphne and the discovery that she has not stopped loving him. Finally, both his farewell call to Riley and his own knowledge of the gulf left in his life by his mother's departure further fuel his guilt about how he has treated his son. Only such a review of the events that precede Kayes's thoughts about returning to Daphne and Curtis will allow a reader to see that Kayes's use of the word *decency* concerns how he should treat his son, not what people think about his affair with a black woman. That Price concludes Kayes's monologue with thoughts of Leah, rather than of Curtis and Daphne, demonstrates how fully Kayes understands the incredible power of his love for Leah and hers for him as he contemplates the loss of that love.

Although Price takes the sad ending of their interracial affair beyond race, even as he shows the difficulty in interpreting their behavior this way, his novella also demonstrates that race relations affected this relationship more than Kayes knows. Because Leah is black, she has not been able to think about a future with Kayes or to ask his intentions. This aspect of their relationship, which the narrator reveals to readers, is one truth that Kayes does not discover, even though he senses less than total intimacy in their relationship: "part of Leah had stayed shut to him, the part of her mind that planned for him" (57). Kayes wonders briefly if his inability to read Leah has anything to do with her race, but he quickly backs away from such thinking, remembering that "he had known old Red like an easy book" (57).

Price interjects hope in a sad story by weaving throughout Kayes's story of interracial love and loss Curtis's story of growth and understanding. Curtis looks like his father, and Price gives their stories several important parallels but also some very significant differences. Like his father, Curtis is tired of Daphne's dependence on him. Like his father, Curtis is attracted to Leah's individuality and independence and takes pleasure in the way she makes him feel like a man. But whereas Kayes does not discuss race or his family with Leah, Leah and Curtis confront these issues directly the first time they meet. Kayes and Curtis each discuss Kayes's interracial affair with a childhood friend, but the circumstances are different. Kayes tells Brutus about his love for Leah, but he will probably never see him again. Curtis admits to his only friend, Cally, that he likes Leah and can even understand why his father has stayed with her. Unlike Kayes in the parallel scene with Brutus, Curtis calls Cally to task when he uses the word "nigger" (47). Kayes risks nothing; Curtis risks a great deal. For Kayes, telling "the truth" feels "like a fruitful island discovered after months at sea" (36–37), but the feeling comes too late for him to tell his son the truth about anything. During the four times Kayes sees Curtis in the six months after he leaves home, they do not talk about anything important. Next to Leah, Kayes thinks he has hurt Curtis, not Daphne, the most; but because father and son never talk honestly, Kayes never knows that Curtis and Leah meet. As a result, Kayes never learns what readers do—that the fact of Kayes's affair with Leah has certainly hurt Curtis, but that an understanding of Leah as a person has also taught him a great deal: "Curtis knew he had learned some large true thing that would lead him into a better life than he'd known till now—less mess, less meanness, fewer people draining his life for blood" (33–34).

Price gives the novella something of a double ending that takes it beyond a tragic story of interracial love lost. In concluding with Curtis's interior monologue and ending the novella with Curtis's dream, Price plays on the title of the book, *The Foreseeable Future,* in which "The Fare to the Moon" is collected. The night Curtis picks up his father's car from Leah's house, an errand that culminates in his frank conversation with Leah, he dreams that a friend, whom he later identifies as Kayes, has led him "home" after he has lost his way in the dark (60). Here Price highlights two thoughts that Kayes cannot reconcile. In living with Leah, Kayes feels he has gotten "lost" (17), but he can no longer think of the house that he lived in with Daphne as "home." As a result of this dilemma, he no longer knows where "home" (20) is. His inability to reconcile these conflicting feelings makes him glad he has been drafted and that the direction of his life is out of his hands. Significantly, Curtis's dream positions Kayes in the role of friend and rescuer leading him home. Although the narrator concludes Curtis's dream by stating that Curtis was "easing himself ahead with childish hope," a few brief sentences later, the narrator concludes the novella with a consoling sentence for readers: "At the least, that sight of a useful father let Curt sleep till Sunday daylight, clear and dry with slow church bells, the first whole day of his grown man's life" (60). With this hopeful sentence, Price tempers his contemporary readers' frustrations with the sad conclusion of the 1940s interracial affair. But it is Leah, whom Curtis meets because of his father's affair, who has really been Curtis's guide. She has turned him away from his mother's cloying concern with reputation and shown him his father's mistake in refusing to speak the truth: "Nobody had dealt with him like this, in his whole life till now—this clean dead-level eye-to-eye truth. He knew he was being rammed forward through time. Any second now, he would be a grown man, tall enough to do what was right" (30). In the "foreseeable future" it appears that Curtis will become the man his father was not able to be.

T. R. Pearson's *Blue Ridge* (2000) is a quirky exception to white male writers' affinity for reworking old stories about interracial love. This contemporary detective novel includes as a subplot the sexual relationship between a white male cop in rural Hogarth, Virginia, and a black female Park Service officer from Washington, D.C., who meet while investigating the murder of a black man on the Appalachian Trail and the defacement of a Confederate statue in town. Pearson uses their relationship in part as a barometer to measure the small-minded people who still inhabit small southern towns like Hogarth, where the locals watch the interracial couple "indelicately and with transparent disapproval." Despite this reaction, Ray Tatum and Kit Carson fall into bed together, mainly, it seems, because they are the only two liberals in town. Their relationship speaks more to creature comforts than emotional involvement, and Pearson views their sex scenes comically through the perspective of Ray's dog, Monroe, who is upset by the commotion of their copulation. In using humor for such a sensitive subject, Pearson breaks new ground.[61] However, the conventions of detective fiction, which dictate that the detective must be free to go where the next job leads, determine the novel's ending. The future of their relationship is left in doubt, because Kit returns to D.C. when they have solved the case. But Kit is willing and Ray is interested, so Pearson leaves readers thinking that this relationship may continue. Sure enough, Kit reappears briefly in *Polar* (2002), but because of the local-yokel point of view that Pearson selects for this sequel, their relationship is seen from a curious distance, and Kit functions as an arresting object of intense "local scrutiny meant to come off as worldly indifference."[62]

Because of its genre, *Blue Ridge* is more about crime solving than interracial love, but Pearson creates a very interesting moment between Kit and Ray, when he seems poised to explore important questions about racial solidarity as well as the viability of their relationship in a small Virginia town. Once they discover the murder victim's arrest record, Ray is surprised that Kit seems uninterested in locating the victim's murderer. Ray tells her he thought she would feel "differently" because "[h]e was one of yours." Kit is disappointed in Ray's racial naïveté at the turn of a new century: "Tell me something, all this yokel

trash around here, are they yours? Are you boys just one big cracker brotherhood?" But her rejoinder does not lead to further discussion.[63] Instead, Kit
abruptly walks away from Ray, and neither racial solidarity nor her abrupt departure is brought up the next time they are together. While Pearson glosses over
a potential difficulty in their relationship, he raises an interesting question for
his readers about the meaning of post–civil rights movement racial solidarity.

Unlike Pearson's Kit, the African American women that McCaig, Kilgo, and
Price create for their white male protagonists to fall in love with are all light-
skinned. Although this choice allows the writers to interrogate the social construction of racial identity, it can also be read as reifying white definitions of
female beauty. Aware that such a charge could be made, McCaig has Marguerite
self-consciously assess this literary practice in historical terms: "'It is curious,
is it not, that the lighter-skinned we are, the more anxious the dominant race
is to mate with us. Those first white men to sleep with the dark-skinned daughters of Africa were such bold pioneers!' She raised her invisible eyebrows mock-
ingly. 'I suppose it is more agreeable to make love with creatures that closely
resemble oneself. Narcissism is one of the South's notable frailties'" (20). In
some respects the black female characters in these white men's texts can also
be seen as examples of nineteenth-century literature's tragic mulatta: beautiful
(according to white definitions), accomplished, and moral, but mistreated.[64]
However, these writers do not fully follow nineteenth-century conventions. Although they do not shy away from depicting white racism's effect on African
Americans, they are intent on showing how racism deforms the lives and
minds of their white characters as well. The female characters are far from simply tragic victims of white men's love; they are depicted as strong, resource-
ful, and imaginative people, unlike the weak white men who love them. They
do not let their lives slip totally out of their control, despite the difficulties of
living in a racist society. Only in McCaig's novel is true love thwarted because
of race, and he uses this plotting device to begin his novel rather than end it,
as so many nineteenth-century novelists usually did. McCaig makes Midge/
Marguerite the mistress of her own fate, although her life never again includes
romance. Kilgo's story, too, picks up at a different point. Years after the beginning of an interracial love affair, his couple's concerns involve "the difficulty
of sustaining a secret passion": "Without a community to turn to, a surrounding circle of family and friends who thought of them as a couple and believed
in their future, they had no refuge from each other's recrimination."[65] Significantly, the white male writers have the African American women initiate the

interracial affairs. Given the southern history of white male aggression toward black women, they may be reluctant to have their white male characters make the first move in stories of interracial attraction. In these new southern historical novels, however, the end of the affair is as heartbreaking for the white man as it was for the tragic mulatta in nineteenth-century northern representations. But even so, these writers do not give up hope for cross-racial understanding; they position it in the next generation.

The way the white man and the black woman begin a love relationship is modified somewhat by white writer Connie Mae Fowler, who makes the attraction mutual and the move to fulfill desire simultaneous. Fowler's woman of color, Soleil Marie Beauvoir, is of mixed Haitian and Seminole Indian ancestry, a racial and ethnic mix crucial to the magical realism Fowler employs in *Sugar Cage* (1992). Although Fowler sets her love story in the more recent past, the tumult of the civil rights era still causes historical events to hang heavy on her interracial couple. But like Reynolds Price, Fowler is concerned with the contemporary social conditions and interpersonal dynamics that threaten interracial love. Magical realism allows her to depict realistically the nightmare of southern racial history and to avoid a predictable conclusion.

Set in the seedy central Florida town of Tiama, "Prison Capital of the World," *Sugar Cage* begins in 1945, spans more than two decades, and examines the race relations of two generations. Like so many other contemporary novelists concerned with race relations, Fowler chooses multiple perspectives to tell her story—a narrative technique that emphasizes the isolation of some characters but encourages readers to see connections that many characters cannot discern. Fowler creates two exceptions to these narrow views: Inez Temple, a poor black woman from Zora Neale Hurston's hometown of Eatonville, and Soleil Marie Beauvoir, a Haitian cane-field worker, are both clairvoyant. Soleil Marie is a voodoo priestess whose powers enable her to "hear the rhythms of love or hate," to protect those she loves from harm, to see goodness "behind the pain."[66] Inez is descended from a line of "good, old-fashioned witches," renowned locally for their "healing teas and protecting rituals" (11). Attempting to gain readers' trust in Inez's magical powers, Fowler begins the novel when Inez encounters Rose and Charlie Looney on their honeymoon, reads the "sugar cage" at the bottom of Rose's empty iced tea glass, and predicts that Rose is "going to let love eat her up" (17). The very next chapter proves Inez right, as readers discover that years later Charlie regularly cheats on Rose. Their violent quarrels have led their son Emory to hit his father, who subsequently banishes Emory to his uncle's sugar cane plantation, where he meets Soleil Marie.

That the most prescient characters in *Sugar Cage* are also the most loving and nurturing makes their ability to see a bigger picture, in both space and time, a significant and important gift. While Inez and Soleil Marie certainly resemble earlier black seers and saviors of deluded white people, Fowler's use of magical realism complicates this familiar literary figure (known in film circles as "the magic Negro") who helps white characters find their souls and fix their lives. Unlike these secondary, often two-dimensional characters, Soleil Marie is not a minor character who uses her magical powers simply to help the white man, but a major character who uses her powers to make a life with Emory possible. The story of interracial love between Emory and Soleil Marie is plotted alongside the domestic saga of Emory's parents and the social activism and domestic service of Inez. Both the civil rights movement and the Vietnam War complicate the domestic dramas of Fowler's working-class characters. The way these plots are intertwined forces readers to compare the similar human emotions and behaviors that underlie these very different public and private struggles. Both domestic disputes and racial strife feed on misunderstanding, fear, and lack of trust. Struggles between races and wars between nations are both fueled by provincial perspectives. At one time or another all nine narrators of *Sugar Cage* are imprisoned to various extents within their own narrow perspectives, and their individual stories are about moving beyond the "cages" in which they find themselves.

Emory and Soleil Marie's relationship is one of the few interracial sexual relationships in contemporary southern literature that ends happily, but Fowler marries southern gothic to magical realism in order to pull it off—thereby highlighting the enormous difficulties to be overcome. Like Dori Sanders in *Clover,* Fowler places her white character in a black world. She also creatively reworks the old plot of plantation fiction. As the only white farm laborer, Emory remains an outsider among the black cane workers until Soleil Marie approaches him. Attracted by Emory's "pretty face" (61), she uses voodoo to draw Emory into her orbit. But readers later learn that he has already noticed her lovely "collarbone" and her "beautiful skin" (108) as they work together in the cane field. Because he is "the only white guy out there," Emory does not believe friendship with his co-workers is a possibility (108). Soleil notices that racial difference has kept Emory isolated from his fellow workers but faults both races: "My people, none of them talked to Uncle's Boy. But to them he didn't either. Like he was not in our world. But that was just a lie my scared sweetness told himself" (61). That Emory actually lives and works in her world provides the compassionate young woman with the opportunity to seek out the lonely young man and gradually get to know him. Fowler makes clear that Emory would not have approached Soleil Marie while living with his parents in their segregated world in Tiama. Because he is in her world, his stereotypes about black identity and behavior are challenged every day: "I wondered how a colored girl who grew up whacking cane could say all her words so much better than me. It's not that it made me jealous, no. But I'd be lying if I said it did not shake me" (114).

Fowler places the white character in a black working-class world so that Emory can see other aspects of Soleil Marie's life at close range: her callused, chapped hands and her one-room shack with "no running water, no toilet, no bathtub, no electricity" (116). Emory experiences guilt at the conditions of Soleil Marie's life and immediately plans to return and fix her broken screen door. But he also delights in her sensuous response to life—her bare mattress piled high with pillows, her one-room house filled with candles and suffused with the scent of herbs. Emory has heard his Uncle J.W. refer to the Haitian migrant workers as "weird niggers" because of their customs, but when Emory encounters those customs in the presence of the Haitian woman with whom he is infatuated, he reacts to them differently: "But what could be wrong with dipping my hands in water mixed with a few flowers?" (115). The captivating candlelit world in which Soleil Marie receives Emory and the lyrical way she speaks transform their lovemaking into a magical, metaphorical moment: "We moved, she and I, like the tight body of a great bird. Say I'm crazy, go ahead, but we flew. Soleil Marie was the wings, and me the darting body. . . . Below us swayed the dancing fields. Their sweet smell ruffled through us as we dipped and soared through a sky made beautiful not with stars but with candlelight" (120). Emory's soaring love in this scene seems not so much attraction to the exotic other (although it could be so perceived) as the romantic response of a young man in love for the first time. Emory's continued relationship with Soleil Marie produces an emerging sensitivity to her racial position in the predominately white world.

Communication scholars Anita Foeman and Teresa Nance have pointed out that for an interracial couple, becoming acquainted is both "an interpersonal and cultural experience," which often makes the process more tentative and difficult. For interracial couples to survive, they must become aware of four perspectives: their own, their partner's, and those of their own racial group and their partner's racial group.[67] Fowler explores this process. When Emory and Soleil Marie surreptitiously watch the civil rights march on Washington on his uncle's television, Emory does not understand a sign that reads, "End segregated rules in public schools" (160), but he does not ask her to define the word *segregated* for him. Soleil Marie, however, asks Emory to explain the news announcer's reference to the Emancipation Proclamation. He unthinkingly responds, "You don't know about *that?*" (160). Her reaction is to become alternately defensive, embarrassed, and upset, especially after having to admit that she cannot read. Fowler creates a lengthy scene in which Emory and Soleil Marie are both called on to negotiate the first moment when they see each other as the other. Soleil Marie counters his thoughtless remark from the standpoint of her racial identity: "I can't read your white people's newspapers or your white people's books. But I know more about those fields and swamps, more than you'll ever dream about, Uncle's Boy" (161). When Emory realizes how much he has hurt the pride of the woman he loves, he checks his intended angry response to her outburst, judging that such behavior would be "childish" (160). Instead he rephrases his questions about her background, allows her to save face by admitting his own deficiency in math, and then offers to teach her to read, this time phrasing his offer carefully because he realizes that her revelations have made her feel "vulnerable" (162).

In this detailed scene, Fowler shows how interracial romance not only awakens Emory's racial sensitivity but broadens his racial consciousness as well. For example, while watching the news broadcast, Emory at first does not comprehend the civil rights activists' demand for "decent housing now," but as soon as "a picture of Soleil Marie's house" flashes through his mind—no toilet and no real kitchen—he immediately understands (160). Thinking further, he makes the connection between her living conditions and her illiteracy (in order to survive, she has not been able to go to school) and between her working conditions and her poverty (her labor has made disproportionately more money for his uncle than for her). Emory's specific realization about Soleil Marie's life leads him to think more generally about his other co-workers, some of whom are children who work alongside their parents, all of whom labor long hours at low wages for his "fatcat uncle" (162). Fowler shows that because Emory has lived in a segregated world, he has not been called on to think about either the lives or the civil rights of black people until he sees the issue indelibly written on the face of the young woman he loves: "I hadn't paid much attention to all this civil rights stuff. . . . Civil rights, for all the few seconds I had thought about it, was something that concerned people far removed from me. But suddenly, with my Sweetness's revelation, what these marchers were trying to accomplish took on new meaning" (162). Curbing his own desire to leave for the carnival they planned to attend, he honors Soleil Marie's intense interest in Martin Luther King Jr.'s "I have a dream" speech and allows the power of King's words and the sound of his voice to fill his racist uncle's house.

Until this point in the novel, Fowler's interracial couple live in a world of their own making, meeting clandestinely and remaining insulated from each other's racial communities. With the scene at the Dog Days Carnival, Fowler tests their relationship by forcing them to cope with the white public reaction to an interracial couple. Whereas Alice Walker and Ernest Gaines explore both black and white responses to their interracial couple, Fowler, like Reynolds Price, focuses only on the white response. But Fowler avoids having to deal with a confrontation between Emory and his parents: Emory's racist father dies before he finds out about his son's Haitian lover, and his mother is more tolerant. The carnival scene, however, pushes the couple to another stage in their relationship. They must negotiate a threatening situation as white carnival goers sneer and their children point: "Mama, Daddy, look. That man's holding a nigger's hand!" (167). The setting for this excursion into the larger world is significant. Soleil Marie and Emory are treated like freaks in the carnival's sideshow. Emory negotiates their first threatening situation by accommodation—ignoring the white prejudice and refusing to hold her hand, which he knows would call attention to their status as lovers. Soleil Marie declares that she is "not scared of these stupid people" and is disappointed that Emory is not more confrontational (167). She deems his behavior cowardly and therefore unmanly.

Soleil Marie narrates the carnival scene, and from her position as cultural outsider, a Haitian Catholic who practices voodoo, she points out how different the Dog Days Carnival is from carnivals she has experienced in Haiti, which are filled with "mystery, love, good times" (163). Caribbean carnivals, with their masking and playful subverting of hierarchy and convention, are liberating. In contrast, the Dog Days Carnival, with its freak shows, isolates people and labels their bodily differences grotesque, much as the crowd singles out the interracial couple Emory and Soleil Marie. Soleil Marie's misreading of the snake painted on the House of Horrors as an evil *loa* calls the reader's attention to the essential cruelty of the freak shows, indicating at the same time the cultural difficulties that interracial and interethnic couples experience. To ward off the evil *loa,* Soleil Marie throws a handful of dirt on Emory "for protection" and screams, "Run" (169). Unfamiliar with her beliefs and voodoo practices, Emory misreads Soleil Marie's behavior as hysterical, and their communication breaks down, but because readers view the scene from her perspective, we understand what Emory does not.

At this point, in order to deal with Soleil Marie's fear, Emory changes his strategy of negotiating prejudice to avoidance and decides to escape the crowds who gawk at them by riding the Ferris wheel, where, high above the crowd, they will be able to hold hands. As the ride begins, the operator calls Emory a "nigger-lover" (170), and when it concludes, the operator manipulates the wheel so that they are the last couple left on the ride. Thinking he has the interracial couple fully under his control and intending to punish them for their transgressive behavior, the operator spins the wheel very fast, hoping to scare them. At this point, Fowler creates a Bakhtinian moment for Soleil Marie and Emory, when they are able to make the Dog Days Carnival function more like a Caribbean carnival. Together the couple renders invalid the southern codes and conventions that reduce them to racial objects and their love to something grotesque. For the first time during their evening out, Soleil Marie and Emory face the white challenge to their relationship together, and on their own terms. Initially confused, they choose to delight in their fast ride: "we both, the two of us, laughed sudden, hard and so good. As we flew back to the ground, the sneer on the angry man's face grew huge and monsterlike. But he was a monster without an enemy, because fun this flying race was. . . . we was determined: the angry man, he was not going to win" (172). When the operator tries to scare them further by walking away after stopping them at the top of the Ferris wheel, Soleil Marie and Emory once again turn the threatening situation to their advantage. They take the opportunity to enjoy the beautiful view of the carnival's twinkling lights, and Emory gives Soleil Marie a reading lesson by using the signs they can see, "Tickets" and "Hot Dogs." Like Bakhtin's carnival heroes, they resist the essentializing framework "of *other people's* words."[68] The strategy that they devise to cope with prejudice allows them to establish what communication theorists call "a culture common to them," which helps to "ensure the survival of the relationship."[69] The couple's strategy works as well as any of Soleil Marie's magic potions. It allows them to cement their relationship in a world that would tear it apart. But coping with prejudice is a defensive move, and Fowler does not take her interracial couple beyond that stage.

Fowler plots their romance alongside Martin Luther King Jr.'s career as an activist, thereby suggesting that they embody his hopes and fulfill his dream, at least on a personal level. Early in the novel, after hearing a civil rights activist on the radio, Inez foresees Emory and Soleil Marie's meeting in the cane fields. In the middle of the novel, Soleil Marie realizes she is pregnant with Emory's child about the same time that Emory's mother, Rose, is inspired by hearing King speak: "I decided those words that poured from his sweet face were healing words" (153). But by then Emory has left the plantation to attend his father's funeral in Tiama. Near the end of the novel, Soleil Marie loses her job because she takes a day off to mourn King's death. However, rather than sink further into despair without Emory, she flees the city where she feels caged in order to return to the expansive cane fields she loves. Having given up on Emory's promise to return and not knowing he has been drafted, she reverses course and decides to locate him so that their daughter, Charlite, will have a father. For Fowler, life's unfairness can be paralyzing, but she suggests that unfairness must be met with determination and hope, a philosophy all of her characters come to employ in *Sugar Cage*. Fowler writes an ending for *Sugar Cage* that depends on hope, on the part of both her characters and her readers.

The ending of *Sugar Cage* is as happy as that of any romance novel, but not nearly so predictable, because it depends on magic. With Emory about to die in the Vietnam War, unaware that Soleil Marie has borne him a daughter, readers have given up all hope of a happy ending when Soleil Marie unexpectedly uses voodoo to save him. She and Charlite morph into a heron, fly half way around the world, and swoop down to pluck Emory from the killing fields of Cambodia. Inez's concluding vision of a soldier's return to an old stilt house in the cane fields of Florida gives readers hope that the love between Soleil Marie and Emory has survived both the South's racism and the Vietnam War. But Fowler constructs her novel so that readers must trust in Soleil Marie's magic and Inez's prescience in order to interpret the ending this way. Readers never know for sure whether Emory survives the Vietnam War. We only know that Soleil Marie and Inez very much hope that he does. In Fowler's world, hope arises from an ability to see a broader perspective than one's own and to discern the possibilities in a world preoccupied with prohibitions. That's when magic happens. The difficulty of escaping the burden of southern history is made plain by the fact that Fowler relies on magic to secure a future for her interracial couple. It does seem significant, however, that Fowler, much like Dar

Tomlinson, chooses for her white protagonist a partner of color from the Caribbean, not the American South—thereby making the black lover foreign, rather than African American. This weakens the transgressive act somewhat for both the white partners and white readers.

Recent novels featuring black women and white men by black women writers turn upon the issue of whether the black female protagonist will be perceived by her friends and family as sleeping with the enemy and whether her white lover's family will accept her as a member of their family. For example, in Monica White's 1996 popular romance *Shades of Desire,* Jeremy is a liberal, reconstructed white southerner, and Jasmine, his African American lover, is his equal in intelligence, education, and attractiveness. At first Jasmine and Jeremy each wonder if the other is interesting only as an exotic other. However, these doubts are quickly acknowledged as part of the interracial dating terrain and then rapidly swept aside, because genre conventions of the romance dictate that the lovers will confront more external than internal conflicts. In popular romances, like *Shades of Desire,* it is not the main characters' thinking that must be transformed but that of friends and family members. Even these obstacles to true love, though, create only a minimum amount of discomfort before being swept away. What makes a novel like *Shades of Desire* ultimately unsatisfying is that readers never see the process of transformation: how the black girlfriend who thinks "no white man can satisfy a black woman" comes to realize she is jealous because Jasmine is in love and she is not; how Jasmine's brother who questions her racial "pride" in bringing "a white boy into our parents' home" is converted by working for a predominately white company; or how Jeremy's aloof parents, aristocratic products of the Old South, have come around to the possibility of having biracial grandchildren. In this novel Jasmine's parents bring up all the issues that the interracial couple will have to confront, but love easily conquers all, and the conventions of the romance genre stop Jasmine and Jeremy's story at the altar.[70]

A much more interesting situation in terms of redefining regional and racial identity and reconfiguring race relations occurs in African American writer Shay Youngblood's *Black Girl in Paris* (2000). In this novel a young black woman from Georgia, who is an aspiring writer looking for adventure, goes to Paris in hopes of meeting James Baldwin for a jolt of courage and inspiration. There Eden has a picaresque series of encounters with a variety of people on the Parisian margins but not a single encounter with her literary idol. Instead, the increasingly homesick Eden meets a blues trumpeter and falls in love with the sound of his horn before she discovers that he is white. Ving's music pulls her "home" to Georgia, and once she realizes that he is white, his southern accent succeeds in keeping Eden interested long enough to find out he not only has "soul" but, unlike everyone else, fully understands her creative desires.[71] Although people who hear Ving blow his "soulful and sad" horn wonder if he has "any African blood in him," Youngblood, unlike Eric Jerome Dickey in *Milk in My Coffee,* does not find any African American ancestors in his family tree. Her focus is on the hybridity of culture, rather than its racial genealogy. Ving arranges for Eden to stay with his friends in St. Paul de Vence, where James Baldwin lives. After working as a nude model there to make ends meet, she discovers that Baldwin has been in Paris all along for a theater production of *The Amen Corner* and she has just missed him in both places. Eden drowns her sorrows in her writing and produces the novel we are reading.

At the end of the novel, Youngblood rewards Eden for her efforts with a surprise visit from Ving, who is "as handsome as his music" (232), and a meeting with Baldwin in Paris. While readers do not know what will happen to Ving and Eden's relationship once she returns to Georgia, readers do know that two southerners have had to go to Paris to discover that beneath their "racial" differences there are some regional affinities. When Eden first contemplates going out with Ving, the burden of southern history overwhelms the regional cultural ties that draw her to him. She must overcome the "fear" of white men engendered in her when her father called them "white devils" and her mother warned her to "trust none but Jesus" (149). After Eden and Ving become romantically involved, she must deal with the hostile stares of a few black men and the troubling racist comments from a few white people. But because she is away from the South, away from the demands of family and friends, she feels "free" to act as she desires, rather than as her southern black community dictates: "I remembered that I was in Paris and there was no one to judge my actions, no one to remind me of my disloyalty to the race, to accuse me of losing my blackness, no one to remind me of the master-slave relationship. I was a free woman and could choose whom and what I wanted" (150). Journalist Itabari Njeri has termed the monolithic definitions of blackness, from which Eden longs to be free, "the last plantation." She argues that "even as we are victimized by the ethos of slave masters and their descendants, we often define ourselves and operate in terms that speak to the psychological slavery that leaves the mind the last plantation."[72]

Readers' responses on Internet Web sites to interracial romance novels mirror Eden's search. They are testimonials both to the hunger for positive portrayals of contemporary interracial love and to the transformative power of fiction. Comments such as this one appear regularly: "It was good to read about interracial romance without all the stereotypes as to why black men choose white women or why black women choose white men." In *Shades of Desire* Jasmine and Jeremy early in their relationship rent the video *Guess Who's Coming to Dinner* (1967), in order to bolster their courage to continue their love affair in the face of strong opposition from family and friends, both black and white. From the Internet comments about novels like *Shades of Desire*, it is evident that readers use popular romances to validate their life choices and work through the challenges of interracial dating, in the way that Jasmine and Jeremy use *Guess Who's Coming to Dinner*.[73] And yet these same readers seem to long for something more than the typical popular romance plot: "We would love to see how their lives work out."[74] The next step would seem to be a literature treating the life of interracial couples beyond the beginnings of interracial love: raising children, balancing work and family life, and locating a supportive community. Starting, rather than ending, the southern interracial love story with a wedding and setting interracial gay and lesbian love stories in the South are new plots begging to be written.[75] But writers, both black and white, native and nonnative to the South, apparently still have a lot of rewriting to do to bring past southern interracial intimacy into perspective. At present there is an explosion of wounded novels about interracial love that revisit past taboos and expose continuing psychic burdens. There are no happily-ever-afters in these novels. Only in romance novels does interracial love conquer all in the South, and so far only Genesis Press is supplying readers with this fantasy. That the topic continues to be controversial seems evident. The signs range from the real-life effort that Margaret Mitchell's estate expended, unsuccessfully, to stop publication of Alice Randall's *The Wind Done Gone* with its love affair between R (Rhett) and the biracial half sister of Other (Scarlett) to all the objections to interracial dating made by the fictional friends and families of protagonists in contemporary romance novels. Serious literature about interracial love set in the contemporary South will be written only when the burden of southern history does not weigh so heavily on writers' imaginations and only by writers who are bound neither by strict genre conventions nor by stereotypes about the South.

CHAPTER 5

Rethinking the One-Drop Rule

Race and Identity

They are *me.* Would she always have to remind herself?
—ROSELLEN BROWN, *HALF A HEART*

Despite golf phenomenon Tiger Woods's public identification of himself as Cablinasian—a contraction of Caucasian, Black, Indian, and Asian—and despite spirited debates about the new 2000 census, which allowed respondents to check more than one race or ethnic category, the practice of individuals with African ancestry identifying as racially mixed has only recently resurfaced in American society. This is especially true in the South, where the one-drop rule still reigns supreme. On the 2000 census, for example, of respondents with African American ancestry, in Mississippi less than 1 percent identified themselves as racially mixed, as compared with 13.8 percent in Massachusetts and 9.9 percent in California.[1] In *Dark of the Moon* (1999), a detective novel by P. J. Parish, the biracial protagonist leaves his job as a policeman in Michigan to return to the small town Black Pool, Mississippi, where his mother is dying. There he discovers that he has undergone an identity change as well as a career move: "Half white . . . or was it half black? He was never sure, and didn't really care, unless someone or something forced him to think about it. Here in Black Pool, it seemed there was no question. He was black."[2] In the 1990s the racially mixed character made a small but significant reappearance in American fiction from popular novels to serious literature, particularly among white writers. Alyce Miller includes trouble-filled stories about mixed-race teenagers in *The Nature of Longing* (1994), but novelists as different as Reynolds Price and Jay McInerney have embraced the mixed-race child as a symbol of hope. The children who unexpectedly appear at the conclusions of Price's *The Promise of Rest* (1995) and McInerney's *The Last of the Savages* (1996) are both products of the interracial love of southerners, although neither is conceived in or lives in the South. One is born in New York, the other in Los Angeles—both cosmopolitan cities more hospitable to people who eventually might choose to identify as racially mixed, rather than to assume, more conventionally, the racial identity of the minority parent. In some respects, both Price's and McInerney's symbolic use of the racially mixed figure seems, although hopeful, little more than the deus ex machina du jour for readers weary of the culture wars and identity politics.[3]

As Barbara Ladd observes, the mulatto, more than any other literary figure, embodies "the threats and promises of integration in a racist culture."[4] Before the Civil War white writers, attempting to paint slavery in the best light, excluded mulattos from their romantic plantation fiction, just as most white people turned a blind eye to the racially mixed slaves on southern plantations. Writers of slave narratives, however, almost always emphasized the existence of racial mixing. Abolitionists from outside the South used the mulatto character to condemn slavery, sometimes in ideologically problematic ways. Black and white writers scripted plots about tragic mulattos who were unacknowledged by their white fathers and subjected to undeserved suffering, or they wrote of tragic octoroons who were brought up white only to be sold into slavery when their white fathers died.[5] After emancipation, supposedly "scientific" theories about the biology of race and the racial degeneration of mixed people allowed racist whites to promote the one-drop rule for black identity in an attempt to maintain white racial purity and solidify white power and privilege. The rule was based on the belief that each race had its own blood type, which corresponded to physical characteristics and behavior. While the upper South had for all intents and purposes adhered to the one-drop rule since the Revolutionary War, in the lower South, particularly around Charleston and New Orleans, racially mixed people constituted a distinct third racial class, made up in part by the freed slave offspring of white fathers.[6] But after the Civil War, entrenched racism led to a steadily growing affinity between mulattos and blacks, although for a couple of generations some mixed people continued to pass as "white" or to foster the idea of a light-skinned "black" elite. Black writers tended to condemn both avenues in their fiction. They cast those who were passing as unhappy, fearful loners, and they portrayed the black bourgeoisie as misguided imitators of "white" culture and values. Writers like Charles Chesnutt and James Weldon Johnson painted more nuanced portraits; but in general, black writers reserved heroic status for racially mixed characters who identified as black. They often portrayed these characters as race leaders, because they were more educated than other black characters. While a few white writers who grew up in the South, such as Mark Twain and George Washington Cable, were ahead of their time in using the mulatto to demonstrate the social construction of race, most, like Thomas Dixon, marked the mulatto as a racial degenerate or an "African savage." In the early twentieth century William Faulkner reacted to southern preoccupation with white purity and to white hysteria about invisible blackness by creating such conflicted characters as Charles Etienne Saint-Valery Bon, an octoroon unsure about where his racial allegiance lay, and Joe Christmas, an orphan uncertain about his racial identity. After the civil rights movement, novels with racially mixed characters decreased dramatically as black racial pride increased.

In Faulkner's *Go Down, Moses* (1942), young Ike McCaslin is appalled to discover his slave-owning grandfather's miscegenation and incest. But as an old man, Ike is arguably even more horrified by the idea that the nameless woman of "Delta Autumn" might demand from his cousin Roth the acknowledgment that old Carothers McCaslin denied Eunice, the slave he impregnated, and their daughter Tomasina. For Ike, the sight of the baby in the light-skinned black woman's arms brings back the repressed transgressions of McCaslin family history that he thought he had put behind him; for Faulkner, the young woman and her mixed-race child signal the inevitability of cross-racial desire despite laws against miscegenation. Not at all ready for interracial marriage in the early 1940s, Ike silently protests, "*maybe in a thousand or two thousand years in America. . . . But not now! Not now!*"[7] Demographer Barry Edmonston believes that racial and ethnic blending in the United States will occur more quickly, in a matter of centuries rather than millennia. He projects that by 2050, 21 percent of the U.S. population will be of mixed ancestry.[8] How these people choose to define themselves in the new millennium will surely be affected by the new instructions on the 2000 census, which sought for the first time since 1920 not to identify U.S. citizens monoracially.[9] A higher-than-expected number of blacks checked more than one race in the 2000 census; one person in twenty (1.76 million people) who identified as black also checked at least one other race. Because the multiracial numbers are higher than could have been forecast from mixed-race birth certificates, Urban Institute demographer Jeffrey Passell believes the numbers indicate a "willingness" to acknowledge ancestors whom people might not have acknowledged previously. Other experts think that simple publicity about the new census option increased the numbers.[10] Whatever the reasons, regional differences remain.

Americans have been more accepting of white ethnic intermarriage than racial intermarriage, especially between blacks and whites—a prejudice fueled by miscegenation laws, which were more prevalent and lasted far longer in southern states than in the rest of the country. But the twentieth-century biracial baby boomlet, which began after the 1967 *Loving v. The Commonwealth of Virginia* Supreme Court decision struck down these laws, has steadily grown as American society has gradually become more tolerant of black-white marriages. Researchers have associated increased acceptance with such factors as urban living, liberal ideologies, and being born after World War II and outside the South.[11] In 1968, the year that the National Center for Health Statistics began keeping track, 8,758 births were recorded to interracial black-white couples; by 1991 the number had grown to 52,232, and the center believes that this number is low, because in more than 620,000 births in 1991, the father's race was not specified.[12] Such statistics lead some to suggest that the growing numbers of racially mixed young people represent "the best hope for the future of American race relations."[13] But as much as legal race theorist Patricia J. Williams celebrates "the future of a culturally mixed, biologically miscegenational world," she worries that "we seem genuinely unable to appreciate how much we are already in that happy state of nature."[14] Only a handful of white people, such as Edward Ball, have deliberately searched for the African Americans in their family. A few more African Americans have begun to track down their absent white ancestors—mostly prominently Thomas Jefferson's descendants but also a few with less illustrious white ancestors, such as journalist Neil Henry. Research for *Pearl's Secret: A Black Man's Search for His White Family* (2001) took Henry on an emotional journey and a geographical trek from his immediate upper-class black family in Seattle to his extended working-class white family in rural Louisiana. While the white Beaumonts frankly admitted that if he had come knocking twenty-five years earlier, they probably would not have answered the door, at the end of the twentieth century they were ready to welcome him with open arms—a southern white response that surprised at least one reviewer of *Pearl's Secret*.[15]

My focus in this chapter is on the roles played by racially mixed characters in contemporary southern fiction. As protagonists these characters are called on to negotiate the conflicting heritages of their lives, not just to blend them symbolically, and they must do so in the historically freighted racial climate of the South. Currently the figure of the tragic mulatto lives on in southern characters who grow up thinking they are white and discover they have African

American ancestry, whereas the figure of the mulatto as pragmatic race leader has dominated for those who know of their mixed ancestry but identify as black. In recent southern fiction, the "white" biracial character's nightmare comes in contemplating a loss of white social status in a society where racism lingers; the "black" biracial character's dream depends on gaining wealth through inheritance when the missing white parent can be publicly identified. This asymmetry in fictional treatment occurs when the parents of African American descent are absent or silent for the "white" racially mixed characters, as in John Gregory Brown's *Decorations in a Ruined Cemetery* (1994), and when the white fathers are not present for the "black" biracial characters, as in Ernest Gaines's "Bloodline" (1968) and Bebe Moore Campbell's *Your Blues Ain't like Mine* (1992). Only when the biracial character has a public and personal relationship with both parents, as in Rosellen Brown's *Half a Heart* (2000), does a new twenty-first-century figure emerge—the "deliberately biracial" character.[16] Unlike Danzy Senna's *Caucasia* (1998), none of these southern novels are written by authors who identify as biracial, although southern mixed-race writers are emerging, like poet Natasha Trethewey, who was raised in Mississippi; playwright Jerome Hairston, originally from Virginia; and songwriter-turned-novelist Alice Randall, who grew up in Washington, D.C. But given the biracial baby boomlet of the late 1960s, the number of interracial couples living in the South, and the recent interest in hidden racial roots, a southern or South-interested Danzy Senna is surely looking for a publisher as I write. Furthermore, given the influx of Latinos and Asians into the South in the 1990s, biracial black-white identity will soon be superseded by other biracial identities and even more complex multiracial identities, like that of Tiger Woods.

The vision and the rhetoric of the civil rights movement perhaps provided the impetus for Ernest Gaines to write the novella "Bloodline" in 1968, a revision of the mulatto fiction written by the generation of writers preceding him. In both William Faulkner's *Absalom, Absalom!* (1936) and Langston Hughes's "Father and Son" (1933), the mulatto son of a white father seeks acknowledgment of paternity, but neither receives it, and both lie dead at the end of the narratives. Although the mulatto plays a tragic role in both works, these fictions have significant differences. Faulkner's Charles Bon dies at the hand of his white half brother who learns of Bon's plan to seek revenge by marrying his white half sister—or so his story is constructed by the young white men, Quentin and Shreve, who imagine it years later. Hughes's Bert Lewis takes his revenge more directly by strangling his father and then committing suicide to avoid the inevitable retaliatory lynching. Faulkner's Charles Bon, according to the white men who imagine his story, seeks only private acknowledgment of paternity and perhaps a belated bit of fatherly love. Hughes's Bert Lewis demands much more: his father's surname as well as his plantation. Although both men are spurned by their white fathers,[17] only the African American writer's mulatto character seeks both his birthright and public acknowledgment of his paternity. This difference is a significant and important one, for the black writer thus emphasizes how southern laws against miscegenation construct both race and class identities.[18] By legislating against interracial marriages, southern states ensured that the offspring of interracial unions would be legally illegitimate, and states like Louisiana went even further to limit the possibility of children with African ancestry inheriting from white fathers. Only with the white father's voluntary public and legal acknowledgment could a child of color inherit any part of his estate. In the late 1960s, with a variety of new civil rights laws being passed and cases concerning the legal discrimination against illegitimate offspring making their way to the Supreme Court,[19] Gaines envisioned a more hopeful ending for his racially mixed character, Christian Laurent, than Faulkner and Hughes did for theirs.

But Christian Laurent's beginning recalls that of his southern literary predecessors. Nicknamed Copper because of his skin color, he was conceived in a ditch, where the white plantation owner, Walter Laurent, raped his mother, a black laborer. Following southern racial custom, Copper grows up as the son of the black man who was his mother's husband, but his true paternity is an open secret among local blacks and whites. As a young man Copper threatens to kill Walter Laurent for continuing to take advantage of his mother, but she protects her son from his own anger by fleeing north. After her death, Copper's stepfather refuses to care for him because he is the son of a white man, and Copper finds himself alone to fend for himself, like his mulatto predecessors. He is preoccupied at first by the injustice done to him, but eventually, motivated by the racial discrimination he observes everywhere he goes, Copper returns to the South with potent new weapons that his literary predecessors did not possess. The rhetoric and the ideas of the civil rights movement allow him to imagine a more satisfying revenge for past injustices. Although his white father is dead, Copper demands that his father's brother, Frank Laurent, publicly acknowledge his true identity and thus make it possible for him to claim some portion of his birthright, the Louisiana plantation that Walter has left to Frank.

Gaines sets "Bloodline" during a time of transition when the promise of the civil rights movement has begun to threaten the practices of Jim Crow in the South. In a parallel move, Gaines weakens Frank Laurent, the lone white authority figure, with a heart condition and positions him as the only white character in the novella, the last of a dying breed. Infirm from a recent heart attack and uninterested in farming, Frank and the old black people find themselves in an oddly codependent situation. He depends on them to care for him, and they depend on him to provide them free housing. But Copper's return changes the dynamic. Demanding that Frank acknowledge their family relationship but refusing to go through Frank's back door to ask him, Copper challenges both the laws and the customs governing race relations. Gaines depicts the interplay between the two as a struggle between exceptionally strong-willed men who share some of the same genes. The black narrator, Felix, notes, "He was no more scared of Frank than Frank was scared of him. They was both Laurents. A Laurent wasn't supposed to be scared of any man" (203). The black people who knew Copper as a boy make much of the fact that he resembles his father Walter both physically and personally. He is similarly tall, slim, and left-handed as well as equally defiant and stubborn. Obviously trying to discredit flawed theories about race and identity, Gaines bases Copper's resemblance to Walter on a variety of genetic markers, not race alone.

Gaines constructs the novella as a chess match between the old order and the new, between Frank, the old white man armed with outmoded Jim Crow laws, and Copper, the young black man bolstered by new ideas about race and civil rights. Although Frank tries to call the shots as he has always done, demanding that Copper come to the big house and explain why he has returned to the plantation, Copper maintains his dignity and forces Frank to come to the quarters to get his questions answered. In this reversal, Gaines moves the white man onto the black man's turf and positions the two men so that Copper, who leans against the porch railing, looks down on Frank in the chair. In small ways Copper gains some advantage over the ailing Frank. He begins by taking advantage of Frank's question "When did this birthright notion come into your head?"[20] to start with Walter Laurent's rape of his mother, a strategy that allows him to catalog not only personal injustices but society's racism over decades. By refusing to answer Frank's most pressing question about his present intentions until Frank calls him by his given name, instead of his skin color, Copper succeeds in getting Frank to call him "Christian" (207). By persisting in calling Frank "Uncle" and by refusing to allow Frank to be rude to him—to treat him like one of his "niggers"—Copper demands that he acknowledge their kinship. Finally Frank capitulates and calls him "Nephew." This appellation amounts to public acknowledgment of Copper's paternity if the laws ever change, because Frank's black handyman Felix is a witness, albeit a potentially weak one in a white-run legal system. While Felix assumes that Frank capitulates because "he re'lized he wasn't being a gentleman" (215), Gaines suggests that the looming threat of a physical response from Copper may have intimidated Frank.

But Frank will only go so far, and he has the current law to back him up: "you know because your mon was black you can't claim a damn thing. Not only birthright, you can't even claim a cat" (206). Although Frank eventually admits Walter's injustices to Copper's mother and the other black laborers, Frank refuses to give Copper a share of the land. Thus Frank takes only the easy first step toward change by acknowledging wrongs done. He leaves the repeal of discriminatory inheritance laws to the next generation of southerners and the reversal of unfair family matters to the next generation of Laurents. Gaines's portrait of Frank Laurent is a profile in cowardice. Frank allows his professed desire for a change in race relations to be crushed by the burden of southern tradition: "I didn't write the rules. I came and found them, and I shall die and leave them. They will be changed, of course; they will be changed, and soon, I hope. But I will not be the one to change them" (199). Frank attempts to hide his own cowardice in not changing his will behind the largesse of paternalism: "as long as I'm here I'm going to do all I can to make up for what he did to these here in the quarters. I'm going to give them shelter and food, medicine when they're sick, a place to worship God. When they die, I'm going to give them a little plot of ground in which to be buried" (216). But Gaines makes it clear that when such white paternalism masquerades as amelioration, it strips black people of future self-sufficiency. For Frank has said that when his niece inherits the plantation, she will manage it differently, evicting blacks from the property and increasing the Cajun presence. Only by owning the land will the black people be able to live and work there after Frank's death, a fact Copper clearly understands. Frank's self-serving paternalism gives them only enough land to bury their dead, a paradoxical monument to their own lost way of life farming the land.

Gaines's construction of the novella's plot proves the error in Frank's thinking that "neither one of us is going to change [the rules], not singly" (216). When Copper defies just one custom governing black-white relationships, other customs begin to fall behind it, like so many dominos. Almost before Frank realizes it, his most trusted old black retainers are also breaking the rules governing interracial relationships as they try to help him understand Copper. For the first time, Frank's handyman Felix sits with him in the library to help him strategize about how to make Copper come to the back door. Felix suggests that Copper might come if Felix told him that his "uncle" Frank wanted to speak with him (166). Gaines captures the changing nature of Frank's relationship with Felix by having Felix punctuate their disagreements with the charged remark, "You're the authority." By merely uttering this phrase, Felix attacks the hierarchy of their relationship even while acknowledging it. When Frank's black housekeeper, Amalia, who is Copper's aunt, realizes that if Copper owns the land, the black people will not have to worry about being evicted at Frank's death, she courageously follows Felix's lead by also speaking the truth of Copper's paternity. When Frank refers to Copper as her nephew, she says "softly, with her head down," "Us nephew" (175). With such incremental changes, Gaines suggests that "rules" can be changed "singly" if individuals dare to defy them.

Although Frank may appear to have won the battle with Copper over land ownership by not changing his will, the ending to Gaines's novella is not closed. By giving Copper the last word, Gaines indicates that men like Copper will eventually win the war, "Tell my aunt I've gone. But tell her I'll come back. And tell her when I do, she'll never have to go through your back door ever again." An interesting blend of southern gentleman and militant activist, Copper offers to help his Uncle Frank to his car, even as he tells him his "days are over." Copper exits bowing to his uncle but walking away from him "the way soldiers walk." He vows to return and claim by any means necessary what is due him as Walter Laurent's son: "I'll take my share. I won't beg for it. . . . I'll take it or I'll bathe this whole plantation in blood" (217). Some critics, like some characters in the novella, have used such remarks, as well as Copper's habit of pressing his temples and staring into space, to question his sanity, but his behavior suggests not so much insanity as preoccupation with finding a way to redress white injustice. These critics base their arguments on the novella's position in the story collection and Gaines's position on violence, but an examination of Gaines's other "crazy" characters, of the historical context when "Bloodline" was written, and of Copper's place in the literary history of the mulatto, along with an awareness of Louisiana laws governing the right of inheritance, suggests a more complex assessment.[21]

According to Louisiana laws, public acknowledgment of paternity had to come first—hence Copper's seemingly maniacal insistence that Frank publicly recognize their kinship. Copper's single-minded self-possession and his refusal to be shown disrespect win Felix's respect and eventually Frank's, just as similar behavior wins Marcus the respect of the older generation of blacks who fear change in *Of Love and Dust*. In both works the other characters, black and white, view Copper's and Marcus's flaunting of racial customs as "crazy," not only because such behavior is out of the ordinary but also because it can get a black man killed. Copper's use of force with the black men whom Frank dispatches to summon him is troubling, but Gaines is careful to explain such behavior, though not to justify its use. First Felix, whose narrative voice is one of reason, judges Copper's behavior self-defense when Frank asks. Then Copper, citing the violence of southern race relations, explains his violent behavior to Frank as a psychologist might: "you have imbedded the stick and the chair in their minds for so long, they can't hear anything else. I needed it to get their attention. I think I have it now—and I won't have to use it any more. From now on I'll use the simplest words. Simple words, Uncle; a thing you thought they would never understand" (209). Revising southern white racists' link between African ancestry and savagery, Gaines has Copper assign "barbarity" (209) to the white society, which constructed a racist social order based on black powerlessness and undergirded by intimidation, beatings, and lynchings. Copper's final militant promise to return and use violence if his demands are not met should be read in light of the rhetoric of civil rights activists who were wearying of Martin Luther King Jr.'s dependence on nonviolence during the time Gaines was writing the novella.

A self-proclaimed "General," Copper resembles an earlier figure of the mulatto as race leader, a man with more cosmopolitan experiences than most black people who chooses to identify with the black masses in order to lead them. Copper's crisp army khakis, his highly polished shoes, and his specialized combatant's language hint at the mental liberation from Jim Crow that serving in the U.S. Army afforded many southern blacks before and after World War II. Undaunted by Frank's refusal to give him any land, Copper plans to continue his fight for reparations not only for biracial people like himself, but for millions of others "not my color, but without homes, without birthrights, just like me" (213). In no way does Copper want to use his color or his white father's last name to set himself apart from other black people, as Creoles of color had done in Louisiana, a behavior Gaines criticizes repeatedly in his fiction, most notably in his first novel, *Catherine Carmier*. The only time Copper refers to his race, he identifies himself as "black" (212). Unlike earlier mulatto race leaders who returned south as educators, ministers, or lawyers to fight the good cause,[22] Copper finds more promise in the practical weapon of land ownership, the main source of economic power in rural Louisiana, where Gaines grew up. By highlighting the fact that the civil rights of southern blacks, especially those of biracial descent, sometimes included property rights, Gaines uses "Bloodline" (with its deceptively "simple words") to foreground the legal connections between racial identity and socioeconomic class in the South—the legacy that shadows many southern blacks to this day. In the late 1990s some black leaders renewed calls for economic reparations for slavery, and black farmers successfully challenged banks and sued government agencies for discriminatory practices that had cost them their farms.[23]

In the popular novel *Your Blues Ain't like Mine* (1992), African American writer Bebe Moore Campbell creates a much happier ending from the same fictional materials Gaines uses in "Bloodline." Like Copper, Ida Long, the biracial child of a black domestic, seeks her birthright when she learns of her white father's identity; and like Copper, Ida is an assertive person much like her father, who just happens to be the richest man in town—although Gaines's sugarcane plantation has been updated into a catfish farm. Because of a happy accident late in the novel, Ida finds photographs of Stonewall Pinochet with her and her mother. Since Ida's discovery occurs after Pinochet's death, she does not have to confront a practicing racist but rather her white half brother, Clayton Pinochet, who is a closet liberal. Clayton has lacked the courage to defy his rich father: he has not worked openly in the civil rights movement or married his long-time black mistress. But Clayton has worked behind the scenes—tutoring black boys, such as Ida's son, and tipping off northern reporters to the lynching of a black teenager, an incident Campbell models on Emmett Till's murder, which I discuss in chapter 1. Through the years, Clayton has come to know Ida as a friend and to admire her as a community activist, long before she tells him she is his half sister. Because of their mutual friendship, he is quick to acknowledge their family relationship, at least privately, but much slower to share his father's wealth. By including in this property the extremely lucrative New Plantation Catfish Farm and Processing Plant, where Ida works for low wages in harsh conditions, Campbell ties owning property to controlling one's fate, just as Gaines does in "Bloodline."

As befits her popular form, Campbell makes Ida's road to gaining her birthright easier than Copper's, for the white man comes to moral consciousness by himself. When Clayton cannot placate Ida with cash, she decides to sue with the help of a Harvard-educated black lawyer. Clayton seeks assistance from his father's attorney, but Clayton's moment of awareness comes when the lawyer invites him to assume his father's old position among the town's white powerbrokers, the so-called "Honorable Men of Hopewell." Clayton realizes then that fighting Ida's claim would necessitate calling on the white racist establishment that he has always despised and from which his father's death has finally freed him. In a scene reminiscent of Huck Finn's decision to go to hell rather than betray the escaped slave Jim, Clayton announces with a self-conscious irony that Huck did not have, "Waldo, I am not an honorable man."[24] He then throws in his lot with Ida for a grand finale of black-activist desires fulfilled. Clayton decides not only to give Ida her rightful inheritance but to make common cause with her in changing the town's unjust institutions. Readers last glimpse Clayton joining Ida and her co-workers on the picket line at the catfish processing plant.

In portraying Ida as a racially mixed activist who identifies as black, Campbell positions her, as Gaines does Copper, in a long line of light-skinned race leaders. But in doing so, Campbell endows Ida with a few 1990s twists. Unlike black writers at the end of the nineteenth century, such as Frances Harper, Campbell does not portray her racially mixed protagonist as exactly like middle-class white people but rather positions her white characters in the working class with Ida. To reach her position as race leader, Ida must overcome *not* the old black elitist pride in being light-skinned that afflicted some of her literary predecessors but a contemporary shame that her skin is not dark enough and her hair not nappy enough. Her white features draw the unwanted attention of white men and silently sabotage potential friendships with black women, who "don't trust a high-yellow woman with good hair around their men" (107). Psychologists explain shame as a painful feeling of inferiority based on the discrepancy between ideal and identity.[25] Campbell gives Ida a dark-skinned lover who is a civil rights activist from New York. He serves multiple functions, although not the expected one of husband. Nat erases Ida's shame by displacing it onto her white father; he validates her blackness with his attraction to her as a person, not to her white features; and he instructs her in social activism, which allows her to transcend her color. Finally, Campbell gives Ida a wider influence than earlier "race" leaders. For in agitating to change the working conditions for the catfish processing plant workers, Ida emerges as a leader for both blacks and whites and a role model for the daughter of the white man who murdered Armstrong, the Emmett Till character. In part because labor unions are rare in the South, such an interracial alliance along class lines is an equally rare occurrence, a fact that led one reviewer to conclude that "the ending tries to force an upbeat notion onto what is a bleak reality."[26] While Gaines's ending is certainly more realistic than Campbell's, both African American writers choose the same activist role and the same legal and financial goals for their racially mixed protagonists. Their fictions make reparations not simply a handout for past social injustices but a rightful inheritance withheld.

Raymond Andrews takes another tack with his parodic examinations of racial identity in *Appalachee Red* (1978). Michael Kreyling argues convincingly that Andrews's "cool handling of hot subject matter hints that what has been seen as first-order realism must now be thought of as trope."[27] The first of a trilogy of novels set in fictional Muskhogean County, Georgia, *Appalachee Red* provides a symbolic romp through the power struggles not only between blacks and whites, but also between blacks and blacks (accommodationists versus activists). The novel also functions as an intertextual shooting gallery filled with icons of the southern literary pantheon. Just to give one major example, Andrews's biracial protagonist, Red, succeeds where Faulkner's Charles Bon failed: he drives off into the sunset in a black Cadillac with his besotted white half sister beside him. Named for his skin color, Red is the son of a white planter and a black servant. Not at all the predictable realist or modernist psychological interrogation of biracial identity, *Appalachee Red* is a pyrotechnic send-up of southern racial labeling, which means that the biracial character is "Red," his much darker half brother is "Blue," and the local sheriff is Boots "White"—glaringly white after receiving Red's election gift of a white cowboy outfit and a white horse. Raymond Andrews's take on racial politics is much like Albert Murray's, who has consistently maintained, long before it was fashionable, that Americans are cultural mulattos. Andrews's main characters taken together are American—red, white, and blue—and he thinks they should be so identified, not narrowly labeled as either black or white. To signify even further the hybridity of Americans, the southern sheriff wears a western outfit.[28]

Growing up in Madison, Georgia, in a family of sharecroppers, Raymond Andrews and his older brother Benny were labeled other from both sides of the color line. Very light-skinned, the Andrews brothers looked white, and Benny told a reporter they had difficulty finding seats on segregated buses; "nobody, black or white, back or front," wanted to sit next to them in the 1940s. They were the first "black" boys in their area to go to high school, the first to go to college, and the first to become artists. Having tried all his life to get beyond race as the South defined it, Raymond Andrews grew bitter because reviewers could not get beyond narrow notions about race when reading his work: "I am finally beginning to realize the truth. No one wants my work because it deals *too much* with Americans. . . . Conservative whites want no part of it whatsoever as they are who decides what did and didn't happen in America's history. Liberal whites don't want to offend the blacks by suggesting that some of their members got honky blood. And blacks want to believe that every American black is pure African or he's not true black. I'm writing about a part of black history nobody wants to talk or know about."[29] In November 1991, a few months after he wrote this diary entry, Raymond Andrews committed suicide. Only now, over a decade later, readers may be ready to appreciate his work in all its literary, historical, and political complexity.

In *Decorations in a Ruined Cemetery* (1994), which is set in New Orleans in 1965 but framed in the present, John Gregory Brown uses modernist techniques to dismantle southern myths of white racial purity, even as he resurrects the tragic mulatto figure that Raymond Andrews made such sport of. *Decorations in a Ruined Cemetery* is one of the few contemporary novels about passing; another is Donald McCaig's historical novel *Jacob's Ladder* (1998), which I discuss in chapter 4. Significantly, both are by white writers who use the passing plot to question white racial purity, rather than simply to advocate black racial equality, as their nineteenth-century predecessors did. Given the complex history of racial and ethnic mixing in New Orleans, where Brown grew up, it is perhaps not surprising that he resuscitated and revised the passing plot. Anthropologist Virginia Dominguez, who did fieldwork in Louisiana during the period Brown writes about, notes that "suspicion is part of everyday life in Louisiana": "Whites often grow up afraid to know their own genealogies. Many admit that as children they often stared at the skin below their fingernails and through a mirror at the white of their eyes to see if there was any 'touch of the tarbrush.'" Creoles of color whom Dominguez interviewed claimed that the "purity" of white Creole ancestry is "imaginary," and they privately delighted in stories questioning it. She found that when questions have arisen about the racial purity of their ancestry, some "white" Creole families have left Louisiana for California or Chicago or New England rather than face continued rumors.[30]

Brown structures his novel around such a moment of discovery. Meredith Eagen, whom readers initially assume is "white," tells the story of how she comes to understand why her hair is curlier and her skin a bit darker than her twin brother's. As befits the discovery of a family secret, Meredith's story progresses both backward and forward, and it unravels from three different perspectives: Meredith's backward glance at her twelfth year, when her father, Thomas, left his second wife, Catherine; Catherine's letters to Meredith, written after the separation; and aging black family servant Murphy Warrington's third-person perspective. From Catherine's revelations about Meredith's paternal grandmother Mollie, Meredith learns she is racially mixed. From Murphy's revelations to Catherine, Meredith discovers why Mollie left her husband and young son Thomas, a fact not even Meredith's father has known. When Thomas was only eight, his mother had an affair with Murphy and left town after discovering she was pregnant. As an adult, Meredith finds parallels between her own melancholia and her father's that seem connected not so much to the truth of her mixed ancestry as to a debilitating uncertainty about how to give it meaning. Meredith is thirty-seven, but her life remains on hold. She still lives, alone and withdrawn, in the house she grew up in; however, her father's death has activated her determination to make sense of her life.

Philosopher and artist Adrian Piper, who is racially mixed but light enough to be mistaken as white, contends that "among politically committed and enlightened whites the inability to acknowledge their probable African ancestry is the last outpost of racism. It is the litmus test that separates those who have the courage of their convictions from those who merely subscribe to them and that measures the depth of our dependence on a presumed superiority." In *Decorations in a Ruined Cemetery* the "white" characters who discover that their ancestry is mixed seem not so much doomed by their own desire to feel superior to black people as daunted by the racism of their society—fearful of a loss of "social regard and respect" that Piper describes from personal experience as "practically unbearable."[31] When first Thomas Eagen and then his daughter Meredith learn of their black ancestry, they continue to live publicly as white. Privately, however, they come to view themselves as "passing," which creates a chronic, debilitating existential problem, even though no performance of race is involved. Unlike other racially mixed characters, who must leave the place where their identity is known in order to pass as white, Brown's Eagens are passing in place; this makes them the perfect vehicle for Brown to question the purity of white identity and the courage of white liberal convictions. However, like other passers, they face a crucial question: how is the racially mixed individual "to forge an identity and satisfying social role within a two-caste society"?[32] To varying degrees, Thomas and Meredith each fear misunderstanding and exposure, which would result in loss of status. Such fears make intimate relationships difficult to sustain or even to embark on. But at the same time each one yearns for a close relationship, needing to share the secret but also, in that very act of imagined confession, making abandonment a possibility. The Eagens' passing in place exposes whiteness, as Americans understand it, to be a fiction. It also illuminates the power of the social narrative of white superiority to construct identity and the knowledge of mixed ancestry to complicate definitions of the self.

The central problem in a novel of passing is "whether or not the passer can achieve a healthy identity,"[33] and most often the fictional solution has been for the passer who has African ancestry to embrace a black identity. Thomas Eagen and his daughter Meredith never take this step and live filled with unhappiness and consumed by "regret," a word frequently repeated. Unlike Campbell's Ida, who for years experiences shame in the black community because her mixed ancestry calls attention to her parents' illicit affair, Thomas and Meredith experience guilt, a painful feeling of responsibility for hiding their mixed ancestry, even though they do not seem to question their white identity.[34] They both seem plagued by the questions that the old black servant Murphy believes tormented Meredith's father: "What if his skin had been a few shades darker? What if the world had given him no choice but to live a black man's life, set himself up in a black man's house and work a black man's job? What if he'd had no choice but to lay down with a black woman who in time would hand to him his own black children, and these children would then pay the same price for their blackness he'd have been asked to pay?"[35] Thomas's periodic restlessness recalls Etienne Bon's and Joe Christmas's movements back and forth between black and white communities in an attempt to find themselves. But an important difference is that Thomas never lives openly as a "black" man, even though he does not shun black people or black culture. He frequents black jazz clubs, sometimes to sing, and he fills his home with the music of black jazz artists, encouraging his son Lowell to cultivate his passion for their music. Thomas commutes between the white neighborhood where he lives and the poor black neighborhood where he practices medicine, a choice that is harmful to his family's finances but beneficial to the poor black people, who cannot afford health care—a choice that Catherine speculates is motivated by Thomas's guilt at hiding his African ancestry. When Thomas leaves Catherine, he moves to this black neighborhood, installing his children in the sparsely furnished living quarters above his office. There Thomas has a brief fling with a woman whom Murphy speculates must be black, since Thomas's mother, Mollie, had an affair with him, which he believes was an attempt to reconnect with her blackness. Brown gives readers only one quick glimpse of Thomas's lover, a beautiful thin dark-haired woman, and he does not identify her racially. Thus he demonstrates with yet another character that racial ancestry is not always written on the body, or, as Amy Robinson has argued, "the visible is never easily or simply a guarantor of truth."[36] With neither the change in neighborhood nor the change in sexual partner does Thomas publicly redefine his identity or his children's. He continues to let his white skin speak for him publicly and protect him from white racism, even as his silence on the matter torments him privately.

Thomas experiences continued guilt because of the discrepancy between the liberal ideology he grew up with and the life he lives. After his mother leaves when he is a boy, his father tells him that she is a "Negro," but he assures him this does not mean anything (134). For Mr. Eagen, an Irish immigrant to America and a northern emigrant to the South, Mollie's mixed ancestry is not an issue. His main point, of course, is that a person's race should not be an issue, and yet he knows only too well its devastating consequences. Because he and Mollie both failed to concern themselves with the South's preoccupation with race, they were ostracized, his business was boycotted, and the Klan burned crosses on their lawn. In dismissing the social significance of Mollie's race, he fails to instruct his son in how to deal with the social construction of race. As he grows up, Thomas sees that race matters, but he does not know "what to do with that information" or how to think of himself or how to position himself in a world divided between black and white (134). His strongest regret is that his mother, whom he dearly loved, was not around to serve as a model. Her absence means that Thomas never learns how to talk about race or racial identity with his own children. Instead he says nothing, and a sad, painful cycle repeats itself.

Brown does not make Thomas Eagen one of his narrators or filter characters, a choice that underlines not only his failure to answer his daughter's first

questions at twelve or her last at thirty-seven before he dies, but also his ultimate failure to answer the questions he asked Catherine in the first year of their
marriage: "My mother was a Negro, okay. What was I supposed to do? I still
don't have an answer to that. What am I supposed to do?" (134). Readers understand Thomas Eagen only partially and indirectly. In a letter to Meredith,
Catherine relays Thomas's most paradoxical conversation about race, in which
he reveals that he does not want to be thought a racist, but neither does he
want to think of himself as black: "'I don't want you thinking I'm ashamed because my mother was a Negro,' he said. 'That's not the case, Cathy. . . . I'm
ashamed because I haven't found the place for that fact,' he said" (135). Given
that Thomas tells Murphy he is leaving Catherine because she has failed to understand him, being understood seems to be what Thomas needs most. Cathy's
reassurances that his mixed ancestry "doesn't mean anything" (135) smack of
his father's naïveté and set their marriage on the wrong course in its first year.
Given that Thomas defines for Catherine, a North Carolinian, the intricacies
of racial identity in New Orleans by using historical examples that show how
his children would have been labeled and discriminated against, racism seems
to be what Thomas fears most for Lowell and Meredith or for a child he and
Catherine might have. Racism is what his father has not prepared him for, and
indeed racism is what he eventually encounters from Catherine. Believing
Thomas has been unfaithful to her and angry at him for not wanting the child
she is carrying, Catherine explains in a letter to Meredith that she returned the
terrible hurt she felt by striking at Thomas's most obvious vulnerability. Like
Alice Walker's Lynne, Catherine calls Thomas a "nigger" in a moment of anger,
even though she has said she hates the word. She blames his unhappiness on
his failure to come to terms with his mixed identity, and she accuses him of re-
lieving his psychic pain through his charity to poor blacks and, when that fails,
spreading pain to his family.

　　To spare his children the pain he has experienced may be Thomas Eagen's
excuse in hiding the truth from his children. And yet as Brown plots the novel,
the truth can never really be hidden. Meredith suffers a life of anguish and regret similar to her father's once she learns the truth from Catherine, and
Meredith blames her father, as he did his father, for not telling her how to deal
with the information. As a child Meredith learned racism from her bigoted
school friends before learning of her mixed ancestry. Thus at first she fears the
black men she encounters in the black neighborhood they move to after her
father leaves Catherine, although after a few weeks, she finds pleasure in the

care and company of the black people she gets to know there. However, apprehensive about what her white friends will say, she tells no one about her new life or her new feelings about black people. The contents of *Decorations in a Ruined Cemetery* are ostensibly Meredith's attempt, twenty-five years later, to piece together the story her father has never told her. Her father's death frees her to explore her family's history and genealogy in her journal, but she does not succeed at thirty-seven any more than she did at twelve, or any more than her father ever did, in publicly telling the truth of her mixed ancestry. When Meredith finishes writing her family history, she predicts that she will not be able to tell a future husband and child the truth of her racial ancestry. This means, of course, that another generation may well be surprised with information about their ancestry that no one has had the courage to tell them. Meredith is reluctant to divulge her secret for she fears that if she tells anyone, that person will not love her. Most especially she fears that if she tells a man who has grown to love her, he will leave her. This is the cautionary tale she has gleaned from the way Catherine relates the breakup of her marriage to Thomas. More than Meredith wants a husband, she, like Catherine, wants a child, because she wants someone to need her, thinking "that would be enough" to bring "certainty" in her world (231). But the novel provides no evidence that Meredith will ever have a relationship that might produce this child.

Crushed by the loss of her stepmother and paralyzed by the thought of losing the status that accompanies her white identity, Meredith has lived in retreat from the world, unable to begin a meaningful relationship with anyone. She has holed up in her father's office building on Magazine Street, but now that her father is dead, she plans to move to her grandfather's home in Mandeville, where Thomas retreated after his father's death. Like Faulkner's Joe Christmas, she is searching for "peace," just as her father did before her (33, 244). In moving to Mandeville, Meredith hopes to find the "peace" (135) her grandfather found there after Mollie left him. But Mr. Eagen found peace because of his faith, which allowed him to accept the loss of his wife Mollie as God's will and encouraged him to do good works, like sculpting concrete gravestones for poor black people. Meredith concludes her family story and Brown concludes the novel by explaining that Meredith hopes to find peace in writing about the past.

Meredith's twin brother, Lowell, is the only racially mixed character in this novel who is untroubled by passing as white; indeed, given his seeming lack of conflict, one could ask if he is passing. He seems to have accepted the meaning he has given his life and is not questioning his identity. From the beginning of the family's move to Magazine Street, he interacts with black people with ease, although at this point he does not know of his mixed ancestry. He spends his spare time in his new black neighborhood drawing black faces, just as he has spent his time in his old white neighborhood listening to black music. Readers never know exactly how much Lowell knows of the family history, although we do know that when he asks a question about what Meredith has learned from Murphy, she promises to tell him "later," even as their father remains silent (235). Meredith assumes that as an adult Lowell's creature comforts as a successful architect and family man insulate him from the existential quandaries that plague her. But is she correct? Her father had similar comforts, and he was not insulated. Might Lowell have a different temperament that enables him not to be preoccupied with the questions that torment her? Is he less inclined to melancholy than his grandmother, father, or sister? Is he more optimistic, more like his grandfather? As Meredith says, "he is able to find some measure of faith and belief in the goodness of life, its pleasures and rewards, no matter its pain and disappointments" (104). Or is he simply less political? Lowell is a shadowy figure in this novel, and John Gregory Brown has not given him a narrative voice. Thus it is difficult to determine whether Lowell Eagen is in flight from his mixed ancestry or whether he has landed safely by scripting a new narrative. The former seems more likely than the latter, since Brown does not write his adult life in any detail. By including two generations of children who are raised as white and who pass for white, Brown suggests that passing is the most likely route even an unprejudiced person who had grown up as "white" would take if he or she discovered African ancestry, whether in 1965 or 1990. By giving his anguished protagonist Meredith a twin who seems to experience no psychological or social problems, Brown reminds us of the ease with which race can be forgotten when someone looks white. But he also signals the difficulty in discerning the causes for people's behavior.

The novel, with its many secrets, takes readers around and around, as we, along with the characters, try to understand the motives that lie behind actions, only to become even more perplexed when we discover that some of the facts we are basing our premises on are false. It is very difficult to feel certain that we completely understand anyone in this novel. We understand the adult Meredith only through her thoughts, while we understand her father mainly through his actions. Neither are enough to discern motives. It is tempting to ascribe the angst of passing as the sole cause of Meredith's unhappiness, just because it seems the sole cause of her father's unhappiness. In her anger Catherine ties her marital problem to Thomas's inability to deal with his mixed heritage, and Murphy at one point agrees with her assessment. But Catherine also suggests that Thomas's restlessness may have more to do with "a dissatisfaction of the spirit" that he inherited from Mollie, "that must have been coursing through his veins the moment he was born" (157). First Murphy says that he still does not know why Mollie had an affair with him—was it incompatibility with her husband or simply a propensity toward restlessness—but later he explains the affair in terms of race.

Over and over Brown questions whether racial identity matters as much as we think it does, only to demonstrate its paradoxical significance when his black and white characters read and misunderstand each other's actions because they have viewed them through the prism of race. For example, Murphy assumes that Catherine thinks of him in the race-neutral terms of "handyman," in order to avoid thinking of him in racially charged terms as "the Eagen family's old black domestic" (82). So Murphy plays that role when she brings some broken chairs to his house; ostensibly she has come to ask him to fix the chairs, but really the chairs are a pretext for asking him about her husband's first marriage. Each is actually partially right, but at the same time somewhat wrong, about the other's motives, all because they filter their responses through multiple levels of race relations as they have evolved in southern history. This Byzantine way of interrelating makes discerning true motives close to impossible. As Catherine says, "maybe the greatest shame of the separation between the different races in this world, between white and black, is that we're left blind and groping as a direct result, unable to sort out the qualities of character that we use to make our judgments about those we meet" (157). Brown puts his readers in the position his characters are in: hopelessly uncertain but desperately seeking to understand, wanting to take characters at their word but doubtful whether they know their own minds or understand another's motives. One thing Brown makes clear is that in conversations with Murphy, both Catherine and Thomas miss the benefit of his analysis of race relations or human relations because neither makes him feel enough like an equal to tell them what he is really thinking. This loss seems especially troubling for Thomas, because he so much regrets not having had conversations about race with his mother. In order to begin such a conversation, Murphy wants Thomas to do what he has resisted: "talk to me nigger to nigger, one black man to another. I wished he could find whatever it was in himself of his mother's color that she'd passed down to him, no matter her absence, and let that rule the roost" (174). While Thomas admits to Murphy that his mother was a "nigger" and to Catherine that she was a "Negro," which he tells her means that some might call him a "nigger" or more accurately a "mulatto," he never applies any of these terms to himself (185, 134, 132).

A witty and potentially revealing vignette sparkles at the center of this sad novel; it takes place during the upsetting first two weeks, when Meredith has just lost her home and her beloved stepmother, but before she has found out about her mixed ancestry. Gabrielle, a racially mixed shopkeeper whom Meredith adores, tells her the story of two old white women from Virginia who come into her shop on Magazine Street looking for antique linen for a granddaughter's wedding present. When they learn that the Gabrielle whose name is on the front door is a black woman, they back out of the store without buying, saying, "We thought you'd be French." Holding both of her arms up in front of her eyes, Gabrielle retorts, "You mean I'm not?" (142), insinuating, of course, that ethnic (and racial) ancestry is not always written on the body, but also that she has every right to define herself, not be defined by white people. In 1965 Gabrielle is not allowed the fullness of her identity, and in 1990 Meredith will not assume the fullness of her identity.

Los Angeles journalist Itabari Njeri argues that African Americans should acknowledge their racially mixed identity because an affirmation of their complex ancestry would reduce colorism, by making normal "what is erroneously treated as an exotic and, consequently, divisive characteristic among African Americans."[37] John Gregory Brown, like Donald McCaig, seems to be suggesting something similar for whites—that they must give up the myth of white racial purity to help bridge the racial divide in this country. But this desire is evident more in the form of his novel and his narrator's yearnings than in the outcome of the plot. If we are moving toward new ways of thinking about race in twenty-first-century America, such novels as *Decorations in a Ruined Cemetery* suggest that contemporary New Orleans, despite its Creole history, is not as cosmopolitan as Los Angeles, its western equivalent, which Farai Chideya has termed "America's multiracial mecca."[38] *Decorations in a Ruined Cemetery* demonstrates that racial identity as white southerners think they know it is a fiction and that the race relations they so politely practice are a tortured masquerade. Fifty years later, John Gregory Brown has not so much revised William

Faulkner's story of a "white" person's anguish about hidden blackness as removed the violence.

As Lise Funderburg has pointed out, "a paradox of the one-drop rule is that it is never a two-way street": "one can be black and have 'white blood' (even to the point of having a white parent. . .), but one cannot be white *and* have 'black blood.'" Funderburg believes that none of the biracial people willing to be interviewed for her book about biracial Americans identify as white because their inclusion in her book would have "jeopardized their white status."[39] To clarify, I would add that a person can have one drop of Native American blood or Asian blood and still be white. The history of slavery and legal segregation created a unique difference between minority groups and played a special role in the way we think about race in America. Social customs created this thinking and American laws have perpetuated it: beginning with antebellum laws that classified all children born to slave mothers as slaves, continuing with the postemancipation obsession with racial identity, and extending to various twentieth-century practices—from the way the U.S. census relied on hypodescent from 1920 to 2000 to the fact that until 1989 hospitals assigned babies the racial status of the nonwhite parent.[40] Recently researchers of attitudes about mixed-race identity have discerned an interesting new paradox: as European Americans have become more willing to bend the one-drop rule, many African Americans have held firmly to it, even though they would admit that most African Americans are racially mixed. Their reasons are many and understandable. In an ongoing struggle against white power and privilege and in an attempt to maintain cultural plurality, African Americans do not want to dilute their numbers.[41] Many do not know the identity of their nonblack ancestors, or if they do, they want nothing to do with a kinship begun by rape or with white kin who refuse to acknowledge the family relationship. Others do not acknowledge mixed ancestry for ideological reasons—because they do not want to appear as if they, like some light-skinned African Americans in the past, are ashamed of a black identity.[42]

Those few who do identify as biracial or multiracial most often, like Tiger Woods, have parents who are socially recognized as belonging to different races. The present desire of some racially mixed individuals to so identify has met with concern about how their offspring will identify, with worries that such attempts to solve anomalies may create others, and with questions about whether new classifications may worsen race relations or end racial classification prematurely.[43] Representing the Association of Multi-Ethnic Americans, Carlos Fernandez has attempted to address important minority issues. Understanding African American concerns about civil rights enforcement and distribution of government services, Fernandez successfully argued before the U.S. Congress that the issue of entitlement programs being directly tied to population numbers can be finessed by allowing racially and ethnically mixed people to indicate all classifications that apply to their identity, as was eventually done on the 2000 census. Fernandez's view of other arguments that brand intermarriage as disloyal and multiracial identity as threatening to racial unity is that they deny multiracial and multiethnic people the basic human rights to identify themselves and to honor both parents.[44] Maureen Reddy, who readily identifies herself as "a white feminist mother of black children," understands the social practices of racial identification but believes that "to see a biracial person simply as black is to reduce complexity, to deny his/her real heritage, and to make interracial families invisible."[45] This way of thinking has been spurred on by the maturation of the 1960s biracial babies, by record numbers of recent immigrants of color, and by new ideas about multiculturalism and postmodern constructions of identity. Racially mixed individuals have only just begun to write about their experiences.[46]

In *Half a Heart* Rosellen Brown examines Miriam Vener's 1980s attempt to assuage white liberal guilt by tracking down Veronica Reece, the child of her interracial love affair with Eljay Reece, a music professor at a black college in Mississippi, where she taught briefly during the 1960s. Brown loosely based Parnassus College on Tougaloo, where she and her husband taught from 1965 to 1967. Born in Philadelphia and educated in New York and Boston, Brown returned to the South in the 1980s and taught at the University of Houston for a number of years.[47] Brown leavens her take on contemporary racism and identity politics with the hopeful story of interracial reconciliation between mother and daughter. In Veronica "Ronnee" Reece, Brown creates a biracial protagonist who, like Gaines's Copper and Campbell's Ida, identifies as black and seeks remuneration from the missing white parent. But Ronnee is different in that her reunion with her white mother sets her on a course to forge what Lise Funderburg would term "a self-concept that is deliberately biracial."[48] In Miriam, Brown creates a white Jewish southerner who is passing in a way—hiding her racial politics and her interracial sexual history.[49] In her marriage to Barry Vener, an ophthalmologist, Miriam has retreated to the white bourgeois world in which she grew up in order to recover from the emotional turmoil of her breakup with Eljay and the devastating loss of her infant daughter to his care. Now living the sheltered life of an upper-middle-class housewife, Miriam allows her liberal social views to flicker only occasionally in smug remarks about keeping her three children in Houston's public schools and in the generous checks made out to good causes. Although her wealth, social status, and three children with Barry partially insulate her from the debilitating self-scrutiny that John Gregory Brown's Meredith suffers, Miriam is subject to periodic depressions caused by the guilt of giving up Veronica and the cowardice of sublimating her former activism in philanthropy. The novel opens during one of those periods. With her children away at summer camp, her mother in declining health, and a chance sighting of a lovely mixed-race teenager, Miriam experiences a depression so heart-wrenching that she feels compelled to track down Veronica.

By pairing Miriam and Veronica as protagonists, Brown nudges readers to consider Ronnee as passing also. Brown's decision to alternate the narration of *Half a Heart* between Miriam's consciousness and Ronnee's allows her to illuminate the evolution in their thinking about each other, about racial identity, and about race relations. Their dual perspectives also function to expose the thoughts and feelings that Miriam and Ronnee hide from each other as they negotiate their new relationship—a technique that Brown surely hoped would speak the unspoken for both black and white readers. The reviews of *Half a Heart* were mixed, a fact *Time* magazine reviewer Paul Gray would not find surprising, since he forecast that "[s]ome whites and some blacks may dislike parts of what they read, which will only demonstrate that Brown is writing very close to the bone."[50]

While registering a complaint about the identity constraints of the one-drop rule, Brown does not ignore the racist beliefs that generated the practice or the current social pressures that perpetuate it. As a result, she constructs her story without making a total end run around racism, which Eric Lott believes occurs in recent theorizing about identity politics and mixed-race identity. He worries that arguments that separate culture from politics and move Americans too quickly beyond racial solidarities to multiracial identities overlook the work that still needs to be done to eliminate racism.[51] Although cloistered in her gated community, Miriam has not been unaware of her financial privilege, because of the great contrast between her present life and her memories of the poor Mississippi town where she attempted to practice her political beliefs as an idealistic history teacher at a black college. But Brown shows her to be less aware of whiteness as a social norm, of the race consciousness and racism that black people experience daily, and of the hidden racism among her friends and family members. In numerous ways, reconnecting with Ronnee gives Miriam "a new way of looking at what she'd taken for granted."[52] Miriam finds that no matter how liberal she is, she has much to learn in order to understand her eighteen-year-old biracial daughter. In memoirs, Jane Lazarre and Maureen Reddy have both detailed how their experiences as white mothers of biracial children attuned them to racism's many ramifications and awakened them, as Reddy writes, "to the reasons for the bitterness and hostility many blacks feel toward whites."[53]

The way Brown geographically divides Miriam's lessons in race consciousness and race relations is significant. In New Hampshire, where the Veners have vacationed to escape Houston's brutal summers, Miriam finds she has actually been able to forget about Veronica. Not until she sees her beloved northern town through Ronnee's eyes the day they meet—"white houses, white fences, white faces" (66)—does Miriam become aware of its absolute "whiteness," which is, of course, the very homogeneity that has allowed her not to think about Ronnee when vacationing there. Two incidents in New Hampshire reveal the difference between Miriam's and Ronnee's perceptions of interpersonal relationships across the color line. The first day they unexpectedly run into a friend of Miriam's in the grocery store, but Miriam does not introduce Ronnee as her daughter. Sensing Ronnee's hurt feelings, Miriam later denies that her silence has had anything to do with race. Alone, Miriam rationalizes her behavior at length—going on for over two pages about the social awkwardness of explaining her secret past and thus her secret self to her summer friend. In contrast, in the next chapter Ronnee assesses the incident quickly in a couple of bitter sentences: "So this mother of hers, surprise, was just another white woman who couldn't face unpleasant facts. But it was one thing not to need anything of this *mother,* she thought, seething, playing the word *mother* around in her mouth, all its street ironies sour on her tongue" (93). White readers may find the hostility of Ronnee's perspective surprising, given how she has disguised the depth of her feelings from her mother, but this hidden anger is exactly what Brown is trying to expose. That is what makes her alternating interior monologues so effective. Derrick Bell explains the insidious effect of racism this way: "Because bias is masked in unofficial practices and 'neutral' standards, we must wrestle with the question whether race or some individual fail-

ing has cost us the job, denied us the promotion, or prompted our being rejected as tenants for an apartment. Either conclusion breeds frustration and
alienation—and a rage we dare not show to others or admit to ourselves."[54]

The second troubling incident occurs when Ronnee tries to use Miriam's
credit card at a local store and the shopkeeper refuses it, telling her he knows
she is not Miriam's daughter. Miriam's first response once again is to deny that
racism is involved in the shopkeeper's reaction: she leaps to his defense and
explains his actions as those of a thoughtful acquaintance trying to protect her
interests. Miriam's reaction provokes Ronnee's angry response: "This just shows
you don't know *any*thing about the kind of shit we have to put up with" (185).
Confronted with the fury of this outburst, Miriam finally understands as she
has been unable to before that "logic was an affront" and that a more appropriate reaction would have been sympathy with her daughter's feelings (185).
Brown punctuates this incident and others similar to it with Miriam's recol-
lections about how the humiliations from whites that Ronnee's father Eljay experienced in the 1960s were magnified when she witnessed them. Miriam
knows that her whiteness has shielded her from such humiliations, but not
until she spends time with Ronnee does she realize that white-skin privilege
has also shielded her from daily consciousness of race. While Miriam has at
first not been able to see the New Hampshire incidents as related to race in any
way, Ronnee, weighed down by the history of American race relations, is quick
to assume that each is a racial incident. Brown is not so much interested in
whose interpretation of these incidents is correct as she is in showing readers
how the lens through which they view the world is tinted by their skin color
and in convincing readers that this reason, if no other, makes the incidents
race-related. Brown makes it Miriam's responsibility to learn about what it
means to be black, not Ronnee's to teach her, but Brown employs Jewel, a black
teacher who befriended Miriam at Parnassus College, as a ready reference of
sorts when Miriam needs an interpreter or some advice.

For the less subtle lessons in race relations and for incidents that can be seen
only as racist, Rosellen Brown takes her characters south, a move some readers have viewed as stereotypical and others as revealing problems in race relations that liberal white southerners do not want to admit.[55] Brown begins her
dissection of race relations in the new South with Miriam's aging mother, who
assumes Ronnee is a nurse's aid because of her skin color. Advancing
Alzheimer's disease has stripped away her polite veneer of southern manners,
with the result that she talks about black people in language Miriam has never

heard her use before—words such as "schwartze" and "nigger" that Miriam thought her mother "deplored" (30). This development forces Miriam to face the fact that her mother has always thought in these terms but censored them from her speech. Brown goes on to portray some of the professional, educated white southerners in Miriam's own generation as hypocrites of a different sort, liberal in theory but not in practice. They voice support for liberal causes, but most send their children to private schools and live in segregated neighborhoods. They attend the party Miriam hosts in Ronnee's honor, but some of them talk about her behind her back. They allow their teenage children to socialize with Ronnee but do not want their sons to date her. Miriam's assessment of these friends hits the mark: "Their response to Ronnee she would not have predicted, but up close and in the family was obviously not the same as abstract and safely elsewhere" (323).

The white teenagers are more liberal in practice than their parents, although they have had so little interaction with minorities in their predominately white private schools that they too traffic in stereotypes. To Lisa, who is an underground activist for illegal immigrants, Ronnee's racial ancestry means that she will automatically want to get involved in helping the "underdog" (298). To Lisa's handsome brother Jordan, Ronnee presents a unique opportunity to punch an exotic notch in his already well-tooled sexual belt: "You are so rare. You make me dizzy" (280). Jordan figures in Ronnee's own secret plans for sexual experimentation across the color line, but the significant difference between Jordan and Ronnee is in their contact with the other. Jordan's motives are clearer to Ronnee than hers are to him, because she knows white people from her school, while he knows black people from television ("Bill Cosby is a good representative") and his advanced placement English class ("Toni Morrison. Zora What's-her-name" [278]). Jordan thinks that "ninety percent—of the problems between the races come from unfamiliarity and that's all" (280). He believes that with a major in sociology, which will teach him about people, and another in political science, which will teach him how to get things done, he can change the world. The difficulties that Ronnee and her mother have in understanding each other prove Ronnee's assessment more accurate: "You can keep your politicians and your sociology double major, it's going to take a lot more than familiarity to make white folks comfortable with us. And vice versa" (281).

In coming into contact with such variations of white racism, Ronnee reacts differently depending on the circumstances, choosing her fights carefully—tenderly ministering to Miriam's senile mother's physical needs, rising above the awkwardness of the behavior of Miriam's friends, but directly confronting her own peers in very frank exchanges. In each of these encounters, Brown has Ronnee think of Eljay, because he has taught her how to protect herself against white racism, even though he has hardened her against white people in the process. During the time she spends with her mother, Ronnee learns that she needs to become more aware of whites as individuals. Slowly she retrains herself not to think of whiteness as the cause of every white person's offensive or regrettable action. For example, the night Jordan takes her to a sleazy motel for sex, Ronnee finds she is more accurate if she assesses his behavior in terms other than his race: "If they'd only been in a civilized place, she'd have walked away from this crude, arrogant, self-absorbed boy—not white boy, she lectured herself. Just *boy*" (302).

Brown's technique of having both Ronnee and Miriam call attention to their own stereotypical thinking seems a deliberate attempt to heighten readers' awareness to how stereotypes operate and how insidious they are. For example, when Ronnee, who needs money for college, first contemplates meeting her mother, two facts about her—that she is white and that she lives in Texas—lead Ronnee to picture "a cash cow, a big woman with big hair, horselike if not cow-like, responsible for *her* size, wearing a white cowboy hat and boots and something made of denim with a fringe" (86). Knowing the cultural inflections of Houston, more southern than western, for example, would have only minimally changed Ronnee's racial and geographic profiling, because she fails to factor in her mother's religion, her former civil rights activity, the grief she felt when Eljay kidnapped her infant daughter (Ronnee), or her current guilt. That readers have already met Miriam and know these facts only heightens the impact of Brown's technique. All it takes is the sight of Miriam—"the small, well-exercised, carefully manicured woman who strode out of the dark of the hall in classy sandals, really good clothes, that pricey hairdo" (89)—to make Ronnee realize how popular culture has governed her imagination. Brown makes such revisionary thinking mandatory for Miriam as well. Because Miriam has experienced a wider range of people than her daughter has, she knows from the day they meet that "everything was qualified, everything particular. There was no such thing as a Black Girl, let alone a Half-Black Girl, From Brooklyn" (64). But more than once Miriam has to remind herself that just because her daughter is half black does not mean she will be interested in political or social causes.

In *Half a Heart,* Rosellen Brown is as interested in how Americans define racial identity as she is in how blacks and whites interact. Through a flashback to Ronnee's experiences growing up in New York, Brown suggests why America's insistence on monoracial identity can pose problems for the mixed-race child. Despite the fact that Eljay has raised Ronnee to identify as black, her light skin elicits a different story, which changes depending on whether her interlocutor is white or black. In the New York public school Ronnee attends, the black students label her "a snob and a house nigger," terms that reflect color-coded class hierarchy within the black community, a cruel by-product of slavery's many evils. They call her "white" because of her studiousness and her desire to please her teachers (76), a paradoxical attempt by black teenagers to control how race is defined in the very schools that have failed them by defining them as incapable. Seeing "academic success as unattainable," the black students "protect themselves by deciding school is unimportant."[56] Brown forces readers to consider how many popular notions about racial identity are really based on what Paul Gilroy calls "oppositional identities" that are created by racist stereotypes. He argues that "cultural versions of race are no less brutal than the biological."[57]

When teenage black boys sexually harass her, Ronnee takes matters in her own hands by winning a scholarship to a very selective, but predominantly white, private school—only to be viewed by her father as abandoning her "people" and going over to the "enemies." The insensitivity of his remark is measured by the pain of Ronnee's rejoinder, "half of me is those enemies" (79). Adrian Piper explains the persistence of such polarized thinking by arguing that the history of race relations has created a dynamic in which "blacks and whites alike seem to be unable to accord worth to others outside their in-group affiliations without feeling that they are taking it away from themselves."[58] Because of such thinking, Ronnee has come to think of her genes as "born fighting" (91), an image that reverberates with the emotional toll taken on Ronnee's health. Brown figures the social construction of race as stressful—whether it is expressed as black appeals to racial authenticity,[59] or white presumption of differences that do not exist, or white blindness to the causes of differences that do. At the public school, stress from black students' accusations that she is not black enough produces the physical sensation of "drowning" (77) and actually increases her asthma attacks, while the polite wariness she encounters in the predominately white private school creates a social uneasiness that makes her feel "sick," as if she had "a chronic low-grade illness" (76). Being forced to disown part of her racial identity no matter whom she is with, Ronnee's search for self becomes far more painful than normal adolescent angst.[60] For her, for example, all dating is interracial. In casting her biracial character as a budding actress, Brown refigures passing as doubly complex because both blacks and whites require Ronnee to play a role different from her biracial identity, one that often conflicts with it.

Brown's plot enacts the pitfalls that occur, as Diana Fuss has argued, when racial identity is theorized as a strict opposition between essentialism and social construction.[61] Knowing that Ronnee will be seen as black because of society's arbitrary one-drop rule, Eljay convinces Miriam when Ronnee is an infant that she will be better off with him because he can best teach her not only about black culture but also about white racism. Believing whiteness is a socially constructed category of oppression rather than a culture, Eljay, like some contemporary whiteness theorists, teaches Ronnee that whiteness is "a nothing, an absence, a ghostliness." Furthermore, he deceives Ronnee into thinking that her mother abandoned her. In practice, Eljay's lessons about black self-worth essentialize blackness and ironically result in Ronnee judging herself "slightly incomplete in her blackness, flawed" (84).

In order to position Ronnee outside of this American context so that she will be forced to see that her racial identity is constructed, Brown creates an encounter for her with an African student, Nkoma. He fancies Ronnee and she him, but he will not date her because his parents expect him to marry a pure-blooded black woman. Nkoma's definition of race exactly reverses America's one-drop rule, equating blackness with purity and whiteness with hybridity. While Ronnee views black identity as "culture" and thinks of herself as black, Nkoma views black identity as "blood" and sees her as white (82). Rather than labeling Ronnee "tainted," as she labels herself, Nkoma terms her "ineligible" as a potential mate, a term Ronnee likes because it seems more scientific than judgmental (83–84). Nkoma's different perspective causes Ronnee to see that whiteness does have a "presence" in her identity after all, which makes her interested in discovering what its presence might mean for her. Nkoma's flattery in comparing her beauty to that of a "hybrid flower" and his finger under her chin, intended to bolster her spirits, make Ronnee aware of an aspect of her identity she has not considered: "any American girl, black or white" would see his patronizing gestures as "foreign" (84).

From this point on, Ronnee revises her thinking about "all" black people, just as later in Houston when surrounded by white people, she attempts not to generalize about whites. For example, during the party Miriam hosts to introduce Ronnee to family friends, Ronnee first assumes that the guests are dull because they are white, only to check herself by remembering that her father's friends are "artists, most of them, more funky, difficult, noisy, profane than the majority of people, color beside the point" (251). Throughout the novel Brown plays with pronouns, because both Miriam and Ronnee must rethink who is "we" and who is "they." Brown's use of this device culminates in Ronnee's remark near the end of the novel when she watches the Jewish children at her half sister Evie's summer camp: "*They* are *me.* Would she always have to remind herself?" (384). As she wonders if she could ever understand the Hebrew service these children are conducting, her answer combines both the hope of connection, for she sees the other as part of herself, and the habit of separation, for she has not known of the relationship for eighteen years.

Being at her mother's house in Houston allows Ronnie to contemplate who she would have been if she had grown up in her mother's luxurious lap in a white suburb: "Would she, Veronica Whoever, have been white, then?" (217). Drawing on her memory of a class discussion about "essence" and "existence" and "which came first," Ronnee initially thinks her "existence" would not have been that different, apart from having more money. Given her mother's liberal values and work during the civil rights movement, Ronnee knows Miriam would have exposed her to black history and culture and would have sent her to the same type of safe, slightly integrated school she chose for herself in New York. Thus, she thinks her mother "would have kept her black. Neatly, exactly half black. As much as she could." But knowing that in Houston she feels "on the other side of . . . something," Ronnee finally realizes that because her mother is white and Jewish, she would have acquired a different perspective on the world, which would have made her "existence" very different. While fully focused on building a relationship with her mother that will produce the much-needed money for her tuition at Stanford, Ronnee works part time on trying to determine her own "essence," the "nub of her" that lay like a "small jewel somewhere" obscured beneath her racial "existence" (217–18).

Brown suggests that Ronnee catches sight of her "essence" in physical similarities to her mother that remind her of their genetic connections—shared mannerisms and hair texture, a similarity that surprises Ronnee because she does not think of white women as having "bad hair" (269). Miriam's friend Jewel notices a similarity in temperament—that each seems to think she "deserves rejection" (275). It is in their biological relationship that Brown begins to figure the "presence" of Ronnee's whiteness; "blood" and "genes" are words that both Ronnee and Miriam keep returning to in their thinking. But it is the work of developing an ongoing mother-daughter relationship that will sustain this presence. Ronnee's initial revulsion at her mother's desperation to have a relationship with her mellows into pride at Miriam's decision to host a party in her honor and to defy her husband's sense of propriety by doing so.

Brown constructs the plot so that Ronnee, much like Dori Sanders's Clover, must live with her mother for a while in order to see her as a "real" person (378) with complex emotions and deep feelings, instead of a "seditty white lady" (90). By the time Eljay lets Miriam know that Ronnee wanted to meet her solely for financial reasons, Ronnee has been with her mother long enough at least to sense the bond that she longed for as a child but that as a teenager she began to think she no longer needed. As Ronnee ponders the possibility of losing her mother's love when Miriam learns of her ulterior motives, Ronnee thinks that "her mother was the only one, in the end, who didn't see her color first, and she would miss that" (394). She compares her mother's and father's comments about skin color: Miriam's yearning for her physical body, her "little brown shoulders," after her father stole her away contrasts with Eljay's ideological exhortations, "Black Girl! Bearer of our racial destiny. Counter in the struggle" (394). This thought causes Ronnee to leap to the conclusion that her mother, in contrast to her father, has understood her "essence," while her father has been preoccupied with "existence." Ronnee's second thought about her mother's definition of identity more nearly hits the mark Rosellen Brown seems to be aiming for in this novel: "Essence and existence, *she'd* have said they were indivisible" (394).

The lengthy telephone conversation between Ronnee's parents near the end of the novel parallels the only other conversation they had about their daughter's identity, eighteen years before, when existence seemed to win out over essence. Then Eljay convinced Miriam that because whites would see Veronica as black, he could better prepare her to deal with white perceptions of black identity and white racism. Eighteen years later they reach a different conclusion about their daughter's identity, one that echoes the 1990s debate about how the 2000 census should categorize identity. Miriam asks Eljay, "[A]re you willing to let 'your girl' be what she is?" (368). Genetically Ronnee is not simply black, although her father has raised her as a black woman. And Ronnee's ability to negotiate the minefield of prejudice in Houston testifies to Eljay's talent in equipping her with the self-esteem and social skills she needs to live in a world that is only a bit more ready for her than it was for Faulkner's Etienne Bon. But Eljay's promise to allow Ronnee to get to know her white family and ultimately to choose her own racial identity is predicated on the enjoinder that Miriam not force Ronnee into a lawsuit against the Houston police for their racism and neglect of Ronnee's asthma. In other words, Eljay is willing to allow Ronnee to be half white, if Miriam won't force her into political activism simply because she is half black. He reminds Miriam that Ronnee is also a teenager—self-absorbed and self-conscious—who would be more hurt by a lawsuit than helped by it when her sexual relationship with Jordan became embarrassing public knowledge.

When Ronnee learns that her father has revealed her mercenary motives, she assumes Miriam will not want anything more to do with her. In a move that seems weakly motivated, although thematically necessary, Ronnee goes to California so that she can at least meet her half sister Evie before departing the Vener family forever. In this final scene, which takes place at Evie's Jewish summer camp, the family relationship between Ronnee and Evie supercedes racial identity—evidence perhaps of a liberal white desire to think beyond the one-drop rule, but a desire Brown attributes to Ronnee as well. Miriam has scaled back her 1960s thoughts of Ronnee as a "gift" to the world (141) and now thinks of Ronnee as a "a gift" (267) to Evie, who has always wanted a sister. Miriam hopes that Ronnee and Evie's relationship will be "untainted" with the tensions and misunderstandings that have characterized her own relationship with Ronnee. But to keep the relationship untainted, Brown must fall back on ten-year-old Evie's youthful innocence and her excitement about having a sister to even the family feuds between her and her two brothers. Aware of her brothers' fear of black people but uncertain of the reason, Evie dispenses with any scary connotations by viewing Ronnee's skin color literally—"you aren't black at all, really. You're sort of—coppery" (389). Stripping skin color of society's ideological constructs recalls her mother's view of the infant Ronnee's "little brown shoulders." But Evie's explanation makes Ronnee realize that she has much to teach her sister about race relations and demonstrates that Rosellen Brown resists making her biracial child into an idealistic symbol of improved race relations, even as she positions her securely within the white half of her family as well as the black.

In an interview Rosellen Brown termed the ending to *Half a Heart* "hopeful but unfinished."[62] The novel concludes with a telephone call in which Miriam expresses worry about Ronnee's disappearance, and Ronnee responds with the one word Miriam has been longing to hear, "Mom?" (402). That Ronnee delivers this intimate word of relationship as a question implies that she wants Miriam to be much more than the "cash cow" she first envisioned but that she wonders if Miriam is still interested in their blood tie, given Ronnee's betrayal of Miriam's trust. Because Brown ends her novel by having Ronnee say the one word she had never expected to utter and the one word Miriam had hoped to hear, it is difficult for a reader not to complete Brown's "unfinished" ending. Because of that one word, readers may well assume that each character will get what she most wanted from the other and more. Throughout the novel, comparisons of Ronnee to Cinderella and Miriam to Sleeping Beauty both point up the difficulties of their less-than-fairy-tale reunion and self-consciously predict the problems some readers may have with a tidy ending to a psychologically complex narrative about race relations. Technically Brown is right to say that her ending is open, for readers do not know whether Miriam will put her rekindled passion for social activism to a broader use or whether Ronnee's life will be as charmed as Tiger Woods's life seems to be most of the time. Nor do we know for sure whether Miriam and Ronnee will continue their relationship. The question mark signals that uncertainty. What readers do know is how riddled with mixed motives and misunderstandings their relationship has been so far. We also know that Ronnee will not be trying out her new biracial identity at a southern university, but at Stanford on the more cosmopolitan West Coast.

In her new thinking about racial identity, Ronnee finds herself looking for a guide at Evie's camp, where she spots "a boy darker than she was with telltale hair, his warm-brown neck lovely against his white Izod shirt. What, she wished she knew, was his story, and how did he like it?" (385). Ronnee's desire to know the "story" of this mixed-race child parallels the growing desire for stories about biracial identity, which is evident in the immediate attention given such very recent works as *Half a Heart;* Rebecca Walker's memoir, *Black, White, and Jewish;* Danzy Senna's novel *Caucasia;* Jerome Hairston's play *a.m. Sunday;* and Natasha Trethewey's *Bellocq's Ophelia.* Throughout *Half a Heart,* Brown gives Ronnee and Miriam an awareness of the difficulty of writing a new "script" for their relationship (57, 89), which may be a self-conscious nod toward Brown's new plot for the mixed-race character. In imagining an interracial story about mother-daughter love regained, Rosellen Brown is writing beyond the ending of the tragic mulatta, whose story concluded with romantic love lost. In *Half a Heart* Jordan auditions Ronnee for that old part by telling her that his mother cried when she learned they were dating: "Like she's already seeing her little grandchildren and they're, what, octaroons? No, wait. Quadroons." But Ronnee refuses the role: "Jesus, those words! That's right out of the Reconstruction or something. What are we, in New Orleans, and I'm the Tragic Fucking Mulatto?" (291). At the end of the novel Brown also gives Ronnee two choices that Gaines's Copper and Campbell's Ida did not have: the chance to have a relationship with the white parent and the opportunity to identify herself. In answer to Evie's pointed question, "Are you a—um—black?" Ronnee says, "half," without hesitation (387). By representing Ronnee as "deliberately mixed" and including the exchange between Jordan and Ronnee, Brown seems to be calling for an end to stories about the tragic mulatto. But by choosing a biracial character who has grown up black and decides with her mother's support to explore her "white side" (249), Rosellen Brown makes it easier to jettison that old southern character type than John Gregory Brown found it to be when he focused on a racially mixed protagonist who looks and identifies white in a society where prejudice against blacks lingers.

The sad, secret history of interracial sexual relationships in the South still plays a role in contemporary fiction about mixed-race characters. In none of the works by Ernest Gaines, Bebe Moore Campbell, or John Gregory Brown does the mixed character actually get to talk to the missing parent or grandparent; rather, these characters must negotiate their mixed ancestry with someone at least once removed, uncle or half brother or stepmother. The ending of Rosellen Brown's *Half a Heart* suggests that the growing presence of both parents in the racially mixed child's life may help to change the one-drop rule, even if concerns about black solidarity and white purity have not totally exited the stage. However, Ronnee's conflicts in *Half a Heart* show that existential angst, if not tragedy, will continue to plague racially mixed people as long as society's demand to define them clashes with their attempts to define themselves.

CHAPTER 6

Still Separate after All These Years

Place and Community

I thought all that was over and settled. Everything's integrated, right?

—JOSEPHINE HUMPHREYS, *DREAMS OF SLEEP*

In March 2001 the *Washington Post* reported that David Holton, the owner of Perry Package Store and Lounge in rural Florida, had been racially segregating his clientele since 1970—whites listening to country music in the large front lounge and blacks listening to the blues in a small back room with a concrete floor and folding chairs. When asked to explain this practice, Holton maintained that the arrangement reflected his customers' choices, but a waitress revealed that she had been advised to steer black patrons to the back if the white people in the lounge were "rednecks." To outsiders, particularly the Maryland congressman directed to the back room in 2001, Holton's shocking discriminatory practices called to mind "the struggles of the 1950s and '60s, when restrooms were labeled 'white' and 'colored,' restaurants and motels could refuse service with impunity, and blacks were relegated to the back of the bus." But to residents in Perry, the segregated bar was old news, a town fixture they thought would never go away.[1] While it may be comforting to look on such an establishment and mind-set as an aberration in the twenty-first-century South, as simply a rare throwback to the bad old days, contemporary novelists have recently been asking readers to look more closely—not only in such rural backwaters but in the South's metropolitan areas as well.

In the first half of the twentieth century, many southern blacks escaped legal segregation by leaving the South—moving to New York and Washington, D.C., to Chicago and Detroit. But by the end of the century, cities in the Northeast and the Midwest had the highest levels of black-white residential segregation and racial isolation in the United States, which is not to say that segregation does not persist in the South's largest metropolitan areas as well, especially in cities like Atlanta and New Orleans.[2] However, the 2000 U.S. Census figures revealed that people in the fastest-growing regions of the country—the South and the West—are more likely to live in integrated neighborhoods than those who live elsewhere in the country. As career opportunities draw young professionals to the South and as more baby boomers retire to the South, blacks and whites in these demographic groups are moving to the same new housing developments, thus creating some neighborhoods integrated from their inception, particularly in the suburbs and smaller cities. Owing to a distinctive southern metropolitan development, in which white developers created black suburbs on the urban fringe and white suburbs expanded into rural black areas, southern metropolitan areas have never been as highly segregated as their northern counterparts, where blacks are more confined to the urban core and less scattered in outlying metropolitan areas. When segregation levels are measured at the block level rather than the tract level, however, segregation is higher in the South.[3]

Demographer William Frey believes that return migration to the South, particularly in the 1990s, is helping "to realign relationships between the races, creating a more equal balance" in a region once best known for its racial problems.[4] But given past patterns of white flight from newly integrated neighborhoods, it is too soon to say whether this new pattern will hold and produce the effects Frey imagines. While studies show that blacks would prefer to live in neighborhoods that are one-third to two-thirds black, whites become anxious or fearful when integration progresses beyond "managed tokenism." Although public opinion polls show white support for integration, the "discomfort level" of whites rises when black families make up more than 5 or 6 percent of a neighborhood. For example, the formerly integrated middle-class Atlanta neighborhood of Cascade Heights, where former mayor Andrew Young lived, is almost all black today.[5]

In *American Apartheid*, sociologists Douglas S. Massey and Nancy Denton argue that "by the end of the 1970s residential segregation became the forgotten factor in American race relations."[6] But southern novelists have not forgotten. Josephine Humphreys, Tom Wolfe, Toni Cade Bambara, Christine Wiltz, Elizabeth Spencer, and Randall Kenan have all used a wide-angle lens to examine the residential and social segregation that persists despite the growing number of interracial friendships. They represent contemporary race relations as being closer to Booker T. Washington's 1890s promise of economic cooperation but social separation than to Martin Luther King Jr.'s 1960s dream of a "beloved community." In 1944 Gunnar Myrdal argued that where residential segregation is extreme, cross-racial understanding is not possible. Massey and Denton have recuperated his argument, pointing out that "most Americans vaguely realize that urban America is still a residentially segregated society, but few appreciate the depth of black segregation or the degree to which it is maintained by ongoing institutional arrangement and contemporary individual actions."[7] Because the reasons for residential segregation are complex and lie beyond any one individual's ability to change them,[8] the conclusions of these novels do not contain as much optimism for improved race relations as those novels discussed in previous chapters, which zoom in on relationships between individuals. Of the writers interested in community dynamics, only Christine Wiltz envisions the beginning of a small interracial group that exhibits King's ideals of responsibility, connectedness, generosity of spirit, and respect across racial lines. Nonetheless, by the end of *Glass House* the future of this fledgling integrated community is left in doubt. These contemporary southern novels give readers a complex sense of social segregation, an "unfortunate holdover from a racist past,"[9] which today plagues the United States, not just the South.

Urban Spaces, Racial Enclaves

As time passes and the history of the civil rights movement recedes, race relations have come to seem less troubling to some, more a vexing issue between individuals than a pressing social problem. In *A Country of Strangers*, David Shipler argues that "a diminished sense of history diminishes the sense of responsibility for racial ills." As a region, the South for decades felt the responsibility for racial ills more than the rest of the nation, but Steve Suitts, the former executive director of the Southern Regional Council, believes that dynamic has recently changed. Suitts, who is white, points out that because his generation of white southerners grew up during the civil rights movement, they knew that their fathers and grandfathers were complicit in southern segregation, and hence many felt a personal responsibility for segregation. Now, he says, young white southerners who listen to black music and look up to black athletes no longer feel any "personal responsibility for the fact that 60 percent of the black kids in this country, or in my state [Georgia] are poor."[10] No wonder urban southern novelists who remember the civil rights movement are reminding readers of white complicity in black poverty and residential segregation in the present.

In Josephine Humphreys's *Dreams of Sleep* (1984), when Will Reese, a native Charlestonian, tells newcomer Duncan Nesmith that the city may be in for "a doozy of a racial war," in an attempt to discourage him from building a pirate theme park near the historic district, the white real estate developer from Ohio is taken aback: "I thought all that was over and settled. Everything's integrated, right?" Compared with Duncan's obliviousness to the legacy of legal segregation, Will's brief explanation that much of Charleston's black population is economically and spatially "trapped" is at least informed, if not motivated, by racial sensitivity.[11] In the 1990s Tom Wolfe, Toni Cade Bambara, and Christine Wiltz joined Humphreys in fictionalizing the urban South's racial divide, trying to shake readers, especially white readers, out of the complacency and ignorance that Duncan exhibits. Communication scholars Leonard Steinhorn and Barbara Diggs-Brown believe that the majority of white Americans have a view similar to Duncan's. They argue that television has given white Americans an illusion of integration that "enables whites to live in a world with blacks without having to do so in fact": "It provides a form of safe intimacy without any of the risks. It offers a clean and easy way for whites to establish and nourish what they see as their bona fide commitment to fairness, tolerance, and color-blindness." But according to Steinhorn and Diggs-Brown, what "television giveth, in the form of the virtual community that transcends race, . . . it taketh away, by reinforcing an association between blacks and crime that makes real community building all but impossible."[12] Southern urban writers are making segregation visible through their varied urban settings. While they do not flinch from describing the dangers in inner-city ghettos, they break the media's simplistic link between poor black people and crime, pointing their pens at public policies and private prejudices that still simmer behind polite facades in uptown mansions and gated McMansions in the suburbs.

Collectively, they have begun to establish conventions for the urban southern novel; perhaps most important among them is the use of multiple perspectives. For example, by presenting her New Orleans story through the diverse perspectives of residents who live in the housing projects as well as those who occupy the mansions uptown, Christine Wiltz suggests that all readers, like all her characters, have something to learn about the people on the other side of town. Bambara and Wolfe complicate Wiltz's rich white–poor black paradigm with class divisions on both sides of the color line. Each of these writers has great fun parodying the ubiquitous urban guided tours, which render invisible past racism as well as its present-day manifestations. In Wolfe's *A Man in Full* (1998) the black mayor conducts a tour starting predictably in lily-white Buckhead but concluding in South Atlanta's poorest black neighborhood—a hypersegregated portion of the city that was lopped off the tourist maps printed for the 1996 Olympics. Humphreys deconstructs the sanitized architectural and historical bus tour of Charleston in *Rich in Love* (1987) by having a black character fill the official tour guide's silences with the expunged history: "Here is where they hung the pirates. . . . Here is where they hung the Negroes."[13] In *Those Bones Are Not My Child* (1999), Bambara provides an alternative tour, set up by a black-owned tour company. During the period of the Atlanta child murders, the narrator imagines a parodic addendum: "Got the Merchandise Mart, the World Trade Congress Center, the world's tallest hotel. . . . Got funeral wreaths fading on doors in our neighborhoods. . . . We got names, dates, events boxed, locked, and buried. Got walls erected against question and challenge."[14] These urban novelists all draw attention to specific streets in Charleston, Atlanta, and New Orleans that still serve as very real color lines spatially segregating whites from blacks by neighborhoods, even though workplaces have been integrated for decades. When schools figure in these novels, they are rarely integrated—a reminder that after the Brown decision, white families fled to outlying predominantly white suburbia or turned to hastily formed segregationist academies and private parochial schools.

In *Dreams of Sleep* Josephine Humphreys juxtaposes Charleston's historic waterfront homes, with their double piazzas designed to catch the sea breezes, and the cheaply built, generic public housing projects that spatially segregate Charleston's poor blacks. Humphreys represents the city's de facto segregated housing as creating the very opposite of the South's celebrated sense of community.[15] Humphreys's female protagonist, Alice Reese, and her husband, Will, live in a "transitional neighborhood," a recently all-black, formerly all-Jewish, neighborhood, which white people are beginning to gentrify. As a result this part of town—between the architecturally exquisite white Battery and the prefabricated mostly black projects—is an accidentally integrated neighborhood of old houses in varying states of repair. But as Alice says, "neighborhood" is a misnomer, since people keep to themselves. The Reeses' recently restored home is a fortress, walled and gated to keep out their neighbors—"students, homosexuals, and Navy people" who live "in groups not identifiable as families"

(7)—and the black people who live in the nearby projects. Because of the city's residential segregation, the projects are a "hidden world" (135) to white people —avoided because feared, feared because unknown. When Will's mother, a real estate agent, hears of a rape anywhere in town, she automatically assumes Alice is at risk just because she lives near the projects. This climate of fear means that Alice detours around the projects when running her daily errands, even though her route would be shorter if she drove or walked through them.

When Alice hires Iris, a poor white babysitter, in order to escape the boredom of being a stay-at-home mother, Humphreys appears to be creating a situation in which Alice will also enlarge the spatial boundaries that create her racial isolation. Because Iris grew up in the projects, she naturally walks through the area to get to Alice's house. While Alice perceives Iris's choice as brave, Iris sees it as unremarkable, "just something I've always done" (132). This new and unexpected point of view nudges Alice to do the previously unthinkable and take the shortest route to the supermarket. Several trips through this previously "hidden world" of the projects neutralize her fears and make the place less foreign: "Children skitter down the sidewalk ahead of her, walking home from school with bookbags, cheerleading pompoms, cans of Pepsi" (135). At the same time, Alice despairs at the lack of progress made since the civil rights movement in moving urban blacks out of poverty. Although she vows not to give up hope, she does nothing to initiate a public crusade against poverty or to start a private rebellion against segregation—she doesn't even speak to the black people she passes on her walks.

Humphreys does not totally sidestep this explosive issue, however, although she restricts her exploration of the ghetto to Iris's perspective. Ironically, Alice sees Iris as "unburdened by a sense of history or home or kin" (129) because she is a poor white teenager who no longer lives with her dysfunctional family. But Iris has her own regionally induced hang-ups, which most directly relate to my focus on race relations and urban space. Her best friend is Emory, a young black artist whom she grew up with in the projects. He is the only person in her life she does not have to care for, the only person who actually looks out for her, the one person who brings her joy. Although Iris is clearly drawn to Emory, she turns him down when he asks her to move to Atlanta with him, because she cannot envision a future with him. Iris arrives at this understanding when Alice speaks about her own inability to be adventuresome: "It's more than the physical task. It's . . . a vision of yourself. If you don't see yourself as being able to do it, then you can't no matter how easy it is" (203). Iris likes to think that she has turned down Emory for his own good, not wanting to ruin his future as a painter by turning his life into the furtive, marginal existence that she perceives other interracial couples live—"at the Laundromat or the bus stop at odd morning hours when married people aren't ordinarily seen together" (200). However, outside of Charleston, as she and Alice drive toward Florida during the night of Alice's aborted flight from her empty marriage to Will, Iris's imagination soars unchecked when she thinks of Emory: "She would enroll in a community college. And at night they'd work two jobs and save their money. It would be the life he wanted, and the kind of scenery artists like to paint, sun and water, orange trees" (207). Humphreys shows how one's thinking is influenced by place, for back in Charleston, Iris cannot sustain her vision of interracial love. After seeing Emory one last time, Iris realizes that she will "never get to another place" (226). Humphreys, who grew up in Charleston, has said that "Charleston is a place that demanded your loyalty," and she represents that demand as pressure "to follow the rules of the town," which involve traditional thinking about regional myths, ancestry, gender roles, and race relations.[16]

In the end Iris cannot follow the advice she says she would give Alice's daughters: "Always choose love over safety if you can tell the difference" (217). Doing battle with Iris's deep personal desire for Emory (love) is a stronger desire for social approval (safety), which manifests itself as anger both at him, "for being black and for being her best friend, two things he ought never to have been" (156), and at her mother, for having raised her in the projects, having put her in a place where, she says, "the one friend I had was always a danger to me" (225). Humphreys suggests that simply living in an integrated neighborhood is not enough to overcome society's pervasive racial mind-set. Iris is determined to move her mother out of the projects, not because of the stigma of poverty, but because of the stigma of race: "Other people who couldn't understand it was only time that had put Fay there and left her stranded, might think of other causes. A white woman who would live like that would have to be a whore or feebleminded, somebody abandoned by her own people. Even the black people would think this" (151). Similarly, Iris fights her desire to go with Emory based on what she knows white Charlestonians would think of their union, not on what anyone she loves or respects has actually said to her, although it is clear to readers that Emory's foster mother worries about their relationship even though she loves Iris. Iris's mother insinuates that if Iris had a sexual relationship with Emory, it would not bother her, as long as Iris uses birth control: "It's nigger babies I'm warning you against, Iris. Not love" (18). Such mixed messages add up to an emotional conflict that keeps Iris in Charleston, even as she contemplates visiting Emory in Atlanta.

As a couple, Iris and Emory are better suited to each other than Alice and Will are, who after separate existential conflicts settle back into a banal life together out of inertia. For Humphreys the mutual affection between Iris and Emory is a subplot, but one that resonates in ironic ways if readers compare the two relationships. Humphreys does not facilitate this comparison, however, as readers never see Charleston or race relations or the projects through Emory's eyes, a significant omission in a southern urban narrative. The reader looks only through the eyes of the white characters: Alice, Will, and Iris. The author's concerns about how to live in a city that is beautiful and historic but traditional and segregated resonate deeply in the background of this novel, but her narrative of social and residential segregation recedes as the domestic dramas take center stage. Yet she is not oblivious to the potential for the city's continued social segregation to produce its own drama. During one of Alice's solitary walks through the projects, she wonders: "Was the whole civil rights movement nothing but a minor disturbance in the succession of years? White people have started telling jokes again. Blacks and whites live farther apart than ever, like the double curve of a hyperbolic function, two human worlds of identical misery and passion but occupying opposite quadrants, nonintersecting. In a way, equal but separate. One day something will blow up, but Alice doesn't know whether it will be the world or the South or the Reese family" (134).

In the next decade, Christine Wiltz, Tom Wolfe, and Toni Cade Bambara began to explore in much more detail the hidden southern urban narrative territory that Humphreys exposed in *Dreams of Sleep*. Their 1990s novels dramatize the potential and real urban "blowups" created by residential segregation, racial isolation, economic disparity, and unspoken prejudice. Humphreys's Emory dreams of Atlanta as a place where he could become a successful artist and live openly with Iris. But Wolfe and Bambara depict such a dream of an integrated Atlanta as a mirage, even though of all the U.S. metropolitan areas, Atlanta has become "the premier African American magnet."[17] They satirize the symbolically constituted interracial community that Atlanta's government and business leaders have attempted to create with the slogan the "City Too Busy to Hate." Such contemporary urban advertising smacks of the narratives of evasion that Scott Romine has argued enabled previous generations of southern white male writers to maintain myths of southern community.[18]

Given Tom Wolfe's considerable abilities as a social satirist, *A Man in Full* is much more than a novel about black-white relationships, but it is in this context that I examine it.[19] In an interview with the *Baltimore Sun* conducted after *A Man in Full* was published, Wolfe criticized white writers' safe approach to race relations:

> People—white writers, anyway—are terribly afraid of it. It's OK to raise the issue of the friction between the two races if, in the course of the story, there arrives some wise person, preferably from the streets, who shows everyone the error of his ways and leads everyone off to a glorious finale. Or you can have the reluctant buddy movie. They really hate each other at the beginning but by the end they have become bosom pals. This is literary etiquette. It all has to work out harmoniously. Alas, modern life is not like that. I think you can do it, write about racial antagonisms in America, if you do it objectively, do the research, the reporting. And you get it right.[20]

With such remarks Wolfe insinuates that in *A Man in Full* he has gotten race relations "right." While it seems most Atlantans think his "racial dynamics" could be more nuanced, most also agree with the reviewer for the *Atlanta Journal-Constitution* that Wolfe understands "the basic social compact" of the city.[21]

Fictionalizing a real-life example of how black opposition to a major highway through South Atlanta was overcome, Wolfe has Wesley Jordan, Atlanta's fictional black mayor, explain this compact to his lawyer friend, Roger White II: "So they've got this lawyer who's their spokesman, the white people do, and he starts his pitch, and he's talking about Atlanta's place in the regional economy and the global village and the cosmos and one thing and another and Isaac interrupts him and says, 'Scuse me, brother, but you mind if I speed things up and get right to the checked flag? You got the money, and we got the power. We want some money.'"[22] In *A Man in Full* Wolfe shows blacks and whites periodically working together to achieve different goals, meeting only briefly to formulate the terms of their exchange. In this example, the white businessmen, who live in suburbs outside the city or to the north in tony Buckhead, get their fast road through the ghetto, while impoverished blacks who live in South Atlanta get "day-care centers, youth centers, health clinics, parks, swimming pools" as compensation (212). Although the "Atlanta way" benefits black people in ways they could not rely on when whites controlled city politics,[23] Wolfe's point is that Atlanta's motto, "City Too Busy to Hate," masks the city's continued residential and social segregation. Furthermore, while Wolfe shows white businessmen and black leaders ostensibly trying to prevent racial conflict that could tarnish Atlanta's image, he also suggests that these same individuals manipulate underlying racial tensions for their own gain. Real estate developer Charlie Croker orchestrates a racial incident to drive down the price of land in outlying Cherokee County, and Mayor Jordan exaggerates the significance of an incident involving interracial fisticuffs in order to spotlight his ability to restore calm to the city. As for amiable social relationships across the color line, none exist in this novel.

Wolfe uses Atlanta's racially codependent leaders to shape his narrative. His characters are white businessmen and bankers, black government officials and lawyers, who play important roles in perpetuating the city's social compact. Wolfe chooses an interracial sexual incident to expose the "racial fault line" (524) papered over by the city's motto. Inman Armholster, a Buckhead resident who is one of Atlanta's richest businessmen, accuses Fareek Fanon, a football star for Georgia Tech who grew up in one of Atlanta's poorest and worst neighborhoods, of raping his daughter. The impetus to resolve this cross-racial incident mirrors the usual workings of the city's social compact. Georgia Tech's white coach Buck McNutter calls on Roger White II for legal assistance in this incident because of his friendship with Mayor Wes Jordan. Mayor Jordan suggests that perhaps good old boy Charlie Croker could help defuse the situation, because he bridges the social divide, being both a prominent businessman and a former Tech football hero. Cross-racial cooperation is needed, but only for mutually exclusive goals: Charlie's multimillion-dollar debts will be refinanced if he makes a public statement calling for calm in the Fanon case, product endorsements will once again flow Fareek's way if he is exonerated, Coach McNutter's lucrative job at Georgia Tech will be saved if his star player can be kept out of jail, Roger's desire to prove he is not "too white" will be fulfilled by coming to the aid of a "brother," and Mayor Jordan's attention to Fareek will shore up lagging inner-city support for his reelection. The light-skinned, well-educated Jordan has been labeled "a beige half-brother" by his opponent, a former NBA player and social activist who is darker-skinned.

Wolfe carefully maps the separate social spheres for his readers. We get an aerial overview early in the novel as Charlie, the rich white real estate developer, looks down proprietorially on greater Atlanta from his private jet. From on high he exults in the fact that he and other white developers have constructed what Joel Garreau calls edge cities, where growth occurs "not in the heart of the metropolis, not in the old Downtown or Midtown, but out on the edges in vast commercial clusters served by highways" (68). As a result fewer than four hundred thousand people, three-quarters of whom are black, actually live in the city limits, but 3.5 million people, most of whom are white, have abandoned the city to poor blacks and moved to the suburbs that developers like Charlie have created. The upper-class white characters in this novel never cross Ponce de Leon Street to go south into Atlanta's black neighborhoods. In the scenes filtered from their perspectives, nameless black characters glide through their lives, silently serving them as waiters in upscale restaurants, as parking attendants at the exclusive Piedmont Driving Club, as butlers, maids, and gardeners in their Buckhead mansions. Significantly, it is to the old role of southern planter that Charlie turns when socially uncertain and to his plantation, an older center of southern economic power, that he retreats when his New South creditors turn predatory. Charlie is oblivious to the hypersegregation that his handiwork has created in Atlanta and unconcerned about the separate racial spheres he perpetuates on his twenty-nine-thousand-acre plantation in rural Georgia, where black retainers enact roles right out of the nineteenth century.

Although contrived, a driving tour of Atlanta that Mayor Jordan gives Roger White II allows readers another view of the city and an opportunity to put the tryst between Fareek Fanon and Elizabeth Armholster into economic, racial, and spatial perspective. The Armholster mansion, decked out in "sheer homage to conspicuous consumption" (203) in the geographically elevated white enclave of Buckhead, is miles away and a world apart from the gutted, rundown, crack-infested black ghetto where Fareek grew up fatherless. The mayor's tour is really a tour de force, giving Wolfe ample opportunity to flex his satiric muscle as he skewers everything from the corporate skyscrapers of Peachtree Street, straining for international influence, to the ghetto where black boys, the "Jailhouse Fashion plates, were Frankensteining it, rocking like Druids away from the crack house and around the corner" (219). But the tour is also an important thematic device; it allows Wolfe to present Atlanta as a city divided by economic disparity and racial isolation, still suffering from the legacy of racism, which means that a rich white coed can turn a college hookup with a football star into a rape by a black man, when her white friends walk in on her in Fareek's bed.

By withholding until the end of the novel Elizabeth's private admission that she has lied to her father about the incident, Wolfe encourages readers to examine their own perhaps premature conclusions about what really happened. An *Atlanta Journal-Constitution* reviewer objected to Wolfe's use of this old southern story: in a city that has withstood the missing and murdered children crisis and bombings at the Olympic Park and abortion clinics, he argued, an alleged interracial date rape would not "endanger the public peace."[24] But a fictional tempest in a teapot about interracial sex serves a number of Wolfe's purposes, from undermining Atlanta's pretensions as an international city to revealing its very real racial segregation and its reticence to speak frankly about race relations. As banker Ray Peepgass says, "[e]ven though everybody (*le tout Atlanta*) was wild about the topic, you had to walk a very narrow, very academic, sociological disinterested line, or else you were guilty of . . . a breach of etiquette. It was sheer . . . bad manners. It showed poor . . . intellectual upbringing" (599). Ray's opinions here mirror Wolfe's impatience with what he calls the "literary etiquette" of representing race relations, and Wolfe's reference to manners suggests that he believes they still perform the old southern social work of hiding truths about race relations. In *A Man in Full*, Wolfe attempts to voice the truths about race that Atlantans, black and white, fail to speak.

But if good race relations and proper racial etiquette are a performance for whites, Wolfe presents performance of black identity as an additional burden for African Americans. In the first chapter Roger White II—lover of expensive Italian suits, luxury Japanese automobiles, and European classical music—is marooned in the middle of a Freaknic traffic jam. All around him black college students celebrate spring break—young women shake their "booty" to rap music and young men bear their butts to the white faces "peering down" on them from the exclusive Piedmont Driving Club (22). Caught in a Du Boisian moment, Roger is alternately drawn to the students' unfettered exuberance and appalled by their tasteless behavior, worried about what white people will think. Roger's ambivalence mirrors his own conflicted feelings—worry that he will be late for an appointment with a prominent white man, Coach Buck McNutter, and anger at being so concerned about it. Wolfe portrays Roger as a socially conservative African American with upper-class tastes who shied away from social activism and African culture in his college days. Roger's tastes and values have been shaped by his desire to assimilate into the white world, where he is now a lawyer in a prestigious otherwise-white firm. Roger perceives the students' "ghetto rags" and in-your-face behavior as an upper-middle-class performance of blackness, dependent on the authenticity of the vernacular, which allows them to feel like "true bloods" as they cruise the streets in Camaros and BMWs purchased by their fathers (20–21). But at the same time, Roger is perennially preoccupied with his own presentation of self: carefully dressing up to meet white businessman Charlie Croker but dressing down to attend a political rally at a black church in South Atlanta. Roger looks on clothing as "sartorial armor" (587), much as both his creator, Tom Wolfe, and his idol, Booker T. Washington, do. While literary critic Houston Baker views Washington as a black dandy, "all dressed up without any fully modern, urban place to go,"[25] Wolfe represents Washington's late-twentieth-century successor, the urbane Roger, as having fully arrived, but with a double case of performance anxiety.

Roger is uncomfortable both in white society and in all but a narrow upper-class stratum of black society. In fact, the only time readers see him truly comfortable is behind closed doors with Mayor Wes Jordan, his Morehouse College fraternity brother. When Roger is with the white members of his law firm, he worries about appearing "too black," but with black acquaintances not of his social class, he fears that his aesthetic tastes and upper-middle-class values will identify him as "too white" and that his position in a predominantly white law firm will call into question his racial solidarity. For example, at the first press conference in support of Fareek, Roger ends up saying more than he knows is prudent as soon as he spots a black reporter. Eager not to come off as Roger Too White, his Morehouse nickname, Roger insinuates that a possible motive in the false rumors about Fareek may have been white resentment at black success. After the press conference a mental review of his performance overwhelms Roger, as he goes back and forth between thinking that by mentioning Nietzsche he has appeared too learned (which he equates with "too white") to black television viewers and too angry (which he equates with "too black") to white viewers by bringing up Nietzsche's theory of *ressentiment*. Roger's analysis reveals as much about his own mind-set as about anyone else's.

The white people Roger works with appear as ghostly, albeit powerful, figures who, while they share his economic class, make him tense and uncomfortable. He feels he must be constantly vigilant in order to read their interpretations of his behavior. Since Roger is the token black lawyer at the prestigious corporate firm Wringer Fleasom & Tick, he fears betraying behaviors or attitudes that his white partners have stereotypically associated with black people; his is the stressful state that Patricia Williams calls "the clanging symbolism of self."[26] Roger is wound tighter than a spinning top because of these pressures, and Wolfe portrays him as retreating to the comfort of a segregated black neighborhood after long, tense days working with white people. Although Roger and Wes could afford housing in the northern white section of the city or the surrounding white suburbs, both men still live in South Atlanta in an upscale all-black neighborhood on Niskey Lake, west of the black middle-class neighborhood, now a ghetto, where they grew up. Wolfe presents such residential segregation as self-selected, alluding to the degree to which black exhaustion with double consciousness and black discomfort with white people factor into their choice. What Steinhorn and Diggs-Brown have to say about such segregation is relevant here:

> The fact that whites see this retreat as self-segregation or as a race-conscious rejection of integration is ironic to most blacks, who seek this racial safe haven partly because they do not believe whites are capable of interacting with them in anything but a race-conscious way. As blacks see it, the only way to transcend race is to be with people capable of transcending it, and few whites seem to qualify. To whites, it may sound illogical to hear that predominantly black environments are nonracial rather than race-conscious, but to blacks it makes perfect sense—much the same way whites don't think twice about being around all whites.[27]

For the most part, the chapters in *A Man in Full* are as segregated as the city's neighborhoods. The scenes in which Roger White appears are the only ones in which blacks and whites interact as social equals. Because he is a black man who has assimilated into white culture, Roger serves as a mediator of sorts between white and black worlds, but Wolfe presents 1990s interracial encounters even among social equals as highly charged, very different from Gail Godwin's optimistic portrayals in *A Mother and Two Daughters* (1982). Wolfe's black and white characters are psychologically entangled in much the same way that David Shipler describes in *A Country of Strangers*: "Even as we look upon each other like strangers from afar, we are trapped in each other's imaginations."[28] When Roger has his initial meeting with Charlie Croker to propose restructuring Charlie's debts if he will support Fareek Fanon, Wolfe represents Roger as filled with racially charged emotions: resentment that Charlie gained his fame as a football player without ever competing against black players and anger that Charlie owns a plantation simulating southern slave society, but also apprehension because by meeting Charlie at his office in Croker Concourse, "he was now . . . deep into the alien country of Atlanta's white establishment"

(587). The scene between the two men is rife with misreadings and rereadings based on race. The black man reads the white man's body language for signs of prejudice and disrespect and as a result misreads Charlie's fatigue as boredom. The white man, so struck by the fact that Roger has "no black accent at all" (589), gets distracted from the matters at hand and begins to rethink speech as a racial identifier.

Wolfe begins and ends *A Man in Full* with Roger's references to Booker T. Washington's 1895 Atlanta Compromise speech, thus framing his contemporary story in such a way as to force readers to compare 1990s race relations with Washington's prediction: "He said the white man will *never* like you! He said he'll never treat you fair out of the goodness of his heart! He'll treat you fair only after you've made something out of yourself and your career and your community and he's dying to do business with you!" (25). At the end of the novel, Roger's successful work with the Fanon case brings fame to his law firm, which results in the black owner of a highly successful restaurant chain asking Roger's white firm to represent his business. Although the white partners are overjoyed at getting this large account, Roger is cynical about what the deal means for race relations. Feeling that his unfashionable interest in Booker T. Washington in the 1960s has been vindicated by the 1990s "Atlanta way," Roger underlines the hypocrisy for Wes Jordan: "The white lawyers at Wringer Fleasom couldn't care less about African Americans singly or in the aggregate. But in Atlanta not even the bigots want to *look* old-fashioned" (783). Roger's growing cynicism about race relations seems to reflect Wolfe's view, for even as Roger's new prominence in the black community catapults him into position to run for mayor when Wes's term ends, Wolfe makes it clear that Wes has reached the end of his political career: "There's no place for a black mayor of Atlanta to go. When you start talking about being governor or senator, the white folks' reluctance to appear old-fashioned somehow evaporates" (785). As he leaves the mayor's office, Roger utters the novel's last words, "I'll be back" (787).

As for Charlie Croker's end, Wolfe redeems him from the excesses of new South materialism ("This is Atlanta—where 'honor' is the things you possess" [680]). Charlie's home-care aid Conrad introduces him to the teachings of Epictetus, whose philosophy enables him to see a way out of his moral dilemma—deciding whether to save himself from bankruptcy by standing up for Fareek, whom he does not admire, or to succumb to bankruptcy by standing by his friend Inman Armholster, who has falsely accused Fareek of rape. For weeks, Charlie feels trapped because either choice will render him a pariah in

Atlanta society. Stoic philosophy leads Charlie back to older notions of honor: "One of the few freedoms that we have as human beings that cannot be taken away from us is the freedom to assent to what is true and to deny what is false" (766). Charlie forgoes any deals that will save his plantation and his business from bankruptcy and offers not a simple statement of support for Fareek but what he believes to be the complex truth: "he's arrogant, he's obnoxious, he's impertinent, he thinks the world owes him whatever he wants—but you can't necessarily jump from that to say he'd *do* whatever he wants. Besides, my information is that sexual customs are a lot different today from what they were when I was young" (765). Charlie's public pronouncement not only breaks the agreement Charlie made with Roger to fully support Fareek at the news conference; it breaks the compact between black politicians and white businessmen. In some respects Charlie's newfound Stoic philosophy really amounts to little more than the old Stoic pessimism that upper-class southern whites embraced to cope with the demise of their own hierarchical society. In his 1956 essay "Stoicism in the South," Walker Percy describes their fascination with Stoicism, even mentioning Epictetus, but rather than embracing Stoicism's pessimism in the tumultuous 1950s and 1960s, Walker Percy chose Christian optimism and renounced the South's outmoded love affair with hierarchy.[29]

In 1998 Tom Wolfe seems to straddle the fence. He knows that Charlie Croker is the last of the good old boys, yet as John Updike points out in his review of the novel, Wolfe respects "the old macho notion of Southern manhood—narrow, maybe, and bigoted, but also gallant and life-loving—and traces its collapse with a certain regret."[30] The excess of making Charlie a Stoic evangelist spreading Epictetus's word about personal integrity throughout rural Georgia, the Florida Panhandle, and southern Alabama and willing to sign a contract for a syndication deal with Fox Broadcasting undercuts what Wolfe surely sees as Charlie's newfound integrity. But such an over-the-top ending allows the somewhat conservative Wolfe not to look too conservative. However, his rehabilitation of Charlie Croker as a politically incorrect Stoic seems to prove Mary Gordon right. After the publication of Wolfe's *Bonfire of the Vanities,* she wrote in *Harper's* that Wolfe is "merely doing for literature what he did for painting and architecture: speaking from a position that comforts the uneasy, taking up a role that has done well by him in the past—the thinking man's 'redneck.'"[31]

But if there is a peculiar ambiguity in Wolfe's portrait of Charlie Croker, there is an equally odd ambiguity in his portrait of Roger White. Wolfe leaves readers wondering what to make of Roger's victory in the game of Atlanta race relations that Wolfe depicts as fraught with hypocrisy—the very opposite of Charlie's reclaiming his integrity by refusing to play the game. Although Wolfe presents Roger's dawning interest in African American affairs and African art as positive, he depicts his interest in Fareek's case as rooted in self-interest— an attempt to solidify his racial identity. After all, Roger's assessment of Fareek, an opinion Wes shares, is not very different from Charlie's. He simply does not voice it: "Roger Too White had never seen one of these people up close before, but here stood an example of one of the worst role models black youth could emulate: the big-time athlete, the mercenary for hire who assumes that the world owes him money and sex, and lots of both, whenever he wants it, and that he will be immune, whatever happens" (34). The better Roger learns to play by the rules of Atlanta's race relations game, which Wolfe suggests means occasionally "playing the race card" (582), the more he emerges as "Roger Black," "a man of the world" (787)—possible successor to Mayor Wes Jordan. Wes has succeeded in his bid for reelection by using the incident involving Fareek to shore up his black support, and he is already strategizing about how to improve Roger's image in South Atlanta by omitting the fact that he lives in a mansion on Niskey Lake. Given Roger's belief that Booker T. Washington was right, he seems understandably little inclined to put much effort into integration, the futility of his current effort having only increased his anger over the years.

Although Wolfe seems strangely unconcerned that Roger may be ready to give up on integration, he is troubled by Roger's gravitation to a supposedly more authentic black identity. Like Paul Gilroy, Wolfe would rather see identity based on affinity than on predetermined sameness.[32] For example, the night that Roger and his wife, Henrietta, attend the symphony, Wolfe provides readers with a look through Roger's eyes at what it would be like to be a black man who could ignore race in an integrated setting. Roger interprets fellow concert goers' stares as proof that they recognize him as the lawyer who appeared on television. An avid music lover, Roger compares the eclectic program to a multicourse meal, suggesting to his wife that Stravinsky's *Rite of Spring* is the heavy main course and Scott Joplin's jaunty "Maple Leaf Ray" is the dessert, "a nice little piece of chocolate" presented to the audience for consuming their Stravinsky. But the experiment in color-blindness can go no further. Both Roger's need to make sure his wife does not attach a double meaning to "chocolate" and his hope that his amusing analogy will show the "white folks" he is not "ill at ease" (654) illustrate Wolfe's belief that a black man's racial coping skills are rarely idle. When Roger's wife assesses the evening, she puts race in what Wolfe believes is its true place in Atlanta as the primary signifier: Joplin is added to the program because he is black; people stare at Roger because he and his wife are the only black couple in the audience. Wolfe confirms Henrietta's interpretation as the correct one by next having readers observe Roger through white eyes. Martha Croker, Charlie's ex-wife, notices Roger because he is the only black man in the concert hall, not because she saw him on television. Just as Mayor Jordan does not go to the High Museum because "our people have no interest in seeing their black Mayor at one of these celebrations of white cultural chauvinism" (208), Wolfe hints that Roger will probably forgo the symphony in the future. After experiencing the concert through Henrietta's eyes, he feels "like a blind fool—dragging her off to these white 'cultural' events" (656). Wolfe leaves no doubt that given Roger's love of classical music, giving up such concerts in the future would be another form of cultural blindness. Thus Wolfe represents Roger's transformation into "Roger Not a Bit Too White" (732) as also a loss. But because Wolfe registers the transformation only in psychological terms, he appears to neglect the very socioeconomic processes that foster such racialized thinking, which earlier in the novel he seemed to be laying the groundwork for. Choosing Conrad, a white boy from Oakland, as his working-class filter character, rather than a black boy from South Atlanta, certainly allows Wolfe to show the reach of Charlie Crocker's empire at its height, but it does little to explain the ramifications of Atlanta's social compact in the ghetto.

Wolfe can position himself as the lone white racial realist because he avoids making his black and white characters "bosom pals" and giving readers a "glorious finale" of racial reconciliation. But Wolfe's goal in *A Man in Full* seems different from the aims of the other writers I have discussed. While Wolfe measures contemporary southern race relations by poking fun at Atlanta's boosterism and hypocrisies, other writers use narrative to imagine how a new reality might be achieved. In tackling the big picture, Wolfe chauffeurs readers on a highly entertaining tour of Atlanta, during which readers become adept at penetrating Atlanta's "integration illusion." But Wolfe is writing social satire, despite his dislike of the term; he illuminates types rather than dismantling stereotypes. Preferring to think of himself as an old-fashioned realist, Wolfe repeatedly denies that *A Man in Full* is a satire: "I've tried as best I could . . . just to capture Atlanta as it is. I have never liked the word satire. If I got it right, the book is Atlanta."[33] Certainly *A Man in Full* captures many aspects of Atlanta, but it also omits others, either by chance or by design, which makes the place Wolfe's Atlanta, not simply Atlanta. Wolfgang Iser's theory about mimesis is relevant here: "In the Aristotelian sense, the function of representation is twofold: (1) to render the constitutive forms of nature perceivable; and (2) to complete what nature has left incomplete. In either case mimesis, though of paramount importance, cannot be confined to mere imitation of what is, since the process of elucidation and of completion both require a performative activity if apparent absences are to be moved into presence."[34]

Wolfe's interest in exposing Atlanta's pretensions and in elucidating Atlanta's power brokers (both black and white) proceeds at the expense of exploring how Atlanta's larger socioeconomic forces shape some of the lower-class characters whose appearances he describes with such relish. I think particularly of Fareek Fanon, the one significant male character in this novel about contemporary manhood and race relations whose consciousness Wolfe does not enter and whose home and neighborhood readers see only briefly on Mayor Jordan's tour. Readers experience the black ghetto only through upper-middle-class black eyes, for although Wes and Roger once lived in the inner city, it was not a ghetto then. Readers know what Fareek looks like, acts like, and sounds like, but we know very little of what he feels or thinks and nothing of how he came to be that way. In a 1972 article, Wolfe discussed the "extraordinary power" of point of view, "giving the reader the feeling of being inside the character's mind and experiencing the emotional reality of the scene as he experiences it."[35] Wolfe gives readers such an experience with his other major characters, but not Fareek (or for that matter, Charlie's very young trophy wife, Serena). As a result, even though on his tour Mayor Jordan shows Roger how far Fareek has come and Coach McNutter reminds Charlie "that nobody ever taught him about everyday common courtesy" (627), readers are not given enough information to fully understand the significance of the details Wolfe delights in piling on—Fareek's sartorial style (gold chains, diamond earrings, and homey jeans), his wary, hostile look, his dreadful posture, and his talk of "hubba ho's." Readers only know that we have seen young men like this before on the mayor's quick tour of the ghetto.

What role has the culture of segregation that Wolfe maps so carefully played in shaping Fareek?[36] Is Fareek's attitude and affect a product of the so-called culture of poverty? Or is Fareek in part shaped by a subordinated group's oppositional culture that devalues behaviors and attitudes of the dominant group? Or some combination? Without the kind of understanding of Fareek's background that readers have of Charlie Croker's poor rural roots, readers leave this novel without really understanding Fareek, even though Wolfe's ending suggests that Charlie has courageously told all. Interestingly, the one time in *A Man in Full* when Stoicism's teachings prove problematic for Charlie's unlikely mentor Conrad, who has spent some time in prison, is the day Conrad decides to help a homosexual whom the other inmates are picking on. Conrad chooses not to turn away from this man as Epictetus's teachings would have him do: "If a man is unfortunate, remember that his misfortune is his own fault" (481). While Epictetus gives Charlie the courage to tell the truth as he sees it about Fareek and to forgo his worldly goods in the process, Epictetus's teachings about the unfortunate seem to mislead Charlie in the same way they did previous generations of white southerners, such as Walker Percy's uncle, William Alexander Percy. But the question for many readers may be, Where have the Stoics led Wolfe in his assessment of Atlanta's race relations?

In *Those Bones Are Not My Child* (1999), Toni Cade Bambara focuses on an impoverished area of the city that Wolfe only chauffeurs readers through, and she introduces readers to a segment of Atlanta's population that Wolfe merely pathologizes. One of Bambara's middle-class African American characters sees the unfortunate differently than Epictetus because she works with the poor in Africa, yet even she admits that "a part of me is always thinking that they must have called it down on themselves somehow."[37] But Bambara is determined to disabuse her readers of such a simple notion. Because the narrative arises out of a particularly sensitive time, Atlanta's missing and murdered children crisis, *Those Bones Are Not My Child* overflows with characters' suspicions of each other. Bambara's Atlanta, like Wolfe's, is divided by race, but because her focus is on the disfranchised, she sets her story in South Atlanta and reveals the city's dual civic institutions: two police organizations (Fraternal Order and Afro-American Patrolmen's League), two investigative teams for the murders (the city's official Task Force and the black community's volunteer Committee to Stop Children's Murders—STOP), and two newspapers (the *Atlanta Journal-Constitution* and the *Call,* a publication authored by and for the black community).

Bambara is as eager as Wolfe to point up the discrepancy between media image and real life in the "City Too Busy to Hate." Bambara repeatedly calls attention to the facile slogans and rehearsed remarks of public officials that stand in for the hard work needed to address the city's racial suspicion and segregated enclaves. She makes readers aware of how such "rhetorical integration" can seduce Atlantans, particularly whites, into thinking they have achieved the real thing.[38] She directs readers' attention to the difference between the "self-consciously integrated" group of businessmen out for a quick lunch in the park and the "integrated group of civil-rights workers" planning a conference on poverty (167, 361). The businessmen, with their sports jackets slung over their shoulders, look "exactly like the models on the glossy Atlanta brochures: City Too Busy to Hate," but they are no more at ease with one another than Wolfe's Charlie Croker and Roger White. The way the businessmen "talked overloud and worked hard at laughing" reveals that what might look like friendship is performance. In contrast, the truly integrated group—"progressives from the Highlander Center and the local Southern Regional Council, and clergy who identified with the *Catholic Worker* tradition"—are at ease with each other, not so much because they are working together, which the businessmen do also, but because they have common goals and a common vision for their community. A glimpse of this group provides Bambara's protagonist Zala, whose child is missing, with some small "hope that maybe the whole world wasn't crazy damn mad" (361). But the world in which readers dwell in *Those Bones Are Not My Child* is the "crazy damn mad" world, not the socially aware, socially just world that the real-life Southern Regional Council is working to create.

To reveal the tawdry facts behind Atlanta's glossy image, Bambara sets *Those Bones Are Not My Child* in a poor black neighborhood in South Atlanta near Washington Park. For Bambara, this area exemplifies how poor black people's attempts to live a decent life and to protect their children compete with the needs of City Hall and corporate Atlanta to maintain a public image of good race relations. From the first chapter readers dwell in the confusion, humiliation, and frustration that Zala Spencer experiences as she seeks help from a variety of government agencies in finding her twelve-year-old son. Bambara certainly does not shy away from the big picture, drawing ever larger concentric circles around her fictional family, to drive home the fact that prejudice against people of color, especially those who are poor, is not simply a local phenomenon but a national and international one also. Thus, while Wolfe calls attention to Atlanta's pretensions as a cosmopolitan city of international commerce, Bambara makes international parallels to its human rights violations. One issue of the *Call* points out similarities between criminal cases in New Cross, England, and Atlanta: "slow acknowledgment of the crime, blame-the-victim, denial of racist motives, the Black-man-as-culprit ploy, and the discrediting of people's right to mobilize, organize, and investigate" (423).

During the period between September 1979 and June 1981, when more than forty black children were kidnapped, sexually assaulted, and murdered, Bambara was living in Atlanta, her mother's hometown. She became obsessed with the crisis and disillusioned with the way the authorities were handling it. Like others, she was incredulous when the criminal justice system charged one man, Wayne Williams, who did not resemble any of the descriptions of suspects, with the murder of two adult males and then hitched to his "coattails as many [other] cases as the law would allow" (7). Because Bambara thought of writing as a way "to engage in struggle," as "a real instrument for transformation politics,"[39] she became her community's interpreter. To that end, she wrestled for well over a decade with a massive manuscript, which she hoped would transform the public's thinking about a case that most white people believed had been solved and that most black people knew had not.

When Bambara died of cancer in 1995 before *Those Bones Are Not My Child* had been edited to her satisfaction, her friend Toni Morrison took up the task. Morrison said that her determination to see the book into print was "fueled" by the public attention given Tom Wolfe's *A Man in Full* and the fact that "[n]o one is talking about Atlanta from the point of view of these people who knew it—not the political way, not the way the marketers knew it, but on the streets, in the houses, in the schools."[40] Morrison shortened the manuscript by two hundred pages, a length finally acceptable to Random House. Most reviewers, however, wished Morrison had cut another two hundred pages, especially from the incredibly dense two chapters in the middle of the novel. These chapters detail all the leads that black volunteers followed to discern the six patterns in the killings: "Klan-type slaughter, cult-type ritual murder, child-porn thrill killing, drug-related vengeance, commando/mercenary training, and overlapping combinations."[41] Even the most attentive reader can get lost in the plethora of names, acronyms, and theories and bogged down by the transcriptions of tapes and documentary films. While Bambara clearly wanted readers to be aware of the tremendous amount of research performed by citizen volunteers and to sense the overwhelming frustrations they experienced when the police ignored their leads, we will never know how much frustration she wanted readers to experience in processing this information.

The novel bears evidence of Bambara's concern with reader response. She alludes periodically to reader response throughout the novel, but most often in chapters 4 and 5, the very chapters that sometimes read like transcriptions of Bambara's voluminous journals. For example, one character after reading the galleys for the latest issue of the *Call* says, "This material tends to overwhelm" (421). Bambara does aid her readers by bracketing her emotionally charged fiction about the Spencer family's missing child with a nonfiction prologue and an epilogue summarizing the facts of the real case as well as her fears and frustrations in writing about it. An editorial in the *Call* exhorting black Atlantans not to "be sidetracked by charges of racist paranoia or appeals to good race relations" (419) parallels her own concerns with reactions to black concerns in the Atlanta missing and murdered children case. In a calculated way, Bambara attempts to address the concerns of several different groups of readers: white readers, like the various city officials, predisposed to see black people as paranoid if they voice concerns with racism and injustice; black readers like Zala's rich sister-in-law, worried that criticism of black leaders, like Atlanta's mayor, would be disloyal and hurt their cause; and black readers like Zala, who feel powerless but who do not want to be labeled paranoid or disloyal if they question the authorities, no matter their race.

Bambara depicts the poor black community's circling their wagons not so much as nationalism or separatism, as some might allege, but simply as survival. Feeling accused by the police, stereotyped by the media, and ignored by City Hall, despite the presence there of the city's first black mayor, the black neighborhood and a few white supporters organize to do their own investigating and reporting. Their independent efforts pay off, as perhaps Bambara surely hoped hers would in writing this novel. While the *Atlanta Journal-Constitution* buries in its back pages brief stories of the missing and murdered children, the *Call* mobilizes black residents with impressive investigative reporting and spirited editorials. While the police investigators ignore Zala's pertinent questions and the Missing Persons Bureau loses the paperwork on her son, Zala's friends and neighbors gather evidence and talk to witnesses. Bambara is keen to show that such activism pays off, for only when the volunteer investigators amass enough information to embarrass the official investigative bureaus does City Hall finally treat the missing and murdered children case as other than routine. And only when STOP holds a rally in Washington, D.C., to spotlight the assaults on black people all over the country is the first Atlanta suspect arrested, even though the neighborhood residents have supplied enough evidence for the police to have brought in several people for questioning. It is, after all, not the police or the special task force, but Zala and

Spense's doggedness that leads them to Sonny's kidnapper. Their leadership and activism solve the mystery of their son's year-long disappearance and his mysterious midnight excursions after his return home.

By the end of the novel, Zala, who worried that city officials would perceive her zeal as hysteria, has become a community leader. Bambara includes the full text of Zala's short speech to her community, which functions as a summary of the novel's message to readers who feel powerless. Despite Wayne Williams's incarceration, Zala exhorts her listeners to work to have the Atlanta missing and murdered children case reopened, and she encourages them not to be manipulated into silence by the fear of being called "paranoid" by white people or a "traitor to the race" by black people in positions of power (660). Zala also urges the most disillusioned not to be so cynical as to shun the very institutions they are suspicious of: "what we're after is a congressional investigation spearheaded, perhaps by the Black Caucus, with the parents calling the witnesses and asking the questions" (661). Although driven to grassroots leadership for personal reasons, Zala remains active for the good of her community. Testimony to Bambara's faith in the power of imaginative literature is the inspiration Zala finds in a line of poetry that she remembers during a time of deep despair: "Take heart, sometimes the light at the end is caught in the bend of the tunnel" (122).

The fictional story of the Spencer family, through which Bambara weaves the tangled threads of the real Atlanta missing and murdered children case, enables those readers who might find themselves alleging "racist paranoia" to rethink this accusation. Bambara shows that race is not the only factor involved in the black community's theories about the children's murders. One of Zala's friends who is a seer thinks cult members are responsible for the murders; the black female police officer who offers the most help thinks the facts of the case suggest a porn ring. Significantly, the solution to Bambara's fictional case does not appear to involve race hatred, at least not directly, but rather child molesting. The man who kidnaps and molests Sonny lives in the black neighborhood, a theory Zala fleetingly entertains at one point. In *Those Bones Are Not My Child,* Bambara shows how both present preoccupations and past injustices influence the hypotheses her characters posit. For example, Zala's neighbor who is a nurse reminds folks that the Atlanta Center for Disease Control monitored the Tuskegee Experiment. Toni Morrison points out that Bambara does not make Zala simply a virtuous victim.[42] Zala drinks periodically to escape her problems, and they are overwhelming—overwork, children to feed, rent overdue, incompletes in two courses at Georgia State, a periodically absent husband, and a missing son. As she grows more and more preoccupied with Sonny's disappearance, she occasionally neglects her younger children, who then assume the care of their house and their mother. Zala also hides certain evidence from the police that she thinks does not present her son in the best light, such as an unfamiliar photo of Sonny, which looks "challenging in some way, sexual" (108).

But Bambara also reveals the very real institutional racism and individual prejudice that Zala experiences. In attempting to locate Sonny, Zala encounters both race and class prejudice from a wide variety of people—ranging from an insensitive white policeman to a busy black female officer in the Division of Missing Persons. For example, one white cop's stereotypical line of questioning—"Well, ma'am, what about the boy's father? Do they all have the same father" (42)—is clearly humiliating. One reviewer remarked, "Their casual reception of her concerns is both believable and beyond understanding."[43] Everywhere Zala goes, others define her experience for her, and even when they do not, she carries a running commentary in her head, just as Wolfe's Roger White does. At the Division of Missing Persons, Zala's son is labeled a "runaway" even as she insists otherwise. Knowing full well how the media stereotype black single mothers as "lazy" and how the Atlanta Task Force in particular has termed the mothers of missing and murdered children "female hysterics," Zala strains to answer questions with language and behavior that will show she does not fit either stereotype. She uses "we," even though she and her husband, Spense, are estranged, because she knows "a woman with no 'we' didn't even get served by waiters" (66). She lists three work phone numbers to exhibit her own work ethic, only to be pegged a neglectful mother for never being home. Zala is subsequently referred to a social worker. At the same time that Bambara allows readers to experience this frustrating scene from Zala's perspective, she plants details that make Zala rethink her reactions. The female officer explains that *runaway* is a technical term, and by "lowering her voice" the officer is actually giving Zala a tip that being assigned a social worker has proved effective in getting help to locate missing children, even though this should not be the case (69). If Zala is perhaps a bit too sensitive in this situation, Bambara calls on readers to understand why: continual humiliation and stereotyping, no matter how unintentional, have put her on guard. Racism causes race consciousness.

The South's history of slavery, segregation, and racism rears its ugly head frequently and in unexpected ways in *Those Bones Are Not My Child*. When Sonny is found, he is ashamed at having been molested and at first refuses to tell his parents what has happened to him. But behind closed doors at his grandmother's Alabama farmhouse, Sonny concocts a southern gothic horror story to scare his siblings, a tale of being "sold to a slave gang of boys and forced to work on a plantation" by two white men (528), a familiar southern narrative that absolves Sonny of the sexual guilt he is feeling. Bad memories of racial discrimination and cycles of revenge and retaliation during her childhood in Alabama cause Zala to see racial motivations whenever behavior appears illogical: "Were they [Atlanta authorities] lying, were they stupid, or were they just playing things close to the chest? . . . Had the children been killed because they were Black, or would she say because the murderers were white? Had the authorities marginalized Dettlinger [a supportive cop] because he was white, because the high command was Black?" (149). Spense becomes convinced that the Klan is involved, especially after the day care center is bombed during the week of the Klan's convention in nearby Cobb County. The difficulty in getting full police cooperation and the media's attention suggests to Spense that some members of the police force or the city government, or both, may be colluding with the Klan or certainly suppressing news about Klan activity. Spense tells his son Kofi when he asks if his father knows who might be killing the children, "I've got thirty-two years' worth of informed suspicions" (304).

While Bambara does not indicate which theory might be correct (indeed, she suggests that multiple killers with multiple motives may be the perpetrators), she gives readers enough evidence to see that the missing and murdered children case should not have been closed with Wayne Williams's arrest. Bambara said in a letter about the novel, "I don't attempt to 'solve' the case but rather point up how plausible the 12 theories are given this country and the situation of all children in it, most especially poor kids, and particularly poor black kids."[44] Bambara seems to have left some facts in her fictional story up for interpretation as well, perhaps to underline the fact that the case may never be solved, perhaps to show American readers how race preoccupies us. Bambara, much like Toni Morrison in the story "Recitatif," chooses not to identify the kidnappers by race but gives her readers clues that can be interpreted either way: Mr. Gittens, Sonny's molester, is Zala's landlord, and his accomplice Maisie has olive skin and dark wavy hair. They live close enough for Sonny to revisit them, after he has been returned to his family, which suggests they are African American; however, elsewhere in the novel Bambara mentions that two white men have been arrested for running a porn ring in a black neighborhood. While readers know for sure by the end of the novel who kidnapped Sonny and why, we cannot be absolutely sure of the single fact Americans continue to find so significant, the race or races of the perpetrators.

If any paranoia exists in poor black neighborhoods, Bambara illustrates why it might be there. But perhaps as importantly, Bambara, much like Wolfe, demonstrates that paranoia pervades City Hall, where those in power, white or black, are afraid Atlanta's New South mask will slip and reveal the face of old southern racial tensions. Once readers of *Those Bones Are Not My Child* have seen the massive amount of evidence the black volunteers gathered and how few white people were involved in the effort, they are likely to view the city's slogan "Let's Keep Pulling Together, Atlanta," engineered especially for that crisis, as ridiculously empty rhetoric (461). Although the public service spot featured by the local television station shows black and white citizens of all ages in a tug-of-war against an invisible team, Bambara's cast of characters suggests otherwise. Only two characters who are identified as white play even minor roles in helping the black community during this crisis, and only the fictional Teo has a speaking part. Teo, Spense's friend, is a Vietnam veteran who assists STOP by infiltrating Klan meetings. The other white character is real-life Atlanta policeman Dettlinger, who figured out the geographical pattern of the attacks. Thus, by the time readers encounter this slogan created for the crisis, Bambara must have hoped they would not fall victim to "the integration illusion" it attempts to foster, even if they were previously taken in by Atlanta's motto "City Too Busy to Hate." Bambara shows those readers who are afraid to criticize the black mayor that City Hall's evasions ironically undermine race relations further by reinforcing the lack of trust poor blacks have for government officials who ignore their humanity and render their neighborhoods invisible when attention to them does not suit the officials' agenda.

Those Bones Are Not My Child contains a figure that Patricia Yaeger has identified as ubiquitous in earlier rural southern fiction, the dead black body, or what she terms "the throwaway body: the quick translation of white-on-black murder into economic terms, the quicker translation of black-on-black murder into nothing."[45] This black throwaway figure still appears in contemporary urban settings where poor, often unemployed, black people are warehoused out of sight in housing projects or the local jail. Like Bambara, white novelist Christine Wiltz humanizes such throwaway bodies by giving them names and by narrating their lives, but she does not sentimentalize them. She shows, as Benjamin DeMott argues, that "a brutalized population will inevitably include some who come to behave like brutes," which "in turn makes it easier for the brutalizers to see themselves as policers, not causers, of brutishness."[46] Of recent writers about race relations in the urban South, only Wiltz attempts to imagine a way out of this vicious circle and into an integrated community. Her solution involves the choices of private citizens rather than the policies of government leaders and government institutions. As Bambara did for *Those Bones Are Not My Child,* Wiltz found the catalyst for her novel *Glass House* (1994) in a historical incident that strained race relations. In 1980 a policeman was killed near the Algiers-Fisher housing project across the river from New Orleans. Although there were no witnesses to the shooting, the police brutally questioned residents of the housing project and eventually killed three people.[47] In *Those Bones Are Not My Child,* Bambara actually links the Atlanta child murders and the Algiers-Fisher housing project murders in order to suggest a national pattern of explaining "away the murders" of poor black people, or treating them like throwaway bodies (549).

In the first chapter of *Glass House,* Wiltz lays out a grid of city streets that orients readers to her view of urban segregation as well as to her vision of how integration might be nurtured. Wiltz's fictional Convent Street connects the mansions of uptown New Orleans to the Convent Street Housing Project. The wide crossing street, St. Charles Avenue, serves as a "buffer zone between the very rich and the very poor," or as is so often the case in urban America, between white and black.[48] Wiltz uses these streets to illustrate how the lives of rich whites and poor blacks are linked, despite their spatial separation. The connection has been obscured, making for Balkanized communities and a dysfunctional relationship that few white characters, and perhaps few white readers, fully understand. While black women from the projects regularly cross St. Charles to support their families by working for low wages in the uptown mansions, only a few white characters ever enter the projects, and then only to assert their authority as police officers or social workers. Most upper-class whites view the Convent Street Housing Project only from their television screens, and the negative media coverage verifies their stereotyped images of poor black people as drug dealers and welfare queens.[49] Wiltz suggests that such omnipresent negative media images, combined with isolated events, have produced a climate of white fear that through a twist of faulty logic has become a fear of black men and a grave misunderstanding of the culture of poverty, which has evolved into a lack of sympathy for poor black people.[50] From the vantage point of their uptown neighborhood, white characters see themselves as victims and black people as the enemy, as in this exchange at a dinner party:

> Lyle went on, "They're all armed so we have to be armed too."
> "They've declared war on us," Mona said belligerently.

The dinner is a homecoming party for Thea Tamborella, who, after living for ten years in Massachusetts, has returned to New Orleans, just briefly she thinks, in order to settle the estate of her Aunt Althea. Lyle Hindermann, the host, encourages her to buy a handgun, pointedly placing "a gun on the white tablecloth next to the bowl of yellow flowers, at the base of a silver candlestick" (53). This odd juxtaposition of objects reflects the uneasy way people like Lyle and Sandy Hindermann live in their newly renovated and well-fortified "plantation-like" houses (48).

But Wiltz depicts the Hindermanns as victims of their own social myopia, not of the black people they fear. Theirs is one of the glass houses of Wiltz's title, with "the curtains open so that the windows were tantalizing showcases for the tempting life inside" (48). Wiltz makes sure that readers have already seen New Orleans race relations through the eyes of those who live in the projects before we enter the opulent home of the Hindermanns. She presents the Convent Street Housing Project as both "a dangerous place to live," filled with "jobless people whose hope of finding work dwindled as the jobs themselves did" (18), and as a place filled with people trying to live a decent life. The trajectory of Wiltz's plot suggests that they are caught in a culture of poverty, which sociologists for decades have thought promotes "patterns of behavior inconsistent with socioeconomic advancement," but which the popular media and some scholars have severed from its roots in unemployment, social immobility, and residential segregation.[51] In *Glass House* Wiltz regrafts the culture of poverty onto those roots. Through the eyes of characters who live in the projects, like Janine and Burgess, Sherree and Dexter, readers see both the cycle of unemployment, illiteracy, and unwed childbearing that entraps them and their often heroic attempts to break free. Wiltz represents the women as more thoughtful than the men in their attempts to escape the vicious cycles: learning to read, looking for work, babysitting each other's children. The men become victims of a misguided masculinity that sends them down blind alleys in search of power over their own lives, whether through guns or money, fancy cars or expensive clothes, or a special relationship with a drug lord. Unlike

Wolfe, Wiltz enables readers to experience the motivating factors for the behavior and appearance of her poor black characters.

One of the ways Wiltz tries to get readers to think differently about the problem is by revealing similarities in lives that readers may only think of as different, and she manages this without erasing the important differences of white power and privilege. White characters, like Lyle Hindermann, prove themselves "muy macho" when they don police uniforms (67), much like the black men in leather in the ghetto. Both Dexter's girlfriend Sherree and Lyle's wife Sandy find such hypermasculine behavior off-putting and disturbing. Lyle, obsessed with apprehending criminals, commits a criminal act himself when his single-minded pursuit of drug dealers causes him to kill an innocent woman. People in both wealthy and poor neighborhoods are afraid: whites are afraid of black crime and blacks are afraid of white injustice. As a result, both whites and blacks hide out, becoming prisoners of sorts in their homes: the whites in "electronic cells" protected by alarm systems, the blacks in "red-brick square buildings like a cell," barricaded against raids by both the police and the project drug lords (36, 19). People in both neighborhoods have nightmares about being pursued: Thea by a threatening dark man and Burgess by the police. At an early stage in their dating relationships both Sherree in the ghetto and Thea uptown prematurely think of inviting their lovers to live with them so that they will feel safer. Each group is angered by the other's stereotypes: the black maid Delzora resents being confronted with suspicion by white police officers when she reports the death of her employer; Thea resents Burgess's assumptions about how safe her life is compared with his in the ghetto. Both black and white characters long for life to be better in New Orleans, a city they all love, but their difficulty, Wiltz suggests, is finding a way out of the segregated communities in which they are trapped.

Wiltz, who began her career writing detective fiction, intricately constructs her plot in interlocking ways to point up the hidden connections between rich whites and poor blacks. For example, when a rash of burglaries occur in a white-flight neighborhood across a drainage canal from New Orleans, the local white sheriff calls a press conference to announce that "any suspicious-looking black males seen in all-white neighborhoods would be stopped and questioned, especially those driving shabby, disreputable cars" (116). Angered by such blatant racial profiling, Dexter organizes a parade of black men in old cars, radios blaring and flashy streamers trailing from their antennas. They cruise through Jefferson Parish, with Dexter as their grand marshal, resplendent in glove-soft, blue leather and ensconced in a customized white Cadillac. What white people like Lyle see as unmotivated lawlessness, Wiltz portrays through a character like Dexter as total frustration with the white power structure. The attention Dexter calls to himself with his clothes and his car leads weekend deputy Lyle Hindermann to assume mistakenly that Dexter is the drug kingpin in the projects.

The structural ironies Wiltz uses in plotting *Glass House* create an overwhelming impression of the difficulty of breaking the cycles in which the characters are caught. Sherree's precaution of having Dexter move in with her for safety actually leads to her death when Lyle mistakenly shoots her after tracking Dexter to her apartment. In a similar series of related incidents, the cleanup effort that the real drug dealer Burgess masterminds in the housing project results in his death. His minimal but noticeable changes—fresh paint, repairs, a communal garden, and a child care center—attract the attention of the police, who know that the city has not provided the money for these improvements. Burgess's well-meaning but unorthodox urban renewal leads the police to assume that drug money is involved, a suspicion that results in the police harassing Dexter and Burgess going underground. This outcome, of course, brings a halt to Burgess's improvements and his moderating presence in the projects, making way for a rival gang to terrorize people and ultimately kill him. Because Wiltz's white protagonist, Thea, knows Burgess and Dexter and Lyle, she can see the connections between what appear to be unconnected events, leading her to an important realization about the city's "collective fate," which she comes to see as "bigger than any one person's fate, or even one race's fate, bigger than them all" (141). Similarly, Wiltz prods readers, as we follow the cause-and-effect plot structure, to discern the underlying causes for urban violence and racial tensions, just as we might look for clues in one of her murder mysteries.

Wiltz creates two characters who bridge the divide between these two segregated neighborhoods: Thea, the white woman who was raised in an uptown home, and Burgess, the black drug dealer who grew up in the Convent Street Housing Project. Wiltz makes their unlikely friendship plausible because they knew each other as children, when Burgess's mother Delzora worked as a maid for Thea's Aunt Althea. Using money made from dealing drugs elsewhere, Burgess returns to play Robin Hood in the projects—employing the men who live there to make needed repairs and paying one woman to care for the children so that the other women can work and go to school. After a failed marriage in Massachusetts, Thea returns simply to collect her inheritance from her aunt's estate but is ensnared by her old hometown. Instead of hiring the white architect and contractor whom her high school friend Sandy Hindermann suggests to renovate her aunt's house, Thea follows Delzora's advice and engages Burgess and his eclectic crew. Despite her time in the North, at first Thea seems a likely convert to Lyle Hindermann's prejudiced views and siege mentality, since black men robbed and murdered her parents in their New Orleans grocery store when she was a child. But their death actually put Thea in a position to get to know a black person as more than a servant, a familiar plot in white southern fiction that is employed more complexly here. After her parents' death, Thea moved in with her Aunt Althea, who, temperamentally unsuited to mothering, passed the role on to Delzora. This relationship not only gave Thea some of the love she had lost but prevented the mental leap from anger at the black men who killed her parents to hatred of all black people.

Wiltz suggests that people who live segregated lives may be more susceptible to such subliminal leaps in logic, for she traces Lyle's obsession with black crime to the time he saw a white neighbor robbed at gunpoint by a black man. Because of Thea's parents' Italian ethnicity and her middle-class social status as a child, Thea was never fully accepted in high school as a member of Lyle and Sandy's upper-class white crowd. For all of these reasons, Thea is able to resist the Hindermanns' current influence. When Lyle once again offers Thea a gun, she refuses it, reminding him that the police think her parents were killed with the very gun that her father kept in the grocery store. When Sandy tries to convince her to fire Burgess and his crew because their work is unknown in her social set, Thea remains loyal to them, reminding Sandy that "if Burgess and his carpenter never get any work, how will they ever have anything to show?" (99). Both Lyle's prejudice against black people and Sandy's preference for white contractors hurt black people's chances in New Orleans. Wiltz makes plain that Thea's determination to follow her own course is not easy given the Hindermanns' constant chorus of fear and distrust, as well as the very real threat of crime in her neighborhood. Lyle's preoccupation with crime at the dinner party provokes a troubled sleep for Thea that churns up "old childhood fears" (60), and when her high school boyfriend Bobby is mugged as he leaves her house that very evening, Thea is shaken. But she is not deterred. That she remains alone in employing a black contractor and that Lyle kills an innocent black woman suggest how the behavior of white people is implicated in the escalating crime rate and in the racial tensions that the Hindermanns and their friends perceive to be a black problem.

The chapter that Wiltz juxtaposes with these disconcerting incidents serves as a possible explanation of why Thea on her return does not become prejudiced like Lyle and Sandy. Every day the house that she has inherited is filled with black people, most significantly Burgess, whose company she enjoys. The smells from Delzora's cooking, the sounds of the crew's laughter and blues music, and Burgess's quick ironic wit and his easy banter with Bobby, who becomes Thea's lover, make "the house feel alive" in a way that it never felt when Thea lived there with her stern and bigoted Aunt Althea. The ongoing days spent in this way recall for Thea a fantasy she used to have as a child—"that she lived here with her family, her mother at the stove cooking, her father singing Italian arias in another part of the house" (69). While this fantasy recollection may seem to evoke the old southern white myth that black servants were members of the family, Wiltz does not idealize Thea's relationship with Delzora. Rather, she shows their relationship to be very different from her aunt's relationship with Delzora and from the Hindermanns' relationship with the nameless black woman who cares for their children. Delzora is Thea's maid, but she is also an older woman to whom she looks for advice, someone who knows her family history, and the mother of her friend Burgess. As a result, the presence of Delzora, Burgess, and Bobby in her home not surprisingly evokes the "feeling of warmth, of safety" that families can provide (69). Thus, when Lyle insists that Thea get an alarm system, that she accept the gun he periodically offers, and that she monitor the comings and goings of all these black people in her house, she refuses to be swept up in his scare tactics.

Wiltz allows readers' hopes to mount that a fledging integrated community will emerge. Thea's friendship with Burgess and his successful renovation of her house have led to his friendship with Bobby, which leads to more legitimate work renovating a rental property Bobby owns and the possibility of renting that house from Bobby when he is done—all of which adds up to a legitimate contracting business and a new life outside the projects with his lover Janine and the child they are expecting. As an angry sixteen-year-old, Burgess taunted his mother with her status as a maid in a white woman's house and certainly sees the irony when he comes to work there too. But he also sees that being Thea's contractor is different, not "like a comedown in life to him" but "full of possibilities" (158). Wiltz sets up a situation to test Thea's trust as well as her ability to manage fear when Thea accidentally discovers that Burgess is a drug dealer, information that threatens to turn Burgess into a type. She overhears a heated conversation he has with his mother, in which Delzora questions his misapplication of the Christian virtues she taught him—arguing that he has tainted his good works in the projects by using drug money to implement them. Because Thea has been subconsciously using her friendship with Burgess to confront her own confused feelings about her parents' deaths and her aunt's prejudice, this information about Burgess sets Thea back by rekindling old fears.

Two oddly similar incidents help Thea and readers, especially white readers, understand the Catch-22 of contemporary race relations: how dis-ease creates dis-ease, how fear begets fear, and how each can be misperceived. The first incident involves Sonny Johnson, who knocks on Thea's door one evening soliciting signatures and funds for SAFE, a group that promotes safety in New Orleans. As a young black man in an all-white neighborhood during a period of racial tension, Sonny knows that white people will probably fear him, so he makes an awkward joke: "I'm not sellin anything and I promise—I'm safe" (76). But his quip fails to conceal his worry about how Thea will treat him. Thus, during their brief encounter his nervousness makes Thea nervous—a reaction that in turn only increases Sonny's nervousness, which then makes Thea second-guess her trusting nature and wonder if she has misjudged Sonny's good intentions. Because of these fleeting misgivings, later when she sees Sonny lying spread-eagled against a police car, her first thought is that he must have committed a crime. But she quickly realizes that she is witnessing a crime—racial harassment—just one of the many scenes of re-vision in *Glass House*. The second instructional incident involves her new dog, Roux, who growls only at Jared, one of the painters. Delzora wonders if Roux dislikes black men, but Thea points out that Roux does not growl at other black workers and that Jared is the only worker in Burgess's crew who is afraid of dogs. In helping Thea make sense of the incident, Delzora suggests that fear can be misread as intimidation: "When somebody's that afraid, I guess they be pretty scary themselves" (109). With each incident Wiltz demonstrates how in a society so preoccupied with race, race can be a false signifier.

While Wiltz uses Thea to reveal the anatomy of white fear, she uses Burgess to reveal the anatomy of black rage. Because these incidents enable Thea to understand how fear works and because she sees Burgess as more than simply a drug dealer, given their shared personal history, their business relationship, and their growing friendship, she decides to meet with him even after she learns of his illegal activities. Her unexpected welcome disrupts the pattern of response Burgess expects and makes him feel comfortable enough to try to explain how he can be both a lawbreaker and a benevolent community leader. During this conversation, Burgess makes several presumptuous remarks about white people, which anger Thea. He stereotypes her ("someone like you"), and he assumes that she cannot understand "black reality" because she lives in a totally different world—"you white; you safe" (160). Her response is to remind him that although *he* may feel safe in her house that *she* does not feel safe there because Bobby was mugged outside and because her parents were murdered in an incident in which drug use may have prompted the violence. Wiltz employs this conversation to shed light on what each does not understand about the other's reality—whites do not understand why poor blacks might be led to crime, and poor blacks do not understand why whites might stereotype them as criminals. Although her anger kindles his, Burgess knows that if unchecked anger escalates into rage, it will block his ability to care about making her understand him and it will frighten Thea, pushing them further apart. It is significant that he moderates his anger because he knows her and because he cares about their relationship. With their frank exchange, in which they talk through their anger and apologize for misunderstandings, Wiltz models the possibility of productive interracial dialogue.

This scene works to show that understanding is possible, but the perspective on negotiating racial conflict is definitely white: blacks should allow whites to express anger without accusing them of racism, blacks should moderate their own anger toward whites, and "old anger" should be banned from current situations. Before they talk, Thea leads Burgess onto the porch where they used to play until her aunt discovered them and called a halt to their relationship. The memory of what occurred there causes "a hot spot of rage" to rise in Burgess's chest, but Wiltz represents Burgess as consciously dismissing the "old anger" as unproductive (159). Given the many venues Wiltz explores in this novel, it is not surprising that she chooses Thea's house for frank dialogue about unspoken racial tensions. For it holds memories of the past that must be understood, and it is the only place where blacks and whites have come together at work, at meals, and at play. Furthermore, Thea and Burgess each want the other to understand, and both are open to a different point of view. Sociologists have determined that simple integration is not enough to deconstruct stereotypes and that contact between the races may strengthen prejudice if the contact occurs between unequals who have different goals and very different cultures. The chemistry is exactly right between Burgess and Thea because of their shared history, their growing friendship, their mutual goal, and their willingness to look beyond easy stereotypes.[52]

Given the mutual attraction between Thea and Burgess, theirs is the type of interracial relationship that would have become a romance in another novel. Setting their first meeting in the romantic gazebo in Thea's garden, Wiltz encourages readers to speculate about such possibilities. In an interview, Wiltz says that she even considered such a plot development but rejected it because it would have been unrealistic to have her two characters relate romantically after so many years apart.[53] By delineating their relationship as one of friendship and business, Wiltz joins Elizabeth Spencer in her novella "The Business Venture" (1987) in expanding the possibilities for relationships between black men and white women in fiction. And yet the undercurrent of emotional attraction between these two characters makes readers unable to forget why they never became childhood sweethearts. Because Aunt Althea was a racist, she forbade Delzora from bringing Burgess to work on Saturdays when she realized that the children were playing together. Because of white racism, Thea and Burgess never attended the same school; Aunt Althea sent her to a private school. Thea's ignorance, even as an adult, of the reason Burgess stopped coming to her aunt's house provides unexpected evidence of liberal white obliviousness to the discrimination blacks encounter.

Wiltz's penultimate chapter is filtered through Burgess's perspective, and for the first time readers see the "self-loathing" of this charming, talented, but misguided man, who wants to provide a decent life for his pregnant girlfriend and belatedly glimpses a new life "full of possibilities" (187, 158). While Thea must come to terms with the white fear that fuels racial injustice, Burgess must come to terms with the fact that he made the wrong choices as a young man. Through such a realization, Wiltz points to Burgess's responsibility for his actions but simultaneously shows how self-perpetuating the culture of poverty can be. In watching young boys in the projects play a circle game involving little plastic baggies filled with grass, powder, and rocks, Burgess thinks "he could see his whole life in that ghostly circle, a tight, claustrophobic life with few choices: deal drugs or be poor. And whatever the choice, live with fear and die young, younger than the people who lived outside this world of danger and violence" (151). Delzora calls the Convent Street Housing Project "a prison for lifers" (18). Burgess's realization that he had more choices than he thought comes just when he begins to see a way out of the ghetto's debilitating mindset and when together he and Thea begin to escape the social segregation of their city. But it is too late.

Like Wolfe and Bambara, Wiltz paints the city government's reaction to the city's racial problems as political expedience, although New Orleans, as Wiltz depicts it, is not as effective as Atlanta in providing a modicum of services for inner-city inhabitants. When the black mayor realizes his reelection is in jeopardy because of the outrage in the Convent Street Housing Project over Sherree's death, he forces the white chief of police to resign. Federal officials begin a lengthy probe into civil rights violations, but by the end of the novel, blacks and whites in the city have grown more divided, and the outrage among blacks has only increased white fear. Readers of *Glass House* see fear close enough to understand how fear provokes fear and misunderstanding generates more misunderstanding. Most importantly, readers should be able to discern how white people's misconceptions, even if not outright prejudices, are a large part of the problem, because they influence not just personal interactions but institutional practices as well. Readers dwell in the possibility of racial integration in Thea's home and in her way of doing business.

But as readers, we leave the novel much as we began it, with Delzora still traveling the same street—and thus we are not sure how far Wiltz has taken us. Burgess's son will grow up without a father, just as Burgess did, and Janine will be a single mother, just like her mother before her. The small hope held out for readers at the end of this novel is that Thea and Bobby, unlike Thea's aunt, will welcome Delzora's grandson into their home to play with the child they are expecting. But this hope must be read between the lines of a chapter that ends with Delzora's hopeless summary of the events: "It's a shame what we all do to each other, a terrible, terrible shame." Although optimism for improved race relations is deferred to the next generation, *Glass House* provides readers with "a brief time when things had been different, when people had been tied together with a common thread of hope instead of drifting off by themselves in despair" (189). That Wiltz concludes *Glass House* with no easy solutions underlines the fact that residential segregation, institutional racism, and the long legacy of prejudice will not be changed by the goodwill of a few good people. However, Wiltz, much like Bambara with Zala, does suggest that Thea's and Janine's considered decisions to stay in New Orleans because the city is their "home" (9, 156) and to conduct their lives differently from those around them is an admirable place to start. But it is a commitment they will have to remake every day in a segregated city where both blacks and whites are armed. Wiltz represents gun violence as dangerous not only to individuals but to the future of race relations. And yet by concluding her novel with Delzora's paradoxical musings—"Nothing had changed but everything had changed" (189)—Wiltz suggests that to fixate only on the big picture is to devalue the individual initiatives that might help to change it.

When *A Man in Full* appeared in 1998, Tom Wolfe seemed unaware that southern women writers had already begun to plow the literary terrain of urban "racial antagonisms" that he believed was his own virgin territory.[54] Humphreys, Bambara, and Wiltz explore urban race relations with distinctive perspectives that lie somewhere between Wolfe's satirical overview, which reveals urban social segregation and racial types but misses interracial relationships that do not fit the broad pattern of segregation, and the domestic close-ups of other writers, like John Gregory Brown and Dori Sanders, who frame interracial intimacies but do not always employ a lens quite wide enough for the big picture. Bambara and Wiltz, and to a lesser extent Humphreys, bring the racial antagonisms of the city streets into the domestic scene, although only Bambara takes her black mother into the streets, where she becomes a grassroots leader for social change. Bambara's message is similar to NAACP president Julian Bond's. In an overview of the rise of SNCC, he reminds his readers, "It took but one woman's courage to start a movement in Montgomery, the bravery of four young men in Greensboro to set the South on fire."[55]

Rural Places, Compartmentalized Lives

When Christine Wiltz's Thea returns to New Orleans in the 1980s after a ten-year sojourn in Massachusetts, she refuses to live the segregated life that her old social set works to maintain. Although Thea has no real impact on the overall social dynamic of New Orleans race relations, neither does she become a pariah in New Orleans for her liberal racial views and black friends. The city's population is large enough and diverse enough for her not to have to depend on her old social group for a sense of community. Rather, Thea gravitates to a few like-minded individuals, black and white, who constitute the beginnings a small but integrated group. Such is not always the case when fiction about race and community is set in rural areas and small towns. Neither Elizabeth Spencer's Nelle and Robin in "The Business Venture" (1987) nor Randall Kenan's Horace in *A Visitation of Spirits* (1989) are as fortunate as Thea. While a small population usually ensures that completely isolated racial enclaves do not exist, social segregation still poisons any real sense of a shared community. Eileen, the white narrator of "The Business Venture," points out that black people "were all around us, had always been, living around us, waiting on us, sharing our lives, brought up with us"; however, she does not have even one black friend.[56] Characters of both races in these contemporary rural fictions know almost everyone in their small towns, white and black. But for this same reason, finding people willing to ignore what family and friends think about race and to put aside the old practices of social segregation is difficult. In order to live in a rural community resistant to change, characters who embrace integration compartmentalize their lives in ways that Thea is not required to do. If they do not, they face open hostility, as Laidlaw and Redmon do in Madison Smartt Bell's *Soldier's Joy*, or communal manipulation and marginalization, as Spencer's Nelle and Robin do in "The Business Venture."

To emphasize the power of place to affect individuals, Spencer presents Nelle and Robin's interracial business venture through the eyes of the town gossip, Eileen, who, as secretary to the only lawyer in town, is strategically positioned both to hear the town's dirt and to dish it out. Because Eileen's "crowd" of young white married couples has always been at the apex of the town's social ladder, Eileen absolves herself of any blame for Nelle's marginalization: "It still upsets me to think of all the gossip that went on that year, and at the same time I have to blame Nelle Townshend for it, not so much for starting it, but for being so unconscious about it. She had stepped out of line and she didn't even bother to notice" (128). Nelle disregards the roles that white women from prominent families are expected to play in tiny Tyler, Mississippi. She shows no interest in marriage, she attends art theory seminars at the University of Southern Mississippi, she runs a dry cleaning business out of her family's Victorian home, and most egregiously, she takes as her business partner a black Vietnam veteran, Robin Byers. Eileen's gossip about Nelle and Robin exemplifies the white community's use of narrative as coercion and self-protection in the name of concern for others. Eileen recounts what she and her crowd have done to coax their friend Nelle back within the bounds of respectable white female behavior, but she also recirculates the half-truths and lies about Nelle and Robin that disturb and titillate Tyler, stories even Eileen herself does not really believe. Eileen's own actions to rein in Nelle range from indirect, setting her up with Grey, an old flame and the most eligible white bachelor in town, to direct, warning her that people are gossiping about the nature of her relationship with Robin. Because Nelle must care for her aging mother in a town with very few employment options, she finds her old crowd's attempts to divert her from her work ludicrous: "I've got no time for anything but worrying about customers and money" (138). In a desperate attempt to control Nelle's

behavior, Grey's brother John helps bring an injunction against the dry cleaning business, alleging that the fumes are a health hazard. The white community's concern with integration remains unspoken, although they freely acknowledge among themselves that the injunction has nothing to do with
anyone's physical health. As Nelle's lawyer says, "[t]he fumes in this case have
got nothing to do with dry cleaning" (145). In 1976 the white community in
the small town of Tyler is still trying to ignore the changes the civil rights
movement has wrought, and Eileen's crowd, with their distinction for having
a good time, never talk "about race relations because it spoiled things too
much" (136). Nelle's business venture with Robin disrupts the usual pattern
of gender and race relations; therefore, her behavior threatens the dynamics of
her social group, since "the crowd" has always thought and acted like "one person" and has spoken with "one voice." Not surprisingly, Eileen judges Nelle a
"betrayer" (127), and a male member of the group declares her "too independent," incredulous that "she thinks she can live her own life" (129). The
men wish that she had a man—father, uncle, brother, husband—to look after
her, but mostly to control her. The gossip about Nelle heightens the group's
self-consciousness—its "consciousness of 'outside' (inhabited by those talked
about) and 'inside' (the temporarily secure territory of the talkers)."[57] By the
end of the novella the crowd's social leader is already auditioning new couples
to take Grey and Nelle's place, should the group's last-ditch efforts fail to keep
them together and thus to contain Nelle within the confines of appropriate
ladylike behavior.

"The Business Venture" not only takes small-town gossip as its subject but
also employs gossip as its form, with the result that readers must engage in a
variety of speculations about Nelle and also eventually about Eileen, the
narrator and chief gossipmonger. Although the group thinks of gossip as
"information-sharing," the information exchanged falls "into recognizable patterns," which, according to Patricia Meyers Spacks, "derive from cultural history."[58] In part Eileen's gossip about Nelle and Robin takes the shape of a romance narrative, because the crowd cannot conceive of any other relationship
for a man and a woman who spend so much time together. Eileen's gossip follows this pattern partly because of the way Nelle and Robin disregard traditional
customs for interracial interaction: she goes out to his house at night, and he
sometimes rides in the front seat of her car. But also Eileen's narrative assumes
this shape for personal reasons, because unconsciously she needs to ruin Nelle's
reputation in order to safeguard her own marriage to Charlie, who is a first-

class womanizer. Eileen proves to be an unreliable narrator, who is not so much naive as unwilling to face unpleasant truths about her husband. She uses town talk about Nelle and Robin to distract her and her listeners from Charlie's latest indiscretions and their own rocky marriage: "Busying my thoughts about all this, I had been forgetting Charlie" (131). But the narrative pattern of Eileen's life intertwines with Nelle's after she hears that Nelle's mother fired a warning shot at Charlie when she spotted him on her property. Eileen then thinks back to the time she saw Nelle driving with someone she could not identify on a wooded back road, and she wonders if the passenger was Robin or Charlie. Later Eileen draws attention to the fact that Nelle and Robin both separately went to the coast before the judge heard the case against their dry cleaning plant, but she makes nothing of the fact that Charlie was away at that time as well.

At the beginning of the novella, readers are put in the position of listening to some juicy gossip without knowing a thing about the person gossiping. Spencer strategically structures Eileen's storytelling so that readers must learn about Eileen in order to interpret the story she is sharing. We must discover the truth about Charlie that Eileen is hiding from herself in order to be reasonably certain we understand the relationship between Nelle and Robin. At first readers may misread Eileen's complicated interest in Nelle's fate, because she withholds the crucial fact that Charlie and Nelle were romantically involved the summer that he started dating Eileen—during a time when Nelle was preoccupied with her sister's illness and subsequent death. Readers learn about their thwarted love affair very late in the novella, and then only because a disappointed Grey flings it in Eileen's face. This exchange occurs after the dinner party fails to rekindle his relationship with Nelle but ignites an old spark between Nelle and Charlie. In telling Nelle and Robin's story, Eileen withholds crucial facts because they disrupt her society's conventional cultural narratives about race and gender. In the story of her marriage, she withholds information to protect her pride and to prevent herself from becoming the subject of town gossip.

While Eileen confesses privately (to the reader) that she does not think Nelle and Robin are lovers, she repeatedly injects the innuendo of romance into her public story, giving readers enough hard evidence to view their relationship as a business venture but enough circumstantial evidence to wonder if it could be a romance. Right after the hearing about the dry cleaning business in which the judge finds in favor of Nelle and Robin, Eileen takes a shortcut home and sees them literally dancing for joy in Nelle's backyard—"whirling each other around, like two schoolchildren." Eileen instantly recognizes the clandestine moment as one of "pure joy." Just as quickly she revises their childlike innocence and rereads their behavior through another trope, thinking they could have been "old lovers . . . too happy at some piece of luck to really stop to talk about it." Her final reading of the incident—through the lens of changing race relations—is the most complex interpretation and perhaps the most accurate: "I didn't think they were lovers. But they were into a triumph of the sort that lovers feel. They had acted as they pleased. They were above everything. They lived in another world because of a dry cleaning business" (146). Significantly, Eileen does not tell anyone what she has witnessed because she thinks, "It was too complicated for any two people to know about it" (147). In part Eileen's thoughts are so place-bound—"We couldn't jump out of our own skins, or those of our parents, grandparents, and those before them" (135)—that she cannot imagine her opinions about Nelle and Robin helping to transform the way the white people in Tyler think about integration.

But because Eileen withholds from her friends the knowledge that Robin is Nelle's "real partner" and "not just her hired help" (130), the townspeople continue to misread their relationship. Eileen's failure to explain ends up threatening the very calm that she is attempting to orchestrate. Spencer's narrative strategy demonstrates the two faces of gossip that Patricia Meyers Spacks has delineated—private "educative possibilities" and public "social destructiveness." In contrast with Eileen's public gossip with her crowd—the stories that circulate freely—Nelle's private gossip with the reader takes place between two people in a context of implied trust that her story will go no further.[59] By exchanging information with the reader that she has not exchanged with her friends, Eileen employs gossip in the second mode, which allows her to reflect upon her own ideas about black people and integration as well as on her marriage and which allows Spencer to involve white readers in a more broadminded view about integration than some may have been accustomed to entertain. But the outcome of the novella illustrates that withholding the truth for what one perceives to be safety's sake can actually increase the possibility of danger, both for the subjects of one's gossip and for oneself. Hearing the gossip about Nelle and Robin makes Charlie resume his proprietary interest in Nelle. Jealousy overrules caution, and in the last few lines of the novella, he phones Nelle from home and makes threats against Robin: "If you really are foolin' around with that black bastard, he's answering to *me*" (159). Overhearing this call renders Eileen too upset to tell herself a story that will let Charlie off the hook, which brings an end to her storytelling and to the gossip she has shared with the reader.

In her analysis of how gossip works, Spacks argues that "to transmit a narrative about other people briefly takes possession of their lives"; that dynamic is evident in Nelle's and Robin's attempts to shake off the town's efforts to control their lives. In order to disguise their equal partnership from a white community that is growing increasingly suspicious, they use old southern customs regulating interracial contact as a shield behind which to build their business and hide their friendship. Robin rides in the backseat of her car and takes to calling her "Miss Nelle," with the result that black children in the local school accost Robin's daughter and call him a "Tom." Except for Nelle, the townspeople, white and black, have never seen the Robin that readers observe during the hearing—the smart businessman, dressed like "an assistant university dean," whose testimony causes the judge to find in their favor (141). Only once at the hearing, and then inadvertently, does Nelle speak the "we" that characterizes her partnership with Robin, and this "we" stands in stark contrast to the "we" of the white "crowd" that Eileen constantly invokes (144, 135). Certainly Robin and his wife are never invited to the parties hosted by Nelle's social set. Because Nelle and Robin do not conduct their business publicly as equal partners, but instead meet clandestinely at Robin's house outside of Tyler or drive separately to Biloxi to jointly purchase new equipment, their behavior causes the very speculation of an illicit liaison that they are trying to avoid. Significantly, it is when Nelle is acting the role most expected of her—Grey's sexy date—that Charlie falls in love with her again.

When Nelle and Robin try to hide the truth of their relationship by performing old social roles, they fragment their own identities. Even though Spencer does not enter the consciousness of either Nelle or Robin, she suggests their social schizophrenia and psychological fragmentation with both their performance of racial hierarchy and the duality of their physical appearances. Nelle is represented in two extremes: the preoccupied business owner oblivious of her appearance, with mussed hair and no makeup, and the sexual object of the male gaze at the dinner party, provocative in new high-heeled sandals and an eye-catching red silk shawl. Robin looks different depending upon which side of his face a viewer is positioned on: "From one side he could look positively frightening, as he had a long white scar running down the side of his cheek. . . . The other side of Robin Byers's face was regular, smooth, and while not especially handsome it was good-humored and likeable. All in all, he looked intelligent and conscientious" (141). This difference in the ways Spencer portrays Robin's and Nelle's dual identities suggests that the white woman can control how she appears to white people, but that the black man cannot exert such control. In this small southern town, a black body is so visibly marked by race that it is as if it were permanently scarred. Whether the black man is judged by the color of his skin or the content of his character depends totally on the viewer's ideology about race.

While neither Nelle nor Robin openly lives the truth of their interracial relationship, the very fact of it changes the community, whether the community chooses to acknowledge it or not. Early in the novella, Eileen says, "We felt weakened because of her" (157). At the end, Eileen admits, "We are all hanging on a golden thread, but who has got the other end? Dreaming or awake, I'm praying it will hold us all suspended" (159). Spencer's novella demonstrates the unlikelihood of such social stasis after the sixties, no matter white people's desire. Eileen's gossip about Nelle and Robin suggests that love of place in the 1970s South had less to do with the virtues of rootedness that Eudora Welty extolled than with the "white anxieties about the changing South" that Patricia Yaeger brought to light in *Dirt and Desire*.[60] Words do indeed make communities,[61] and while Eileen fails to use her words to remake her community, Spencer succeeds quite cleverly. In his review of "The Business Venture," Madison Smartt Bell praises Spencer's ability to supply a "slice of social history" rather than creating "only a story of racial unrest": "Ms. Spencer has a master's touch for rendering the spirit of the setting, not only the landscape and architecture, but the traditions and social manners that make a place what it is for the people who inhabit it." In explaining how "locale is inextricably involved with what happens in the story," Bell quotes Eileen's description of her crowd's symbiotic relationship: "We were all like one person, walking around different ways, but in some permanent way breathing together, feeling the same reactions, thinking each other's thoughts. What do you call that if not love?" (127). In response to this question, Bell answers, "suffocation, possibly, and yet in essence it's both."[62]

Like Spencer and Bell himself in *Soldier's Joy*, Randall Kenan examines how place can shape destiny and how a community's love can both support and suffocate individuals. In *A Visitation of Spirits* (1989), Kenan captures the soul of rural Tims Creek, North Carolina, a fictional town patterned after Chinquapin, where he grew up. Kenan focuses on the narrow-mindedness of the black community, and unlike Spencer, he employs the perspectives of characters on the margins as well as those at the town's center. The second-person pronoun that Kenan switches to in his conclusion, "Requiem for Tobacco," challenges readers to consider whether any community that is "bound together . . . as one" can be nurturing of individuals who are different and thus whether unity in the black community actually exists: "You've heard of these things, I'm sure? Didn't you see it in a play or read it in a book."[63]

Kenan's main filter characters are cousins, Jimmy Greene and Horace Cross, descendants of the most prominent black family in Tims Creek. Although Jimmy is older than Horace, they have a lot in common: both are brilliant sons of unwed mothers who fled rural North Carolina, both are raised by their grandparents, both grow up in the Baptist Church, both are intellectually curious and socially well-mannered. Both eventually question the ways of their family and the black community, but neither wants to leave the place—the physical landscape—he loves. Their lives follow different trajectories because of their relationship to the black community's values, which suggests Kenan's purpose in creating these character doubles. Jimmy rebels in college, drinking and engaging in promiscuous sex far away from the prying eyes of family and community. He then returns to Tims Creek and fulfills his family's high expectations by becoming both the first principal of the newly integrated elementary school and the minister of First Baptist of Tims Creek, a church built on land donated by his great-great-grandfather. In contrast, Horace, although he is a very good student, becomes a disappointment to his family because his friends are a group of privileged white boys he meets at the integrated public high school. He becomes a disappointment to himself because of his hidden sexual orientation, which his Baptist upbringing teaches him is abnormal and sinful. John Howard has pointed out that while religious persecution of homosexuals occurs all over the United States, religious belief—particularly Protestant evangelicalism—proves especially significant for southern homosexuals, because "the religiosity of many lesbian and gay Southerners means religion is anything but a one-way, oppressive force."[64]

Kenan structures *A Visitation of Spirits* as a braided narrative: Horace's review of his life on the night before his suicide alternates with a typical day in Jimmy's life a year later. Jimmy's portion of the novel includes confessions of his sins of commission and omission—his guilt for not having prevented Horace's suicide and for having given the appearance of perfect probity himself. Horace's attempts to find a community in rural Tims Creek that will respect the many facets of his identity are interspersed with Jimmy's emerging struggle to teach compassion and tolerance to Horace's family, which clearly failed Horace. Both men hide the truth. At first Horace lies to himself about his sexual orientation, and later he hides his homosexual affairs from his family and the black community. Jimmy hides the truth about his youthful indiscretions, and in a way reminiscent of Spencer's Eileen, he later hides the truth about his wife Anne's adulterous affairs from readers as well, thus making him look, especially to Horace, like a model citizen, and his life like a piece of perfection. Significantly, Jimmy never tells Horace that Anne once wondered if Jimmy was gay.

The overview of Horace's life the night before his death allows readers to see how he has moved from group to group, seeking a community of people who will acknowledge the fullness of his identity as a gay black intellectual. Horace's diverse interests—from the Flip Wilson show and Pink Floyd to Camus and physics—reveal an eclectic cultural and intellectual life. His ability to get along with a variety of people in his integrated high school suggests that he is ready to broaden his social circle beyond the segregated black community of his grandparents. But his grandparents are understandably wary of rural whites who once openly discriminated against them, and they are cautious about differences within the black community that might threaten the racial solidarity that enabled them to rebel against the South's Jim Crow laws. In high school Horace acts on desires he has held in check and secretly begins a sexual relationship with Gideon, a gay black classmate. Later, when Horace's grandfather publicly expresses pride in his academic accomplishments, Horace feels guilty about this clandestine relationship. In need of assurance about his normality, he turns his back on Gideon. He becomes an athlete, joins several high school clubs, and even has somewhat reassuring, although uninteresting, sex with a black girl. But when Horace's school activities and advanced placement classes foster friendships with white teenagers, his black friends and his family question Horace's racial identity.

A summer job for a theater group brings Horace into contact with a group of handsome, cosmopolitan gay actors, which causes him once again to confront his sexual orientation but also to feel self-conscious about his rural roots and his dark skin. His unrequited love for a light-skinned upper-class black actor from Washington, D.C., makes Horace feel too dark and too provincial, but a summer of merely casual sex with Antonio, a gay man of mixed Italian and Puerto Rican ancestry from Brooklyn, leaves Horace emotionally unsatisfied. Finally in his senior year, Horace feels he has "found a group" of like-minded friends who are bright, interesting, and "quick to set themselves apart from the tedious banality of East York Senior High School," because they have lived outside the South in cities such as New York and San Francisco. Although Horace finds these white guys intellectually stimulating, he is uncertain of their motives in befriending him. He wonders if they are "accepting him merely as a reaction to the traditional racial bias of the area," to show their "lack of prejudice" (237). When his black friends call him "Oreo" and his family subsequently puts a halt to his interaction with "them no-account white boys," Horace begins to plan his exit from Tims Creek (239, 186).

However, Horace's attachment to North Carolina is so strong (he feels "[h]e had to stay here" [11]) that rather than move away, he turns to the occult, deciding after much deliberation to transfigure himself into an indigenous bird. When his fantastic attempt to become a red-tailed hawk fails, Horace assumes suicide is his only alternative until he hears a demonic voice commanding him to kill both the bigoted whites and the homophobic black minister. In several fantasy scenes, two apparitions bearing Horace's face enact roles that Horace could assume in North Carolina: a black-robed figure wielding a scimitar against his foes and a black actor dressed as a harlequin and made up as a mime in white greasepaint. The cloaked figure resembles Horace's much-beloved comic book superheroes who seek justice but represent a life of vengeance. With both horror and fascination, Horace watches the cloaked figure decapitate the homophobic minister. The actor, a figure conjured from Horace's memories of the summer theater company, suggests a life in the public eye, perhaps one of social activism, since he offers Horace a vintage topcoat worn by "an educated, crusading reconstructionist minister from the North who, along with the carpetbaggers, had been sent to make sure the slaves got their due" (226). But Horace's Baptist conscience refuses the superhero's "salvation" through violence (168) and the actor's possibility of "redemption" through becoming a new "savior" (234). Robert McRuer argues convincingly that the actor represents the constructedness of identities and thus truly *is* Horace's redemption but that "Horace is unable to recognize and deploy that concept against the multiple communities that surround him."[65] While Horace's family has made sure that he understands how white racism constructs blackness, the black community has not interrogated the social construction of homosexuality. Kenan portrays the black church, the very institution that mobilized the black community prior to and during the civil rights movement, as currently failing its homosexual members. Although Jimmy, representative of a younger generation of pastors, attempts to assuage Horace's guilt by dismissing his attraction to men as simply adolescent sexual experimentation, he reinforces Horace's notion that homosexuality is sinful. As a result Horace never realizes that the teaching of his church, not he, is wrong. He dies thinking he has sinned, but Kenan ends the novel with Jimmy and thus makes readers painfully aware of the role Jimmy has played in Horace's death.

Horace's attempt to compartmentalize various aspects of his life as he searches for a community in which he feels comfortable echoes the identity conflicts of mixed-race protagonists who shuttle back and forth between two racial communities. Horace could, of course, go to New York, as Randall Kenan himself did for a time, but Kenan's point is that he should not have to. So Kenan places Horace in the untenable position of not wanting to leave North Carolina but not able to be himself there. McRuer has detailed the ways in which *A Visitation of Spirits* makes explicit the homosexual issues that James Baldwin deals with more indirectly in *Go Tell It on the Mountain*. But Kenan alludes to a southern white literary predecessor as well when he places Horace, like Joe Christmas, in the headlights of an oncoming vehicle—naked, armed, and confused but certain something is going to happen to him. Kenan says that he has dealt with the anxiety of Faulkner's influence by "intermingling those things that are most real" to him, by thinking of his work as "a continuation" of Faulkner.[66] Similar to the racial politics in Faulkner's Jefferson, Mississippi, which result in Joe Christmas's death, the identity politics of Tims Creek, North Carolina, kill Horace, although Horace himself pulls the trigger. In *A Visitation of Spirits,* all of the groups that Horace seeks solace from are looking for sameness; no one group will accept the diversity that is always present within individuals. While the smart, liberal white boys come closest to accepting the multifaceted Horace, even they do not know of his sexual orientation.

Two scenes in which Horace's lovers apply the epithet *faggot* convey Kenan's point about narrowly defining individuals. In the scene in which a religiously repentant Horace spurns his high school lover Gideon, Gideon tells him, "You're a faggot. You can run, you can hide, but when the shit comes down . . . you suck cock, you don't eat pussy." Horace's response, "You're sickening," is an attempt to deny his own homosexuality as he turns away from Gideon (164). By the time his actor lover Antonio uses the same epithet, Horace's response is significantly different, which suggests that he has accepted his homosexuality, even though he stills views it as sinful. Horace's rejoinder to Antonio's taunt, "Don't like to be called what you are?" reflects a refusal to be defined solely by his sexuality: "What I *am* is brilliant" (224–25). In concluding the novel with Horace's suicide, Kenan suggests that Horace's friends and family, indeed all of Tims Creek, need to learn what Eve Sedgwick teaches in *Epistemology of the Closet*—that even those people who seem most like us are different in some way.[67] Kenan demonstrates that identity politics, of any stripe, can function to create community but that communities so formed continue to function only by negating differences of the individuals within them. As McRuer points out, Kenan's rural black gay protagonist disrupts and decenters numerous hegemonies: heterosexual, southern white, urban gay.[68]

Kenan frames the story of Horace's suicide with what at first seem to be two nostalgic reveries of southern black rural life. The communal hog killing that opens the novel and the tobacco harvest that closes it resonate in multiple ways. Juxtaposed with Horace's horror story of contemporary identity politics, these pastoral scenes reveal that the old rural communal ways, with their back-breaking labor and gender-role-specific jobs, were not idyllic. But these scenes simultaneously remind readers that individuals express their humanity when in community with each other. By using such pastoral scenes to frame a contemporary story replete with fast food and mechanical harvesters, Kenan points up how the rural South is changing but also how much further such places must be transformed before they will truly be home to all who grow up there.

This is where Jimmy's role as the other protagonist in *A Visitation of Spirits* becomes so significant. While Horace is haunted by apparitions and demonic voices on the night of his death, Jimmy is haunted by those black people for whom he and the black community have failed to show tolerance and compassion—his own unwed mother, who returns briefly for her mother's funeral, but especially Horace, whom he talked to right before his suicide. Although Jimmy does not directly admit his guilt about Horace's death, his sense of personal "triumph" (40) dissipates in situations that trigger his memory of Horace. These remembered events are so vivid that they erupt into Jimmy's prose confessions as short dramatic scenes: the morning Jimmy failed to talk Horace out of committing suicide, the afternoon following the church service when he failed to validate Horace's sexual orientation, and the evening at Thanksgiving dinner when he failed to discourage the Cross family from making Horace give up his white friends. Although the older generation of African Americans does not alter its views on homosexuality, by the end of the novel Jimmy does—terming Horace's love of men "a simple, normal deviation" (188). By listing the paradigm-shifting books that Jimmy has been reading, Kenan suggests that books have played a key role in Jimmy's enlightenment: "Augustine and Erasmus. Maybe Freud, or Jung, or Foucault. Black history: Franklin, Quarles, Fanon. Occasionally fiction" (44). Kenan must have hoped his own novel would have a similar effect on some of his readers.

A Visitation of Spirits contains some seemingly gratuitous scenes that take place a year after Horace's suicide when Jimmy takes his great-aunt Ruth Cross and his great-uncle Zeke Cross, Horace's grandfather, to visit a dying cousin in the hospital. The narration of this trip is intertwined with the narration of Horace's last hours on earth, a juxtaposition that creates an ironic commentary on the Cross family's attempt to control Horace's life. On the way to Fayetteville, readers have access to Zeke's and Ruth's memories, which reveal hidden fallibilities and potential rebellions that neither has shared with Horace or Jimmy. We discover that Zeke, a deacon in the Baptist Church, has been unfaithful to his wife and that neither he nor his sister-in-law Ruth has been particularly happy in their marriages. As a younger man, Zeke measured himself against his father and came up short far too often, although he finally realizes that it is all right to be different. Readers know that Horace has done the same, measuring himself against Zeke and despairing that he will never be like him. By having Zeke and Horace use the same language to think about their parental figures, Kenan calls attention to the fact that Zeke has failed his grandson by misrepresenting himself.

During the day-trip that takes Ruth and Zeke out of their black enclave, Kenan also calls on readers to notice the difference between Horace's attitude toward white people and Zeke's and Ruth's. At the fateful Thanksgiving dinner a year before, Horace accuses his family of being "bigots" (186), but the family matriarch corrects him: "You have no idea what bigotry is. No idea what prejudging is. No idea what hate is" (187). Certainly the virulent racism and legal discrimination that Horace's grandparents and their generation experienced do not compare to the generalizations Horace's family members level against Horace's white friends, but the series of interracial scenes that occur a year after his suicide suggest that Horace's family members need to examine their own prejudices. At the hospital Ruth is perturbed by the addled chatter of a old woman she calls a "no-mannered white fool," with whom her cousin Asa must share the room (127). But during lunch Ruth gets so worked up in arguing with Zeke about the Cross family's pretensions that she calls as much attention to herself in the café as the "no-mannered" white woman did in Asa's hospital room. The similarity of these outbursts, which Kenan directs readers' attention to with similar language, and the two scenes that follow exemplify what Debbora Battaglia has called the "collaborative practice" of identity formation. Battaglia argues that a reified self is "continually defeated by mutable entanglements with other subjects' histories, experiences, self-representation; with their texts, conduct, gestures, objectifications."[69]

Kenan fashions this portion of his novel to test his readers, particularly his black readers, by creating two scenes involving local white people that take place after the hospital visit. When Jimmy, Zeke, and Ruth stop for lunch after their visit to the hospital, the young white woman who waits on them is rude. In the café scene Kenan leaves ambiguous the reason for the waitress's rudeness, much as Elizabeth Cox does with her store clerk in *Night Talk*. Ruth is very hard to please, but given the white racism she has experienced in her lifetime, Ruth could assume the waitress's behavior stems from prejudice. The very next scene, which also involves a working-class white family, cautions against such an easy assumption. It takes place in a service station, where Jimmy, Zeke, and Ruth find themselves after their car breaks down. Kenan surprises readers by having the white family show Zeke and Ruth more compassion than they have shown each other all day long. The mechanic promises to have their car finished in a couple of hours, even venturing to crack a joke about their luck. Although his wife looks like another "no-mannered" lower-class woman, with her greasy black hair and *True Confessions* magazine, she sympathizes with Jimmy, Ruth, and Zeke about Asa's illness and commiserates with them for having to spend a cold, rainy afternoon in a service station. To boost their spirits, she even brews a communal pot of coffee, and the couple's young daughter with a wink throws Ruth off guard by offering to teach her how to play pinball. Their behavior thwarts Ruth's expectation of racism, against which she has established her superior character all day. Instead, a cold and weary Ruth instinctively pronounces the woman's coffee "mighty good" (203), a statement that contradicts her petty essentialist declaration at the café: "White folks don't know how to cook no how" (193). Most surprisingly, Ruth agrees to the white girl's offer of a pinball lesson and quickly becomes so immersed in the game that she exhibits a "glee" Jimmy has never seen (205). In this scene identity becomes what Paul Gilroy has called "an ongoing process of self-making and social interaction" instead of "a thing to be possessed and displayed."[70] With this unexpected scene, Kenan hints at the need for a broader understanding of community as "a group of people living in the same locality."[71]

In an interview Kenan said, "It seemed, and it seems . . . that for that community to change they have to understand the devastation that they're wreaking on certain people."[72] Kenan gives his readers this experience in *A Visitation of Spirits*. And because he has made Jimmy principal of an integrated high school and minister of First Baptist Church, Kenan has put him in positions of authority with the potential to change his community as well, the one hopeful sign in a novel that ends with a suicide. Early in *A Visitation of Spirits*, readers learn that Jimmy's brother, a lawyer in Washington, and his sister, a doctoral candidate in architecture at Berkeley, have both encouraged him to leave North Carolina. His reply, "If we all 'get out,' who will stay?" (35), accrues a great deal of significance by the end of the novel. Jimmy's choice mirrors the real-life choices of black and white southerners in the sixties who became civil rights activists, and it parallels the fictional decisions of characters in *Glass House, Those Bones Are Not My Child,* and "The Business Venture" who choose to stay and make a difference in their communities. Read together, Randall Kenan and Elizabeth Spencer demonstrate how the social pressure to segregate racially can come from both sides of the color line and can torment those individuals who would like to cross. Their protagonists are psychologically bruised by family and friends, but both authors suggest that the characters' defiance of small-town racial customs reverberates in positive ways they never know.

James Baldwin concludes *The Evidence of Things Not Seen,* his meditation on the Atlanta child murders, with an attempt "to excavate the meaning of the word *community,*" which as he understands it "simply means our endless connection with and responsibility for, each other." He points out that "in the twentieth century, and in the modern State, the idea—the sense—of community has been submerged for a very long time. In the United States, the idea of community scarcely means anything anymore, as far as I can tell, except among the submerged, the 'lowly': the Native American, the Mexican, the Puerto Rican, the Black."[73] Toni Cade Bambara, Christine Wiltz, Elizabeth Spencer, and Randall Kenan attempt to show readers how their discrete racial communities are ultimately connected and how the health and well-being of both their communities and the individuals within them depend on a broader sense of community and a more complex understanding of identity. While all of the writers I have discussed in this chapter give readers a wake-up call about the problems of segregation, whatever its cause, Bambara, Wiltz, Spencer, and Kenan suggest through their character-activists a course of action. Their works remind readers that "sustained personal interaction" can be "the best inoculation against distrust and fear."[74] However, they show that consciousness of racism is not sufficient: that fundamental changes need to be made in social, economic, and government institutions that wittingly or unwittingly encourage behaviors that perpetuate racism.

Whereas an earlier generation of southern writers, black and white, challenged the mythic unity of southern communities in order to lay bare their racial divisions, these contemporary writers challenge the mythic sameness of racial communities and the contemporary connotation of community as a special interest group. In doing so they open up a sight line that points the way back to a broader definition of community, which involves not simply a group of people who live in the same locality and under the same government but a group of people who *because* they live in the same locality share common interests and connections. None of these writers go so far as to envision Martin Luther King Jr.'s "beloved community." But most hold out some hope for change by illustrating the power of the imagination to find hidden passages across racial fault lines and to chart new courses for race relations through the very acts of "reconciliation" and "redemption" King called for in 1956.[75] Thus readers are encouraged to keep his dream alive. And yet despite individual successes, these writers maintain no illusions that their communities are integrated, and thus neither can readers. Just as the fictions of cross-racial relationships progress toward a happy ending but are brought up short by reverberations from within the society, so these fictions of community end unhappily, even as they contain isolated tales of hope. They could not do otherwise and allow readers to dwell in new possibilities even as they tell the complicated story of race relations in the South, and in the United States, at the end of the twentieth century.

Appendix: Fiction Discussed

1967
Ernest J. Gaines, *Of Love and Dust*

1968
Ernest J. Gaines, "Bloodline"

1976
Alice Walker, *Meridian*

1977
Alice Walker, "Advancing Luna—and Ida B. Wells"

1978
Raymond Andrews, *Appalachee Red*

1979
Barbara Chase-Riboud, *Sally Hemings*
Ellen Douglas, *The Rock Cried Out*

1982
Rita Mae Brown, *Southern Discomfort*
Gail Godwin, *A Mother and Two Daughters*

1983
Ernest Gaines, *A Gathering of Old Men*

1984
Josephine Humphreys, *Dreams of Sleep*

1986
Sherley Anne Williams, *Dessa Rose*

1987
Elizabeth Spencer, "The Business Venture"

1988
Ellen Douglas, *Can't Quit You, Baby*

1989
Madison Smartt Bell, *Soldier's Joy*
Larry Brown, *Dirty Work*
Randall Kenan, *A Visitation of Spirits*

1990
Dori Sanders, *Clover*

1991
Reynolds Price, "The Fare to the Moon"

1992
Bebe Moore Campbell, *Your Blues Ain't like Mine*
Thulani Davis, *1959*
Connie Mae Fowler, *Sugar Cage*
Randall Kenan, *Let the Dead Bury Their Dead*
Nanci Kincaid, *Crossing Blood*

1993
Mark Childress, *Crazy in Alabama*
Ernest Gaines, *A Lesson before Dying*
Lewis Nordan, *Wolf Whistle*

1994
John Gregory Brown, *Decorations in a Ruined Cemetery*
Julius Lester, *And All Our Wounds Forgiven*
Christine Wiltz, *Glass House*

1995
Albert French, *Holly*
Myra McLarey, *Water from the Well*

1996
Monica White, *Shades of Desire*

1997
Elizabeth Cox, *Night Talk*

1998
James Kilgo, *Daughter of My People*
Donald McCaig, *Jacob's Ladder: A Story of Virginia during the War*
Dar Tomlinson, *Forbidden Quest*
Tom Wolfe, *A Man in Full*

1999
Toni Cade Bambara, *Those Bones Are Not My Child*

2000
Rosellen Brown, *Half a Heart*
T. R. Pearson, *Blue Ridge*
Shay Youngblood, *Black Girl in Paris*

2001
Anthony Grooms, *Bombingham*

Notes

Introduction

1. David Nicholson, "Driving Old Dixie Down: A Northern Black Confronts His Southern Discomfort and Finds a New American Dream," *Washington Post*, April 24, 1994, C1.

2. Tony Horwitz, *Confederates in the Attic: Dispatches from the Unfinished Civil War* (New York: Pantheon Books, 1998).

3. Patricia J. Williams, *Seeing a Color-Blind Future: The Paradox of Race* (New York: Farrar, Straus, and Giroux, 1998), 56.

4. During a lecture at the Christopher Newport University Writers Conference in Newport News, Virginia, April 16, 1994, Dori Sanders explained the origin of the idea for her novel.

5. Humphreys made this remark during a conversation with students at the University of Richmond, November 4, 1998.

6. Michael O'Brien, *The Idea of the American South, 1920–1941* (Baltimore: Johns Hopkins University Press, 1979), xii. Patricia Yaeger, *Dirt and Desire: Reconstructing Southern Women's Writing, 1930–1990* (Chicago: University of Chicago Press, 2000), xi, xii.

7. Michael Omi and Howard Winant, *Racial Formation in the United States from the 1960s to the 1980s* (New York: Routledge and Kegan Paul, 1986), 68.

8. Albion W. Tourgée, "The South as a Field for Fiction," *Forum* 6 (December 1888): 404.

9. Maureen Ryan analyzes this collection and other fiction about Vietnamese Americans in "Outsiders with Inside Information: The Vietnamese in the Fiction of the Contemporary American South," in *South to a New Place: Region, Literature, Culture*, ed. Suzanne W. Jones and Sharon Monteith (Baton Rouge: Louisiana State University Press, 2002), 235–52.

10. Susan Choi, *The Foreign Student* (1998; New York: HarperPerennial, 1999), 53.

11. Donald Noble, "The Future of Southern Writing," in *The History of Southern Literature*, ed. Louis D. Rubin Jr., Blyden Jackson, Rayburn S. Moore, Lewis P. Simpson, and Thomas Daniel Young (Baton Rouge: Louisiana State University Press, 1985), 587.

12. Michael Kreyling, *Inventing Southern Literature* (Jackson: University of Mississippi Press, 1998), 110.

13. I use Fred Hobson's phrase from *But Now I See: The White Southern Racial Conversion Narrative* (Baton Rouge: Louisiana State University Press, 1999). While Hobson analyzes memoir and autobiography, the paradigm is prominent in fiction by southern whites as well, particularly modernist fiction published after the Civil War up through the 1960s.

14. See Suzanne W. Jones, "I'll Take My Land: Contemporary Southern Agrarians," in Jones and Monteith, 121–46.

15. I echo the distinction that Larry McClain pointed out between two western writers, Texans Rolando Hinojosa and Larry McMurtry, in "The Rhetoric of Regional Representation: American Fiction and the Politics of Cultural Dissent," *Genre* 27.3 (fall 1994): 249.

16. Don O'Briant, "Anger at Klan Fuels New Novel," *Atlanta Journal-Constitution,* June 12, 1989, B1.

17. Julian Borger, "Papa, I Have to Know What You Were Doing," *Guardian* (London), May 7, 2001, Features, 6.

18. David K. Shipler, "Bombingham Revisited," *New York Times Book Review,* March 18, 2001, 8.

19. Linda Martín Alcoff, "What Should White People Do?" *Hypatia* 13.3 (summer 1998): 21, 25.

20. After a trip to Africa, Eddy Harris, a black journalist from New York, recounts in *South of Haunted Dreams* (New York: Simon and Schuster, 1993) how he discovered his cultural roots in the American South.

21. Nell Irvin Painter, "'The South' and 'the Negro': The Rhetoric of Race Relations and Real Life," in *The South for New Southerners,* ed. Paul D. Escott and David R. Goldfield (Chapel Hill: University of North Carolina Press, 1991), 43.

22. Thadious M. Davis, "Expanding the Limits: The Intersection of Race and Region," *Southern Literary Journal* 20.2 (spring 1988): 6.

23. Anthony Grooms, *Bombingham* (New York: Free Press, 2001), 131.

24. R. Jeffery Smith reports on the analysis of U.S. Census figures for 2000 in "Reversing a Long Pattern, Blacks Are Heading South," *Washington Post,* May 5, 2001, A1, A10. The region the U.S. government defines as the South for census purposes includes Delaware; Maryland; Washington, D.C.; Virginia; North Carolina; South Carolina; Georgia; Florida; Alabama; Mississippi; Louisiana; Texas; Oklahoma; Arkansas; Tennessee; Kentucky; and West Virginia.

25. Leonard Steinhorn and Barbara Diggs-Brown, *By the Color of Our Skin: The Illusion of Integration and the Reality of Race* (1999; New York: Plume, 2000), 5.

26. David K. Shipler, *A Country of Strangers: Blacks and Whites in America* (New York: Knopf, 1997), 314–15, 271.

27. Richard Morin, "Misperceptions Cloud Whites' View of Blacks," *Washington Post,* July 11, 2001, A1, A7. The survey was conducted by the *Washington Post,* the Henry J. Kaiser Family Foundation, and Harvard University.

28. Benjamin DeMott, *The Trouble with Friendship: Why Americans Can't Think Straight about Race* (1995; New Haven: Yale University Press, 1998), 23, 22, 5.

29. Megan Rosenfeld, "In South Africa, Learning to Forgive and Remember," *Washington Post,* June 11, 2001, C1, C5.

30. DeMott, 123, 120.

31. Andrew Hacker, *Two Nations: Black and White, Separate, Hostile, Unequal* (New York: Scribner's, 1992); Stephan Thernstrom and Abigail Thernstrom, *America in Black and White: One Nation, Indivisible* (New York: Simon and Schuster, 1997); Shelby Steele, *The Content of Our Character: A New Vision of Race in America* (New York: St. Martin's Press, 1990); Douglas S. Massey and Nancy A. Denton, *American Apartheid: Segregation and the Making of the Underclass* (Cambridge, Mass.: Harvard University Press, 1993).

32. Steinhorn and Diggs-Brown, 90, 25.

33. Mikhail Bakhtin, *Problems of Dostoevsky's Poetics,* ed. and trans. Caryl Emerson (Minneapolis: University of Minnesota Press, 1984), 287.

34. Wolfgang Iser, *Prospecting: From Reader Response to Literary Anthropology* (Baltimore: Johns Hopkins University Press, 1989), 280.

35. See Kenneth W. Warren's introduction to his *Black and White Strangers: Race and American Literary Realism* (Chicago: University of Chicago Press, 1993) for an excellent and more detailed summary and analysis of this debate.

36. Henry Louis Gates Jr., *Figures in Black: Words, Signs, and the "Racial" Self* (New York: Oxford University Press, 1987), 45.

37. Wolfgang Iser, *The Implied Reader* (Baltimore: Johns Hopkins University Press, 1974), 294.

38. Sanders shared these responses with me at the Christopher Newport University Writers Conference in Newport News, Virginia, April 15–16, 1994.

39. Wolfgang Iser, "Do I Write for an Audience?," *PMLA* 115.3 (May 2000): 313–14. Peter Rabinowitz, *Before Reading: Narrative Conventions and the Politics of Interpretation* (Ithaca, N.Y.: Cornell University Press, 1987).

40. Elizabeth Kastor, "Southern Seeds of a First Novel," *Washington Post,* May 6, 1990, F1, F9.

41. Alison Light, "Fear of the Happy Ending: *The Color Purple,* Reading and Racism," in *Plotting Change: Contemporary Women's Fiction,* ed. Linda Anderson (London: Edward Arnold, 1990), 92.

42. Steinhorn and Diggs-Brown, 105. Despite their pessimism about the possibilities for integration, they give a few examples of sustained integration. Shaker Heights, Ohio, has carefully engineered residential integration, Corning Glass has made quality of life a priority in order to retain African American employees, and "white women in the military are seven times more likely to marry black men than white women who never served, and white men are three times more likely to marry black women" (22).

43. DeMott, 7.

44. Pierre Nora, "Between Memory and History," in *Realms of Memory: Rethinking the French Past,* directed by Pierre Nora, trans. Arthur Goldhammer (New York: Columbia University Press, 1996), 20.

45. Audre Lorde, "Age, Race, Class, and Sex" in *Sister Outsider* (Trumansburg, N.Y.: Crossing Press, 1984), 123.

46. Ralph Ellison, William Styron, Robert Penn Warren, and C. Vann Woodward, "A Discussion: The Uses of History in Fiction," *Southern Literary Journal* 1.2 (spring 1969): 70.

47. Iser, "Do I Write?" 313–14.

CHAPTER 1: Lost Childhoods

1. In *Testimony: Crises of Witnessing in Literature, Psychoanalysis, and History* (New York: Routledge, 1992), Shoshana Felman and Dori Laub argue that witnessing is composed of memory "that has been overwhelmed by occurrences that have not settled into understanding or remembrance, acts that cannot be constructed as knowledge nor assimilated into full cognition, events in excess of our frames of reference" (5).

2. Hugh Davis Graham, "Since 1965: The South and Civil Rights," in *The South as an American Problem,* ed. Larry J. Griffin and Don H. Doyle (Athens: University of Georgia Press, 1995), 154.

3. To distinguish between the narrative agent telling the story (the narrator) and the character's consciousness perceiving the events and feelings when fiction is narrated in third person, I use Seymour Chatman's term *filter character.* Gérard Genette makes the same distinction between narration and focalization as Chatman does, but Genette uses the term *focalizer* rather than *filter character.* Gérard Genette, *Narrative Discourse* (1972; Ithaca, N.Y.: Cornell University Press, 1980); Seymour Chatman, *Story and Discourse* (Ithaca, N.Y.: Cornell University Press, 1978).

4. Elizabeth Goodenough, Mark A. Heberle, and Naomi Sokoloff, eds., *Infant Tongues: The Voice of the Child in Literature* (Detroit: Wayne State University Press, 1994), 4.

5. Mark Twain, *Adventures of Huckleberry Finn,* ed. Walter Blair and Victor Fischer (Berkeley: University of California Press, 1985), xx.

6. Lillian Smith, *Killers of the Dream* (1949; New York: Norton, 1978), 39.

7. Felman and Laub, 108.

8. Anthony Grooms, *Bombingham* (New York: Free Press, 2001), 22. Subsequent citations are indicated parenthetically in the text.

9. Bebe Moore Campbell, *Your Blues Ain't like Mine* (1992; New York: Ballantine Books, 1993), 43. Subsequent citations are indicated parenthetically in the text.

10. Juan Williams, *Eyes on the Prize: America's Civil Rights Years, 1954–1965* (New York: Penguin Books, 1987), 38–39.

11. Williams, 46. The historical summary in the next paragraph comes from information in *Eyes on the Prize* (38–57) and in John Dittmer's *Local People: The Struggle for Civil Rights in Mississippi* (Urbana: University of Illinois Press, 1995), 55–58.

12. Dittmer, 58.

13. In *Mississippi: An American Journey* (New York: Alfred A. Knopf, 1996), 43, Anthony Walton points out this link that I elaborate on here.

14. Laurel Graeber, "It's about Childhood," *New York Times Book Review,* September 20, 1992, 13.

15. In his 1996 portrait *Mississippi,* Anthony Walton depicts rural race relations as closer to polite tolerance, and in her study of African Americans returning to the rural Carolinas, anthropologist Carol Stack detects some white resistance to their new ideas. See Walton; and Carol Stack, *Call to Home: African Americans Reclaim the Rural South* (New York: Basic Books, 1996).

16. Anonymous Reviewer for *Kirkus Reviews,* June 15, 1992; and John Katzenbach, "Ricochets in Their Hearts," *Washington Post,* October 10, 1992, D10.

17. Lewis Nordan, *Wolf Whistle* (Chapel Hill: Algonquin Books, 1993), 259. Subsequent citations are indicated parenthetically in the text.

18. Russell Ingram and Mark Ledbetter, "An Interview with Lewis Nordan," *Missouri Review* 20.1 (1997): 84.

19. While few writers today, black or white, would argue for racial exclusivity in writing about race relations or for presenting only the racial perspective of the author, the controversy surrounding the publication of William Styron's *The Confessions of Nat Turner* still reverberates. Intellectual historian Richard King believes that it "scared off white novelists from writing about the Movement or black figures for a good long time." Richard King, "Politics and Fictional Representation: The Case of the Civil Rights Movement" in *The Making of Martin Luther King and the Civil Rights Movement,* ed. Brian Ward and Tony Badger (London: Macmillan, 1996), 168. He places the vehemence of the ten black writers' response in the cultural context of black nationalists expelling white civil rights

workers from the Student Nonviolent Coordinating Committee (SNCC) in 1966. But King does not let Styron off the hook; he defines Styron's problem as a failure of moral deference: "The upshot is that, while white Americans can write about the African-American experience, they should do so only after considerable thought and care. They must in short 'earn' that right. But the opposite is true as well: blacks must take the trouble to understand the 'white' culture they think they know so well" (167). I would only add to King's development of context that the editor of *William Styron's Nat Turner: Ten Black Writers Respond* (Boston: Beacon Press, 1968), John Henrik Clarke, gave a presentation at the Dillard University conference, which called for the ouster of white civil rights workers from SNCC.

20. Randall Kenan, "Review of *Wolf Whistle*," *Nation*, November 15, 1993, 594.

21. See Nordan's own discussion of this image in Ingram and Ledbetter, 75.

22. See Ingram and Ledbetter, 76; and Sam Staggs's interview with Lewis Nordan in *Publishers Weekly*, October 18, 1993, 50.

23. Dittmer, 58.

24. Julian Bond, "The Movement We Helped to Make," in *Long Time Gone: Sixties America Then and Now*, ed. Alexander Bloom (New York: Oxford University Press, 2001), 33.

25. Patricia Holt, "Wacked-Out Racism in Sleeper Summer Novel," *San Francisco Chronicle*, August 23, 1993, E8. E-mail correspondence with Thulani Davis on April 8, 2002, and with Tony Grooms on April 10, 2002.

26. Diane Roberts, "Atlanta Author Mines the Eras of Vietnam and Civil Rights," *Atlanta Journal-Constitution*, October 28, 2001, 6B.

27. Holt, E8.

28. Walton, 55.

29. Melissa Fay Greene, "One Girl's Awakening to Racism," *Washington Post*, January 30, 1992, C2.

30. Thulani Davis, *1959* (1992; New York: HarperPerennial, 1993), 3. Subsequent citations are indicated parenthetically in the text.

31. Pierre Nora, "Between Memory and History," in *Realms of Memory: Rethinking the French Past* (New York: Columbia University Press, 1996), 1, 14.

32. J. Harvie Wilkinson, *From Brown to Bakke: The Supreme Court and School Integration, 1854–1978* (New York: Oxford University Press, 1976), 46.

33. Nordan, 211. This scene is something of a tour de force, in that at the same time Nordan critiques southern customs, he parodies the outside reporters' dispatches as narrow-minded and their attempts to write "pure-dee poetic" descriptions as ridiculous: "They wrote that the scenery itself was hostile. *The scenery is as oppressive as the moss that hangs from the cypress trees,* they wrote. *The silence is like taut skin,* they wrote, *and the faint heart startles, when that silence is cracked by the hiss of a suddenly opened Coke*" (213).

34. Patricia Hampl, *I Could Tell You Stories* (New York: W. W. Norton, 1999), 33.

35. Robert Plunket, "The Head in the Tupperware Bowl," *New York Times Book Review*, August 22, 1993, 7; Garland Reeves, "Vagabond Novelist Mark Childress Grew in Literary Soil," *Cleveland Plain Dealer*, September 12, 1993, Arts 12; Patricia Holt, "Southern Lunacy Meets Hollywood, *San Francisco Chronicle Sunday Review*, August 8, 1993, 1. At least one reviewer saw the "southern" elements as the "southern" writer's stock in trade. See Hank Klibanoff, "One Too Many Plot Lines in a Southern Novel as Nutty As It Needs to Be," *Philadelphia Inquirer*, August 8, 1993, H2.

36. Take, for example, Bobby Birdwell, who in May 2002 finally testified against

Bobby Frank Cherry in the Birmingham church bombing trial. He said that the racist hatred he heard at home and in Cherry's kitchen made him afraid of what might happen to him if he told on Cherry in 1963. Birdwell was eleven at the time. See Rick Bragg, "Prosecutors Try to Recreate Birmingham's '63 Nightmare," *New York Times*, May 15, 2002, A1.

37. Mark Childress, *Crazy in Alabama* (New York: Ballantine Books, 1993), 101. Subsequent citations are indicated parenthetically in the text.

38. When *Crazy in Alabama* became a major motion picture in 1999, Childress wrote the screenplay, thus broadening the audience for his narrative; but perhaps because the film was coproduced by Melanie Griffith and directed by her husband, Antonia Banderas, Lucille's story seems to get more screen time than Peejoe's. Perhaps distilling a 400–page novel, with two plot lines, into a 100–page screenplay was a feat that not even its creator could accomplish. The zaniness survives, at least in Lucille's plot, but Childress's fresh perspective on a white child's experience of the movement loses its originality. Furthermore, with so few major motion pictures about the civil rights movement, yet another with the white character as the protagonist in what looks like the familiar white racial conversion narrative was understandably "troubling" for several reviewers. See Elfrieda Abbe, "*Crazy in Alabama* a Quirky Equation That Doesn't Add Up," *Milwaukee Journal Sentinel*, October 22, 1999, News 8; John Keenan, "Banderas Disappoints in Directorial Debut," *Omaha World-Herald*, October 23, 1999, Living 67.

39. J. A. Appleyard, *Becoming a Reader: The Experience of Fiction from Childhood to Adulthood* (New York: Cambridge University Press, 1990), 16, 14.

40. Ruth Frankenberg, "Growing Up White: Feminism, Racism, and the Social Geography of Childhood," *Feminist Review* 45 (autumn 1993): 55. Her research into the social geography of childhood informs my discussion of *Crossing Blood*.

41. Nanci Kincaid, *Crossing Blood* (1992; New York: Avon Books, 1994), 11. Subsequent citations are indicated parenthetically in the text.

42. Frankenberg, 61.

43. Frankenberg, 54.

44. Paula Gallant Eckard, "Decoding Black and White: Race, Gender, and Language in *Crossing Blood*," *CLA Journal* 41.2 (December 1997): 183.

45. Audre Lorde, "The Master's Tools Will Never Dismantle the Master's House," in her *Sister Outsider: Essays and Speeches* (Trumansburg, N.Y.: Crossing Press, 1984), 112.

46. Martin Swales, *The German Bildungsroman from Wieland to Hesse* (Princeton, N.J.: Princeton University Press, 1978), 23.

47. Dori Sanders, *Clover* (1990; New York: Fawcett Columbine, 1991), 33. Subsequent citations are indicated parenthetically in the text

48. For a discussion of the difference in these concepts, see Thomas F. Pettigrew, "Integration and Pluralism," in *Eliminating Racism: Profiles in Controversy*, ed. Phyllis A. Katz and Dalmas A. Taylor (New York: Plenum Press, 1988), 19–30.

49. Evelyn C. White, "Racial Drama from a Child's Viewpoint," *San Francisco Chronicle*, April 18, 1990, E4. Reviews in major newspapers across the country were overwhelmingly favorable. See also Margaret Camp for the *Washington Post*, April 5, 1990, Jennifer Hill for the *Atlanta Journal-Constitution*, March 25, 1990, Susan Larson for the *New Orleans Times Picayune*, October 21, 1990, Andy Solomon for the *Chicago Tribune*, April 1, 1990, and Jack Sullivan for the *New York Times*, May 20, 1990. Of major newspaper reviewers, only Ursula Hegi for the *Los Angeles Times*, April 15, 1990, was critical. Although she terms the story "powerful" and the voice "authentic," she judges the

major characters superficial and the ending forced (BR2). The title of her review, "So Who Needs a White Stepmother?" is hardly in keeping with the spirit and resolution of the novel and seems to reflect the reviewer's feelings rather than the novelist's.

50. Elizabeth Kastor, "Southern Seeds of a First Novel," *Washington Post,* May 6, 1990, F9.

51. Michael Omi and Harold Winant, *Racial Formation in the United States: From the 1960s to the 1980s* (New York: Routledge and Kegan Paul, 1986), 62.

52. For a history of this controversy, see Rachel F. Moran, *Interracial Intimacy: The Regulation of Race and Romance* (Chicago: University of Chicago Press, 2001).

53. See Gary Saul Morson's analysis of Bakhtin's theories in "Bakhtin and the Present Moment," *American Scholar* 60 (spring 1991): 201–22.

54. In April and October 1995, I had several conversations with Dori Sanders about *Clover* and its reception.

55. See Diana Fuss's discussion of Althusser and of the difficulties of understanding one's own experience in *Essentially Speaking: Feminism, Nature, and Difference* (New York: Routledge, 1989), 114. See Louis Althusser, "A Letter on Art in Reply to André Daspre," in *Lenin and Philosophy,* trans. Ben Brewster (New York: Monthly Review Press, 1971).

CHAPTER 2: Dismantling Stereotypes

1. Audre Lorde, "Age, Race, Class, and Sex: Women Redefining Difference," in *Sister Outsider* (Trumansburg, N.Y.: Crossing Press, 1984), 115, 123.

2. Alice Walker, *In Search of our Mothers' Gardens* (New York: Harcourt Brace Jovanovich, 1983), xi.

3. See Barbara Christian, "Trajectories of Self-Definition: Placing Contemporary Afro-American Women's Fiction," in *Conjuring: Black Women, Fiction, and Literary Tradition,* ed. Marjorie Pryse and Hortense J. Spillers (Bloomington: Indiana University Press, 1985), 233–48.

4. See the first chapters of Anne Goodwyn Jones, *Tomorrow Is Another Day: The Woman Writer in the South, 1859–1936* (Baton Rouge: Louisiana State University Press, 1981); and Hazel Carby, *Reconstructing Womanhood: The Emergence of the Afro-American Woman Novelist* (New York: Oxford University Press, 1987), for good summaries about the origins of these conventions.

5. Irving H. Bartlett and C. Glenn Cambor, "The History and Psychodynamic of Southern Womanhood," *Women's Studies* 2 (1974): 19.

6. Minrose Gwin, *Black and White Women of the Old South: The Peculiar Sisterhood in American Literature* (Knoxville: University of Tennessee Press, 1985), 4.

7. Mark Snyder, "Self-Fulfilling Stereotypes," in *Race, Class, and Gender in the United States,* ed. Paula S. Rothenberg (New York: St. Martin's Press, 1998), 455. This article first appeared in *Psychology Today,* July 1982, 60–68.

8. Mary Chesnut, *A Diary from Dixie,* ed. Ben Ames Williams (Cambridge: Harvard University Press, 1980), 21.

9. Carby, 27.

10. Toni Morrison, "What the Black Woman Asks about Women's Lib," *New York Times Magazine,* August 22, 1971, 15.

11. For example, Sue Thrasher, who grew up on a farm and whose mother worked in a factory in Tennessee, did not find that *The Feminine Mystique* spoke to her. See her

memoir, "Circle of Trust," in *Deep in Our Hearts: Nine White Women in the Freedom Movement* (Athens: University of Georgia Press, 2000), 251.

12. Morrison, 64.

13. Gloria L. Joseph and Jill Lewis, *Common Differences* (Garden City, N.Y.: Anchor, 1981), 40.

14. Alice Walker, *Meridian* (1976; New York: Washington Square Press, 1977), 130. Subsequent citations are indicated parenthetically in the text.

15. See Sara Evans, "Women's Consciousness and the Southern Black Movement," in *Speaking for Ourselves*, ed. Maxine Alexander (New York: Pantheon, 1977), 240; and Paula Giddings, *When and Where I Enter: The Impact of Black Women on Race and Sex in America* (New York: William Morrow, 1984), 296.

16. Penny Patch, "Sweet Tea at Shoney's," in *Deep in Our Hearts*, 155.

17. Barbara Christian, "Novels for Everyday Use: The Novels of Alice Walker," in *Black Women Novelists: The Development of a Tradition, 1892–1976*, by Barbara Christian (Westport, Conn.: Greenwood Press, 1980), 223.

18. Judith Andre, "Stereotypes: Conceptual and Normative Considerations," in *Racism and Sexism*, ed. Paula S. Rothenberg (New York: St. Martin's Press, 1988), 259.

19. Pamela Barnett, paper presented at MLA conference, December 29, 2001, New Orleans. See also Pamela E. Barnett, "'Miscegenation,' Rape, and 'Race' in Alice Walker's *Meridian*," *Southern Quarterly* 39.3 (spring 2001): 65–81.

20. bell hooks, *Yearning: Race, Gender, and Cultural Politics* (Boston: South End Press, 1990), 58. See also Michele Wallace's challenge to black male sexualized discourse in *Black Macho and the Myth of the Superwoman* (New York: Dial Press, 1979).

21. For example, compare the rather pessimistic reading by Nancy Porter in "Women's Interracial Friendships and Visions of Community in *Meridian, The Salt Eaters, Civil Wars,* and *Dessa Rose*," in *Tradition and the Talents of Women*, ed. Florence Howe (Urbana: University of Illinois Press, 1991), 251–67, with the more optimistic readings of Elizabeth Schultz in "Out of the Woods and into the World: A Study of Interracial Friendships between Women in American Novels," in Pryse and Spillers, 67–85; and Barbara Christian in her *Black Women Novelists*, 231–32.

22. Maureen Reddy, *Crossing the Color Line: Race, Parenting, and Culture* (New Brunswick, N.J.: Rutgers University Press, 1994), 169.

23. Alphonso Pickney, *The Committed: White Activists in the Civil Rights Movement* (New Haven, Conn.: College and University Press, 1968), 34. I am indebted to Margaret Edds for finding this source and for insights from her fine unpublished essay comparing literary depictions of white women in the movement with historical accounts. See *Deep in Our Hearts* for memoirs that not only break the silence of white women in the movement but also dismantle popular notions about why these women became civil rights activists.

24. Alice Walker, "Letters Forum: Anti-Semitism," *Ms.*, February 1983, 13.

25. Barbara Smith, "Between a Rock and a Hard Place: Relationships between Black and Jewish Women," in *Yours in Struggle: Three Feminist Perspectives on Anti-Semitism and Racism*, by Elly Bulkin, Minnie Bruce Pratt, and Barbara Smith (Brooklyn: Long Haul Press, 1984), 65–87.

26. Mary King, *Freedom Song: A Personal Story of the 1960s Civil Rights Movement* (New York: William Morrow, 1987), 540. I am grateful to Margaret Edds for pointing out this text.

27. Alice Walker, "Advancing Luna—and Ida B. Wells," in *You Can't Keep a Good*

Woman Down: Stories, by Alice Walker (New York: Harcourt Brace Jovanovich, 1981), 102. Subsequent citations are indicated parenthetically in the text.

28. Dorothy Sterling, *Black Foremothers* (New York: Feminist Press, 1979), 60–117.

29. Linda Hutcheon, *The Politics of Postmodernism* (New York: Routledge, 1989), 41.

30. Gail Godwin, "The Southern Belle," *Ms.,* July 1975, 52.

31. Gail Godwin, *A Mother and Two Daughters* (1982; New York: Avon Books, 1983), 145. Subsequent citations are indicated parenthetically in the text.

32. Gwin, 11.

33. Carolyn Rhodes, "Gail Godwin and Southern Womanhood," in *Women Writers of the Contemporary South,* ed. Peggy Whitman Prenshaw (Jackson: University Press of Mississippi, 1984), 64.

34. María C. Lugones with Pat Alake Rosezelle, "Sisterhood and Friendship as Feminist Models," in *The Knowledge Explosion: Generations of Feminist Scholarship,* ed. Cheris Kramarae and Dale Spender (New York: Teachers College Press, 1992), 410.

35. Reddy, 169.

36. Benjamin DeMott, *The Trouble with Friendship: Why Americans Can't Think Straight about Race* (1995; New Haven: Yale University Press, 1998), 133.

37. Schultz, 75.

38. When I gave talks in public libraries about Godwin's treatment of racial stereotypes and race relations in this novel, many adults told me that they did not remember these sections of the novel. Six of eleven major reviewers of the novel made no mention of race relations, including Anne Tyler for the *New Republic* and Jonathan Yardley for the *Washington Post.* See Walter Clemons, *Newsweek,* January 11, 1982, 62–3; Jonathan Yardley, *Washington Post Book World,* December 13, 1981, 3; Caroline Moorehead, *Spectator,* February 6, 1982, 26; Anne Tyler, *New Republic,* February 17, 1982, 39–40; Laura Geringer, *Saturday Review,* January 1982; and Dannye Romine, *New Orleans Times Picayune,* February 21, 1982, sec. 3, p. 5. Five other reviewers do mention that Renee is black; however, all but one tend to dismiss this aspect of the novel as superficial. See Edmund Fuller, *Wall Street Journal,* January 11, 1982, 26; Brigitte Weeks, *Ms.,* January 1982, 39, 41; Paul Gray, *Time,* January 25, 1982, 72; Jennifer Uglow, *Times Literary Supplement,* March 5, 1982, 246; Josephine Hendin, *New York Times Book Review,* January 10, 1982, 3, 16. Only Edmund Fuller writes of Renee's role as "significant" and the "changing South" as an important "part of the picture" of the novel (26).

39. Godwin, "The Southern Belle," 52.

40. Sherley Anne Williams, *Dessa Rose* (1986; New York: Berkeley Books, 1987), x. Subsequent citations are indicated parenthetically in the text.

41. Mona Gable, "Understanding the Impossible," *Los Angeles Times Magazine,* December 7, 1986, D7.

42. Jean W. Ross, "Contemporary Authors Interview with Sherley Anne Williams" (October 29, 1987), *Contemporary Authors, New Revision Series* (Detroit: Gale Research Company, 1987), 25:495.

43. Katherine Bucknell, "Slave to the Slaves," *Times Literary Supplement,* July 17, 1987, 765. In a positive review of Gloria Naylor's *Mama Day,* David Nicholson compared *Dessa Rose* unfavorably, terming it a retreat into "an imaginary, idealized past." *Washington Post Book World,* February 28, 1988, 5.

44. Boyd Tonkin, *New Statesman,* April 24, 1987, 29; Michele Wallace, "Slaves of History," *Women's Review of Books,* October 1986, 4.

45. Marta E. Sánchez, "The Estrangement Effect in Sherley Anne Williams' *Dessa Rose*," *Genders* 15 (winter 1992): 28.

46. Patricia Devine, "Stereotypes and Prejudice: Their Automatic and Controlled Components," *Journal of Personality and Social Psychology* 56.1 (1989): 5–18.

47. See Deborah E. McDowell, "Negotiating between Tenses: Witnessing Slavery after Freedom—*Dessa Rose*," in *Slavery and the Literary Imagination*, ed. Deborah E. McDowell and Arnold Rampersad (Baltimore: John Hopkins University Press, 1989), 152–53.

48. Diana Fuss, *Essentially Speaking: Feminism, Nature, and Difference* (New York: Routledge, 1989), 33.

49. Smith, 79.

50. McDowell, 151.

51. Gwin, 109.

52. See Sharon Monteith's analysis of *Can't Quit You, Baby* in *Advancing Sisterhood? Interracial Friendships in Contemporary Southern Fiction* (Athens: University of Georgia Press, 2000).

53. Betty Tardieu, "'I'm in That Secular World, Even Though I Keep Looking Around for Someplace Else to Be': Interview with Ellen Douglas," *Southern Quarterly* 33.4 (summer 1995): 25. See also Jerry Speir, "Of Novels and the Novelist: An Interview with Ellen Douglas," *University of Mississippi Studies in English* 5 (fall 1984–87): 238.

54. Tardieu, 25.

55. Judith Rollins, *Between Women: Domestics and Their Employers* (Philadelphia: Temple University Press, 1985), 221.

56. See David Katzman, *Seven Days a Week: Women and Domestic Service in Industrializing America* (New York: Oxford University Press, 1978), 200; and Rollins, 221–22.

57. While such narratives are no longer found in serious literature, they still circulate in privately printed southern memoirs. See Gray Rowell Henry, "It Took a Village" (Surry County, Va.: Historical Society, 2001).

58. Speir, 237.

59. Ellen Douglas, *Can't Quit You, Baby* (1988; New York: Penguin, 1989), 5, 4. Subsequent citations are indicated parenthetically in the text.

60. Jane Flax, *Thinking Fragments: Psychoanalysis, Feminism, and Postmodernism in the Contemporary West* (Berkeley: University of California Press, 1990), 177.

61. Toni Morrison, *Playing in the Dark: Whiteness and the Literary Imagination* (New York: Vintage, 1993), xii.

62. Shirley M. Jordan, *Broken Silences: Interviews with Black and White Women Writers* (New Brunswick, N.J.: Rutgers University Press, 1993), 55.

63. Jan Shoemaker, "Ellen Douglas: Reconstructing the Subject in 'Hold On' and *Can't Quit You, Baby*," *Southern Quarterly* 33.4 (summer 1995): 96.

64. Ann M. Bomberger, "The Servant and the Served: Ellen Douglas's *Can't Quit You, Baby*," *Southern Literary Journal* 31.1 (fall 1998): 26.

65. Karen J. Jacobsen, "Disrupting the Legacy of Silence: Ellen Douglas's *Can't Quit You, Baby*," *Southern Literary Journal* 32.3 (spring 2000): 37. The quotation from bell hooks appears in "Where Is the Love: Political Bonding between Black and White Women," in her *Killing Rage: Ending Racism* (New York: Henry Holt, 1995), 219.

66. Reddy, 168–69, argues that novels by black women—*Meridian, Dessa Rose*, and *Beloved*—advocate such dual activism.

67. Allison Xantha Miller, "The Trouble with Friendship," *Newsday,* November 2, 1997, B14.

68. Patricia J. Williams, *Seeing a Color-Blind Future: The Paradox of Race* (New York: Farrar, Straus, and Giroux, 1998), 27.

69. Elizabeth Cox, *Night Talk* (St. Paul: Gray Wolf Press, 1997), 233. Subsequent citations are indicated parenthetically in the text.

70. "Survey Data on Diversity and Race," *Hedgehog Review* 3.1 (spring 2001): 125–27. In 1996 the Institute for Advanced Studies in Culture and the Gallup Organization conducted the survey that produced these findings.

71. P. J. Williams, 27.

72. Monteith, 5.

73. Lugones with Rosezelle, 408.

74. P. J. Williams, 7.

75. Lugones with Rosezelle, 410.

CHAPTER 3: Refighting Old Wars

1. J. Glenn Gray, *The Warriors* (New York: Harper Torchbooks, 1959), 27.

2. See Robert A. Strikwerda and Larry May's comparison of male comradeship and female friendship in "Male Friendship and Intimacy," *Hypatia* 7.3 (summer 1992): 110–25.

3. See Chris Goodrich's review of *Dirty Work* in *Publisher's Weekly,* June 23, 1989, 32; and Susan Wood's review in the *Houston Post,* August 27, 1989, C6. See also Greg Johnson's review in the *Atlanta Journal-Constitution,* September 3, 1989, L10.

4. Strikwerda and May, 112.

5. Allen Tate, "A Southern Mode of the Imagination," in his *Essays of Four Decades* (Chicago: University of Chicago Press, 1968), 583.

6. Larry Brown, *Dirty Work* (1989; New York: Vintage Books, 1990), 120. Subsequent citations are indicated parenthetically in the text.

7. Deborah Tannen, *You Just Don't Understand: Women and Men in Conversation* (1990; New York: Ballantine Books, 1991), 49–53.

8. Madison Smartt Bell, *Soldier's Joy* (1989; New York: Penguin Books, 1990), 339. Subsequent citations are indicated parenthetically in the text.

9. Strikwerda and May, 115.

10. Susan Pollak and Carol Gilligan, "Images of Violence in Thematic Apperception Test Stories," *Journal of Personality and Social Psychology* 42 (1982): 159–67.

11. Mikhail M. Bakhtin, *Problems of Doestoevsky's Poetics,* ed. and trans. Caryl Emerson (Minneapolis: University of Minnesota Press, 1984), 287.

12. Mikhail M. Bakhtin, "Discourse in the Novel," in *The Dialogic Imagination: Four Essays,* by M. M. Bakhtin, ed. Michael Holquist, trans. Michael Holquist and Caryl Emerson (Houston: University of Texas Press, 1981), 338.

13. Madison Smartt Bell, "An Essay Introducing His Work in Rather a Lunatic Fashion," *Chattahoochee Review* 12.1 (fall 1991): 1–3.

14. Mary Louise Weaks, "An Interview with Madison Smartt Bell," *Southern Review* 30.1 (January 1994): 5–10.

15. Weaks, 5, 8.

16. Greg Johnson, "Two Numbed Vietnam Vets Turn to the Soil," *Chicago Tribune,* June 4, 1989, 14, 5.

17. Winston Groom, "Fighting the Enemy from Tonkin to Tennessee," *Los Angeles Times*, July 2, 1989, B2.

18. David Bradley, "The Battles Didn't End with the War," *New York Times Book Review*, July 2, 1989, 3, 23; and David Nicholson, "Tennessee Mountain Nervous Breakdown," *Washington Post Book World*, June 25, 1989, 5.

19. Bradley, 23.

20. Don O'Briant, "Anger at Klan Fuels New Novel," *Atlanta Journal-Constitution*, June 12, 1988, B1.

21. Bruce Allen, "'Joy' and Pain in the Backwoods," *USA Today*, July 28, 1989, D5.

22. See "Active Patriot Groups in the U.S. in 1996," *Intelligence Report: Klan Watch and Militia Task Force* 86 (spring 1997): 18–19; and "Hate Groups in the United States in 1996," *Intelligence Report: Klan Watch and Militia Task Force* 85 (winter 1997): 20–21.

23. James William Gibson, *Warrior Dreams: Paramilitary Culture in Post-Vietnam America* (New York: Hill and Wang, 1994), 196.

24. Dov Cohen and Richard E. Nisbett, "Self-Protection and the Culture of Honor: Explaining Southern Violence," *Personality and Social Psychology Bulletin* 20.5 (October 1994): 562. This study determined that "although southerners were more likely to endorse violence to protect and restore order, they were not more likely to endorse violence to bring about change" (554), which might explain why there has been more paramilitary activity in the West than in the South.

25. Madison Smartt Bell, "Literature and Pleasure: Bridging the Gap," *Antaeus* 59 (autumn 1987): 134.

26. Bell, "An Essay," 8.

27. Bell, "An Essay," 13.

28. Bell, "Literature and Pleasure," 134.

29. Joel Williamson, *A Rage for Order: Black/White Relations in the American South since Emancipation* (New York: Oxford University Press, 1986), 11.

30. Williamson, 15–16.

31. Ernest Gaines, *A Gathering of Old Men* (New York: Random House, 1983), 15. Subsequent citations are indicated parenthetically in the text.

32. bell hooks, *Yearning: Race, Gender, and Cultural Politics* (Boston: South End Press, 1990), 63. Cooper Thompson, "A New Vision of Masculinity," in *Race, Class, and Gender in the United States: An Integrated Study*, 4th ed., ed. Paula S. Rothenburg (New York: St. Martin's Press, 1998), 560–61.

33. In an interview with *Washington Post* reporter Ken Ringle ("A Southern Road to Freedom," July 20, 1993), Gaines describes the contradictory nature of growing up black in rural Louisiana in the 1930s and 1940s: "There's such beauty in this place. Such peace, and such beauty. As a kid here there were times I was the freest kid in the world, and times I was in de facto slavery. There were places I couldn't go, things I couldn't say, questions I couldn't ask. You had to work for nothing and take what they gave you. Yet at the same time, you had all the fields to run in, the river to fish in, the swamp to hunt in. . . . I was freer than any white kid, and at the same time, not free at all. What a paradox" (D1).

34. Hazel V. Carby, *Reconstructing Womanhood: The Emergence of the Afro-American Woman Novelist* (New York: Oxford University Press, 1987), 35.

35. See Clyde W. Franklin II, "Black Male–Black Female Conflict: Individually Caused and Culturally Nurtured," in Kimmel and Messner.

36. In an editorial in the *Washington Post,* "The Problem with Peace Movements," February 17, 1991, C7, Arun Gandhi quotes these lines from his grandfather's letter.

37. Bob Connell, "Masculinity, Violence, and War," in Kimmel and Messner, 197.

38. Patricia Devine, "Stereotypes and Prejudice: Their Automatic and Controlled Components," *Journal of Personality and Social Psychology* 56.1 (1989): 5–18. For further discussion of the complex dynamic of stereotypes, see Leonard Steinhorn and Barbara Diggs-Brown, *By the Color of Our Skin: The Illusion of Integration and the Reality of Race* (1999; New York: Plume, 2000), chap. 5, "What Keeps Us Apart?"

39. See Bertram Wyatt-Brown, *Southern Honor: Ethics and Behavior in the Old South* (New York: Oxford University Press, 1986), chaps. 2 and 3.

40. Wyatt-Brown, 22.

41. Gaines's vision here is similar to Cooper Thompson's in "A New Vision of Masculinity."

42. Williamson, 182, 98–99. See Thomas F. Gossett, *Race: The History of an Idea in America* (Dallas: Southern Methodist University Press, 1963), for a discussion of the "scholarly" articles that articulated the racist ideas that Dixon popularized.

43. James Riener, "Rereading American Literature from a Men's Studies Perspective: Some Implications," in *The Making of Masculinities,* ed. Harry Brod (Boston: Allen and Unwin, 1987), 292.

44. In an interview with Ken Ringle, Gaines revealed that *A Lesson before Dying* "is the product of a lifetime of nightmares about execution," not so much because he is against capital punishment, but because he is "obsessed with wondering what it must be like to know in advance the exact moment one is going to die" (Ringle, D2).

45. Riener, 292.

46. Marcia Gaudet and Carl Wooton, *Porch Talk with Ernest Gaines: Conversations on the Writer's Craft* (Baton Rouge: Louisiana State University Press, 1990), 118.

47. Gaudet and Wooton, 97.

48. Gaudet and Wooton, 97.

49. Gaudet and Wooton, 98.

50. Peter Rabinowitz, *Before Reading: Narrative Conventions and the Politics of Interpretation* (Ithaca, N.Y.: Cornell University Press, 1987), 111.

51. Gaudet and Wooton, 97.

52. Here I use Rachel Blau DuPlessis's phrase and her theories about the endings of women's narratives in *Writing beyond the Ending: Narrative Strategies of Twentieth-Century Women Writers* (Bloomington: Indiana University Press, 1985) to help me think about the endings of men's narratives.

53. Thompson, 560.

54. Ernest Gaines, *A Lesson before Dying* (New York: Random House, 1993), 6–7. Subsequent citations are indicated parenthetically in the text.

55. Ringle, D2.

56. Gaudet and Wooton, 22.

57. Gaines wonders if he would have become an embittered teacher if he had not left the South and gone to school in California, where his writing talents were nurtured (Gaudet and Wooton, 48). In his fiction Gaines vacillates in his depictions of teachers: from the flattering portrait of Madame Bayonne, in *Catherine Carmier,* who is the only person who understands Jackson's frustrations and desires, to the unflattering portrait of Matthew Antoine and the apolitical teachers in *In My Father's House* (1978), who have

lost interest in the civil rights movement. Gaines's portrait of Grant combines the heroism of social activism, as in *The Autobiography of Miss Jane Pitman* (1971), with the duties of teaching, thus broadening the definition of both teacher and activist.

58. hooks, 63–64.

59. The exchange between Reverend Ambrose and Grant mirrors Gaines's own ambivalence toward organized religion, which surfaces in other portrayals of less-than-admirable ministers, such as Reverend Jameson in *A Gathering of Old Men*, the only old man reluctant to support Mathu.

60. Ernest J. Gaines, *The Autobiography of Miss Jane Pitman* (New York: Bantam Books, 1971), v.

61. Michael Kreyling, *Inventing Southern Literature* (Jackson: University of Mississippi Press, 1998), 98.

62. Renato Rosaldo, *Culture and Truth: The Remaking of Social Analysis* (Boston: Beacon Press, 1989), 206–7.

CHAPTER 4: Tabooed Romance

1. See Peter Wallenstein, *Tell the Court I Love My Wife: Race, Marriage, and Law: An American History* (New York: Palgrave, 2002); Rachel Moran, *Interracial Intimacy: The Regulation of Race and Romance* (Chicago: University of Chicago Press, 2001); and R. E. Roberts, "Black-White Inter-Marriage in the United States," in *Inside the Mixed Marriage*, ed. W. R. Johnson and D. M. Warren (Lanham, Md.: University Press of America, 1994).

2. Statistics about intermarriage in this paragraph are from Darryl Fears and Claudia Deane, "Biracial Couples Report Tolerance," *Washington Post*, July 5, 2001, A1, A4; and from Robert Suro, "Mixed Doubles," *American Demographics* 21.11 (November 1999): 57–62. For international comparisons, see T. F. Pettigrew, "Integration and Pluralism," in *Eliminating Racism: Profiles in Controversy*, ed. Phyllis A. Katz and Dalmas A. Taylor (New York: Plenum, 1988), 26. Results of *Interrace*'s questionnaire are reported in *Jet*, October 6, 1997, 25.

3. Werner Sollors, *Neither Black nor White Yet Both: Thematic Explorations in Interracial Literature* (New York: Oxford University Press, 1997), 337.

4. Eric Jerome Dickey, *Milk in My Coffee* (1998; New York: Signet, 1999), 19, 42, 343, 344. Dickey's July 11, 1999, comment on the novel's Amazon.com Web site that the story is "FICTIONAL" suggests an uneasiness that readers may think he is dating interracially.

5. The census of 1960 counted 51,409 black-white couples in the United States; the next decade saw an increase of 63 percent in interracial marriages, according to James E. Blackwell, "Social and Legal Dimensions of Interracial Liaisons," in *The Black Male in America: Perspectives on His Status in Contemporary Society*, ed. Doris Y. Wilkinson and Ronald Taylor (Chicago: Nelson-Hall, 1977), 232–33. Many who intermarried during this decade had higher incomes and more education than previous interracial couples.

6. Stanley O. Gaines Jr., Diana I. Rios, Cherlyn S. Granrose, Katrina L. Bledsoe, Karlyn R. Farris, Mary S. Page Youn, and Ben F. Garcia, "Romanticism and Interpersonal Resource Exchange among African American–Anglo and Other Interracial Couples," *Journal of Black Psychology* 25.4 (November 1999): 466.

7. Statistics about divorce come from S. O. Gaines Jr. and J. H. Liu, "Romanticism and Interpersonal Resource Exchange among Interethnic/Interracial Couples," in S. O.

Gaines Jr., *Culture, Ethnicity, and Personal Relationship Processes* (New York: Routledge, 1997). 483.

8. Gaines et al., 483.

9. Dave Curtin, "Writing Class Sparks Woman's New Career," *Denver Post,* February 21, 1999, A29.

10. bell hooks, *Yearning: Race, Gender, and Cultural Politics* (Boston: South End Press, 1990), 57–58.

11. Sollors, 358–59.

12. bell hooks and Anuradha Dingwaney, review of *Mississippi Masala, Z. Magazine,* July–August 1992, 41.

13. David R. Goldfield, *Black, White, and Southern: Race Relations and Southern Culture, 1940 to the Present* (Baton Rouge: Louisiana State University Press, 1990), 212–14. Orville Vernon Burton, "Race Relations in the Rural South since 1945," in *The Rural South since World War II,* ed. R. Douglas Hurt (Baton Rouge: Louisiana State University Press, 1998), 30–31.

14. Two articles that focus on the significance of the narration are John Edgar Wideman, "Of Love and Dust: A Reconsideration," *Callaloo* 1.3 (May 1978): 76–84; and Herman Beavers, "Tilling the Soil to Find Ourselves: Labor, Memory, and Identity in Ernest J. Gaines's *Of Love and Dust,"* in *Memory and Cultural Politics: New Approaches to American Ethnic Literature,* ed. Amritjit Singh, Joseph T. Skerrett Jr., and Robert E. Hogan (Boston: Northeastern University Press, 1996), 121–39.

15. Anita Kathy Foeman and Teresa Nance, "From Miscegenation to Multiculturalism: Perceptions and Stages of Interracial Relationship Development," *Journal of Black Studies* 29.4 (March 1999): 542–43.

16. Ernest J. Gaines, *Of Love and Dust* (New York: Random House, 1967), 142. Subsequent citations are indicated parenthetically in the text.

17. See Wideman, 76–84.

18. Foeman and Nance, 543–45.

19. David Lionel Smith, "Bloodlines and Patriarchs: *Of Love and Dust* and Its Revisions of Faulkner," in *Critical Reflections on the Fiction of Ernest J. Gaines,* ed. David C. Estes (Athens: University of Georgia Press, 1994), 48.

20. Joseph Griffin delineates some of these comparisons in "Good News: Sacrifice and Redemption in *Of Love and Dust,"* *Modern Language Studies* 18.3 (summer 1988): 75–85. Griffin is especially interested in pointing out the similarities between Marcus and Bonbon, which help highlight the very important differences in their behavior at the end of the novel.

21. In this practice, the South in 1948 was no different than it had been a century before. See James Kinney, *Amalgamation! Race, Sex, and Rhetoric in the Nineteenth-Century American Novel* (Westport, Conn.: Greenwood Press, 1985), 230.

22. Martin Luther King Jr., *Where Do We Go from Here: Chaos or Community?* (Boston: Beacon Books, 1968), 109.

23. Albert French, *Holly* (New York: Viking Penguin, 1995).

24. Sollors, 353.

25. Randall Kenan, *Let the Dead Bury Their Dead* (New York: Harcourt Brace, 1992), 180, 184, 187.

26. Reynolds Price also situates his interracial homosexual lovers outside the South in *The Promise of Rest* (New York: Scribner's, 1995). Significantly, in both "The Founda-

tions of the Earth" and *The Promise of Rest,* no scenes are actually about the lovers. In each work the black gay man has died.

27. Alice Walker, *Meridian* (1976; New York: Washington Square Press, 1977), 140, 157. Subsequent citations are indicated parenthetically in the text.

28. In a recent memoir Penny Patch, a white SNCC member from New York who had an interracial affair in Mississippi recalls that by the end of 1964 SNCC did not tolerate interracial sexual relationships and that black people involved in them were accused of "backsliding" and white people were excluded; only a couple of years later, SNCC purged all white organizers from its ranks. Penny Patch, "Sweet Tea at Shoney's," in *Deep in Our Hearts: Nine White Women in the Freedom Movement* (Athens: University of Georgia Press, 2000), 160, 155.

29. Alice Walker, *The Way Forward Is with a Broken Heart* (New York: Random House, 2000), 67, 29. Walker meditates on her relationship with Leventhal in both fiction and nonfiction pieces in this collection.

30. See Rachel DuPlessis, *Writing beyond the Ending: Narrative Strategies of Twentieth-Century Women Writers* (Bloomington: Indiana University Press, 1985), 158–61.

31. Sherley Anne Williams, *Dessa Rose* (1986; New York: Berkley Books, 1987), 129. Subsequent citations are indicated parenthetically in the text.

32. See Anna Maria Chupa, *Anne, the White Woman in Contemporary African-American Fiction: Archetypes, Stereotypes, and Characterizations* (Westport, Conn.: Greenwood Press, 1990), 88; and Susan Willis, *Specifying: Black Women Writing the American Experience* (Madison: University of Wisconsin Press, 1987), 126.

33. Michael A. Fletcher, "Degrees of Separation," *Washington Post,* June 25, 2002, A1, A10. While more women than men were awarded college degrees in 2002 (57% women), the percentage was higher for African American women, with two women for every man earning a bachelor's degree. This trend, which began in the 1980s, has steadily increased and has led demographers and education researchers to worry that the lopsided graduation rate may create social problems in the future.

34. This statistic in the research of University of Michigan psychologist Ruby Beale was reported in "Fresh Talk about Race" by Richard Morin in the *Washington Post,* June 29, 1997, C5. Beale believed that two facts of life conspire to create this concern: "Disproportionately more black women than white say they can't find acceptable mates, and the overwhelming majority of interracial couples involve a black man and a white woman. Thus Beale said, 'it seems that for many, they see an increase in interracial couples as a decrease in their chances of finding a partner.'"

35. Bebe Moore Campbell, "Black Men, White Women: A Sister Relinquishes Her Anger," in *Wild Women Don't Wear No Blues: Black Women Writers on Love, Men, and Sex,* ed. Marita Golden (New York: Doubleday, 1993), 125.

36. Julius Lester, *And All Our Wounds Forgiven* (1994; New York: Harcourt, Brace, 1996), 2. Subsequent citations are indicated parenthetically in the text.

37. Julius Lester, *Look Out, Whitey! Black Power's Gon' Get Your Mama!* (New York: Dial Press, 1968), 106.

38. Sharon Monteith, "Revisiting the 1960s in Contemporary Fiction: 'Where do we go from here?'" in *Gender in the Civil Rights Movement,* ed. Peter J. Ling and Sharon Monteith (New York: Garland, 1999), 230.

39. Arnold Rampersad, "A Black Leader and His Movement," *Newsday,* June 29, 1994, B3.

40. Both Arnold Rampersad and Lorene Carey, who reviewed the novel for the *Philadelphia Inquirer,* July 3, 1994, E1, found Lisa unbelievably perfect. But David Nicholson, writing for the *Washington Post,* July 12, 1994, E1, placed Lester alongside Faulkner and Ellison in his ability to write about race and sex.

41. Martha Hodes, *White Women, Black Men* (New Haven: Yale University Press, 1997).

42. Rita Mae Brown, *Southern Discomfort* (New York: Harper and Row, 1982), 1.

43. Myra McLarey, *Water from the Well* (New York: Atlantic Monthly Press, 1995), 13. Subsequent citations are indicated parenthetically in the text.

44. Ellen Douglas, *The Rock Cried Out* (1979; Baton Rouge: Louisiana State University Press, 1994), 130, 135–36. Subsequent citations are indicated parenthetically in the text.

45. Dar Tomlinson, *Forbidden Quest* (Columbus, Mississippi: Genesis Press, 1998), 31. Subsequent citations are indicated parenthetically in the text.

46. hooks, 29.

47. Discussions in December 2001 with Velma Pollard, Jamaican writer and literary critic, revealed problems in Tomlinson's use of Jamaican characters and culture. Pollard says that while men of mixed race like Paul Michael are quite common in Jamaica, their eyes are gray or gray-green, and if they are Rastafarians, they call their lovers "queens," no matter the race. By eliding the Rastafarian practice of placing a lover on a pedestal with Paul Michael's assurance to Cally that she will be thought of as a queen because she is white, Tomlinson both falsely suggests a white racial hierarchy in Jamaica and simplifies Jamaican culture by conflating Rastafarian practices with Jamaican cultural conventions. Paul Michael is not a Rastafarian. Labeling the biracial Paul Michael a "pink," as Tomlinson does, is also incorrect, since in Jamaica mixed people are identified as either "red" or "brown" depending on their hair texture, but never pink.

48. See Annette Gordon-Reed, *Thomas Jefferson and Sally Hemings: An American Controversy* (Charlottesville: University Press of Virginia, 1997); Jan Ellen Lewis and Peter S. Onuf, *Sally Hemings and Thomas Jefferson: History, Memory, and Civic Culture* (Charlottesville: University Press of Virginia, 1999); Eugene A. Foster, M. A. Jobling, P. G. Taylor, P. Donnelly, P. deKnijft, Rene Mierenet, T. Zerjal, and C. Tyler-Smith, "Jefferson Fathered Slave's Last Child," *Nature,* November 5, 1998; and the Thomas Jefferson Memorial Foundation's research report, made public on January 26, 2000, which concluded that based on new research there is "a high probability that Thomas Jefferson fathered Eston Hemings, and that he most likely was the father of all six of Sally Hemings's children." http://www.monticello.org/plantation/hemingscontro/ hemings_report.html.

49. Gordon-Reed, 4.

50. hooks, 58.

51. Barbara Chase-Riboud, *Sally Hemings* (New York: Viking Press, 1979), 8. Subsequent citations are indicated parenthetically in the text.

52. See Norman N. Holland, *Five Readers Reading* (New Haven: Yale University Press, 1975).

53. Ralph Ellison, William Styron, Robert Penn Warren, and C. Vann Woodward, "A Discussion: The Uses of History in Fiction," *Southern Literary Journal* 1.2 (spring 1969): 70. See Sharon Monteith's excellent overview of the treatment of the Jefferson-Hemings story in film and fiction, "America's Domestic Aliens: African Americans and the Issue of Citizenship in the Jefferson/Hemings Story in Fiction and Film," in *Alien Identities: Exploring Difference in Film and Fiction,* ed. Deborah Cartmell, I. Q. Hunter, Heidi Kaye, and Imelda Whelehan (London: Pluto Press, 1999), 31–48.

54. Donald McCaig, *Jacob's Ladder: A Story of Virginia during the War* (New York: W. W. Norton, 1998), 69. Subsequent citations are indicated parenthetically in the text and the notes.

55. Eric Sundquist, *To Wake the Nations* (Cambridge, Mass.: Belknap Press of Harvard University Press, 1993), 398.

56. McCaig gives this information in his acknowledgments (522).

57. James Kilgo, *Daughter of My People* (Athens: University of Georgia Press, 1998), 123–24. Subsequent citations are indicated parenthetically in the text.

58. In his acknowledgments James Kilgo writes that "*Daughter of My People* is based on events that occurred in South Carolina during 1918."

59. Reynolds Price, "The Fare to the Moon," in *The Foreseeable Future,* by Reynolds Price (New York: Scribner's, 1991), 14. Subsequent citations are indicated parenthetically in the text.

60. Kinney, 230.

61. T. R. Pearson, *Blue Ridge* (New York: Viking, 2000), 224. In his 1985 study, Kinney states that interracial sex has not been treated humorously (230).

62. T. R. Pearson, *Polar* (New York: Viking, 2002), 103.

63. Pearson, *Blue Ridge,* 194.

64. See Kinney, 47, 90, 111, 194–95, where he offers definitions.

65. Kilgo, 56–57.

66. Connie Mae Fowler, *Sugar Cage* (1992; New York: Washington Square Press, 1993), 61–62. Subsequent citations are indicated parenthetically in the text.

67. Foeman and Nance, 549.

68. Mikhail Bakhtin, *Problems of Dostoevsky's Poetics,* ed. and trans. Caryl Emerson (Minneapolis: University of Minnesota Press, 1984), 59.

69. Foeman and Nance, 552.

70. Monica White, *Shades of Desire* (Columbus, Miss.: Genesis Press, 1996), 8, 92.

71. Shay Youngblood, *Black Girl in Paris* (New York: Riverhead Books, 2000), 141, 146. Subsequent citations are indicated parenthetically in the text.

72. Itabari Njeri, *The Last Plantation: Color, Conflict, and Identity: Reflections of a New World Black* (Boston: Houghton Mifflin, 1997), 8.

73. See readers' comments about Monica White's *Shades of Desire* at http://www .amazon.com/exec/obidos/search-handle-form/002-9323746-2808848 and about Pamela Leigh Starr's *Fate* at http://www.amazon.com/exec/obidos/search-handle-url /index=books&field-author=Starr%2C%20Pamela%20Leigh/002-9323746-2808848.

74. See the comments by Neka Williams, dated August 14, 2000, about *The Color of Love* and by a reader from Ft. Lauderdale, Florida, dated August 19, 1999, about *Shades of Desire,* at www.amazon.com.

75. One early treatment of lesbian interracial love is Ann Allen Shockley's *Loving Her* (1974), but the representation is very indirect. In *Advancing Sisterhood? Interracial Friendships in Contemporary Southern Fiction* (Athens: University of Georgia Press, 2000), Sharon Monteith points out how few southern novels by white women writers focus on interracial lesbian love, with Carol Anne Douglas's *To the Cleveland Station* (1982) being the exception. Other novels, such as Cris South's *Clenched Fists, Burning Crosses* (1984), Lane von Herzen's *Copper Crown* (1991), and W. Glasgow Phillips's *Tuscaloosa* (1994), include interracial lesbian couples in their cast of characters.

CHAPTER 5: **Rethinking the One-Drop Rule**

1. U.S. Census Bureau, "Census 2000 Summary File 1, Census of Population and Housing," U.S. Department of Commerce, Economics and Statistics Administration, digital videodisc, September 2001. Of the states that the census identifies as southern (see chapter 6, note 3), West Virginia, with 8.89 percent, had the highest percentage of respondents with African American ancestry who identified as racially mixed, and Mississippi had the lowest. Other Deep South states, like Louisiana and Alabama, had 1 percent, while southern states on the margins had higher percentages: Virginia with 3.5 percent and Kentucky with 5 percent. Midwest states with large black populations, like Illinois, Indiana, Michigan, and Ohio, had similar percentages to Kentucky and Virginia, while states with lower percentages of black people in their population, like Hawaii, Idaho, New Hampshire, and Vermont, had rates over 30 percent.

2. P. J. Parrish, *Dark of the Moon* (New York: Pinnacle Books, 1999), 28.

3. Price's novel is the concluding one in a trilogy that includes *The Surface of Earth* (1975) and *The Source of Life* (1981); the trilogy spans the twentieth century and concentrates on three generations of the Mayfield family. Another racially mixed character, Grainger, appears in all three of these novels as an important minor character, but he is not publicly embraced as a member of the family. By having Grainger at age 101 meet the beloved mixed child Raven in *The Promise of Rest,* Price signals the change in the Mayfield family and in the South from white sins of racial exploitation to redemption of white racial guilt.

4. Barbara Ladd, *Nationalism and the Color Line in George W. Cable, Mark Twain, and William Faulkner* (Baton Rouge: Louisiana State University Press, 1996), 140.

5. For the history of mulattoes in the United States, see Joel Williamson, *New People: Miscegenation and Mulattoes in the United States* (New York: Free Press, 1980). He explains that a mulatto was a person who was half black and half white, a quadroon was one-quarter black, and an octoroon was one-eighth black. There were a variety of other words, but Anglo Americans did not always make these distinctions, using *mulatto* as a general term for people of mixed black and white ancestry (xii).

6. For the legal history behind the racial demarcation in Louisiana, see Virginia R. Dominguez, *White by Definition: Social Classification in Creole Louisiana* (New Brunswick, N.J.: Rutgers University Press, 1986), chap. 2.

7. William Faulkner, *Go Down, Moses* (1942; New York: Vintage International, 1990), 344. In Faulkner's *Absalom, Absalom!* (1936; New York: Vintage International, 1990), Canadian Shreve McCannon also places racial blending in the distant future but contemplates it with much less emotion: "and so in a few thousand years, I who regard you will also have sprung from the loins of African kings" (302).

8. See Rochelle L. Stanfield, "Blending of America," *National Journal,* September 13, 1997, 1780–82. Edmonston is a demographer for the National Research Council of the American Academy of Sciences.

9. For most of the nineteenth century and up until 1920, the U.S. Census Bureau included the category *mulatto.* More recently Americans have been able to check *other* instead of the five broad groupings adopted in 1977. The five categories were four racial groups—American Indian or Alaskan Native, Asian or Pacific Islander, black, and

white—and one ethnic group, Hispanic origin. But in 2000 the Census Bureau allowed Americans to check all the categories that applied to their identity. This decision was a compromise between parents of multiracial children who wanted simply to add the category *multiracial* and advocates of minority groups concerned that such a category would undermine racial classification altogether, which is used in implementing affirmative action and monitoring desegregation. Canada dropped the racial classification from its census in 1951, and the American Civil Liberties Union tried to get the question about race omitted from the 1960 census, but civil rights legislation in the 1960s depended on such data. See Lawrence Wright, "One Drop of Blood," *New Yorker,* July 25, 1994, 46–55, for an overview of how and why the Census Bureau has changed racial classifications in the last two centuries. He argues convincingly that "by attempting to provide a way for Americans to describe themselves, the categories actually began to shape those identities" (52). Although his article was written before the Census Bureau decided not to add the category *multiracial,* but rather to allow more than one box to be checked, Wright provides a good analysis of issues in the debate. For reactions to the new census forms, see Darryl Fears, "Mixed-Race Question Defies Easy Answers," *Washington Post,* April 16, 2001, A1, A8.

10. D'Vera Cohn and Darryl Fears, "Hispanics Draw Even with Blacks in New Census," *Washington Post,* March 7, 2001, A1, A8. See also D'Vera Cohn, "Multiracial Growth Seen in Census," *Washington Post,* March 13, 2001, A1, A12; and John Meacham, "The New Face of Race," *Newsweek,* September 18, 2000, 38–41.

11. Maria P. P. Root, "The Multiracial Experience: Racial Borders as a Significant Frontier in Race Relations," in *The Multiracial Experience: Racial Borders as the New Frontier,* ed. Maria P. P. Root (Thousand Oaks, Calif.: Sage, 1996), xvi.

12. Lise Funderburg, *Black, White, Other: Biracial Americans Talk about Race and Identity* (New York: William Morrow, 1994), 11–12. F. James Davis reports in *Who Is Black?: One Nation's Definition* (University Park, Pa.: Penn State University Press, 1991) that sociologists and anthropologists have estimated that 75 to 90 percent of black Americans have white ancestry and 1 percent of white Americans have African ancestry, most without knowing it (29). Many whites are not aware of their black ancestry because of passing, which depended on secrecy.

13. Douglas Besharov was so quoted in the *National Journal,* September 13, 1997, 1781. Others from many fields share his belief.

14. Patricia J. Williams, *Seeing a Color-Blind Future: The Paradox of Race* (New York: Farrar, Straus, and Giroux, 1998), 53.

15. Neil Henry, *Pearl's Secret: A Black Man's Search for His White Family* (Berkeley: University of California Press, 2001). Review by Mat Johnson, "Distant Relations," *Washington Post Book World,* April 29, 2001, 9.

16. In her collection of interviews, *Black, White, Other,* Lise Funderburg, whose mother is white and whose father is black, uses this term to identify those people who choose to identify as biracial (15).

17. Judith R. Berzon does not compare these texts, but see her thoughtful analysis of each in *Neither White nor Black: The Mulatto Character in American Fiction* (New York: New York University Press, 1978).

18. Faulkner makes this point better in "The Bear," although I would not say it is his primary concern.

19. See Dominguez, 62–89.

20. Ernest J. Gaines, "Bloodline," in *Bloodline* (1968; New York: W. W. Norton, 1976), 211. Subsequent citations of the novella are indicated parenthetically in the text.

21. See Robert M. Luscher, "The Pulse of *Bloodline*," in *Critical Reflections on the Fiction of Ernest J. Gaines*, ed. David C. Estes (Athens: University of Georgia Press, 1994), for a interesting analysis of the shape of the story collection and of the title story's place in it. Luscher provides an excellent short summary of the research on *Bloodline*. See William Burke, "*Bloodline*: A Black Man's South," *College Language Association Journal* 19.4 (June 1976): 545–58, which situates the collection in historical context.

22. Berzon, chap. 8, "The Mulatto as Race Leader." For example, in T. S. Stribling's *Birthright* (1922), the Harvard-educated mulatto protagonist takes the ideological route of Booker T. Washington and returns to his southern hometown to teach school, hoping to establish a school like Tuskegee; in Willard Savoy's *Alien Land* (1949), the protagonist is a brilliant lawyer who, as leader of the Freedom League, fights for the political and social justice issues that Du Bois championed.

23. See Michael A. Fletcher, "Putting a Price on Slavery's Legacy," *Washington Post*, December 26, 2000, A1, A16–17.

24. Bebe Moore Campbell, *Your Blues Ain't like Mine* (1992; New York: Ballantine Books, 1995), 422. Subsequent citations are indicated parenthetically in the text.

25. Gershen Kaufman, *The Psychology of Shame* (New York: Springer, 1989), 17.

26. John Katzenbach, "Ricochets in Their Hearts," *Washington Post*, October 10, 1992, D10.

27. Michael Kreyling, *Inventing Southern Literature* (Jackson: University Press of Mississippi, 1998), 91.

28. Raymond Andrews, *Appalachee Red* (1978; Athens: University of Georgia Press, 1987).

29. Christopher John Farley, "Artistic Brotherhood," *USA Today*, February 11, 1992, 7D.

30. Dominguez, 158–59.

31. Adrian Piper, "Passing for White, Passing for Black," in *Passing and the Fictions of Identity*, ed. Elaine K. Ginsberg (Durham, N.C.: Duke University Press, 1996), 254, 256.

32. Berzon, 218. See her chapter "The Mulatto as Existential Man."

33. Berzon, 149.

34. For a distinction between the effects of guilt and shame, see Merle A. Fossum and Marilyn J. Mason, *Facing Shame: Families in Recovery* (New York: W. W. Norton, 1986), 21.

35. John Gregory Brown, *Decorations in a Ruined Cemetery* (1994; New York: Avon Books, 1995), 180. Subsequent citations are indicated parenthetically in the text.

36. Amy Robinson, "It Takes One to Know One: Passing and Communities of Common Interest," *Critical Inquiry* 20.4 (summer 1994): 719.

37. See Itabari Njeri, "Sushi and Grits," in *Lure and Loathing: Essays on Race, Identity, and the Ambivalence of Assimilation*, ed. Gerald Early (New York: Penguin Press, 1993), 13–40. She argues that African Americans are a creolized population but that Afrocentrism has wrongly encouraged blacks to think of themselves as an unadulterated ethnic group (37–39).

38. In *The Color of Our Future* (New York: William Morrow, 1999), Farai Chideya argues that southern California is "America's multiracial mecca," but she recognizes that the freeways segregate neighborhoods and people so that some racially mixed people are

supported by the growing multiracial movement, while others find it difficult "to transcend the traditional racial divisions" (43). For Chideya, race is place.

39. Funderburg, 13, 14.

40. Root, xviii.

41. C. Reginald Daniel, "Black and White Identity in the New Millennium: Unsevering the Ties That Bind," in Root, *The Multiracial Experience,* 132.

42. Njeri, 37–38.

43. See Wright, 46–55; Chideya; and Itabari Njeri, *The Last Plantation: Color, Conflict, and Identity: Reflections of a New World Black* (Boston: Houghton Mifflin, 1997).

44. Carlos A. Fernandez, "Government Classification of Multiracial/Multiethnic People," in Root, *The Multiracial Experience,* 29–32. See also Njeri, *The Last Plantation;* and Maria P. P. Root, "A Bill of Rights for Racially Mixed People," as well as other essays in her *Multiracial Experience.*

45. See Maureen Reddy, *Crossing the Color Line: Race, Parenting, and Culture* (New Brunswick, N.J.: Rutgers University Press, 1994), xii–xiii, 99.

46. See Funderburg; Root, *The Multiracial Experience;* Rebecca Walker's memoir *Black, White, and Jewish: Autobiography of a Shifting Self* (New York: Riverhead Books, 2000); and Danzy Senna's novel *Caucasia* (New York: Riverhead Books, 1998).

47. See Melissa Walker's interview with Rosellen Brown in *Contemporary Literature* 27.2 (summer 1986): 145–59. Claiming she did not do "anything the least brave" during her years in Mississippi, Brown describes her work at Tougaloo as bearing "very modest testimony" to her belief in the movement's ideals: "As teachers and later through [my husband's] work with the anti-poverty program we felt we were doing what we could do best. But of course many of our friends were more heavily involved, some full time, and they lived with danger all the time" (150).

48. Funderburg, 15.

49. In *Crossing the Color Line,* Maureen Reddy describes the feeling of "'masquerading' as white in public" when she is not with her black husband and children, and she speculates that this feeling "may be the one thing white partners of black people, and especially white parents of black children, share" (22).

50. Paul Gray, "Study in Living Colors," *Time,* May 8, 2000, 95. See Michiko Kakutani's review in the *New York Times,* May 9, 2000, E8; and Greg Johnson's review in the *Atlanta Journal-Constitution,* June 4, 2000, 10L, both of which fault Brown for employing racial stereotypes. Johnson's review seems unfair in its criticism of Brown for creating "unappealing characters" and "scarcely enough plot to animate a short story."

51. Eric Lott, "The New Cosmopolitanism" *Transition* 72 (1996): 108–35.

52. Rosellen Brown, *Half a Heart* (New York: Farrar, Straus, and Giroux, 2000), 67. Further citations are indicated parenthetically in the text.

53. Reddy, 34. See also Jane Lazarre, *Beyond the Whiteness of Whiteness: Memoir of a White Mother of Black Sons* (Durham, N.C.: Duke University Press, 1996).

54. Derrick Bell, *Faces at the Bottom of the Well: The Permanence of Racism* (New York: Basic Books, 1992), 6.

55. This move has angered some readers, especially some southern readers who posted comments on Amazon.com. However, a Houstonian writes that Brown "accurately and articulately describes the oppressive heat and the insulated neighborhoods to a tee!" See readers' responses on the Amazon.com Web site for *Half a Heart.*

56. Brown's portrait of Ronnee's school experiences parallels James Comer's research in "Educating Poor Minority Children," *Scientific American*, November 1988, 46.

57. Paul Gilroy, *Against Race: Imagining Political Culture beyond the Color Line* (Cambridge, Mass.: Belknap Press of Harvard University Press, 2000), 12, 34.

58. Piper, 255.

59. In *Race Matters* (New York: Vintage Books, 1994), Cornel West bemoans black leaders' refusal "to undermine and dismantle the framework of racial reasoning" that fosters appeals to black authenticity (38).

60. In "Bi-Racial Identity: Children Born to African American and White Couples," *Clinical Social Work* 21.4 (winter 1993): 417–28, Dorcas D. Bowles says her current clinical experiences suggest that the practice of simply labeling biracial (black-white) children black needs to be reexamined, because disowning part of one's ethnic heritage can lead to "feelings of shame, emotional isolation, and depression" (427).

61. See Diana Fuss, *Essentially Speaking: Feminism, Nature, and Difference* (New York: Routledge, 1989), chap. 5.

62. Fritz Lanham, "Black and White Issues," *Houston Chronicle*, May 28, 2000, "Zest" 8.

CHAPTER 6: Still Separate after All These Years

1. Change came on February 3, 2001, when Maryland state legislator Talmadge Branch reported the incident and Florida attorney general Bob Butterworth charged Holton with civil rights violations. See Sue Anne Pressley, "Fla. Bar a Throwback to a Segregated Era," *Washington Post*, March 19, 2001, A3.

2. Douglas S. Massey and Nancy Denton, *American Apartheid: Segregation and the Making of the Underclass* (Cambridge, Mass.: Harvard University Press, 1993), 74. Massey and Denton define *hypersegregation* as a pattern in which four out of five characteristics of segregation occur: unevenness of racial distribution, racial isolation, clustering to form an enclave, concentration within a small geographic area, and centralization at the urban core.

3. See Massey and Denton, chap. 3, "The Persistence of the Ghetto." See also chap. 8, "The Future of the Ghetto," where they note that 1990 census figures put southern cities "10 points below their northern counterparts" in degrees of segregation. While northern cities showed no real change in residential segregation from 1980 to 1990, "significant declines" occurred in six of twelve southern metropolitan areas, although these were offset by an increase in segregation in Greensboro and a "very marked increase" in Birmingham (223). Census figures in 2000 confirm the North-South urban difference Massey and Denton noted.

Information about the 2000 census comes from articles by R. Jeffery Smith, "Reversing a Long Pattern, Blacks Are Heading South," *Washington Post*, May 5, 2001, A1, A10; and by Sarah Cohen and D'Vera Cohn, "Racial Integration's Shifting Patterns," *Washington Post*, April 1, 2001, A1, A10–11. The region the U.S. government defines as the South includes Delaware; Maryland; Washington, D.C.; Virginia; North Carolina; South Carolina; Georgia; Florida; Alabama; Mississippi; Louisiana; Texas; Oklahoma; Arkansas; Tennessee; Kentucky; and West Virginia.

4. Cohen and Cohn, A10.

5. Leonard Steinhorn and Barbara Diggs-Brown, *By the Color of Our Skin: The Illusion of Integration and the Reality of Race* (1999; New York: Plume, 2000), 33–34.

6. Massey and Denton, 4.

7. Massey and Denton, 1. See also Gunnar Myrdal, *An American Dilemma: The Negro Problem and Modern Democracy* (New York: Harper and Brothers, 1944).

8. The reasons that follow are summarized from Massey and Denton, chap. 1, "The Missing Link," and chap. 4, "The Continuing Causes of Segregation." The degree and duration of black segregation is not matched by any other racial and ethnic group in our nation's history. Today institutional racism that fosters residential segregation still exists—manifested, for example, by real estate and rental agencies that steer customers to racial enclaves, city planners who locate public housing in black neighborhoods, and lenders who encourage homogeneous neighborhoods by redlining loan applications. But personal preferences are one of the strongest factors in residential segregation. While blacks prefer neighborhoods that are integrated fifty-fifty, whites prefer neighborhoods that are predominately white by a large margin, which means that some whites begin to leave a neighborhood as soon as one black family moves in, a fact that leaves emerging integrated neighborhoods always in the process of becoming resegregated. Another factor, less frequently mentioned, is the reluctance of black politicians to concern themselves with residential segregation, because it concentrates black votes, which help create safe legislative seats for black politicians. While understanding such motives, Massey and Denton believe that a large price is paid for racial segregation, no matter what the cause, in the decreased incentives for political coalitions and in the particular case of ghettoes forever in social and economic decline, where chances of success are reduced after extended exposure to poverty, joblessness, welfare, drugs, educational failure, and teen pregnancy. See also David J. Armor, "School Busing: A Time for Change," in *Eliminating Racism: Profiles in Controversy*, ed. Phyllis A. Katz and Dalmas A. Taylor (New York: Plenum Press, 1988), 259–80. In chapter 8, "The Future of the Ghetto," in *American Apartheid*, Massy and Denton argue that dismantling residential segregation is the key to real integration and that it depends on strong systematic enforcement of the Fair Housing Act by federal authorities as well as integration maintenance programs that intervene to keep a newly integrated neighborhood from becoming resegregated.

9. Massey and Denton, 1.

10. David K. Shipler, *A Country of Strangers: Blacks and Whites in America* (New York: Alfred A. Knopf, 1997), 187–88. Shipler quotes Suitts.

11. Josephine Humphreys, *Dreams of Sleep* (1984; New York: Penguin, 1985), 179. Subsequent citations are indicated parenthetically in the text.

12. Steinhorn and Diggs-Brown, 156–57.

13. Josephine Humphreys, *Rich in Love* (1987; New York: Penguin, 1992), 195.

14. Toni Cade Bambara, *Those Bones Are Not My Child* (1999; New York: Vintage, 2000), 630–31.

15. In *The Narrative Forms of Southern Community* (Baton Rouge: Louisiana State University Press, 1999), Scott Romine argues that in the past southern white male writers have used their writing to create mythic communities, "to defer reflexivity, to recuperate the autochthonous ideal, and to reclaim the tacit ground that enables the production of an objective social world" (21). In his epilogue, however, he is heartened to observe the "old ideals" of community exhibited in Union, South Carolina, in 1994 when authorities refused to believe a white woman's story that a black man had kidnapped

and then drowned her children (211). In contemporary narrative, though, Romine sees the traditional southern community surviving only: "(1) as a tenuously authentic, autochthonous community available to realist narration," such as in Clyde Edgerton's clichéd *Raney*, "(2) as an oppressive social order necessitating alternative communities or enclaves," such as in Alice Walker's *The Color Purple*, "and (3) as an object of post-modern deconstruction or parody," such as in Lewis Nordan's *Wolf Whistle* (206). Christine Wiltz's novel, along with others such as Sanders's *Clover*, defies these categories and fulfills the promise of examining interracial community in a way that Romine only sees in his real-life example.

16. Alphonse Vinh, "Talking with Josephine Humphreys," *Southern Quarterly* 32.4 (summer 1994): 134. See also Rosemary M. Magee, "Continuity and Separation: An Interview with Josephine Humphreys," *Southern Review* 27.4 (autumn 1991): 792–802. In this 1991 interview, Humphreys says that "the Charleston interest in genealogy and ancestry is partly based on fear of new people, and fear of change and fear of people who have different ideas" (793).

17. Smith, A1.

18. Romine, 3.

19. *A Man in Full* takes into account the fact that the population of the Atlanta metropolitan area is not simply black and white. Wolfe depicts a large immigrant population concentrated in the nearby city of Chamblee, or Chambodia, which, as Martyn Bone argues, contrasts with Atlanta's own idea of its cosmopolitan business identity. See Bone's analysis, "Placing the Postsouthern, 'International City': Atlanta in Tom Wolfe's *A Man in Full*," in *South to a New Place: Region, Literature, Culture*, ed. Suzanne W. Jones and Sharon Monteith (Baton Rouge: Louisiana State University Press, 2002). In my argument about black-white relations in Atlanta, I do not mean to render this international section of the novel "invisible," in a way similar to Mayor Jordan's omission of Asian neighborhoods (see Bone's analysis) in his tour of "two Atlantas, one black and the other white" (195), but rather to focus on the biracial dynamic that currently propels the city's functioning as Wolfe sees it. Interestingly, although Wolfe does not take up this topic, sociologist Michael J. White believes recent evidence from the 2000 census suggests that "as immigrants come in, segregation, if anything, declines between blacks and whites" (quoted in Cohen and Cohn, A11).

20. Michael Pakenham, "The Second Life of Tom Wolfe," *Baltimore Sun*, November 29, 1998, 8F.

21. John Huey, "Wolfe Knows Town, but Not Its Racial Dynamics," *Atlanta Journal-Constitution*, November 5, 1998, 1D.

22. Tom Wolfe, *A Man in Full* (1998; New York: Bantam, 1999), 210–11. Subsequent citations are indicated parenthetically in the text.

23. See Massey and Denton's analysis of segregation and politics (153–60).

24. Huey, 1D.

25. Houston A. Baker Jr., *Turning South Again: Re-Thinking Modernism/Rethinking Booker T.* (Durham, N.C.: Duke University Press, 2001), 75.

26. Patricia J. Williams, *Seeing a Color-Blind Future: The Paradox of Race* (New York: Farrar, Straus, and Giroux, 1998), 27.

27. Steinhorn and Diggs-Brown, 137.

28. Shipler, 561–62.

29. Walker Percy, "Stoicism in the South," in *Signposts in a Strange Land,* ed. Patrick Samway (New York: Farrar, Straus, and Giroux, 1991), 85. Percy's article was originally published in 1956.

30. John Updike, "Awriiiiighhhhhhhhht! Tom Wolfe Looks Hard at America," *New Yorker,* November 9, 1998, 102.

31. Mary Gordon, letter to the editor, *Harper's,* February 1990, 9.

32. Paul Gilroy, *Against Race: Imagining Political Culture beyond the Color Line* (Cambridge, Mass.: Belknap Press of Harvard University Press, 2000), 133.

33. See Pakenham, 8F. See also Tom Wolfe, "Stalking the Billion-Footed Beast: A Literary Manifesto for the New Social Novel," *Harper's,* November 1989, 45–56, and the responses to his manifesto in favor of realistic novels by a variety of writers and readers in succeeding issues of *Harper's.* On the subject of satire versus realism, Madison Smartt Bell's response is pertinent: "The proposition that Wolfe himself (as represented by *The Bonfire of the Vanities*) is a social realist of the same stamp as Honoré de Balzac, Sinclair Lewis, Charles Dickens, William Makepeace Thackery, Fyodor Dostoyevski, and other novelists he cites also needs a second thought. I admire Wolfe as a marvelously inventive and immensely powerful social satirist, which is not quite the same thing" ("Letters," *Harper's,* February 1990, 8).

34. Wolfgang Iser, *Prospecting: From Reader Response to Literary Anthropology* (Baltimore: Johns Hopkins University Press, 1989), 249.

35. Tom Wolfe, "Why They Aren't Writing the Great American Novel Anymore: A Treatise on the Varieties of Realistic Experience," *Esquire,* December 1972, 158.

36. See Massey and Denton, 7–8, 167.

37. Bambara, *Those Bones Are Not My Child,* 560. Subsequent citations are indicated parenthetically in the text.

38. See Steinhorn and Diggs-Brown, chaps. 1 and 9.

39. Toni Cade Bambara, *Deep Sightings and Rescue Missions,* ed. Toni Morrison (New York: Random House, 1996), 219.

40. Valerie Boyd, "Morrison Brings Friend's 'Bones' to Print," *Atlanta Journal-Constitution* (October 17, 1999), 1L.

41. Bambara, "Prologue," in *Those Bones Are Not My Child,* 7. For reviews, see Sven Birkerts, "Death in Atlanta," *New York Times Book Review,* January 2, 2000, 17; Kate Callen, "A Child Is Missing: Plotting Editing Problems Plague Toni Cade Bambara's Final Work," *San Diego Union-Tribune,* October 24, 1999, Books 5; Jonathan Coleman, "Seasons of Sorrow," *Washington Post Book World,* November 21, 1999, 9; John Lowe, "City of Torment: Toni Cade Bambara's *Those Bones Are Not My Child,*" *Washington Times* magazine *The World and I,* February 2000, 267–74. At least one reviewer, Sharon Broussard of the *Cleveland Plain Dealer,* December 19, 1999, felt that the length turned the novel into "a rant of protest," making it "easy to forget the gripping tale Bambara wanted to tell" (15I).

42. In an article, "Writing Atlanta's Nightmare," by Valerie Boyd in the *Atlanta Journal-Constitution,* October 17, 1999, Toni Morrison is quoted as saying that Bambara "loathed, as I do, the sort of simplistic reduction of black people. . . . And she loathed, as I do, that all black people are good, and everybody can eat off their grandmother's floor." Morrison said that "you want to slap Zala because she's not paying attention to her kids, but you understand this is what happens" (3L).

43. Robin Vidimos, "'Bones' Raises Questions on Justice," *Denver Post,* October 24, 1999, H4.

44. Toni Morrison, "Once upon a Time in Atlanta," *Independent* (London), March 26, 2000, 1. In this article Morrison quotes from a letter that Bambara wrote to Melvin Wilk, poet and professor of English at Simmons College in Indiana, dated New Year's Eve 1981–82.

45. Patricia Yaeger, *Dirt and Desire: Reconstructing Southern Women's Writing, 1930–1990* (Chicago: University of Chicago Press, 2000), 76.

46. Benjamin DeMott, *The Trouble with Friendship: Why Americans Can't Think Straight about Race* (1995; New Haven: Yale University Press, 1998), 118.

47. Christine Wiltz talks about the incident in "A Conversation with Chris Wiltz," by Theresa James, *Xavier Review* 15.2 (fall 1995): 14–16.

48. Christine Wiltz, *Glass House* (Baton Rouge: Louisiana State University Press, 1994), 5. Subsequent citations are indicated parenthetically in the text.

49. This image is one Ronald Reagan exploited during his presidential campaign.

50. For an analysis of how popular images of blacks originate and function, see Steinhorn and Diggs-Brown, 170. See Massey and Denton, 4–7, for their explanation of how the connection between culture and economic structure was lost when the popular press picked up Oscar Lewis's idea about a "culture of poverty."

51. Massey and Denton summarize Oscar Lewis's research about the culture of poverty this way: "According to Lewis, this culture originated in endemic unemployment and chronic social immobility, and provided an ideology that allowed poor people to cope with feelings of hopelessness and despair that arose because their chances for socioeconomic success were remote. In individuals, this culture was typified by a lack of impulse control, a strong present-time orientation, and little ability to defer gratification. Among families, it yielded an absence of childhood, an early initiation into sex, a prevalence of free marital unions, and a high incidence of abandonment of mothers and children" (5). See Oscar Lewis, "The Culture of Poverty," *Scientific American,* October 1966, 19–25.

52. See Y. Amir, "The Role of Intergroup Contact in Change of Prejudice and Ethnic Relations," in *Toward the Elimination of Racism,* ed. P. A. Katz (New York: Pergamon Press, 1976). See also Harry C. Triandis, "The Future of Pluralism Revisited," in Katz and Taylor, 31–50.

53. James, 22–23.

54. Wolfe published "a literary manifesto for the new social novel" in *Harper's,* November 1989, taking his fellow contemporary novelists to task for ignoring social realism, particularly "racial strife in the cities" (46). In a subsequent letter to the editor (February 1990), Alison Lurie pointed out that "for Wolfe, literature is an almost exclusively masculine field. His essay names or discusses, at length, by my counting, forty-eight writers, only two of whom are women" (8). As for his charge that novelists have ignored "racial strife in the cities," Mary Gordon, in another February 1990 letter, noted that Wolfe ignored Toni Morrison (9).

55. Julian Bond, "The Movement We Helped to Make," in *Long Time Gone: Sixties America Then and Now,* ed. Alexander Bloom (New York: Oxford University Press, 2001), 22.

56. Elizabeth Spencer, "The Business Venture," in *Jack of Diamonds* (New York: Dutton, 1987), 135. Subsequent citations are indicated parenthetically in the text.

57. Patricia Meyers Spacks, *Gossip* (New York: Alfred A. Knopf, 1985), 5.

58. Spacks, 49.

59. Spacks, 260–61, 5.

60. Yaeger, 14. See Eudora Welty's comments on place in *Conversations with Eudora Welty,* ed. Peggy Prenshaw (Jackson: University Press of Mississippi, 1984).

61. This is Spacks's observation (231).

62. Madison Smartt Bell, "A Bond of Braided Histories," *New York Times,* September 4, 1988, sec. 7, p. 6.

63. Randall Kenan, *A Visitation of Spirits* (New York: Grove Press, 1989), 254, 256. Subsequent citations are indicated parenthetically in the text.

64. John Howard, introduction to *Carryin' On in the Lesbian and Gay South,* ed. John Howard (New York: New York University Press, 1997), 5. In the same volume, Donna Jo Smith in her essay, "Queering the South," cautions against accepting the myth that "it's harder to be queer in the South than in the rest of the nation." She worries about reifying myths of *queer* and *southern* that she argues have had "a significant effect on southern queer experiences" (381).

65. See Robert McRuer, *The Queer Renaissance* (New York: New York University Press, 1997), 85–86.

66. See Charles H. Rowell, "An Interview with Randall Kenan," *Callaloo* 21.1 (winter 1998): 141.

67. Eve Kosofsky Sedgwick, *Epistemology of the Closet* (Berkeley: University of California Press, 1990), 22.

68. McRuer, 72–73.

69. Debbora Battaglia, "Problematizing the Self, a Thematic Introduction," in *Rhetorics of Self-Making,* ed. D. Battaglia, (Berkeley: University of California Press, 1995), 2.

70. Gilroy, 103.

71. *American Heritage Dictionary,* new college ed.

72. V. Hunt, "A Conversation with Randall Kenan," *African American Review* 29 (1995): 416.

73. James Baldwin, *Evidence of Things Not Seen* (New York: Henry Holt, 1995), 123–24.

74. Steinhorn and Diggs-Brown, 40.

75. Martin Luther King Jr., "Facing the Challenge of a New Age," in *A Testament of Hope: The Essential Writings and Speeches of Martin Luther King, Jr.,* ed. James Melvin Washington (1986; New York: Harper Collins, 1991).

Bibliographical Essay

When I began thinking about the representation of race relations in contemporary fiction, one concept I found provocative was Wolfgang Iser's "play theory," delineated in *Prospecting: From Reader Response to Literary Anthropology* (Baltimore: Johns Hopkins University Press, 1989), in which he views literature as an imaginary enactment of human possibilities. But Benjamin DeMott, *The Trouble with Friendship: Why Americans Can't Think Straight about Race* (New Haven: Yale University Press, 1998); and Leonard Steinhorn and Barbara Diggs-Brown, *By the Color of Our Skin: The Illusion of Integration and the Reality of Race* (1999; New York: Plume, 2000), opened my eyes to the potential pitfalls of fiction about interracial relationships if it blinds readers to the larger problems of institutional racism or confuses friendship with integration. I also found helpful a fascinating discussion among Ralph Ellison, William Styron, Robert Penn Warren, and C. Vann Woodward about historical fiction and its ability to tell the truth in "A Discussion: The Uses of History in Fiction," *Southern Literary Journal* 1.2 (spring 1969): 57–90. Shoshana Felman and Dori Laub, in *Testimony: Crises of Witnessing in Literature, Psychoanalysis, and History* (New York: Routledge, 1992), speculate that literature's power is to make the reader a belated witness to history.

In Dana Nelson, *The Word in Black and White: Reading Race in American Literature, 1638–1867* (New York: Oxford University Press, 1976), I found my first model for examining the literary representation of race relations. Toni Morrison's theorizing in *Playing in the Dark: Whiteness and the Literary Imagination* (1992; New York: Vintage, 1993) that race, even in its absence, can structure a novel and Kenneth W. Warren's historical approach to race and genre in *Black and White Strangers: Race and American Literary Realism* (Chicago: University of Chicago Press, 1993) also became crucial texts for thinking about how narratives work to explore issues of race. A model analysis of mixed messages in film and fiction is Diana R. Paulin, "De-Essentializing Interracial Representations: Black and White Border-Crossings in Spike Lee's *Jungle Fever* and Octavia Butler's *Kindred*," *Cultural Critique* 36 (spring 1997): 165–93.

In thinking about how narrative techniques might work to dismantle entrenched notions about race, I found useful theories about language in Henry Louis Gates Jr., *Figures in Black: Words, Signs, and the "Racial" Self* (New York: Oxford University Press, 1987); in Mikhail Bakhtin, *The Dialogic Imagination: Four Essays,* ed. Michael Holquist, trans. Michael Holquist and Caryl Emerson (Houston: University of Texas Press, 1981); and in Mikhail Bakhtin, *Problems of Doestoevsky's Poetics,* ed. and trans. Caryl Emerson (Minneapolis: University of Minnesota Press, 1984). In thinking about strategies to dismantle stereotypes, I found helpful social scientists' theories in *Toward the Elimination of Racism,* ed. P. A. Katz (New York: Pergamon Press, 1976), and in *Eliminating Racism: Profiles in Controversy,* ed. Phyllis A. Katz and Dalmas A. Taylor (New York: Plenum Press, 1988). In *Seeing a Color-Blind Future: The Paradox of Race* (New York: Farrar, Straus, and Giroux, 1998), Patricia J. Williams's examination of the tensions in contemporary interracial interaction is particularly sensitive.

Although they do not focus on representations of race, critics such as Amy Kaplan in *The Social Construction of American Realism* (Chicago: University of Chicago Press, 1988) and Rita Felski in *Beyond Feminist Aesthetics: Feminist Literature and Social Change* (Cambridge, Mass.: Harvard University Press, 1989) underline the dangers of assumptions that rigidly tie ideology to form. Rachel Blau DuPlessis's ideas about women's plots and endings in *Writing beyond the Ending: Narrative Strategies of Twentieth-Century Women Writers* (Bloomington: Indiana University Press, 1985) transfer well to thinking about how new plots involving race relations function, as do Peter Rabinowitz's theories in *Before Reading: Narrative Conventions and the Politics of Interpretation* (Ithaca, N.Y.: Cornell University Press, 1987).

Most helpful in explaining the social construction of race is Michael Omi and Harold Winant, *Racial Formation in the United States: From the 1960s to the 1980s* (New York: Routledge and Kegan Paul, 1986). In her introduction to *Tomorrow Is Another Day: The Woman Writer in the South, 1859–1936* (Baton Rouge: Louisiana State University Press, 1981), Anne Goodwyn Jones gives an excellent summary and analysis of historians' speculations about the origins of southern racial stereotypes. Joel Williamson, *A Rage for Order* (New York: Oxford, 1986), provides a fascinating history of race relations in the South after emancipation. Mark Snyder explains how stereotypes work in "Self-Fulfilling Stereotypes," *Psychology Today,* July 1982, 60–68; and Patricia Devine suggests why personal contact will not always dismantle stereotypes in "Stereotypes and Prejudice: Their Automatic and Controlled Components," *Journal of Personality and Social Psychology* 56.1 (1989): 5–18. Derrick Bell, *Faces at the Bottom of the Well: The Permanence of Racism* (New York: Basic Books, 1992), describes the subtleties of racism. Ruth Frankenberg, "Growing Up White: Feminism, Racism, and the Social Geography of Childhood," *Feminist Review* 45 (autumn 1993): 51–84, delineates a variety of racial social geographies. Minrose Gwin, in "A Theory of Black Women's Texts and White Women's Readings; or, . . . The Necessity of Being Other," and Barbara Christian, in "Response to 'Black Women's Texts,'" have an interesting and provocative exchange about race and reader response (both are in *NWSA Journal* 1.1 [1988]: 21–36). David K. Shipler, *A Country of Strangers: Blacks and Whites in America* (New York: Knopf, 1997), reveals how Americans today think about race and race relations, with blacks proving more comfortable with the subject than whites.

In theorizing whiteness, Linda Martín Alcoff, "What Should White People Do?" *Hypatia* 13.3 (summer 1998): 6–26, is one of the latest in a list of important new studies of whiteness: David Roediger, *The Wages of Whiteness: Race and the Making of the American Working Class* (London: Verso, 1991); Ruth Frankenberg, *White Women, Race Matters: The Social Construction of Whiteness* (London: Routledge, 1993); Eric Lott, *Love and Theft:*

Blackface Minstrelsy and the American Working Class (New York: Oxford University Press, 1993); Theodore Allen, *The Invention of the White Race* (London: Verso, 1994); Mab Segrest, *Memoir of a Race Traitor* (Boston: South End Press, 1994); Ian F. Haney Lopez, *White by Law: The Legal Construction of Race* (New York: New York University Press, 1996); and Grace Elizabeth Hale, *Making Whiteness: The Culture of Segregation in the South, 1890–1940* (New York: Pantheon, 1998).

F. James Davis, *Who Is Black?: One Nation's Definition* (University Park, Pa.: Penn State University Press, 1991); Gerald Early's collection, *Lure and Loathing: Essays on Race, Identity, and the Ambivalence of Assimilation* (New York: Penguin Press, 1993); and Wahneema Lubiano's collection, *The House That Race Built: Black Americans, U.S. Terrain* (New York: Pantheon Books, 1997), analyze definitions of blackness from a variety of perspectives. In "Race into Culture: A Critical Genealogy of Cultural Identity," *Critical Inquiry* 18 (summer 1992): 655–85, Walter Benn Michaels argues that culture has become a way of continuing rather than repudiating racialized thinking. In theorizing blackness, both Itabari Njeri, in *The Last Plantation: Color, Conflict, and Identity: Reflections of a New World Black* (New York: Houghton Mifflin, 1997), and Paul Gilroy, in *Against Race: Imagining Political Culture beyond the Color Line* (Cambridge, Mass.: Harvard University Press, 2000), caution against monolithic definitions of blackness. Randall Kenan, *Walk on Water: Black American Lives at the Turn of the Twenty-First Century* (New York: Alfred A. Knopf, 1999), breaks down such monolithic definitions by providing an account of how a variety of black Americans perceive blackness.

Fred Hobson, *Tell about the South: The Southern Rage to Explain* (Baton Rouge: Louisiana State University Press, 1983); and *But Now I See: The White Southern Racial Conversion Narrative* (Baton Rouge: Louisiana State University Press, 1999); Barbara Ladd, *Nationalism and the Color Line in George Washington Cable, Mark Twain, and William Faulkner* (Baton Rouge: Louisiana State University Press, 1996); and Sharon Monteith, *Advancing Sisterhood? Interracial Friendships in Contemporary Southern Fiction* (Athens: University of Georgia Press, 2000), are pivotal studies in thinking about race and region from the perspective of white writers. Hazel Carby, *Reconstructing Womanhood: The Emergence of the Afro-American Woman Novelist* (New York: Oxford University Press, 1987); Trudier Harris, *From Mammies to Militants* (Philadelphia: Temple University Press, 1982); and Melissa Walker, *Down from the Mountaintop: Black Women's Novels in the Wake of the Civil Rights Movement, 1966–1989* (New Haven: Yale University Press, 1991), are equally important texts from the perspective of black writers. In *Black and White Women of the Old South: The Peculiar Sisterhood in American Literature* (Knoxville: University of Tennessee Press, 1985) and in *Dirt and Desire: Reconstructing Southern Women's Writing, 1930–1990* (Chicago: University of Chicago Press, 2000), Minrose Gwin and Patricia Yaeger, respectively, provide important comparative studies of black and white women authors. Yaeger introduces a new set of categories to illuminate the political in daily life and argues that one of the reasons modern southern women's writing needs to be reexamined is its potential to provoke new ways of thinking about racial epistemologies, an argument that parallels my own thinking about race and contemporary literature set in the South.

In examining the mostly male southern literary renaissance, Richard H. King in *The*

Southern Renaissance: The Cultural Awakening of the American South, 1930–1955 (New York: Oxford University Press, 1980) and Richard Gray in *Writing the South: Ideas of an American Region* (New York: Cambridge University Press, 1986) provide important intellectual histories of the South. Fred Hobson, *The Southern Writers in the Postmodern World* (Athens: University of Georgia Press, 1991); Matthew Guinn, *After Southern Modernism: Fiction of the Contemporary South* (Jackson: University of Mississippi Press, 2000); and Richard Gray, *Southern Aberrations: Writers of the American South and the Problems of Regionalism* (Baton Rouge: Louisiana State University Press, 2000), all take the measure of contemporary southern fiction. Michael Kreyling, *Inventing Southern Literature* (Jackson: University of Mississippi Press, 1998), provocatively questions the way scholars have defined what has come to be known as southern literature. Kreyling's work follows in the tradition of Michael O'Brien, *The Idea of the American South, 1920–1941* (Baltimore: Johns Hopkins University Press, 1979). Kreyling's work and the responses to it have not so much shaped my project as they have made me more conscious about which contemporary stories are set in the American South. Like Susan Donaldson, Anne Jones, and Fred Hobson in their responses to *Inventing Southern Literature* ("A Symposium: The Business of Inventing the South," *Mississippi Quarterly* 52.4 [fall 1999]), Barbara Ladd argues that southern literature should not be seen as an ideological commitment to an orthodox tradition but as a descriptive more inclusive term with the subject constantly changing. Ladd's essay and Scott Romine's postsouthern approach, as well as other theories about regionalism, appear in *South to a New Place: Region, Literature, Culture,* ed. Suzanne W. Jones and Sharon Monteith (Baton Rouge: Louisiana State University Press, 2002).

Nell Irvin Painter, "'The South' and 'the Negro': The Rhetoric of Race Relations and Real Life," in *The South for New Southerners,* ed. Paul D. Escott and David R. Goldfield (Chapel Hill: University of North Carolina Press, 1991), explores the problems in defining a region racially. For analyses of African Americans' reasons for returning to the South, the most helpful are Thadious Davis, "Expanding the Limits: The Intersection of Race and Region," *Southern Literary Journal* 20. 2 (spring 1988): 3–11; David L. Langford, "Going Back Home to the South," *Crisis Magazine,* April 1994; Carol Stack, *Call to Home: African Americans Reclaim the Rural South* (New York: Basic Books, 1996); and James Cobb, "Searching for Southernness: Community and Identity in the Contemporary South," in his *Redefining Southern Culture: Mind and Identity in the Modern South* (Athens: University of Georgia Press, 1999). "African Americans in Southern Rural Regions: The Importance of Legacy," by Louis E. Swanson, Rosalind P. Harris, Jerry R. Skees, and Lionel Williamson, analyzes how the lives of southern African Americans continue to be shaped by the legacy of slavery, sharecropping, and segregation (*Review of Black Political Economy* 22.4 [spring 1994]: 109–24). Orlando Patterson, *Rituals of Blood: Consequences of Slavery in Two American Centuries* (Washington, D.C.: Civitas/Counterpoint, 1998), also argues that the effects of slavery are still evident.

A number of historical works are indispensable to an understanding of the history of the civil rights movement: Numan V. Bartley, *The Rise of Massive Resistance: Race and Politics in the South during the 1950s* (Baton Rouge: Louisiana State University Press, 1969); Taylor Branch, *Parting the Waters: America in the King Years, 1954–63* (New York: Simon and Schuster, 1988); David L. Chappell, *Inside Agitators: White Southerners in the Civil Rights Movement* (Baltimore: Johns Hopkins University Press, 1994); John Dittmer, *Local People: The Struggle for Civil Rights in Mississippi* (Urbana: University of Illinois Press, 1995); David R. Goldfield, *Black, White, and Southern: Race Relations and Southern Culture, 1940 to the Present* (Baton Rouge: Louisiana State University Press, 1990); Stephen J. Whitfield, *A Death in the Delta: The Story of Emmett Till* (Baltimore: Johns Hopkins University Press, 1991); J. Harvie Wilkinson, *From Brown to Bakke: The Supreme Court and School Integration, 1864–1978* (New York: Oxford University Press, 1976); and Juan Williams, *Eyes on the Prize: America's Civil Rights Years, 1954–1965* (New York: Penguin Books, 1987), which is the companion book to the television documentary. The documentary contains invaluable footage of the civil rights movement. The contributors to *Long Time Gone: Sixties America Then and Now,* ed. Alexander Bloom (New York: Oxford University Press, 2001), provide a fascinating retrospective on the sixties, and Hugh Davis Graham assesses the progress in race relations in "Since 1965: The South and Civil Rights," one of a number of provocative essays about the South's relationship with the rest of the nation in *The South as an American Problem,* ed. Larry J. Griffin and Don H. Doyle (Athens: University of Georgia Press, 1995).

Invaluable in understanding the race and gender conflicts within the movement and its aftermath are historian Sara Evans, "Women's Consciousness and the Southern Black Movement," in *Speaking for Ourselves,* ed. Maxine Alexander (New York: Pantheon, 1977); journalist Paula Giddings, *When and Where I Enter: The Impact of Black Women on Race and Sex in America* (New York: William Morrow, 1984); cultural critic bell hooks, *Yearning: Race, Gender and Cultural Politics* (Boston: South End Press, 1990); the memoirs of nine white civil rights activists, *Deep in Our Hearts: Nine White Women in the Freedom Movement* (Athens: University of Georgia Press, 2000); and Michele Wallace, *Black Macho and the Myth of the Superwoman* (New York: Dial Press, 1979).

To aid my thinking about the structure and function of southern novels about childhood, I referred to the introduction to Elizabeth Goodenough, Mark A. Heberle, and Naomi Sokoloff, *Infant Tongues: The Voice of the Child in Literature* (Detroit: Wayne State University Press, 1994); the introduction to Martin Swales, *The German Bildungsroman from Wieland to Hesse* (Princeton, N.J.: Princeton University Press, 1978); and Carol Lazzaro-Weis, "The Female Bildungsroman: Calling It into Question," *NWSA Journal* 2.1 (winter 1990): 16–34. J. A. Appleyard, *Becoming a Reader: The Experience of Fiction from Childhood to Adulthood* (New York: Cambridge University Press, 1990), is helpful in thinking about how children "read" books, the media, and the world around them.

Articles that best explain the controversy about race in the feminist movement and in women's studies programs include Margaret A. Simons, "Racism and Feminism: A Schism in the Sisterhood," *Feminist Studies* 5.2 (summer 1979): 384–401; Maxine Baca Zinn, Lynn Weber Cannon, Elizabeth Higginbotham, and Bonnie Thornton Dill, "The Costs of Exclusionary Practices in Women's Studies," *Signs* 11.2 (winter 1986): 290–303; Marie C. Lugones and Elizabeth V. Spelman, "Have We Got a Theory for You! Feminist Theory, Cultural Imperialism, and the Demand for the Woman's Voice," in *Women and Values,* ed. Marilyn Pearsall (Belmont, Calif.: Wadsworth, 1986).

Attempts to understand and overcome the problem of race relations within the feminist movement include Elly Bulkin, Minnie Bruce Pratt, and Barbara Smith, *Yours in Struggle: Three Feminist Perspectives on Anti-Semitism and Racism* (Brooklyn: Long Haul Press, 1984); bell hooks, "Where Is the Love: Political Bonding between Black and White Women," in her *Killing Rage: Ending Racism* (New York: Henry Holt, 1995); Gloria L. Joseph and Jill Lewis, *Common Differences* (Garden City, N.Y.: Anchor, 1981); Audre Lorde, *Sister Outsider* (Trumansburg, N.Y.: Crossing Press, 1984); and María C. Lugones with Pat Alake Rosezelle, "Sisterhood and Friendship as Feminist Models," in *The Knowledge Explosion: Generations of Feminist Scholarship*, ed. Cheris Kramarae and Dale Spender (New York: Teachers College Press, 1992).

Important literary studies of interracial women's friendships include Monteith, *Advancing Sisterhood?;* Nancy Porter, "Women's Interracial Friendships and Visions of Community in *Meridian, The Salt Eaters, Civil Wars,* and *Dessa Rose,*" in *Tradition and the Talents of Women*, ed. Florence Howe (Urbana: University of Illinois Press, 1991); Maureen Reddy, *Crossing the Color Line: Race, Parenting, and Culture* (New Brunswick, N.J.: Rutgers University Press, 1994); and Elizabeth Schultz, "Out of the Woods and into the World: A Study of Interracial Friendships between Women in American Novels," in *Conjuring: Black Women, Fiction, and Literary Tradition*, ed. Marjorie Pryse and Hortense J. Spillers (Bloomington: Indiana University Press, 1985).

Comprehensive essay collections about masculinity include *The Making of Masculinities*, ed. Harry Brod (Boston: Allen and Unwin, 1987); *Men's Lives*, ed. Michael S. Kimmel and Michael A. Messner (New York: Macmillan, 1989); and *The Black Male in America: Perspectives on His Status in Contemporary Society*, ed. Doris Y. Wilkinson and Ronald Taylor (Chicago: Nelson-Hall, 1977). A collection that examines the blurred boundaries of race, gender, and class is *Race and the Subject of Masculinities*, ed. Harry Stecopoulos and Michael Uebel (Durham, N.C.: Duke University Press, 1997). Essays about black masculinity also appear in Early, *Lure and Loathing*, and Lubiano, *The House That Race Built*. An excellent feminist critique of the intersection of race and gender is hooks, *Yearning*. A provocative feminist analysis of male friendship is Robert A. Strikwerda and Larry May, "Male Friendship and Intimacy," *Hypatia* 7.3 (summer 1992): 110–25. J. Glenn Gray, *The Warriors* (New York: Harper Torchbooks, 1959); and James William Gibson, *Warrior Dreams: Paramilitary Culture in Post-Vietnam America* (New York: Hill and Wang, 1994), are helpful in explaining the military mind-set. Crucial to understanding the history of southern honor is Bertram Wyatt-Brown, *Southern Honor: Ethics and Behavior in the Old South* (New York: Oxford University Press, 1986). Dov Cohen and Richard E. Nisbett update Wyatt-Brown's analysis in "Self-Protection and the Culture of Honor: Explaining Southern Violence," *Personality and Social Psychology Bulletin* 20.5 (October 1994): 551–67. Williamson, *A Rage for Order*, explains how race and violence came to be so interrelated in the South.

Crossing the Line: Interracial Couples in the South, by Robert P. McNamara, Maria Tempenis, and Beth Walton (Westport, Conn.: Praeger, 1999); and *Multiracial Couples: Black and White Voices,* by P. C. Rosenblatt, T. A. Karis, and R. D. Powell (Thousand Oaks, Calif.: Sage, 1995), provide interesting insights into what it is like to be in an interracial couple today. A groundbreaking study about the legal regulation of interracial relationships and the current consequences of that legal history for romance, the family, and racial identity is Rachel F. Moran, *Interracial Intimacy: The Regulation of Race and Romance* (Chicago: University of Chicago Press, 2001). Peter Wallenstein, *Tell the Court I Love My Wife: Race, Marriage, and Law: An American History* (New York: Palgrave, 2002), is an important book about the legal history of interracial romance; and Martha Hodes, *White Women, Black Men* (New Haven: Yale University Press, 1997), provides a social history. As for analysis of nineteenth-century literature that focuses on interracial intimacy, Werner Sollors, *Neither Black nor White Yet Both: Thematic Explorations in Interracial Literature* (New York: Oxford University Press, 1997); and James Kinney, *Amalgamation! Race, Sex, and Rhetoric in the Nineteenth-Century American Novel* (Westport, Conn.: Greenwood Press, 1985), are the most comprehensive.

Joel Williamson, *New People: Miscegenation and Mulattoes in the United States* (New York: Free Press, 1980), is the best history of racially mixed black-white people; and Virginia R. Dominguez, *White by Definition: Social Classification in Creole Louisiana* (New Brunswick, N.J.: Rutgers University Press, 1986), explains the complexities of Louisiana's racial demarcation in great detail. Lawrence Wright, "One Drop of Blood," *New Yorker,* July 25, 1994, 46–55, provides an overview of how and why the Census Bureau has changed racial classifications over the last two centuries. Walter Benn Michaels, *Our America: Nativism, Modernism, and Pluralism* (Durham, N.C.: Duke University Press, 1995), advocates rejecting racial identification altogether; and David Hollinger, *Postethnic America: Beyond Multiculturalism* (New York: Basic Books, 1995), makes the case for voluntary mixed racial and ethnic identities for everyone, in the hope of encouraging more broadly based American communities. In "The New Cosopolitanism," *Transition 72* (1996): 108–35, Eric Lott critiques the use of multiracial identity as upstaging a concern with racism. Farai Chideya, *The Color of Our Future* (New York: William Morrow, 1999), studies emerging multiracialism in California. Two collections of revealing interviews with mixed-race people are *The Multiracial Experience: Racial Borders as the New Frontier,* ed. Maria P. P. Root (Thousand Oaks, Calif.: Sage, 1996); and Lise Funderburg, *Black, White, Other: Biracial Americans Talk about Race and Identity* (New York: William Morrow, 1994).

Gayle Wald, *Crossing the Line: Racial Passing in Twentieth-Century U.S. Literature and Culture* (Durham, N.C.: Duke University Press, 2000), analyzes how the passing plot is used to negotiate identity, agency, and freedom under socially restricted conditions. Elaine K. Ginsberg's collection, *Passing and the Fictions of Identity* (Durham, N.C.: Duke University Press, 1996), contains essays about the politics of passing as it relates not only to race but to gender, nationality, and sexuality; of particular interest in that volume is Adrian Piper's "Passing for White, Passing for Black."

Kinney, *Amalgamation!* provides an exhaustive overview of the mulatto figure in nineteenth-century fiction; an excellent study of the mulatto character up to the 1970s is Judith R. Berzon, *Neither White nor Black: The Mulatto Character in American Fiction* (New York: New York University Press, 1978). Eric J. Sundquist, *To Wake the Nations: Race in the Making of American Literature* (Cambridge, Mass.: Harvard University Press, 1993); and

Susan Gubar, *Racechanges: White Skin, Black Face in American Culture* (New York: Oxford University Press, 1997), provide excellent models for discussions of fiction in their cultural contexts.

In understanding the continuing causes and contemporary consequences of segregation, Douglas S. Massey and Nancy Denton, *American Apartheid: Segregation and the Making of the Underclass* (Cambridge, Mass.: Harvard University Press, 1993), is essential. In *The Narrative Forms of Southern Community* (Baton Rouge: Louisiana State University Press, 1999), Scott Romine explains how earlier generations of southern white male writers used their writing to create mythic communities. An excellent series of articles by D'Vera Cohn in the *Washington Post* (March 7, March 13, April 1, 2001) analyzes what the 2000 census data tells us about the makeup of real American communities today.

Index